Goethe
From My Life
Poetry and Truth
Part Four

Campaign in France 1792
Siege of Mainz

GOETHE

Selected Poems
Faust I & II
Essays on Art and Literature
From My Life: Poetry and Truth (Parts One to Three)
From My Life: Poetry and Truth (Part Four) • Campaign in France 1792 • Siege of Mainz
Italian Journey
Early Verse Dramas and Prose Plays
Verse Plays and Epic
Wilhelm Meister's Apprenticeship
Conversations of German Refugees & Wilhelm Meister's Journeyman Year or The Renunciants
The Sorrows of Young Werther • Elective Affinities • Novella
Scientific Studies

Collected Works in 12 Volumes

Goethe's Collected Works, Volume 5

Johann Wolfgang von

GOETHE

From My Life
Poetry and Truth
Part Four

Translated by Robert R. Heitner
Notes by Thomas P. Saine

Campaign in France 1792/Siege of Mainz

Translated, with an Introduction and Notes,
by Thomas P. Saine

Edited by Thomas P. Saine and Jeffrey L. Sammons

Princeton University Press
Princeton and Oxford

Published by Princeton University Press
41 William Street, Princeton, New Jersey 08540
99 Banbury Road, Oxford OX2 6JX

press.princeton.edu

GPSR Authorized Representative: Easy Access System Europe - Mustamäe tee 50, 10621 Tallinn, Estonia, gpsr.requests@easproject.com

This is volume five in the Collected Works of Johann Wolfgang von Goethe

First published 1987
First Princeton paperback printing, 1994
New paperback and e-book editions, 2026

Paperback ISBN 978-0-691-29222-9
ISBN (epub) 978-0-691-29696-8
ISBN (PDF) 978-0-691-29223-6

Cover images: Courtesy of INTERFOTO / Alamy and Rawpixel

The Library of Congress has cataloged a previous edition of this book as follows:

Goethe, Johann Wolfgang von, 1749–1832.
[Aus meinem Leben. English. Selections]
From my life / Johann Wolfgang von Goethe ; edited by Thomas P. Saine and Jeffrey L. Sammons.
p. cm.—(Princeton paperbacks)
Originally published: New York : Suhrkamp, 1987. (Goethe's collected works ; v. 4–5)
Includes bibliographical references.
Contents: [4] Poetry and truth, pts. 1–3 / translated by Robert R. Heitner ; introduction and notes by Thomas P. Saine—[5] Poetry and truth, pt. 4 / translated by Robert R. Heitner ; notes by Thomas P. Saine. Campaign in France 1792. Siege of Mainz / transated, with an introduction and notes, by Thomas P. Saine.
ISBN 0-691-03797-3 (v. [4]) ISBN 0-691-03798-1 (v. [5] 1. Goethe, Johann Wolfgang von, 1749–1832—Translations into English. 2. Goethe, Johann Wolfgang von, 1749–1832—Biography. 3. Authors, German—18th century—Biography. 4. Authors, German—19th century—Biography. I. Heitner, Robert R. II. Saine, Thomas P. III. Sammons, Jeffrey L. IV. Title. V. Series: Goethe, Johann Wolfgang von, 1749–1832. Works. English. 1994 ; v. 4–5.
PT2026.A1C94 1994 vol. 4–5
[PT2027.A8]
831'.6—dc20
[831'.6]
[B] 94–3217

CONTENTS

FROM MY LIFE
POETRY AND TRUTH

PART FOUR

Foreword

In dealing with the complicated progress of a personal history like the one we have ventured to undertake here, we find ourselves obliged (if certain events are to become intelligible and readable) to separate some things that occurred simultaneously and to condense others that can only be regarded as a series. Thus the whole will be constructed of parts that can be surveyed and assessed judiciously, and to a degree assimilated. With this observation, hoping that it will help to justify our procedure, we embark on the present volume, and we also request our readers to bear in mind that the narrative does not continue exactly where the previous book leaves off. However, all the main threads will gradually be taken up again, for our intention is to present, thoroughly, honestly, and in succession, not only the persons but also the ideas and actions.

Book Sixteen

It is commonly said that misfortunes never come singly, but the same is plainly true of good fortune, and also of other circumstances, which tend to group around us in a harmonious way—whether because some destiny imposes them on us or because human beings have the power of attracting what belongs together.

At any rate, for once it was my experience that everything coincided to promote my outer and inner peace. I enjoyed the former while passively awaiting the outcome of the plans being hatched for me; but the latter came only through the renewal of my studies.

I had not thought about Spinoza in a long time, and now I was driven to him by way of contradiction. I found a little book in our library whose author was vehemently opposed to that unique thinker and, to make an effective beginning, had placed Spinoza's picture opposite the title page with the inscription, *Signum reprobationis in vultu gerens*, which is to say, "His face bears the marks of rejection and confusion." Actually, one could not deny this while looking at the picture, for it was a miserably poor engraving, an absolute caricature. It made me think of how some opponents begin by misrepresenting anyone they disapprove of, after which they attack him as a monster.

However, this little book made no impression on me. I did not like controversy in any case, and always preferred discovering a person's actual thoughts to hearing from someone else what he should have thought. Yet curiosity led me to the article "Spinoza" in Bayle's dictionary,[1] a work which is as estimable and useful for its learning and sagacity as it is ridiculous and harmful for its gossip and twaddle.

The article on Spinoza aroused my displeasure and mistrust. At the very outset the man is termed an atheist and his opinions are roundly condemned; next, however, it is conceded that he was a calmly reflective and very studious man, a good citizen, a communicative person, a quiet individual not involved in public affairs. And so the Bible verse, "By their fruits ye shall know them!" seemed to have been completely forgotten. For how can pernicious principles result in a life pleasing to God and men?

I still remembered the feeling of calm and clarity that had come over me when I once had paged through the posthumous works of that remarkable man. While I could not recall individual details, the impression was still quite distinct, and therefore I hurried to reread those works to which I owed so much; and again the same peaceful breeze wafted toward me. I devoted myself to this reading and felt, as I looked into my inner self, that I had never viewed the world so clearly.

Since this has been such a controversial subject, even in recent times, I would not wish to be misunderstood, and therefore I shall not neglect to insert a few items here about that so much feared, nay, abhorred way of looking at things.

Our physical as well as social life, our manners, habits, worldly wisdom, philosophy, religion, indeed many a chance occurrence, all proclaim to us that we must *renounce*. Many an inward, very personal quality is not destined to be developed for outward use; we are deprived of what we require from without to supplement our existence; and on the other hand, a great deal is thrust upon us that we find alien and burdensome. We are robbed of hard-won gains, of privileges graciously granted, and before we really know what is happening we find ourselves compelled to abandon our personality, at first bit by bit, and then altogether. At the same time, however, it is customary not to have regard for someone who rebels at this; instead, the bitterer the cup, the sweeter the expression one is supposed to assume, so that the tranquil spectator may not be offended by any grimace.

However, nature has equipped the human being with adequate strength, energy, and toughness to accomplish the task. He is aided especially by the indestructible light-mindedness that has been bestowed on him. Thanks to this, he is capable of renouncing an individual thing at any moment, if only at the next he may reach for something else, and so, unconsciously, we are always recreating our whole life. We replace one passion with another. Occupations, inclinations, favorite pursuits, whims, we try them all out only to exclaim at last that all is vanity. No one is horrified by this false, nay, blasphemous saying; indeed it is thought to express something wise and irrefutable. There are only a few persons who have had a premonition about this intolerable feeling, and they have avoided all these partial resignations by resigning themselves totally, once and for all.

The latter make up their minds about what is eternal, necessary, and legitimate and try to form concepts that are imperishable, and indeed are not annulled, but actually confirmed by observation of the transitory. But because there is really something superhuman about this, such persons are generally considered monsters, without respect for God or the world, and they are imagined as having all manner of horns and claws.

My confidence in Spinoza was based on the peaceful effect he had produced in me, and could only be strengthened when I heard my worthy mystics being accused of Spinozism, and when I learned that Leibnitz himself had not escaped this reproach, nay, that Boerhaave, because he was suspected of similar sentiments, had been forced to transfer from theology to medicine.

Let no one imagine, however, that I wanted to subscribe to his writings and literally profess them. For I had already seen all too clearly that no individual understands any other, that the same words have different meanings for everyone, that a conversation or a reading prompts varying trains of thought in various people. And surely we will credit the author of *Werther* and *Faust,* who had been deeply wounded by such misunderstandings, with being less conceited than to think he perfectly understood a man who was Descartes' pupil and through mathematical and rabbinical culture had attained such heights that even today they seem to surpass all other speculative efforts.

What I managed to assimilate of him could be shown quite clearly if the Wandering Jew's visit to Spinoza, which I had devised as a valuable ingredient of that poem, had survived in written form. However, the thought of it pleased me so much, and I liked so much to ponder it in private, that I did not get around to writing anything down. As a result the idea, which would not have been without merit as an incidental jest, became amplified to such a degree that it lost its charm for me and I dismissed it from my mind as burdensome. But now I shall, as succinctly as possible, reveal and describe the extent to which the chief points of my relationship to Spinoza have remained indelible in my memory; for these ideas did exercise a great influence on the further course of my life.

Nature operates according to eternal, necessary laws, which are so divine that the Divinity itself cannot alter them. Unconsciously, all human beings are in perfect agreement about this. Just consider how any natural phenomenon astounds and actually horrifies us if it hints at understanding, reason, or merely free will.

When animals evince something like reason, we cannot get over our astonishment, for as close as we are to them, they still seem to be separated from us by an infinite gulf, and to be relegated to the realm of necessity. Consequently it is little wonder that some thinkers have explained the expert but strictly limited skills of these creatures entirely in terms of mechanics.

When we turn to the plant world, we find still more striking confirmation of our assertion. Consider the sensation that comes over us when the mimosa, upon being touched, folds its pinnate leaves together pair by pair until at last the petiole clicks down as though worked by a joint. The sensation, to which I shall assign no name, is intensified when we observe the *Hedysarum gyrans,* which, without visible external stimulus, raises and lowers its minute leaves as though playing with them—and with our concepts. Let a banana tree be imagined with this talent, alternately raising and lowering its enormous flat leaves by itself, and anyone seeing it for the first time would shrink back in horror. So ingrained in us is the concept of our own superior qualities that we are absolutely unwilling to grant the outside world any part in them, and indeed, if at all possible, we would like to depreciate them even in our own kind.

On the other hand, a similar horror comes over us when we see a man act irrationally contrary to universally acknowledged moral laws, and unwisely contrary to his own and others' best interests. To rid ourselves of this dreadful feeling we immediately transform it into rebuke and loathing and try to free ourselves from such a man either actually or in our thoughts. This point is perceived and granted by everyone, so that it is not necessary for me to labor it further here.

I applied this contrast, which Spinoza stresses so powerfully, in a very curious way to my own nature, and what has been said up to now has really only been intended to clarify what follows.

I had gotten to the point of viewing my indwelling poetic talent altogether as nature, especially since I had been directed to look upon external nature as its subject matter. Of course, a specific occasion could move me to exercise this poetic gift for a particular purpose, but it was at its most joyous and opulent when it burst forth involuntarily, nay, *against* my will.

Through field and woodland swinging,
My little song a-singing,
Is how I passed my day.

It would be the same if I awoke at night, and often I had the urge to imitate one of my predecessors[2] by having a leather doublet made for myself and getting accustomed to capture in the dark, through feeling, whatever had unexpectedly flashed through my mind. I was so used to reciting some little poem to myself, only to forget it again, that more than once I ran to my writing stand and, without even taking the time to straighten out a sheet of paper that was lying there crookedly, actually wrote down a poem on the diagonal from beginning to end, not budging from the spot. In like fashion I also much preferred to reach for a pencil, as the more pliant instrument; for it had been my experience several times that the scraping and spurting of the pen awoke me from my somnambulistic composing and distracted me so much that the little creation died at birth. I had a special regard for such poems because I had more or less the same relationship to them as a hen to her chicks after she has hatched them and they are all cheeping around her. My earlier desire to read these things aloud to my friends was reawakened, but the idea of exchanging them for money offended me.

In this connection I want to mention an incident that occurred somewhat later. When interest in my works kept increasing and there was even demand for a collection of them, which the aforementioned sentiments restrained me from preparing by myself, Himburg[3] took advantage of my hesitation, and to my surprise I received several copies of my collected works in print. With great impudence this unsolicited publisher boasted to me about the great service he had done the public, and in return he offered to send me some Berlin porcelain, if I so desired. The occasion could not but remind me of the fact that Berlin Jews, when they married, had to buy a certain amount of this porcelain, to insure a market for the royal factory. My scorn for the brazen literary pirate took precedence over the chagrin I naturally felt about this robbery. I did not answer him, but while he was doubtless enjoying himself to the full on my property, I took my quiet revenge with the following verses:

Relics of my years spent sweetly dreaming,
Faded flowers, locks of hair once gleaming,
Veils, now slightly creased, discolored ribands,
Melancholy tokens kept when love ends,
To my hearthfire I had scarce consigned them,
When a saucy Sosias purloined them,
Just as though my poetry and merit
Had been willed him duly to inherit;
And the living me shall he then cozen
With his cups and saucers by the dozen?
Gone be porcelain, and pastry too!
Himburgs, I am dead for you.

However, nature, which spontaneously produced such works of greater and lesser extent, sometimes went dormant for a considerable time. There were long periods of time during which I was not able to produce anything even when I wanted to, and I was therefore very bored. In connection with this sharp contrast, the thought occurred to me that perhaps I should use whatever humanity, reason, and sense I possessed in other respects for my own profit and advantage, and that of others. Should not these interim periods be devoted to practical activities, in which I had been engaged before and which were being enjoined on me ever more vigorously, and thus none of my talents be left unemployed? I found these general conclusions to be so much in harmony with my nature and situation that I resolved to act along these lines and thus put an end to my previous wavering and hesitation. It was pleasant for me to think that my lovely natural gift, like something holy, might continue being expended disinterestedly while I was demanding real payment from people for actual services. This observation saved me from the bitterness I might have started to feel when I was forced to see how this most desired and admired talent was being treated in Germany as though it were outside the law and at anyone's mercy.

For it was not only in Berlin that pirated editions were considered permissible and, indeed, amusing. Even the revered Margrave of Baden,[4] who received such high praise for being a virtuous ruler, and Emperor Joseph,[5] who justified so many hopes, showed favor to a Macklot and a Chevalier von Trattner, respectively, and it was declared that both the rights and property of genius should be unconditionally surrendered to tradesmen and manufacturers. Once we complained about this to a visitor from Baden, and he told the following story: The margravine, being an active lady, had established a paper factory, but its wares turned out to be of such poor quality that no one would buy them. Thereupon the publisher Macklot had suggested raising the value of this paper a little by printing poets and prose authors on it, and he said the suggestion had been eagerly accepted.

Although we did not believe this malicious rumor, we enjoyed it to the full. Immediately the name of Macklot became a term of abuse which we invoked repeatedly whenever bad things happened. And thus, while villainy was growing rich on our talents, we light-minded youths, who sometimes even had to borrow money, felt ourselves adequately avenged by a few good sallies.

Happy children and youths wander along in a kind of intoxication, which is especially conspicuous because the dear innocents are hardly capable of noticing, much less recognizing, the nature of their immediate surroundings. They view the world as material to be formed and as a storehouse of things they are entitled to appropriate. Everything belongs to them, everything seems subject to their will, and so they are quite often led astray into a wild and dissolute life. In the better ones, however, this tendency develops into a moral enthusiasm, which occasionally can act as its own stimulus to some genuinely or apparently good action, but also frequently allows itself to be governed, led, and misled.

This was the case with the young man we are talking about, who may have made an odd impression on people but still was received gladly by quite a few of them. From the very first encounter with him one found him to be absolutely open-minded, cheerfully sincere in his conversation, and occasionally precipitous in his actions. Concerning the last, a few anecdotes:

A fierce fire had broken out in Jews' Lane with its very tightly clustered buildings. My general good will, translated into an active desire to help, made me run there just as I was, dressed in good clothes. A breakthrough had been made from All Saints' Lane, and I made use of this entry. There I found a great many persons busy carrying water, hurrying forward with full pails and back with empty ones. It did not take me long to see that it would be twice as effective if they would form a double column along which the pails could be handed back and forth. I picked up two full pails and remained standing as I shouted to others to join me. The persons going forward were relieved of their burden and the ones returning formed a row on the other side. The arrangement was applauded, my exhortations and personal participation found favor, and soon the double file was complete and without a gap from the entry to the fiery goal. However, hardly had their cheerful compliance with my orders instilled a happy, one may say a merry, mood in this efficient living machine, when mischief also entered in and made room for malice. The miserable refugees, dragging away their pitiful possessions on their backs, no sooner met the convenient lane than they had no choice but to go through it, and not without difficulties. Mischievous adolescent boys sprinkled water on them and increased their misery with scorn and rudeness. I put an end to this outrage at once, however, both with gentle persuasion and oratorical reprimands, and no doubt by asking them to consider the clean clothes I was risking here.

Out of curiosity, some friends of mine approached to see the disaster, and they seemed amazed to see their comrade engaged in this damp business while dressed in shoes and silk stockings (for that was the fashion then). I persuaded a few to help, but the others laughed and shook their heads. For a long time we held firm to our position, since willing replacements were found for those who walked away. There was a stream of onlookers, and so my innocent but hazardous undertaking was known to many, and my odd impetuosity became the talk of the town that day.

Such frivolous behavior in response to some good-natured, cheerful whim or other resulted from a blissful self-confidence, which people are prone to criticize as vanity, and our friend attracted attention to himself through other strange instances of it, like the following:

A very severe winter had completely covered the Main with ice, transforming it into a firm floor. The busiest traffic, both of a necessary and of a merrily sociable type, moved over the ice. Limitless skating-runs and wide stretches of smooth ice swarmed with lively groups. I was also there from early morning on, and when my mother drove out later to watch the spectacle I was nearly frozen to the marrow in my light clothing. She sat in the carriage looking very stately in her cloak of fur and red velvet, fastened over her bosom with heavy gold cord and tassels. "Give me your fur, dear Mother!" I suddenly shouted, without stopping to think. "I am terribly cold." She too did not think twice. In a moment I was wearing the cloak, which reached down to my calves and, being crimson, trimmed with sable, and ornamented with gold, did not go at all badly with the brown fur cap I was wearing. In this guise I skated unconcernedly back and forth, and the throng was so great that the strange apparition was not even specially noticed—and yet perhaps to a certain extent, for later it was listed among my anomalies, both seriously and in jest.

A witty Frenchman has said that if some good mind or other has attracted public attention with a meritorious work, everything possible will be done to prevent him from ever producing its like again.

It is so true: something or other good and ingenious is produced in one's quiet, isolated youth, applause is won, but independence is lost. People drag the talented person from concentration into distractions, in the hope of picking off and assimilating some part of his personality.

This was the reason I received many invitations, or rather, not really invitations. A friend or acquaintance would suggest, quite often more than urgently, that he could introduce me here or there. But this amounted to nothing more than satisfying the curiosity of some coterie or family.

Curiosity was aroused by the quasi-stranger, who was declared to be a bear because of his curt refusals, and then again, because of his many talents, to be Voltaire's Huron, Cumberland's West Indian,[6] or a child of nature; and in many families appropriate negotiations were being made to see him.

Among others, a friend requested me one evening to attend a small concert with him which was being held in the house of an eminent Calvinist merchant.[7] It was rather late, but since I liked anything spontaneous I accompanied him, dressed properly, as usual. We entered a room on the ground level, actually the family's spacious salon. The company was numerous, and a grand piano stood in the middle, at which the daughter of the house immediately sat down and began to play with notable skill and grace. I stood at the far end of the piano, so as to get a good look at her person and manner. There was something childlike about her demeanor, and the movements necessary to her playing were unforced and natural.

When her sonata was finished, she came down to the end of the piano just opposite me, and we did no more than greet each other, because a quartet had already begun. At its conclusion I approached a little closer and said a few obliging words, such as how glad I was that my first acquaintance with her had also acquainted me with her talent. She made a polite response to my remarks, and maintained her position, as I did mine. I could see that she was observing me closely and that I was really on display, but I did not mind at all, since I too had been given something very charming to behold. We continued to gaze at each other, and I shall not deny that I began to feel an attraction of the gentlest kind. However, the milling about of the company as it gave its performances prevented any further approach on this evening.

Yet I must confess it was a pleasant feeling when, at my departure, the mother indicated she hoped to see me soon again, and the daughter seemed to chime in with a certain friendliness. I did not neglect to repeat my visits at proper intervals, and we developed an ability to converse very cheerfully and sensibly; but no passionate relationship was foreshadowed.

Meanwhile the now well-established hospitality of our house caused my good parents, and my own self, many an inconvenience. My constant efforts to perceive, recognize, promote, and, where possible, creatively imitate higher things were by no means advanced by this. These people were good, so far as they were pious; but so far as they were active, they were unwise and often unskilled. The piety was of no help to me; the lack of skill confused me. I wrote a careful account of one remarkable case:

At the beginning of the year 1775, Jung, afterwards called Stilling, sent word from the lower Rhine region that he was coming to Frankfurt, having been commissioned to undertake a noteworthy eye operation there. He was welcome to me and my parents, and we offered him lodgings.

Mr. von Lersner,[8] who was a dignified elderly man and universally esteemed because of his tutelage and guidance of young princes, and for his intelligent conduct at court and abroad, had for some time been suffering the misfortune of total blindness, but could not quite give up his longing to be helped. Now, for several years Jung, with pious self-assurance, had been boldly performing many cataract operations in the lower Rhine region, so that he had gained a wide reputation. His sincerity of soul, dependability of character, and simple piety inspired everyone with confidence, and this spread upstream by way of a complex commercial network. Mr. von Lersner and his family, on the advice of a competent physician, resolved to send for this successful eye doctor, even though a Frankfurt merchant, on whom the treatment had not worked, earnestly advised against it. But what did a single case prove against so many successful ones! Jung did come, lured by the prospect of being paid a respectable fee for once, which heretofore had not usually been his experience. He came happily and trustfully, thinking to enhance his reputation, and we looked forward to having such an honest and cheerful companion at table.

After various medical preparations, the cataracts were finally removed from both eyes, and our expectations ran high, since we heard that the patient had been able to see immediately after the operation, until daylight was withheld from him again by a bandage. But obviously Jung was downcast and in low spirits about something. Upon further questioning he admitted to me that he was worried about the outcome of the treatment. Ordinarily, as I knew from having observed it frequently myself in Strassburg, it seemed the easiest thing in the world, and Stilling had succeeded hundreds of times. Once a painless incision had been made in the insensitive cornea, just the slightest pressure would make the opaque lens pop out by itself. The patient would immediately see objects but would have to tolerate having his eyes bandaged until the completion of the cure permitted him full and comfortable use of the precious organ. How many an indigent person to whom Jung had brought this good fortune had wished God's blessing and reward on his benefactor's head! And now this rich man was to make good on that.

Jung admitted that things had not proceeded so easily and fortunately this time: the lens had not popped out, and he had been compelled to go after and actually dislodge it, because it was grown tight. This had involved the use of some force. Now he reproached himself for having operated on the other eye as well. But he had made this very firm resolve to attempt both at once, not imagining such an eventuality; and when it occurred, he had not immediately recovered himself and reflected. Suffice it to say, the second lens was balky too, and only with difficulty could it be dislodged and removed.

The misery of such a good-hearted, well-intentioned, God-fearing man in a case like this admits of no description, no analysis. But perhaps this is the right place to say something in general about dispositions like his.

To work toward the development of his moral culture is the simplest and most expedient task a person can undertake. He has an innate propensity for doing so, and in civil life he is directed, nay, urged toward it by love and common sense.

Stilling was imbued with an ethical-religious feeling of love, and could not exist without communicating it, without having it kindly returned. He required reciprocal affection: where he was unacquainted, he was quiet, and where he was acquainted, but not liked, he was sad. Therefore he was most at ease among well-disposed people of the type who find that their quiet, restricted professional circle is a convenient place for their efforts at perfecting themselves.

Such persons have little trouble ridding themselves of vanity, renouncing ambition for outward honor, learning to speak discreetly, and maintaining an even, friendly behavior toward their colleagues and neighbors.

Often there is a lack of mental clarity underlying this, with modifications in different individuals. Such persons, being stimulated by chance occurrences, give great importance to their experiences in life. They see supernatural intentions in everything and are convinced that God intervenes directly.

In addition, human beings have a certain inclination to persist in their situation, and yet to allow themselves to be pushed and led; and there is a certain irresoluteness about acting on one's own. This is aggravated if very sensible plans come to naught, or if a chance success is achieved through the fortunate coincidence of unforeseen circumstances.

Not only is such a way of life detrimental to alert, manly conduct, but the means of arriving at this condition is also hazardous.

The favorite subject of conversation among these like-minded people is the so-called "rebirth," a kind of conversion which may well have some psychological value. These rebirths are really similar to what we call "aperçus" in scientific and poetic matters, that is, the perception of some great maxim, which is always a brilliant mental feat. One comes to it not through reflection or instruction or tradition, but through intuition. Here it is perception of the moral strength that is anchored in faith and thus can feel proudly secure in the midst of vicissitudes.

Such an aperçu gives its discoverer the greatest joy because it points to the infinite in a novel way; and certainty of belief does not come gradually but arises instantaneously whole and complete. Hence the good old French proverb,

En peu d'heure
Dieu labeure.[9]

Shocking outward events often cause a violent outbreak of such conversions, and people imagine they have seen signs and wonders.

Trust and affection made cordial ties between me and Stilling, for truly I had exerted a good and happy influence on his career, and it was quite in line with his nature to store up in his sensitive, grateful heart everything that was done for him. But at that stage in my life I found his company neither pleasant nor profitable. To be sure, I gladly left it up to everyone to interpret and develop the mystery of his life as he wished; but what seemed too presumptuous to me was Jung's way of ascribing to direct divine intervention every benefit that comes to us from reason in the quixotic course of our lives. Nor could I accept his attitude toward the bad and almost inevitable results of our frivolity and egotism, of our overhastiness or neglect—that these also were divine pedagogy. Therefore I could only listen to our friend, not return him any satisfactory answer. But just as I did with many others, I was willing to let him alone, and continued to shield him from all too worldly-minded individuals who did not hesitate to wound his tender feelings. Thus I kept him from hearing about the witty remark of a waggish fellow who at one point proclaimed quite solemnly, "No! truly, if I were on as good terms with God as Jung is, I would not ask the Supreme Being for money, but for wisdom and good counsel, so that I would not do so many silly things that cost money and bring on years of miserable debt."

For this was certainly not the time for such jokes and mischief. Several days passed amid alternating fear and hope. The former grew, the latter faded and disappeared entirely. The good, patient man's eyes became inflamed, and there was no longer any doubt that the cure had failed.

This put our friend into a state that beggars description. He struggled against deeply felt despair of the worst kind. For what had he not lost in this affair? To begin with, the infinite gratitude of a man with his sight restored, which is the finest reward a physician can have; the confidence of many others in need of help; and his reputation, since his failure in practicing this skill left a family in a helpless situation. Suffice it to say, we played out this Job-like drama from start to finish, with the honest man himself in the role of the scolding friends. He insisted on viewing the incident as a punishment for his previous errors, and he felt impious for having considered himself divinely called to this occupation just because he had stumbled on a method for treating eyes. He reproached himself for not having made a thorough study of this most important specialty, and for having instead handled his cures perfunctorily and at random. Things said about him by unfriendly people now came to his mind, and he began to wonder whether they might not be true. Indeed, such things hurt him all the more since he had to admit that in his life's course he had been guilty of the light-mindedness which is such a danger to pious people, and probably also of egotism and vanity. At such moments he would fall into a reverie, and however much we might try to come to an understanding, the end result was always simply the foregone rational conclusion that God's ways are unfathomable.

It would have been still more damaging to my buoyantly cheerful disposition had I not, in my usual fashion, subjected these mental states to a serious, benevolent examination and analyzed them in my own way. But it grieved me to see my good mother so poorly rewarded for her conscientious domestic efforts, although she remained so even-tempered in her ceaseless activity that she felt no resentment. I felt sorriest for my father. For my sake he had courteously opened a strictly closed household, and he very much enjoyed our lively, indeed paradoxical conversations, especially at table, where the presence of strangers attracted local friends and frequently also persons passing through town. My sundry dialectical polemics gave him great satisfaction and a reason to smile genially. I had the wicked habit of contesting everything that was said, but stuck to my arguments only long enough so that whoever had the last word would surely look foolish. During the last weeks this had been out of the question, for our friend was so unhappy about his principal case that our most joyous and cheerful celebrations of some successful incidental cures could not move him, much less divert his sad mood.

An individual case that made us laugh was that of an old, blind Jewish beggar from the Isenburg estates, who had been led to Frankfurt in extreme misery, and could barely find shelter or wretched nourishment and care. But his tenacious Oriental nature stood him in such good stead that he soon, with rapture, found himself fully cured, and without the slightest difficulty. When he was asked whether the operation had been painful, he answered hyperbolically, "If I had a million eyes, I would have them all operated on in turn, for a penny apiece." As he went on his way he behaved with equal eccentricity in Passage Lane, thanking God in good Old Testament terms and praising the Lord and his envoy, the miracle man. So, going toward the bridge, he slowly walked through this long commercial street. Salesmen and their customers stepped out of the stores, startled by such rare pious enthusiasm being emotionally displayed in public. Everyone's sympathy was aroused, so much so that he, without any demanding or begging, was abundantly showered with gifts of food for his journey.

But in our circle we hardly dared mention a cheerful happening of this kind. For if one could picture that destitute man as very happy, despite his domestic poverty, in his sandy homeland across the Main, in contrast there was on this side a wealthy, worthy man who was without the priceless comfort he had at first hoped for.

Therefore it was mortifying for our good Jung to receive the one thousand gulden which had been unconditionally stipulated and were nobly paid by those generous people. On his return home, this ready money would expunge a part of the debt that weighed on his dreary, nay, wretched circumstances.

And so he parted from us disconsolately, for he foresaw his reception by an anxious wife on his return, and the changed attitude of his well-disposed parents-in-law, who had guaranteed so many debts for this overconfident man and now might think they had made the wrong choice of husband for their daughter. He could already see in advance, in this and that house, peering out of this and that window, the scorn and derision he would have to endure from those who had been hostile to him even in good times. He also needed to be extremely worried about his practice, which had suffered from his absence and was now radically threatened by this catastrophe.

So we let him leave, yet not entirely without hope on our part, for his sturdy nature, supported by his faith in supernatural assistance, could not but inspire his friends with a certain quiet confidence.

Book Seventeen

In returning to the story of my relationship with Lili, I must call to mind the very pleasant hours I spent either alone with her or with her mother present. On the basis of my writings they credited me with what at that time was called "knowledge of the human heart," and in this sense our conversations had a very satisfactory moral content.

But how were we to discuss our inner feelings without opening our hearts to each other? Consequently it was not long before a quiet hour came in which she told me the story of her childhood. She had grown up amid every social advantage and worldly pleasure. From early on her vanity had been aroused and gratified. Unfortunately, no details of this have been preserved. There were further bits of information: she talked about her brothers, her relatives, and her immediate circumstances; only about her mother was she respectfully silent.

But how can one indulge in such confidences without mentioning one's faults? Perhaps hers were not serious, but others disapproved of them nevertheless, and considered these mere shadows to be blemishes. She could not deny being aware of a certain ability on her part to attract other people, which was combined with a certain corresponding tendency to dismiss them again. As we talked this over back and forth we came to a delicate point: she had used this gift on me also, but her punishment was that she was attracted to me in return.

These confessions issued from such a childlike purity of nature that they served to win my heart completely.

Now there developed a mutual need, a habit, of seeing one another. But I had to reconcile myself to seeing her in company, for otherwise how many a day, how many an evening, lasting into the night, I would have forfeited! This was a painful torment for me.

My relationship to her was of person to person, as if to a lovely, cultivated daughter; it resembled my earlier alliances, but was of an even higher kind. But I had not taken external factors into account, such as the mingling and remingling with social affairs. We were ruled by an irresistible desire: I could not be without her, or she without me. But how many days were spoiled and hours wasted!

A recounting of the pleasure excursions that ended in displeasure—the obstructive brother who, when I was supposed to ride back with him, first attended to some business, very slowly and with the greatest imperturbability (out of malice, for all I know), and thereby spoiled the whole rendezvous we had so carefully planned; also other appointments kept and not kept, impatient waiting and disappointment; all these troubles which if related in greater detail in some novel would certainly find sympathetic readers—must be dispensed with here. However, so as to give some degree of immediacy and youthful empathy to this objective portrayal, let a couple of poems be inserted which, although well known, may be especially effective at this point.

Heart, my heart, what's this strange notion?
What oppresses you so sore?
Unfamiliar new commotion!
I scarce know you anymore.
Gone is all that once did gladden,
Gone whatever used to sadden,
Gone both diligence and ease—
Whence, alas, these vagaries?

Tell, what charms so recommend her,
Youthful beauty, lovely form?
Or her glances, true and tender,
Have they taken you by storm?
If I plan a sudden absence,
Steel myself and flee her presence,
Hardly have I started when
Oh! my path leads back again.

Through this silken thread, enchanted
So that it will ever last,
It's my wanton darling granted
'Gainst my will to hold me fast.
Now within her magic province
I must live beneath her dominance.
Great, alas! the change I see!
Love! O Love! please set me free!

Irresistibly, alas, you draw me
To your brilliant light!
Was I not contented when you saw me
In my lonely night?

I, secluded, in my room reclining
Under moonlight's spell,
All enveloped in its ghostly shining,
Into slumber fell.

Dreamt I then of full and golden hours,
Pleasure wholly blest!
For I now had felt the girl's sweet powers
Deep within my breast.

Am I he, whom you, in bright-lit places,
Keep at cards and dice?
Partnering me oft with those whose faces
Turn my heart to ice?

Even spring to me is now less charming,
Blooming in the pasture.
Where you, angel, are, is love all-warming,
Where you are, is nature.

If these songs are sensitively read aloud to oneself, or, still better, sung with feeling, then a breath from those rich, happy hours will certainly waft past.

But let us not take hasty leave of that numerous, brilliant company without first adding a few remarks, especially an elucidation of the concluding lines of the second poem.

She whom I was accustomed to see in her simple, almost uniform house costume now greeted me in the splendor of an elegant, fashionable toilette, and yet she was the same girl as always. Her charm, her friendliness were unaltered, only I might say that her gift of attraction was more in evidence, perhaps because the presence of so many people here gave her occasion to talk more vivaciously, to show herself from several sides, and to adapt herself variously to the approaches of this person or that. Suffice it to say, I could not deny that while on the one hand these strangers were an inconvenience to me, on the other I would not for anything have foregone the pleasure of becoming acquainted with her social graces and of perceiving that she would also be equal to situations of a broader and more general kind.

Although now concealed by finery, this was, after all, the same bosom that had opened its inner core to me, so that I could see into it as clearly as into my own. These were the same lips that had been so ready to describe to me the conditions under which she had grown up and spent her childhood years. Every glance we exchanged, every smile accompanying it, expressed a secret but honorable relationship, and here in the midst of the crowd I was myself amazed by the very human, natural way we had arranged a clandestine but innocent appointment.

With the approach of spring our relationship was to become still more closely knit in the relative freedom afforded by the countryside. Even at that time Offenbach-on-Main showed significant early signs of being a town that would subsequently develop. Beautiful and (for those times) even splendid buildings had already been erected, and Uncle Bernard[10] (whom I shall at once call by his family title) dwelt in the largest of them, which was adjoined by extensive factory buildings. Across from him lived d'Orville,[11] a lively, youngish man of amiable character. Adjacent gardens and terraces leading down to the Main provided a general open access to the lovely surrounding region and greatly delighted everyone entering and tarrying there. No lover could find a more desirable place to indulge his feelings.

I stayed with Johann André,[12] and since this is the place for me to mention this man, who later made a considerable name for himself, I must permit myself a short digression and give some idea of the state of the opera in those days.

Marchand[13] was the theater director in Frankfurt at that time, and he tried to accomplish what he could through his own person. He was in his prime, a tall, handsome, well-built man in whom ease and softness appeared predominant, and therefore he had a rather pleasant stage presence. He possessed about as much voice as was generally required in those days for the performance of musical works, and so he strove to adapt the lesser and greater French operas for us.

He did particularly well as the father in Grétry's opera *Beauty and the Beast,*[14] in which he mimed very effectively in the vision staged behind the gauze curtain.

This opera, a model of its kind, approached the noble style, and was well suited to arouse the tenderest feelings. However, the operatic stage had been taken over by the demon of realism, and operas emerged that featured the trades and various conditions of life. *The Huntsmen, The Cooper,* and others, more than I can tell, had paved the way for André, who chose *The Potter*[15] for himself. He had written the libretto and poured his whole musical talent into this, his own text.

I was lodged at his house, and here I shall say only as much as necessary about this ever-ready poet and composer.

A man of innate, sprightly talent, his real occupation as a resident of Offenbach was that of technician and manufacturer. He wavered between being an orchestra conductor and a dilettante. In the hope of gaining merit as the former he made a serious effort to acquire a thorough grounding in music. As regards the latter, he was inclined to repeat himself endlessly in his compositions.

Among the persons who completed our circle at this time, and proved very effective in enlivening it, must be mentioned Pastor Ewald.[16] While cheerful and witty in company, in private he was very well able to attend to the studies connected with his duties and position; and subsequently he did win honorable repute in the theological field. He must be included as an indispensable member of that circle, a man quick to grasp ideas and reply to them.

On account of Lili's piano playing, our good André became a virtual prisoner of the group. Whether instructing her, criticizing her, or playing selections himself, he was left with few hours of the day or night when he was not taking part in the family activities and daily social round.

Bürger's "Lenore,"[17] at that time the latest novelty and all the rage in Germany, was set to music by André. He loved to play this and did so repeatedly.

I often gave spirited recitations, and was also quite willing to declaim this poem. In those days people were still not bored by repetitious humdrum. If the company was given its choice about which of us two it wanted to hear, the decision often went in my favor.

But all of this, whatever it might be, was for the lovers simply a means of prolonging their time together. They never wanted it to end, and the good Johann André was easily persuaded, by the wheedling of one and then the other, to play without interruption and to continue repeating his music until well past midnight. Thus the two lovers were assured of each other's dear company.

To step out of the house in the early morning was to find oneself in the openest air, but not actually in the country. One saw houses stately enough to have graced a town of that time; gardens laid out in clearly marked divisions with shallow beds of flowers and other ornamental plants; an open vista across the river up to the opposite bank; and often, quite early, a busy floating traffic made up of rafts, skiffs, and guided market ships, a living world gently gliding by that was in harmony with our tender, loving feelings. Even the solitary onward rolling of the gently flowing stream was most refreshing and never failed to cast a decidedly soothing spell over anyone who approached. A bright sky typical of that fairest of seasons overarched the whole, and how pleasant it was for our intimate group to reassemble in the morning, surrounded by such scenes!

However, should this way of life seem altogether too irresponsible and frivolous to some serious-minded reader, let him keep in mind that what is described here as a continuum, for the sake of the narrative, was disagreeably interrupted by days and weeks of abstinence, and even some of intolerable boredom, because of other pursuits and activities.

The men and the women alike were busily occupied in their own spheres of duty. Nor did I delay, in view of my present and future, to attend to my obligations, and still found enough time for the achievements toward which my talent and passion urged me. I owed poetry the earliest morning hours, while the advancing day belonged to practical affairs, which I treated in a quite peculiar way. My father, a thorough, even elegant jurist, personally conducted his affairs, which were imposed on him both by the management of his property and by his connections with valued friends. Although his title of Imperial Councilor prevented him from practicing law, he was available as a friendly legal adviser to many a close associate; however, the documents he prepared had to be signed by an accredited lawyer, who then received a moderate fee for each signature.

My arrival had made this activity of his all the livelier, but it was quite evident to me that he valued my talent more highly than my legal practice and consequently did everything possible to leave me enough time for my literary studies and works. Thorough and capable, but slow in conception and execution, he would study a case file as a private reviewer; then, when we met, he would lay the matter before me. I would complete the drafting of it with such ease that his paternal joy knew no bounds, and once he could not refrain from declaring that if I were not his son he would be envious of me.

These affairs were made still less onerous because we had been joined by an amanuensis[18] whose character and nature, if properly portrayed, could be an addition and adornment to a novel. After some well-utilized school years, during which he mastered Latin and acquired a great deal of other knowledge, an all too frivolous life at the university interrupted his further progress. For a while, sick in body, he dragged himself along in poverty, and only later was helped up into better circumstances by his very beautiful handwriting and his skill in calculation. While being retained by several lawyers, he gradually became adept in the formalities of legal procedure, and his integrity and meticulousness were such that all those he served became his patrons. He had also bound himself to our house and assisted in all matters concerning law and accounts.

This man did his part in regulating our now ever-expanding business, which involved not only legal affairs but also various commissions, orders, and shipments. He knew all the ins and outs at the townhall; he was tolerated in his fashion at the audiences of both burgomasters; and since he had known many new councilors (some of whom had advanced very soon to the rank of juror) in their first days in office, when they were still insecure about what to do, he had earned himself a certain trust, which might almost be called a kind of influence. He was able to use all this for his patrons' benefit, and, while his health required him to restrict his activities, he was always found ready to carry out every commission and every order carefully.

His appearance was not unpleasant, since he was slim of figure and had regular features. He did not behave in a forward manner, but nevertheless showed firm conviction about what was to be done; and he was cheerful and adroit in disposing of obstacles. He was apparently well into his forties, and I still regret (if I may repeat what I said above) not having inserted him as a driving wheel in the mechanism of some novella or other.

In the hope of having partially satisfied my serious-minded readers with this recital, I may surely turn back again to those splendid moments when love and friendship were shown in their finest light.

It is in the nature of such groups that birthdays should be celebrated punctiliously and joyfully, and in a great variety of ways. The following song was composed in honor of Pastor Ewald's birthday:

In all our happy hours,
Inspired by love and wine,
This song shall, in full chorus,
Be sung where'er we dine.
Our God keeps us together,
Who brought us where we sit;
He'll feed our fire of friendship,
For He ignited it.

Since this song has remained popular up to the present day and is happily revived by almost every merry group gathered around a banquet table, we recommend it to posterity as well. May all who sing or recite it get heartfelt pleasure and delight equal to ours when we, unmindful of any world beyond ourselves, believed that our little circle had expanded to become a world of its own.

Now it will be no surprise to hear that Lili's birthday,[19] which was returning for the seventeenth time on June 23, 1775, was to be specially celebrated. She had promised to come to Offenbach at noon, and I must confess that we friends had happily agreed to ban all the traditional complimentary phrases from this festivity. Instead, for her reception and entertainment we had prepared only such loving speeches as would be worthy of her.

Occupied with such pleasant duties, I saw the sun go down, proclaiming good weather for the next day and promising us its shining, happy presence at our feast. But just then Lili's brother George, who could not disguise his feelings, entered the room rather boorishly and bluntly announced that the next day's party was canceled. He himself knew neither how nor why, but his sister was sending word by him that she could not possibly come to Offenbach tomorrow at noon to participate in the celebration planned for her; only toward evening could she hope to manage her arrival. Of course (he said) she felt and was well aware what a sad blow this would be to me and our friends, but she was asking me sincerely, and with all possible urgency, to invent something that would alleviate, nay, remove the unpleasantness of this news, which she was leaving to me to announce. She would be most grateful to me for this.

I was silent for a moment, but immediately composed myself and, as though by divine inspiration, discovered what was to be done. "Hurry, George!" I shouted. "Tell her not to worry, but to do her best to come toward evening, for I promise we shall make a festival out of this very catastrophe." The boy was curious and wanted to know how. This met with my steadfast refusal, although he tried all the tricks and pressure that a sweetheart's brother will presume to employ.

He was hardly gone when I began walking up and down in my room, feeling singularly complacent and expansively happy because this was an opportunity to act in a splendid way as her servant. I bound together several sheets of paper with fine silk cord, as befits a poem written for an occasion, and made haste to write the title:

"She Cometh Not!
A lamentable family drama which, God help us! will be performed in the most natural manner possible in Offenbach-on-Main on June 23, 1775. The action lasts from morn till eventide."

Neither a first draft nor a copy of this farce is extant, and in spite of many inquiries I have never been able to find a trace of it. Therefore I shall have to reconstruct it, which should not be too difficult to do.

The locale is d'Orville's house and garden in Offenbach. The action starts with the domestics, each of whom plays his precise role, so that the arrangements for the festival become perfectly evident. The children, modeled from life, join in, as do the master and mistress with their characteristic activities and supervision. Then, while everything proceeds confusedly with a certain busy haste, in comes the indefatigable composer, neighbor Hans André, who sits down at the piano and summons everyone to listen to and practice his newly completed festival song. He gets the whole household to come, but not for long, since they have urgent business to attend to, and one is called away by the other, one needs the other, and the gardener interrupts to draw attention to the garden and water scenes. There are garlands, ribbons with most decorative inscriptions—nothing is forgotten.

Just as everyone is gathering around these very delightful objects, a messenger enters. (This was a merry sort of errand boy who deserved to play a character role and could tell, from the often too generous tips he received, approximately what the prevailing circumstances were.) He plumes himself on the package he brings, hopes for a glass of wine and a roll, and, after some mischievous refusals, hands over the dispatch. But the man of the house lets his arms drop, the papers fall to the ground, and he exclaims, "Let me get to the table! Let me get to the sideboard! I want to *sweep away!*"

When jovial people forgather their ingenuity expresses itself primarily in symbolic language and gestures. A sort of argot develops which greatly delights the initiated but quite escapes strangers or, if they do notice it, they are annoyed.

Among Lili's most charming peculiarities was one that in word and gesture has been expressed here as *sweeping away,* and it occurred when something objectionable was said or told, especially while we were sitting at table or were near some other flat surface.

The origin of this was in an unmannerly, but infinitely winsome act that she had once performed when a stranger sitting next to her at table brought up something improper. Without changing the expression on her lovely face, she took her right hand and gracefully swept it over the tablecloth, so that everything she touched with this gentle movement was coolly shoved onto the floor. I do not know what it all was: knife, fork, bread, salt cellar, also something of her neighbor's. Everyone was startled, the servants ran up, and no one knew what it meant except those who had taken in the whole scene, and they rejoiced that she had reacted to an impropriety, and quelled it, in such a graceful way.

So here now a symbol was found for repudiating something of a disagreeable nature, which, after all, can occasionally occur in a company which is solid, good, estimable, and well meaning, but not completely cultivated. We all permitted ourselves the gesture of refusal with the right hand, but she herself subsequently had indulged only with moderation and taste in the actual sweeping away of objects.

So when this desire to sweep away, a habit which had become second nature to us, was assigned by the poet to the man of the house as a theatrical gesture, one can see how significant, how effective it was. While he threatens to sweep everything down from every surface, they all hold him back and try to calm him, until at last he falls quite exhausted into an armchair.

"What has happened to her?" they exclaim. "Is she ill? Has someone died?" "Read, read!" d'Orville cries. "It is lying there on the ground." The dispatch is retrieved, they read, and they shout, "She cometh not!"

The great fright had prepared them for a greater one—but she was well after all!—nothing had happened to her!—no member of the family had come to harm. There was hope for the evening.

André, who has continued playing in the meantime, finally comes running up also, consoles them and tries to console himself. Pastor Ewald and his wife likewise enter in their typical way, with chagrin and understanding, with reluctant renunciation and mitigating explanations. However, there is continued confusion until Uncle Bernard, a model of calmness, eventually arrives expecting a good breakfast and a laudable noon banquet and is the only one who can view the matter in the right perspective. He makes some soothing, sensible remarks and reestablishes equilibrium, just as in a Greek tragedy a god, with a few words, can unravel the entanglements of the greatest heroes.

This was all written down with a fluent pen during a part of the night and handed to a messenger, who was instructed to arrive in Offenbach the next morning punctually at ten o'clock with this dispatch.

Seeing the brightest morning light, I woke up, intending and arranging to arrive in Offenbach exactly at noon myself.

I was received with the oddest charivari of responses: they scarcely mentioned the disrupted festival, but instead scolded and grumbled about my portraying them so revealingly. The servants were happy to appear on the same stage with their masters. Only the children, being the most resolute and uncompromising of realists, stubbornly maintained that they had not spoken thus and everything had been different from what was written down here. I soothed them by letting them sample the dessert in advance, and then I was back in their good graces. A jolly midday meal and reduced emphasis on ceremonies put us in the mood for receiving Lili without pomp, but perhaps more graciously for all that. She came and, seeing herself greeted by our cheerful, nay, merry faces, was almost offended that her absence permitted so much cheer. We told her everything, we put on the whole performance for her, and she thanked me in the dear, sweet way that was inimitably hers.

No particular acumen is needed to observe that her absence from the celebration planned for her was not accidental but the result of family discussions pro and con about our relationship. However, this fact affected neither our sentiments nor our behavior in the least.

At this time of the year it was inevitable that a diverse crowd of sociable people should come out from town. Often I could not join the party until late in the evening, and I found Lili apparently sympathetic, but actually rather puzzled. Since I would often stay only a few hours I liked to be of some use to her, either by having executed a greater or lesser commission or by coming to undertake one. And indeed this kind of service is the most delightful thing that can happen to a person, as the old chivalric romances can teach us in their obscure but robust manner. There was no concealing the fact that I was at her beck and call, and her pride in this was quite pardonable. Here both victor and vanquished are triumphant, and both glow with equal pride.

Though often only brief, my periodic influence was always the more effective for that. Johann André always had a supply of music, and I would bring new works of my own and others: poetic and musical blossoms showered down. It was an absolutely brilliant time. A certain exaltation pervaded our group, and there were never any sober moments. Without any question, this was communicated to the others by the relationship between Lili and me, for when affection and passion show forth with the boldness inherent in their nature, timid hearts are inspired with courage and no longer understand why they should make a secret of their similar claims. Consequently it became obvious that some relationships which had been more or less hidden were now being carried on unabashedly. Others, which could not well be admitted, still managed to slip through comfortably under cover of the rest.

If my manifold duties kept me from spending the days with her out there, at least the clear nights made it possible for us to be together for a rather long time in the open air. Souls in love will receive the following anecdote with pleasure.

It was a condition of which the Scripture says, "I sleep, but my heart waketh."[20] The hours of light and darkness were identical, for the light of day could not outshine the light of love, and the night became bright as day through the glow of affection.

We had strolled about till late in the open area, under the clearest starry sky, and after I had accompanied her and the group home to their various doors, taking leave of her last of all, I felt so little like sleeping that I immediately started out on another walk. I went up the high road toward Frankfurt, giving myself over to my thoughts and hopes. I sat down on a bench, in the most unbroken nocturnal quiet, under the dazzlingly starry sky, wanting to think only of myself and her.

Quite near me I became aware of a sound that was hard to identify. It was not a rustling or rushing noise, but when I listened more closely I discovered that it came from under the earth and was the working of little animals. Presumably it was hedgehogs or weasels, or whatever else engages in such activity at that hour.

After that I walked on farther toward town and came to Röder Hill, where I could make out the steps leading up to the vineyards by their chalk-white gleam. I climbed up, sat down, and fell asleep.

When I awoke, dawn had already broken, and I saw that I was opposite the high embankment erected in earlier times as a counterdefense to the hills arising on this side. Sachsenhausen lay before me, and faint mists indicated the course of the river. It was cool, and I welcomed that.

There I waited until the sun, gradually rising in back of me, lit up the opposite shore. It was the region where I would see my beloved again, and I slowly returned to the paradise that surrounded her as she slept.

However, out of love for her I was trying to manage my business affairs and broaden their scope; and as this expanded, my visits to Offenbach became so infrequent that they caused a certain painful embarrassment. Obviously the present was really being neglected and sacrificed for the sake of the future.

Although my prospects were indeed gradually improving, I considered them more significant than they actually were and thought all the more about an early decision, since our relationship was too public to be continued any longer without our feeling uneasy. And, as usually happens in such cases, we did not express ourselves to each other in so many words. But our feeling of unalloyed delight in each other, our absolute conviction that separation was impossible, our equally shared confidence in one another—all that made the atmosphere so serious that I, who had firmly resolved never to begin another long-drawn-out relationship, and yet found myself involved again in this one without any assurance of a happy outcome, really was overcome by a kind of torpor. My only escape from it was to occupy myself more and more with indifferent practical duties, from which, however, I could hope to gain profit and contentment when married to my beloved.

In this curious condition, which, however, has no doubt been painfully experienced by others, a family friend came to our aid who had a very clear understanding of everything pertaining to the persons and circumstances. She was called Mlle Delph,[21] and she and her older sister were at the head of a small trading firm in Heidelberg; at various junctures the larger discount house in Frankfurt had earned her deep gratitude. This odd person with her serious, masculine appearance, who walked straight ahead with a quick, even, forthright step, had known and loved Lili since the latter's childhood. Having been compelled to find her own special place in the world, she knew its ways at least to a certain extent. While she could not actually be called an intriguer, she did watch situations for a long time, quietly mulling over her plans; then she had the gift of recognizing an opportunity, and when she saw that people's sentiments were wavering between doubt and decision, and everything depended on resoluteness, she was capable of acting with so much strength and sturdiness of character that she hardly ever failed to achieve her purpose. In truth, she had no selfish designs. To have done something, completed something, especially to have made a match, was reward enough for her. She had long since perceived our situation, and on repeated visits had investigated it until she at last became convinced that our affection was to be encouraged, that our plans (which, in spite of our sincere efforts, were not being adequately implemented and carried through) would need her support, and that this little love story should very expeditiously be brought to its conclusion.

For many years she had been a trusted friend of Lili's mother. When I introduced her to my family, she succeeded in making a good impression on my parents, for hers was the very sort of brusque personality that is not found offensive in an imperial free city, and, if backed up by intelligence, is even welcomed. She knew our hopes and wishes very well, and saw in them a mandate for her love of wielding influence. To put it briefly, she negotiated with our parents. However she set to work, however she removed the obstacles that may have arisen in opposition to her—suffice it to say, one evening she came to us and brought their consent. "Clasp your hands!" she exclaimed, with her air of pathos and authority. I stood opposite Lili and extended my hand, in which she laid hers slowly, but without hesitation. Then, after drawing a long breath, we eagerly fell into each other's arms.

It was the curious decree of the Supreme Being who rules over us that I too in the course of my wondrous career should experience the feeling of being betrothed.

I may well say that for a man of good morals this is the most pleasant of all memories. It is agreeable to recall those feelings, which are not easy to express and can hardly be explained. One's previous state is completely altered: the harshest disagreements are removed, the most obstinate discords adjusted. Importunate nature, ever-warning reason, tyrannous desires, and prudent law, which formerly opposed us in perpetual conflict, now approach us in amicable agreement. Then, at a generally celebrated pious festivity, the forbidden is required, and the prohibited is elevated to an indispensable duty.

But it will be heard with polite applause that a certain change took place in my attitude from that moment on. Whereas beforehand she had seemed to me beautiful, charming, and attractive, now she appeared worthy and significant. She was a dual person: her grace and charm belonged to me, and I felt that as always; but the merit of her character, her self-assurance, her complete reliability—these remained her own. I viewed them, I understood them, and rejoiced in them as though in a capital sum which would bear interest that I could enjoy along with her for the rest of our lives.

It has long ago been stated with good reason and significance that a situation reaches its climax only to deteriorate rapidly. The parental consent on both sides, which was actually the accomplishment of Mlle Delph, was recognized from now on, tacitly and without further formalities, as authoritative. But as soon as an ideal entity (which is what such a betrothal can really be termed) encounters reality, then, just when one thinks everything is completely settled, a crisis arises. The external world is altogether pitiless and justifiably so, for its claims have to be asserted once and for all. Passion has great self-confidence, but all too often we see it frustrated when faced with reality. Newlyweds, especially in more recent times, cannot expect any honeymoon if they enter upon this state with insufficient possessions. They are immediately menaced by a world full of irreconcilable demands which, if not satisfied, can make a young couple look absurd.

Previously I had been unable to perceive that the means I had chosen in the serious pursuit of my goal were inadequate, because up to a certain point they had sufficed. But now that the goal was in sight, they did not seem completely suitable to either side.

The specious reasoning that passion finds so convenient now began to reveal all its incongruity. My house and the very special aspects of my position in it had to be considered rather soberly. To be sure, there was the underlying consciousness that every arrangement for a daughter-in-law had been made; but what sort of a young woman had they had in mind?

At the end of the third volume we made the acquaintance of one who was undemanding, sweet, sensible, pretty, efficient, even-tempered, affectionate, and imperturbable. She represented the fitting keystone to an arch already constructed and rounded off. But now, if matters were viewed calmly and objectively, it was an undeniable fact that a whole new arch would have to be raised, were this newly-won young woman to fulfill the same function.

Meanwhile this had not yet become clear to me, or to her either. Still, when I looked at myself in the house and thought about bringing her into it, she did not seem to fit there. Just to appear in her circles without making a jarring contrast to the fashion plates there, I had to alter my clothing from time to time, and then alter it again. But that could not be done with household furnishings, not in our stately, rebuilt middle-class house where a now outmoded pomp had led these furnishings backward, as it were.

Therefore, even though their consent had been secured, our parents had not succeeded in starting and developing any mutual relationship: no family connection, different religious customs, different manners! And if my charming girl should want to continue in her way of life to some extent, she would find no opportunity, no place for it, in our house, respectably spacious though it was.

I had previously disregarded all of this, and was lulled and encouraged by the fine prospects from outside that were opening up to me for the attainment of some lucrative position. An active mind establishes itself everywhere; abilities and talents inspire confidence; everyone thinks it is just a question of changing direction. Importunate youth finds favor, and genius is believed capable of doing anything, when it can only do certain things. The intellectual-literary terrain in Germany at that time must really be conceived of as recently cleared land, and among the civic officials there were intelligent men who wanted sturdy tillers and wise husbandmen for the soil that was to be newly cultivated. The well-established and distinguished Masonic lodge itself, with whose most prominent members I had become acquainted through my relationship with Lili, made the appropriate moves toward my acceptance into it. However, out of a feeling of independence which later seemed madness to me, I declined any closer association,[22] not realizing that these men, for all that the bond between them was of a higher nature, could not have failed to advance me toward my goals, which were so nearly related to theirs.

I shall return to the most particular matter.

In towns like Frankfurt there are collective positions, such as those of agent or ruler's agent, which can be infinitely expanded if one is industrious. This kind of office also presented itself to me, and at first glance seemed both profitable and honorable. My suitability for it was assumed, and the three-man chancery I have described could also have handled the work. One suppresses one's doubts, one grasps at anything favorable, one overcomes any wavering by means of furious activity.

Thereby an element of falseness enters into the situation, without, however, diminishing one's passion.

In peacetime the populace surely has no more enjoyable reading material than the public papers which give us quick news about the latest world events. They provide an innocent exercise for the steady, prosperous burgher's partisan spirit, which, considering our limitations, we can never be free of, nor should we be. So every comfortable person, just as when making a wager, creates a random interest for himself, one which involves only intangible gains and losses; and, as in the theater, he feels a very lively, yet only imaginary, sympathy with the fortunes and misfortunes of others. This sympathy often appears to be arbitrary, but actually it is based on moral grounds. For first we give laudable intentions the applause they deserve, and then, carried away by some brilliant success, we turn to the person whose projects we had meant to censure. These times provided us with abundant material for all this.

Frederick II, secure in his might, still seemed to be meting out the fate of Europe and the world. Catherine, a great woman who had considered herself worthy of the throne, gave much latitude to some competent favorites so that they might extend her sovereign power ever more widely. Since her victims were the Turks, whom we usually repay doubly for the scorn with which they look down on us, it did not seem as if humans were being sacrificed when these infidels died by the thousands. The burning of the fleet in the harbor of Cheshme[23] caused general rejoicing throughout the cultivated world, and everyone shared in the triumphal exuberance when a battleship riding at anchor off Leghorn[24] was blown up for the benefit of an artistic study which would preserve an authentic image of that great event. Not long afterwards, a young Nordic king[25] likewise took over the reins of government on his own initiative. No one mourned for the aristocrats whom he suppressed, for the aristocracy in general did not enjoy public favor. By nature it works behind the scenes, and the less it is discussed, the securer it is. In this instance, the young king won still more approval because he had to favor the lower classes and gain their allegiance to counterbalance the upper class.

But the world took an even more active interest when an entire people set about liberating itself. Earlier, we had been glad to watch the same spectacle on a small scale: Corsica had for a long time been the point toward which everyone's eyes were drawn. When Paoli,[26] hampered in the further execution of his patriotic project, traveled to England by way of Germany, he captured everyone's heart. He was a slim, handsome blond man of great charm and friendliness. I saw him at the Bethmann house,[27] where he stayed briefly and with cheerful amiability received a throng of curious people. Now, however, similar scenes were to be repeated in a more remote part of the world. We wished the Americans every success, and the names of Franklin and Washington began to shine and sparkle in the political and wartime sky. Many things were done for the relief of mankind, and now, when even the new, well-meaning king of France[28] showed every intention of devoting himself to the noblest goals and the abolition of various abuses, of introducing a stable national economy, of renouncing all arbitrary power, and of ruling solely with order and justice, then the brightest hopes spread over the whole world, and trusting youth felt assured of a fine, nay, a splendid future for itself and the whole epoch.

However, my interest in all these events was restricted to discussing them in larger social groups. I myself and my more intimate circle did not occupy our time with newspapers and the latest happenings. Our concern was to acquaint ourselves with the human being; humankind in general we gladly left to itself.

The German fatherland's tranquil condition, which had also enveloped my native town for over a hundred years, had been maintained perfectly in spite of various wars and convulsions. A certain degree of contentment was fostered by the fact that the manifold gradations, from the highest to the lowest, from the emperor down to the Jews, seemed to unite rather than to separate all the individual persons. While kings were subordinate to the emperor, their voting right, and the attendant privileges they had obtained and asserted, decidedly redressed the balance for them. However, the first royal rank included some upper nobility, so that they, mindful of their significant prerogatives, could also consider themselves equal, and even in a certain sense superior, to that which was highest. For, indeed, the ecclesiastical electors had precedence before all others and held an uncontested position of esteem as scions of the church hierarchy.

Let us keep in mind the extraordinary advantages which these old established families enjoyed both directly and by way of religious foundations, knightly orders, ministries, confederations, and fraternal societies. Then it is easy to imagine that this great mass of significant people, who felt themselves at once subordinated and coordinated, spent their lives in great satisfaction and well-ordered public activities, and without particular effort prepared a like ease for their progeny and entrusted it to them. Nor was this class deficient in intellectual culture. Advanced military and administrative education had already come to the fore significantly a hundred years earlier and had taken hold in both aristocratic and official circles. But their minds had also been won for literature and philosophy and a loftiness of viewpoint was instilled that was not of particular benefit to the present times.

In Germany it had as yet hardly occurred to anyone to envy that huge privileged class or to begrudge it its fortunate advantages in the world. The middle class had devoted itself peacefully to trade and the sciences and both by this means and the technical knowledge closely related to it had indeed risen to become a significant counterweight. Such activity flourished in towns that were wholly or half free, and their citizens enjoyed a certain tranquil prosperity. Any man who saw his wealth increased or his intellectual activity heightened, especially in the field of law or officialdom, could enjoy a significant general influence. After all, even in the highest imperial courts, and elsewhere as well, a scholars' bench was placed opposite the nobles' bench. The nobles' broader perspective apparently blended easily with the scholars' deeper insight. And in life there was absolutely no trace of rivalry. The nobility felt secure in its time-honored privileges which were out of reach for others, while the middle-class man felt it beneath his dignity to strive for the appearance of having them by putting the preposition *von* before his name. The trader and technician had enough to do in trying to compete modestly with the more swiftly advancing nations. If the usual daily variations can be disregarded, one may surely say that on the whole it was a period of pure endeavor, which had not been possible beforehand and, because of external and internal developments, could not be of long subsequent duration.

At this time I was very much favored by the upper classes. Even though in *Werther* there is an impatient exposure of the unpleasantnesses that arise when two well-defined classes collide, that could be overlooked in view of the book's generally passionate tone, since everyone sensed that no direct attack was intended here.

But with *Götz von Berlichingen* I got into the very good graces of the upper classes. The prevailing literary proprieties may have been violated, but still this was a knowledgeable and skillful portrayal of old German conditions, with the inviolable emperor on top, many gradations between, and a knight who tried to act justly, if not legally, as a private person in that generally lawless situation, and thus got into very bad straits. These complications were not mere fiction, but were presented just as that good, sturdy man had portrayed them in his narrative (consequently no doubt somewhat inclined in his own favor), and in a bright, lively manner which makes them seem a bit modern here and there, but always in his style, nevertheless.

This family was still flourishing and their bond with Franconian knighthood had retained its integrity, even though these connections, like so much else from those times, apparently had grown weaker and less effectual.

Now the little river Jagst and the castle of Jagsthausen suddenly acquired poetic significance. They were visited, as was the townhall in Heilbronn.

It was known that I was meditating about some other events in the history of those times, and many a family with strong roots in that epoch faced the prospect of having their ancestors hauled out, as it were, into the light of day.

A peculiar universal delight results when in some ingenious way a nation is reminded again of its history. It rejoices in the virtues of its forefathers and smiles at their deficiencies, which it thinks it has now long since overcome. Therefore such a presentation cannot fail to awaken interest and approval, and I was privileged to enjoy a manifold reaction of this kind.

Yet it might be worthy of note that among the many people who approached me, that is, among the young men who attached themselves to me, there was not one nobleman. On the other hand, there were some already in their thirties who looked me up, visited me, and showed in their intentions and ambitions a pervasive, joyous hope of educating themselves in a patriotic and more generally humane sense.

At this time interest in the period at the turn of the fifteenth and sixteenth centuries in general had been awakened, and was lively. I came upon the works of Ulrich von Hutten and was amazed to see that in our modern times something seemed to be manifesting itself that was similar to what had emerged in his day. In the aspirations and actions of such men there was an earnest strain of hope that they could develop their patriotic and moral sense to the full.

The following letter from Ulrich von Hutten to Wilibald Pirckheimer[29] might be appropriately placed here.

"What fortune has given us, it usually takes back again, and not only that, but everything else extraneous to a human being is, we see, subject to chance. However, I am striving for honors I would wish to achieve without arousing envy, however that may be; for I am possessed by an intense thirst for fame, and would like to be ennobled as much as possible. I would be in a bad way, dear Wilibald, if I already considered myself a nobleman (although I was born to this rank, to this family, and of such parents) without first ennobling myself by my own efforts. This is the great work I have in mind! I have higher ambitions! not perhaps to see myself elevated to a more aristocratic, more splendid status, but to seek out a source elsewhere from which I could draw a special nobility and not be numbered among the supposed nobles, satisfied like them with what I have received from my ancestors. Instead I want to add something to their accomplishments myself and bequeath this to my descendents.

"Fortune does not determine everything about this, though it has some part in it: how much, I would not care to say. Yet I will admit that I would be glad to experience strokes of fortune that advanced me favorably. This, then, is the goal of my studies and endeavors, and why I strive, contrary in my opinions to those who accept things as they are; for none of that suffices me, who have confessed to you, without your demand or even request, what sort of ambition I have. And so I declare that I do not envy those who have started out from the lowest station in life and have surpassed me. In this respect I am by no means in agreement with the men of my class who are prone to denigrate those whose ability has raised them above their lowly origin. For it is perfectly just that men who have seized the stuff of fame (which we have neglected) for themselves and taken possession of it should receive preference. They may be the sons of fullers or tanners, but they have succeeded in spite of difficulties we would not have faced.

"The ignoramus who envies those who have achieved prominence through their knowledge is not only to be called a fool but is to be numbered among the wretched, nay, the most wretched; and our nobles suffer particularly from this error, because they look askance at such embellishments. For what, by God! is the sense of envying someone who possesses what we spurned? Why did we not study the laws? Why did not we ourselves acquire fine learning and the best arts? In that respect cobblers, fullers, and carters have outrun us. Why did we forsake our post, why did we relinquish the most liberal studies to servants and their filth (be it said to our shame)? Quite justly, the heritage of nobility, which we scorned, has been appropriated and put to good use by anyone who has skill and industry. We wretches! who have neglected something capable of raising any of the lowliest persons above us! Let us finally stop envying and try to attain for ourselves what others, to our shame and disgrace, have presumed to take. Anything being neglected belongs to all; and if we refuse to advance ourselves and instead stay content with much lesser things and languish in darkness and idleness, does this not mean abandoning completely those approaches that are open to everyone, and more accessible to us than to them?

"Every desire for fame is honorable, all struggle for excellence is laudable. But let each class retain its own honor, let each be accorded its own credit! I have no intention of belittling those ancestral portraits, or those elaborate family trees, but whatever value they have, it is not ours unless we first earn it with our merits, and it cannot endure unless the nobility adopts morals suitable to itself. It is in vain that one of those well-fed, corpulent heads of a family shows you the pictures of his ancestors, when he himself is so indolent that he resembles a block of wood more than he does those whose excellence lighted the way for him.

"This is what I have wanted to confide to you, both fully and sincerely, about my ambition and disposition."

I had heard some of my more aristocratic friends and acquaintances utter similarly hearty and forceful sentiments (even though not with such fluency and coherence) with visible results in the form of honest activity. It had become a credo that nobility had to be personally earned, and if any rivalry was shown, it was from above to below.

On the other hand, the rest of us had what we wanted, namely the free and approved use of our naturally endowed talents, which was generally quite possible in our middle-class circumstances.

For in this regard my native town had a unique and insufficiently appreciated situation. Whereas the free imperial cities in the north stood on a foundation of extensive trade, and those to the south, with their diminished commercial status, on one of art and technology, in Frankfurt-on-Main there was a certain complex to be seen that seemed to be knit together of trade, capital, real estate, and delight in knowledge and collections. The Lutheran church was in command. No one was excluded from the magistracy: not the ancient group of co-heirs bearing the name House of Limpurg; not the House of Frauenstein,[30] which had begun as a mere club and had remained loyal to reason during the rebellion of the lower classes; nor any jurist or any other man of wealth and respectability. Even those artisans who had been orderly during the difficult times were eligible for the council, if not for advancement in it. The other constitutional checks and balances, the formal arrangements, and all the other things connected with such a constitution gave many people scope for activity. Meanwhile, in this fortunate geographical location, trade and technology were in no sense hindered from growing.

The higher nobility went about its business unenvied and almost unnoticed. The class just beneath it was required to be somewhat more ambitious: resting on the basis of its old family wealth, it tried to make itself conspicuous by scholarly achievements in law and statecraft.

The so-called Reformed, like the refugee Huguenots in other towns, constituted a distinguished class, and even the fact that they drove out to Bockenheim[31] in their handsome equipages for Sunday services was always a kind of triumph over the ordinary townspeople, whose "privilege" it was to go to church on foot, in fair weather or foul.

The Catholics were scarcely noticed. But they also had become aware of the advantages appropriated by the other two creeds.

Book Eighteen

Returning to literary matters, I must call attention to a circumstance that greatly influenced the German poetry of that era and is to be noted specially because its effect on the whole course of our art of poetry has endured to the present day and will be undiminished in the future.

Since early times the Germans had been accustomed to rhyme, which had the advantage that one could proceed very naively and do little more than count syllables. If, with advancing culture, one instinctively paid some slight attention to the sense and significance of the syllables, that brought praise, which some poets were able to get for themselves. The rhyme showed the end of a poetic sentence, and in shorter lines indicated even the lesser pauses, while a naturally cultivated ear would account for variation and grace. Then, however, rhyme was suddenly done away with, but without consideration of the fact that the syllabic values had not been decided, and indeed were hard to decide. Klopstock led the way, and his efforts and accomplishments are well known. Everyone felt the uncertainty of the matter and became hesitant; and so a rhythmical prose was adopted, in response to the nature movement. Gessner's very lovely idylls opened an endless road. Klopstock wrote *The Battle of Arminius* in prose, as well as *Adam's Death*. A sentimental, elevated style took hold of the theater because of the middle-class tragedies and serious comedies, while on the other hand iambic pentameter, popularized among us by English influence, was reducing poetry to prose. But in general the demands for meter and rhyme could not be given up. Although his principles were uncertain, Ramler applied them strictly to his own works and could not refrain from being equally strict with those not his own. He converted prose into verse and altered and improved the work of others, which earned him little thanks and worsened the confusion. Those poets who used traditional rhyme and tried to observe syllabic values succeeded best. Guided by their natural taste, they obeyed implicit and undecided laws, like Wieland, for example, who for a long time served lesser talents as a model, even though he was inimitable. In any case, procedure remained uncertain, and there was no one, not even among the best, who did not become momentarily confused. The unfortunate result was that this epoch, our age of real poetic genius, produced little that could be called perfect of its kind. For in this respect too, while the time was forward-moving, demanding, and active, it was not reflective and failed to satisfy its own needs.

Yet, to find a ground on which to base ourselves poetically, to discover an element in which to breathe freely, we went back several centuries, where serious capabilities had emerged brilliantly from a chaotic situation. And so we also came to appreciate the poetry of that era. The minnesingers were too remote from us. We would have had to study their language first, and this did not appeal to us. We wanted to live, not to learn.

Hans Sachs,[32] the true master-poet, was closest to us—a genuine talent, indeed not like those old knights and courtiers, but a simple middle-class person, which we also boasted of being. His didactic realism was to our liking, and on many occasions we made use of the same easy meter and conveniently ready rhymes. This manner seemed very well adapted to the poetry of our day, and we found a constant need for it.

If significant works of mine, requiring years, nay, a lifetime of attention and toil, were constructed more or less on such unsteady foundations and for frivolous reasons, one can imagine how wantonly other productions, of an ephemeral nature, sometimes took shape: for example, the poetic epistles, parables, and invectives of all sorts with which we continued to wage internal warfare and to look for external quarrels.

Unless already in print, only a little of this remains. I hope it will be preserved. Short explanatory notes would reveal the origins and intentions more clearly to thinking men.

May those more deeply studious persons who some day set eyes upon these things be so kind as to notice that a sincere endeavor underlay all these eccentricities. Honest wishes strive against presumption, nature against tradition, talent against forms; genius struggles with itself, strength against effeminacy, undeveloped excellence against fully developed mediocrity. Indeed, the entire action can be seen as a skirmish at the outposts following a declaration of war, a skirmish which predicts a violent feud. For, to tell the truth, the battle is still not over, though fifty years have passed; only now it is waged on a higher plane.

Taking my lead from an older German puppet play, I had conceived a mad farce which was to bear the title *The Clown's Wedding*. The plot was as follows: The clown, the orphaned son of a rich peasant, has just attained his majority and wants to marry a rich girl named Ursula Blandina. His guardian, Kilian Aprontop, and the girl's mother, Ursula etc., are extremely pleased by this. Their long-nurtured plan and their dearest wishes are thus at last fulfilled and attained. Not the slightest obstacle is present, and the whole action is concerned merely with the delay which the wedding arrangements and the associated indispensable formalities impose on the young couple's desire to possess each other.

The official bidder of wedding guests steps on stage as the prologue. He makes his banal traditional speech, but ends with the rhyme:

> The inn that's named "The Golden Louse"
> Shall be the wedding banquet house.

To escape reproach for violating the unity of place, I had the above-mentioned inn, gleaming with its insignia, displayed in the background; but it could be pivoted to show all its four sides, with, of course, corresponding changes in the wings closer to the front of the stage.

In the first act the front side facing the street appeared, with its golden insignia projected by a solar microscope; in the second, the garden side showed. The third side faced a little wood, and the fourth a nearby lake, which amounted to a prediction that before long it would cause the stage manager very little trouble to bring a wave effect over the whole stage up to the prompter's box.

With all of this, however, I have not yet stated the really interesting thing about the play: the essential joke was enhanced by the mad trick of giving all the dramatis personae names that consisted of nothing but traditional German terms of opprobrium and aversion. These expressed the character of the individuals at once, and indicated their relationship to the others.

Since we may hope that this present book will be read aloud in good company, and also probably in respectable family circles, we dare not even list the personages by name here, as is commonly done on theater posters; nor at this juncture quote the passages where they most clearly and prominently reveal their characters, even though this would be a very simple, sure way of bringing out merry, teasing, harmless allusions and witty jokes.

But for the sake of experiment we shall insert one page, leaving it to our editors to judge whether it is admissible:

> Cousin Worthless, because of his relationship to the family, had the right to be invited to the festival and no one objected. For even though he was completely unfitted for life, he was there, after all; and since he was there, he could not well be denied. And on such a happy day it was out of place to remember that one had been dissatisfied with him from time to time.
>
> The case of Mr. Scoundrel was a more doubtful matter. To be sure, he had been of use to the family when it had profited him also. But, on the other hand, he had harmed the family too, perhaps for his own advantage, perhaps just because an opportunity presented itself. The more or less intelligent ones voted to admit him, outvoting those who wanted to exclude him.
>
> But now there was still a third person, and it was harder to decide

about him. A no less proper individual in company than other people, he was obliging, agreeable, and in many ways useful; but he had one defect, that is, he could not bear to hear his name. The moment it touched his ear he fell into a heroic rage, which Norsemen call going berserk, made threats right and left to kill everyone, and in his frenzy would both injure and be injured. The second act of the play ended in shambles because of him.

Here was an opportunity to chastise the thievish Macklot which could absolutely not be missed.—Namely, he goes about peddling his Macklotish pulp, and when he perceives that arrangements are being made for a wedding, he cannot resist the urge to be a parasite here too, and to revive his starved guts at other people's expense. He presents himself, Kilian Aprontop investigates his claims, but must turn him away because, as he says, all the guests are acknowledged public figures, whereas this supplicant certainly cannot claim to be one. Macklot tries his best to prove he is just as famous as the others. Since Kilian Aprontop is a strict master of ceremonies, however, and cannot be swayed, that unnamed man, who has recovered from his berserk rage at the conclusion of Act Two, intercedes so desperately for his near-relative, the desperado printer, that the latter is finally accepted by the other guests.

Around this time the Counts von Stolberg[33] presented themselves to pay us a brief visit before touring Switzerland. Thanks to the very early surfacing of my talent in the *Göttingen Poetic Almanach,* I had gotten on the most friendly terms with them and all those young men whose work and ways are quite well known. Rather strange concepts of friendship and love prevailed in those days. Actually it was just lively young men unbosoming themselves to each other and revealing much talent but little cultural development. Such mutual relationships, which of course had the look of intimacy, were considered to be love, genuine affection. Like the others I deceived myself on this point, and suffered for it in more than one way for many years. I have kept a letter of Bürger's from that time which makes it plain that these fellows by no means concerned themselves with morality in esthetic matters. Each one felt an excitement, and believed himself fully authorized to act and compose poetry on this basis.

The brothers arrived, Count Haugwitz[34] with them, and I received them with unfeigned cordiality and due (but not exaggerated) decorum. They put up at an inn, but took most of their meals at our house. The first cheerful gathering turned out very well, but before long some eccentric manifestations emerged.

A special relationship was formed with my mother. In her sturdy, straightforward fashion she found it possible to transport herself right back to the Middle Ages and assume the role of an "Aya"[35] to some Lombardian or Byzantine princess. She was never called anything but "Dame Aya," and she enjoyed the charade, being all the readier to join in our youthful fantasies since she already thought she saw herself reflected in Götz von Berlichingen's good wife.

But this was only the beginning, for after we had sat at table together a few times, and one or two bottles of wine had been drunk, our poetic hatred of tyrants came out and we showed ourselves to be thirsty for the blood of such villains. My father smiled and shook his head. My mother had scarcely heard anything about tyrants in her whole life, although she did remember seeing engravings of such monsters in Gottfried's *Chronicle*: King Cambyses, who, in a father's presence, exults over having shot an arrow into the heart of the latter's little son—such were the things that stuck in her memory. However, to give a cheerful turn to these and similar, ever more violent utterances, she betook herself to her cellar, where the oldest wines were preserved in large well-maintained barrels. No less distinguished vintages were there than 1706, 1719, 1726, and 1748, carefully tended by herself and rarely tapped, only for occasions of solemn significance.

Setting the high-colored wine down in a cut-glass decanter, she now exclaimed, "This is the true blood of tyrants! Enjoy it, but all thoughts of murder are unwelcome in my house!" Thus she pleasantly distracted us and steered us into greater moderation and humaneness.

"Tyrants' blood indeed!" I shouted. "There is no greater tyrant than the one whose heart's blood is being set before you. Enjoy it, but with restraint! For you must guard against being enslaved by its good taste and spirit. The grapevine is the universal tyrant, and ought to be uprooted. Therefore we should choose the holy Lycurgus, the Thracian, and honor him as our patron saint. He attacked his pious work energetically, but was blinded and ruined by the beguiling demon Bacchus, and so deserves first place in the roll of martyrs.

"The grapevine is the worst tyrant of all, simultaneously a hypocrite, a flatterer, and a despot. The first draughts of his blood are appetizing, but one drop irresistibly lures the next one after it. They follow like the pearls in a necklace that one is loath to rip apart."

If by chance I am suspected here of having inserted (as the best historians have done!) a fictitious speech instead of my real discourse, then let me say I wish that a stenographer had immediately taken down this peroration and preserved it for us. The motifs would be found identical, and the flow of words perhaps more graceful and engaging. In any case, the present version wholly lacks the rambling loquacity and superfluity typical of a young man who is conscious of his strength and ability but does not know what he wants to accomplish with them.

In a town like Frankfurt one is in a strange situation: the foreigners constantly traversing it conjure up all the regions of the world and awaken the desire to travel. Even earlier I had become mobile for many a reason, and at this precise moment, when it was important for me to make an attempt at doing without Lili, and when a certain nagging restlessness rendered me incapable of any specific activity, the Stolbergs' invitation to accompany them to Switzerland was welcome. Encouraged by my father's exhortations, since he strongly favored a trip in that direction and recommended that I not pass up an opportunity to cross over into Italy if one presented itself, I quickly resolved to go, and soon everything was packed. I parted from Lili after dropping some hints, but with no farewell. She had become so much a part of me that I really did not think I could leave her.

In a few hours I found myself in Darmstadt with my merry companions. At the local court we were required to conduct ourselves with great propriety, and really Count Haugwitz was our guide and leader in this. He was the youngest of us, well proportioned, of gentle, noble appearance, with a soft, friendly face. He was even tempered and sympathetic but showed such restraint that in comparison to the others he seemed impassive. Therefore he had to put up with all sorts of mockery and name-calling on their part. This might be the case as long as they thought they could behave like children of nature, but when it was a question of propriety and they were required (not altogether to their displeasure) to act the count again, then he was the one able to arrange and manage everything so that we could carry it off, if not with the best, at least with tolerable, repute.

Meanwhile I spent my time with Merck, who had a contrary, Mephistophelian view of my proposed trip, and, after my companions had visited him, he was able to characterize them with merciless perspicacity. He knew me thoroughly in his own way. The invincibly naive amiability of my nature was painful to him, and my everlasting tolerance, my desire to live and let live, was an abomination to him. "Your roaming off with these young fellows," he exclaimed, "is a piece of folly." And then he proceeded to describe them shrewdly, but not altogether correctly. He evinced an absolute lack of kindness, and consequently I felt justified in looking past him, although I did not so much look past him as appreciate the aspects that lay outside his range of vision.

"You will not stay with them long!"—that was the sum of his remarks. At the same time I remember a noteworthy statement, which he later repeated to me and which I repeated to myself, often finding it significant in my life. "Your aim," he said, "your unalterable course, is to give poetic form to reality; the others are trying to give reality to the so-called poetic, the imaginative, and that only results in nonsense." If one grasps the vast difference between these two procedures, and holds it fast and applies it, then one gets much enlightenment about a thousand other things.

Unfortunately, before our group disengaged itself from Darmstadt there was cause for Merck's opinion to be indisputably confirmed.

Among the crazy notions of the time which arose from the concept that a person must try to return to a state of nature was the one of bathing in open waters under the open sky. And our friends, after having endured so much propriety, could not refrain from this impropriety. Darmstadt, situated on a sandy plain without any streams, may nevertheless have a pond nearby, which I have heard about only on this occasion. My hot-blooded and more and more excited friends went to refresh themselves in this fishpond. The sight of naked youths in bright sunshine no doubt was quite a novelty in this region; at any rate, it caused a scandal. Merck repeated his conclusions more emphatically, and I do not deny that I hastened our departure.

In spite of all the good and noble feelings we held in common, a certain difference in our views and behavior showed up already on the way to Mannheim. Leopold Stolberg related passionately how he had been forced to give up a heartfelt attachment to a beautiful English girl, which was why he had undertaken this far journey. If, on the other hand, one wanted to tell him sympathetically that one was also no stranger to such feelings, then his sentiment erupted with youthful extravagance: nothing in the world could equal his passion, his grief, or the beauty and amiability of his sweetheart. If one tried to moderate his assertions with temperate speeches, as is surely permissible among good comrades, this only seemed to make matters worse, and both Count Haugwitz and I were finally obliged to agree to drop this subject. When we arrived in Mannheim, we moved into some nice rooms in a respectable inn. During the dessert of our first noon meal, at which wine had not been spared, Leopold demanded that we drink to his fair one's health, which we did amid considerable clamor. When the glasses were empty, he exclaimed, "But now not another drink may be taken from these hallowed goblets. To drink a second health would be a desecration, and so let us destroy these receptacles!" Thereupon he threw his long-stemmed glass against the wall behind him. The rest of us followed suit, while I imagined I could feel Merck pulling on my collar.

But one childhood trait kept by young people is that they do not bear grudges against good comrades. Ingenuous affection may, to be sure, feel an unpleasant blow, but cannot be wounded.

After these now sacred glasses had been added to our bill, we hurried on to Karlsruhe, confident and cheerful, and took up with a new circle trustingly and light-heartedly. We found Klopstock there,[36] and he very properly exercised his old moral authority over these very devoted pupils of his; and I was also glad to submit to it, with the result that when I was bidden to court with the others I may have acquitted myself tolerably well for a novice. It was rather expected of us to be natural, but also to be significant. The ruling margrave, as one of the senior princes, but especially because of his admirable governmental goals, was a highly respected German regent, and he liked to discuss matters of state economy. The margravine, active and well versed in the arts and various cultural areas, spoke charmingly to indicate that she too had some interest in us. Of course we acted grateful for that, but in private we could not resist making jokes about the poor quality of paper she manufactured and about her patronage of the piratical printer Macklot.

Most significant for me was the fact that the young Duke of Saxe-Weimar and his noble fiancée, Princess Louise of Hesse-Darmstadt,[37] were meeting here to enter formally into marriage, which was also the reason that President von Moser had already arrived. He had to define these important relationships and come to a complete agreement with Count Görtz, the lord high steward. I had the most agreeable conversations with both these high personages, and in our farewell audience they ended by declaring repeatedly that they would both be very pleased to see me soon in Weimar.

A few private conversations with Klopstock filled me with trust and candor toward him, because he was so friendly to me. I read the latest scenes of my *Faust* to him, and he seemed most receptive. Later I heard that he had honored them with marked approval (usually something he could not easily give) in the presence of others, and had expressed the wish to see the play completed.

That uncultivated sort of behavior which at the time was occasionally called "genius-like" was controlled to some extent in Karlsruhe, which was a decorous and, as it were, sacred soil. I parted with my comrades, since I had to make a detour in order to go to Emmendingen, where my brother-in-law was high bailiff. I looked upon this venture of seeing my sister as a real trial. I knew that her life was unhappy, and that this could neither be blamed on her, nor her spouse, nor on the circumstances. She was a peculiar person, and is hard to talk about, but we shall try to summarize here what can be told.

Her lovely figure was an advantage, but her facial features were not, for although they expressed kindness, intelligence, and sympathy distinctly enough they were somewhat lacking in regularity and grace.

Besides, her high and strongly arched forehead made a rather unpleasant impression because of the abominable fashion of combing and forcing the hair away from the face, even though this forehead gave excellent evidence of her moral and intellectual qualities. I can imagine that if she had been able to follow what has been introduced in modern times and had put a cloud of curls around the upper part of her face, and clothed her temples and cheeks with similar ringlets, she would have been more pleased with her reflection in the mirror and have worried no longer about offending others as much as she offended herself. Moreover one must consider the sad fact that her skin was seldom clear, a malady which, by daemonic ill fortune, had afflicted her since childhood, usually on festival days, on days when there were concerts, balls, and invitations of other kinds.

Gradually she had struggled her way through these circumstances, while her other splendid qualities kept developing more and more.

She had a firm, not easily subdued character, a sympathetic and sympathy-seeking soul, superior cultivation of mind, excellent knowledge, as well as talents, mastery of several languages, and a skilled pen, so that, had she only been well favored on the outside, she would have been counted among the most sought-after women of her time.

One more curious thing must be revealed after all of this: her nature harbored not the slightest sensuality. She had grown up beside me and wished to continue spending her life in this sibling harmony. After my return from the university we had remained inseparable, with such heartfelt intimacy that we had our thoughts, feelings, and whims in common, our impressions of everything that happened. When I went to Wetzlar, the solitude seemed unbearable to her, and my friend Schlosser, who was neither a stranger nor repulsive to the dear girl, took my place. Unfortunately, in him the brotherly feeling transformed itself into a decided passion, perhaps his first one, considering his strict, conscientious nature. Here, as they commonly say, was a very convenient, desirable match, which she finally let herself, I may say, be persuaded to accept, after having steadfastly rejected various significant proposals from men who in themselves were not significant, men whom she despised.

I have to confess sincerely that I liked to imagine her, when I sometimes engaged in fancies about her destiny, not as a wife, but as an abbess, the mother superior of a noble convent. She possessed everything that is demanded by such a higher calling, and lacked what the world relentlessly requires. She exercised an altogether irresistible influence over feminine souls: she lovingly attracted young persons and dominated them through the spiritual force of her inner merits. Since she had, in common with me, a general tolerance for what was good and human, with all its oddities, so long as it stopped short of perversity, no one with a peculiarity indicative of some significant natural characteristic needed to conceal it from her or feel abashed in her presence. For this reason our social gatherings, as we have already seen earlier, could always proceed diversely, freely, and pleasantly, even though they sometimes bordered on the audacious. I had her alone to thank for my custom of associating with young women decorously and obligingly without having this immediately lead to a definite restriction and appropriation. Now, however, a perceptive reader who can read between these lines and see what has not been written but only hinted at will begin to understand the solemnity of my feelings as I entered Emmendingen at that time.

But on my departure after a brief stay, what weighed still more heavily on my heart was that my sister had most urgently recommended to me, indeed ordered me, to part from Lili. She herself had suffered badly from a protracted engagement. Schlosser, like the honest man he was, did not become betrothed to her until he was assured of his appointment to the grand duchy of Baden, nay, until he was, so to speak, already appointed. But the actual designation of a place was interminably delayed. If I may reveal what I surmise about this, then I think that our good Schlosser, for all his professional qualifications, had too much uncompromising integrity to be desirable to the sovereign as a servant in direct contact with himself, much less to the ministers as a close coworker. The appointment in Karlsruhe he had hoped and urgently wished for did not materialize. However, the delay was explained for me when the position of high bailiff was vacated in Emmendingen and he was at once transferred there. A distinguished and lucrative office had now been conferred on him, and he showed himself to be fully equal to it. He felt that it quite suited his disposition and methods to be here on his own, to act according to his convictions, and to take responsibility for everything, whether he was praised or blamed.

No objections could be made to this. My sister was obliged to follow him, not to a princely capital, as she had hoped, but instead to a place that could only seem a solitary wilderness to her, and into a dwelling that for all its spaciousness, magisterial quality, and stateliness was completely barren of social life. A few young women of her former circle of friends followed after her, and since the Gerock family[38] was blessed with daughters they took turns visiting her. So, while deprived of many things, at least she could still enjoy the company of some old confidantes.

It was these circumstances and experiences that made her feel justified in enjoining me most earnestly to break with Lili. Although she approved of her highly, she thought it cruel to tear a young woman of this type away from an existence that was lively and active, if not really brilliant, and to bring her into our house. While very nice, it was not suitably appointed for large parties, and she would be between a well-intentioned, taciturn, but didactically inclined father and a mother who in her way was very busy about the house but, once her duties were done and she was comfortably seated at her needlework, did not like to be disturbed in her cozy conversations with selected young persons she was cultivating.

To this she contrasted Lili's situation vividly and clearly, having been told everything about it by me, down to the last detail, partly in letters but partly also in long, impassioned, confidential talks.

Unfortunately, what she presented was nothing more than a detailed, kindly elaboration on a few well-chosen words officiously whispered to her by a friend who was gradually getting a bad reputation as a talebearer.

I could promise her nothing, although I had to admit she had convinced me. I left with that mysterious feeling in my heart which continues to sustain passion, for the child Amor insists on clinging stubbornly to the skirts of departing Hope even after she has begun firmly striding away.

The only thing between there and Zurich that I still distinctly remember is the Rhine Falls at Schaffhausen. Here the mighty plunge of the river clearly marks the first stage of a coming mountainous terrain, and into this we meant to enter. From there we were to toil our way to reach the heights, little by little, stage by stage, and ever upwards.

The view of Lake Zurich that I enjoyed from the gate of the Sword Inn is still present to my mind. I say, from the gate of the inn, because instead of entering I hurried to see Lavater. My reception was cheery and cordial and, I must admit, incomparably charming. His presence could not be imagined other than warm, considerate, beneficent, and uplifting. Although his wife had rather odd features, she looked peaceful and sweetly pious and, like everything else around him, she harmonized perfectly with his manner of life and thought. Our first and almost uninterrupted conversation was about his *Physiognomy*.[39] If I am not mistaken, the first part of this curious work was already completely printed, or at least near completion. It can well be called both inspired and empirical, both methodical and encyclopedic, and my relationship to it was very strange. Lavater wanted the whole world to collaborate and sympathize with him. On his Rhine journey he had already ordered portraits made of a great many notable individuals, so that personal considerations might arouse their interest in a work in which they themselves were scheduled to appear. He managed artists in the same way, inviting each one to send drawings for his purposes. These arrived, but did not precisely serve their ends. Likewise, he had copperplates made right and left, but these also seldom turned out to be characteristic. For his part, he had accomplished a great task and, with money and all sorts of exertion, had made preparations for a significant work which would do physiognomy every honor. And now, when a volume was about to be made of it, when physiognomy, established on theory and demonstrated with examples, was to approach the dignity of a science, not one of the illustrations said what it was supposed to say. The plates had to be criticized and qualified, not even praised, merely admitted, and some practically obliterated by explanations. Since I always tried to find solid footing before taking a step forward, it was one of the most painful tasks I could be assigned to perform. One can judge for oneself. The manuscript text with accompanying illustrations had been sent to me in Frankfurt. I had the right to delete anything that displeased me, and to emend and make additions at will, but of course used it very sparingly. He scolded me just once, when he had included a certain passionate polemic against an unfair critic, and I omitted it, substituting a cheerful nature poem. But later, when he had cooled down, he approved my action.

Let those who page through and even read (they will not regret it!) the four volumes of the *Physiognomy* consider how interesting our meeting was, since most of the illustrations for the work were already drawn and some engraved: these were now displayed and criticized, and we pondered ingenious means to make even the unsuitable items suitable in this case by rendering them instructive.

As I peruse Lavater's work once more, it makes me feel both cheerful and strange, for while I seem to be seeing the shades of people formerly well known to me, they are shades which once vexed and still cannot please me.

However, the potentiality for salvaging, to some degree, this mass of inapt portrayals lay in the decidedly fine talent of the draftsman and engraver Lips. Indeed, he was born for the bold, prosaic depiction of reality that was necessary here. He worked directly under the physiognomist and therefore had to be very careful to satisfy his master's odd demands. The talented peasant lad keenly felt the obligation he owed to this man of the cloth, a citizen of this highly privileged town, and he executed his commission very well.

Since I was lodged separately from my companions, I daily grew more estranged from them, even though not the slightest unpleasantness was involved. We no longer made joint excursions into the country, although we still managed sometimes to meet together in town. With all the arrogance of young counts they too had called on Lavater, and of course they made a somewhat different impression on the adroit physiognomist than on the rest of the world. He gave me his opinion about them, and I remember quite clearly that he exclaimed, speaking of Leopold Stolberg, "I do not know what all of you are talking about. He is a noble, excellent, talented youth, but he has been described to me as a hero, a Hercules, and yet in my whole life I have never seen a softer, tenderer, and, if it comes to that, more easily influenced young man. I am still far from having sure physiognomical insight, but things look very miserable indeed for the whole lot of you."

Interest in Lavater and his physiognomical studies had greatly increased since his trip to the lower Rhine. All sorts of people, returning his visit, thronged to his door, so that he felt somewhat embarrassed about being considered the first among clergymen and intellectuals, and about being viewed as the sole magnet for foreigners. Consequently, so as to avoid all envy and ill will, he would remind and urge all his visitors to show their friendship and regard for the other notable men as well.

In this connection, old Bodmer was the first to be considered, and we had to set out to visit him and pay our youthful respects. He lived on a height overlooking the larger, or old part of town, which was located on the right shore, where the lake compresses its waters to form the river Limmat. We traversed the town and eventually ascended, on increasingly steep pathways, the height behind the walls, where a suburb had grown up in very charming, semi-rural fashion between the fortifications and the old city wall, partly with row houses, partly with detached ones. Here stood Bodmer's house, his abode throughout his life, amid the most open, cheerful surroundings, which, on this lovely, clear day, we had been able to view very pleasurably before entering. We were conducted up one flight of stairs into a completely wood-paneled room, where we were met by a lively old man of middle height. He received us with his habitual greeting to younger visitors: that we should feel complimented because he had delayed his departure from this earthly sphere long enough to be able to welcome us cordially, become acquainted with us, rejoice in our talents, and wish us good fortune in our subsequent careers.

We, in return, extolled his good fortune in having possessed throughout his life, as a poet belonging to the patriarchal world but still in the vicinity of a very cultured town, a truly idyllic dwelling, and in having been able for so many long years, up here in this high, free atmosphere, to find constant solace for his eyes in such a vast prospect.

He did not seem displeased that we asked leave to see the view from his window, which, in the bright sunshine of the finest season of the year, was really quite incomparable. One could see many parts of the "great town" as it sloped downwards, and the "lesser town" across the Limmat, as well as the fertile fields along the river Sihl to the west. Behind us to the left was a section of Lake Zurich with its surface in shining motion and its infinitely varied, alternating mountain and valley shores. Then, dazzled by all this, in the distance one still had the azure series of high mountain ranges to gaze at most longingly, and we ventured to identify their peaks by name.

The extraordinary sight had become routine to him over the years, but the rapture we young men felt over it seemed to please him. He grew, if one may put it thus, ironically sympathetic, and we parted as the best of friends, even though what had mainly occupied our minds was our longing for those blue mountainous heights.

Only now that I am about to take leave of our worthy patriarch do I notice that I have not yet said anything about his face and figure, or his gestures and manner of behavior.

In general, to be sure, I do not think it quite proper for travelers to itemize, as it were, a notable man whom they have visited, as if they were supplying material for an arrest warrant. Nobody considers that one only has a moment, after being admitted, to observe inquisitively, and then only in one's own way. And so the person visited may sometimes actually, sometimes only apparently, be proud or modest, taciturn or loquacious, cheerful or out of humor. In this particular case, however, I would like to excuse myself by saying that Bodmer's venerable person, if described in words, might not readily make a favorable impression. Fortunately, there is Bause's engraving of the portrait by Graff, which perfectly depicts the man as he appeared to us, even with the same quizzical, questioning look.

A special pleasure that was not unexpected but very much hoped for welcomed me in Zurich when I met my young friend Passavant[40] there. This son of a distinguished Reformed family in my native town was living in Switzerland, the fountainhead of that doctrine which he was to proclaim one day as a preacher. Not tall of figure, but agile, his face and general air bespoke a quick, charming resoluteness. His hair and beard were black, his eyes alert, and on the whole he was active, moderate, and sympathetic.

Hardly had we embraced and exchanged our first greetings when he suggested that we visit the small cantons. He had already greatly enjoyed hiking through them, and he wanted me to be charmed and enraptured by the sight of them also.

While I had been discussing the most immediate and important matters with Lavater and we had almost concluded our common business, my lively traveling companions had already set forth on many roads and explored the region in their fashion. Therefore Passavant, who overwhelmed me with his cordial friendship, felt he had earned exclusive right to my company. The others were absent; and it was all the easier for him to lure me into the mountains because I myself was decidedly inclined to make this long-desired tour in complete peace and in my own way. One bright morning we got into a boat and sailed up the splendid lake.

Let me insert a poem which will convey some idea of those happy moments:

And fresh nourishment, fresh blood,
Suck I from this free world;

How sweet this nature is, how good,
Upon whose breast I'm curled!
Our boat is rocked with gentle force
By waves that strike our oar,
And mountains opposite our course
Rise cloud-tipped from the shore.

Eyes, my eyes, why are you lowered?
Golden dreams, must you press forward?
Flee, you dreams, though gold you be,
Here is life and love for me.

On the wave is winking
Many a hovering star,
Downy mists are drinking
Towered peaks afar.
Morning breezes eddy
Round the shadowed lake,
Where ripe fruits, soon ready,
Cool reflections make.

We went ashore at Richterswyl, where Lavater had given us an introduction to Doctor Hotz.[41] As a physician and a highly intelligent, benevolent man, he was venerated in his village and in the whole region, and we believe there is no better way of honoring his memory than to insert a passage from Lavater's *Physiognomy* which delineates him:

"Much finer, but no less cheerful, loyal, honest, dependable, and devoted is the tinted profile below of an excellent fellow citizen of our canton. The outer contour, although it must have lost a great deal, is that of a truly great man.

"The inner part of the nose contrasts with the outer part by being scaled down in size.

"In the eye there is a cheerful, noble, purposeful, but candid spirit, and reflective kindness.

"The cheeks are too poorly drawn to permit the passing of any judgment on them.

"In and around the mouth natural cheerfulness and benevolent goodheartedness with no flabby softness at all.

"I also like how the square, visible jaw stands out from the shadow; it helps to confirm the impression of intelligence, although it is not completely favorable to manly firmness.

"Cheerful, merry, well-built, strong, self-reliant persons without flabbiness or hardness in their outline—always inspire confidence in their integrity."

After enjoying his excellent hospitality and being informed most graciously and profitably about the next stages of our tour, we ascended the hills situated behind this place. When we were about to descend again into the valley of Schindellegi we turned around once more to absorb the charming view over Lake Zurich.

What I felt is indicated by the following lines, which are still preserved in a little notebook just as they were written down then:

If I, lovely Lili, did not love you,
How this sight would fill my heart with bliss!
Yet, and if I, Lili, did not love you,
What were happiness?

I find this little interjection to be more expressive at this point than where it is printed in my collected poems.

The rough roads which led from there to Maria Einsiedeln[42] could not dampen our high spirits. A number of pilgrims whom we had already noticed down by the lake had continued at a regular pace amid prayers and songs and had caught up with us. We let them pass with a salutation, and by summoning us to share their pious goals they enlivened these desolate heights in a charmingly characteristic way. We saw them make a living outline of the winding path along which we also would have to wander, and we seemed to follow more joyfully. In any case, the customs of the Roman church always look imposing and meaningful to the Protestant, for he acknowledges only the original, inward impulse that created them and the human element that transmits them from generation to generation. Thus he penetrates to the kernel and does not concern himself at the moment with the shell, the pericarp, nor, indeed, with the tree itself, its branches, leaves, bark, and roots.

Now we saw the majestic church loom up in a desolate, unwooded valley. The monastery was of wide, stately proportions, standing in the middle of a neatly kept settlement, and could accommodate this great number of multifarious guests in a quite suitable manner.

The little church within the church, the saint's former hermitage, was incrusted with marble and transformed, as much as possible, into a respectable chapel. For me, this little receptacle, reconstructed and with a superstructure of pillars and vaults, was a novelty, something I had never seen before. Inevitably I was aroused to serious reflections, because here a single spark of morality and piety had kindled a gleaming, ever-burning little flame, to which throngs of believers would make the arduous pilgrimage so that they also might ignite their little candles at this sacred fire. Be that as it may, this is an indication that mankind has a boundless need for the same light and warmth which the saint[43] had nurtured and enjoyed with profoundest feeling and surest conviction. We were led into the treasury, which was quite rich and imposing;

but the most eye-catching attraction it offered was some life-size, or even colossal, busts of saints and founders of orders.

But the cabinet opened next was a sight that aroused quite a different sort of attention. It contained ancient and valuable objects which had been dedicated and presented here. Various crowns that were remarkable for their goldsmith work fascinated me, and I examined one of them to the exclusion of the others. It was a spiked crown in the style of olden times, similar to those seen on the heads of ancient queens, but very tastefully designed, and fashioned with great artistry, even the inset colored stones distributed and arranged with extreme skill and selectivity—in sum, a work of the kind one could declare perfect at first sight, without being able to enlarge on this impression in a technically correct way.

In such instances, where art is felt rather than understood, the heart and mind lean to utilization: one would like to own the jewel in order to give someone pleasure. I asked permission to take out the little crown, and as I lifted it up and held it carefully in my hand, my only thought was that I must press it onto Lili's shining curls, lead her to the mirror, and observe both her own joy and the happiness she caused others. Subsequently I have often thought that this scene would surely make a very significant and agreeable sight if portrayed by a talented painter. Then it would be worthwhile being the young king who was winning a bride and a new realm in this manner.

In order that we might see all the monastery's possessions, we were led into a room full of art, curiosities, and specimens of natural history. At the time I had little knowledge of the value of such things. I had not yet been attracted to the science of geognosy, which, though very laudable, dissects our impression of the earth's beautiful surface under the gaze of intellect. Much less had the fantastic science of geology swallowed me up in its labyrinth. Nevertheless, the cleric who was guiding us around urged me to give some heed to the fossilized head of a small wild boar, well preserved in blue shale, which, he said, was highly prized by connoisseurs. Black as it was, it has remained in my memory ever since. It had been found in the region of Rapperswyl, in an area which has been marshy since primeval times and thus could very well receive and preserve such mummies for posterity.

I was attracted quite differently to a copperplate by Martin Schön,[44] kept in a frame behind glass, that depicted the Assumption of Mary. Of course, a perfect example is the only one that can give us an idea of such a master's art, but then, as is the case with any kind of perfection, we are so affected by it that we cannot—however much time may pass in the interim—rid ourselves of the desire to own the same thing and be able to look at it repeatedly. Why should I not get ahead of my story and admit that afterwards I was not satisfied until I too had acquired an excellent print of this engraving?

On June 16, 1775 (for here I first find a date recorded), we started out on a difficult route: wild, stony heights had to be scaled, and, what is more, amidst complete solitude and desolation. In the evening at a quarter to eight we stood opposite the two Schwyzer Hocken,[45] mountain peaks which project mightily into the air next to each other. For the first time we found snow on our trail, but the snow clinging to those jagged, rocky peaks was still from the previous winter. The vast gorges were somberly and awesomely filled with a primeval spruce forest, into which we had to go down. After a short rest we ran briskly, and with reckless abandon, along the footpath which plunged into the depths from rock to rock, from ledge to ledge, and at ten o'clock we arrived in Schwyz. We had grown simultaneously tired and vigorous, ready to fall down and ready to go; we quenched our thirst in great gulps, and felt still more enthusiastic. Let us imagine this young man, who some two years earlier had written *Werther,* and his younger friend, whom that amazing work had inflamed while it was still in manuscript, both of them thrust without conscious intention into something like a state of nature, vividly remembering bygone passions, immersed in present ones, forming ineffectual plans, reveling in the realm of fantasy, secure in their ready strength—then we will have an approximate idea of our condition, which I would not be able to describe, were not the following notation to be found in my journal: "The laughter and happy shouting went on until midnight."

On the morning of the 17th we saw the Schwyzer Hocken from our windows. Cloud upon cloud was rising up on these enormous, irregular natural pyramids. Leaving Schwyz at one o'clock in the afternoon, we proceeded toward Rigi, and at two o'clock the sunlight was splendid over Lake Lowerz. Our sheer delight kept us from seeing anything at all. Two sturdy girls rowed the boat; we found that charming and made no objection. We arrived at the island where, it is said, a tyrant once dwelt. However that may be, a hermit's hut has wedged itself between the ruins.

We climbed the Rigi, and at seven-thirty were standing in the snow next to the shrine of the Virgin; then we went past the chapel and cloister, and to the Ox Inn.

On the morning of Sunday the 18th I sketched the chapel from the Ox. At twelve o'clock we went to the Cold Bath or Spring of the Three Sisters. By a quarter after two we had scaled the height, and we found ourselves in the clouds, which this time was doubly unpleasant for us since they obscured the view and made us wet with falling mist. But when they parted here and there and let us see a clear, splendid, sunlit world, like pictures coming forth and changing within a billowing frame, we no longer deplored these contingent circumstances. For it was a sight never seen before and never to be viewed again, and we tarried a long time in this fairly uncomfortable situation in order to catch sight of a little tip of sunny earth, a narrow stretch of shore, and a patch of lake through the fissures and clefts in this constantly agitated cloud mass.

At eight o'clock in the evening we were back again at the door of the inn and restored our strength with baked fish, and eggs, and plenty of wine.

While the twilight deepened and gradually became night, our ears were engaged by some eerily harmonious sounds: the tinkle of the chapel bells, the splashing of the fountain, the rustling of the shifting breezes, and a hunting horn in the distance—these were salutary, soothing, lulling moments.

On the 19th at six-thirty in the morning we first went upwards, then down to the Lake of the Cantons,[46] to Vitznau, and from there by water to Gersau. We had our midday meal in the inn by the lake. Toward two o'clock we were opposite the Rütli, where the three Tells[47] took their oath; next we went to the ledge where the hero leapt out of the boat, and where, in his honor, the legend of his life and deeds has been immortalized in paintings. At three o'clock we were in Fluelen, where he took ship, and at four o'clock in Altdorf, where he shot the apple.

On this appropriate poetic thread one winds one's way through the labyrinth of these steep walls of rock, which reach down into the water, ignoring us. They, the imperturbable ones, stand there as calmly as the wings of a stage. Fortune or misfortune, merriment or grief affect only the personages on today's playbill.

Such observations, however, were quite beyond the scope of the two young men. They had banished the recent past from their minds, and the future lay before them, as marvelous and inscrutable as the mountains into which they were aspiring to go.

On the 20th we made our way to Amsteg, where baked fish were prepared for us most appetizingly. Here now, in these sufficiently desolate foothills, where the river Reuss surged out of some quite rugged ravines and spilled its cold snow water over the neat gravel banks, I did not refrain from using the wished-for opportunity and refreshed myself in its rushing waters.

At three o'clock we started out again. A train of packhorses was moving in front of us, and we walked with it over a broad snowy mass, only discovering later that this was hollow underneath. Here, in a mountain gorge which ordinarily had to be circuited, the winter snow had been piled up to serve as a shorter, direct road. The water streaming through had gradually hollowed it out, and the mild summer air had melted away more and more of it, until now it connected the two sides like a broad natural bridge. We satisfied our curiosity about this amazing natural phenomenon when, somewhat farther up beyond it, we ventured down into the broader part of the gorge.

As we kept climbing higher, the spruce forests remained in the depths below us, and from time to time the Reuss could be seen through them, foaming over fallen rocks.

At seven-thirty we arrived in Wasen, where we could not drink the heavy, sour, red Lombardian wine until we added water to it and substituted a great deal of sugar for the ingredient that nature had declined to instill in the grapes. The innkeeper displayed some fine crystals, but at that time such nature studies were so far from my mind that I did not care to burden myself with these mountain products, even for the trifling price he asked.

On the 21st at six-thirty we climbed upwards. The rocks grew ever mightier and more terrible, and the way to Devil's Rock and to the view of Devil's Bridge became ever more arduous. My companion elected to rest here, and he encouraged me to sketch the significant views. But while I managed the outlines, there was no depth and no foreground. I had no language for objects such as these. We toiled onward, while the vast desolation seemed to grow ever greater: ledges became mountains, and hollows became abysses. So my guide led me up to the Urseren tunnel,[48] through which I walked a little peevishly, for what we had seen heretofore had been sublime, and this darkness canceled everything out.

But of course my roguish guide had anticipated the joyful astonishment that would overtake me when I emerged. The river, now just moderately foaming, meandered gently here and there through a level valley that was surrounded by mountains but was nevertheless wide enough to invite habitation. Above the neat village of Urseren[49] and its church, which stood facing us on a flat terrain, there rose a little spruce forest, which was held sacred because it protected the settlement at its base from the snow avalanches coming from farther up. The valley's verdant meadows were adorned with small willow trees by the river's edge, and we reveled in a vegetation we had long been deprived of. It was a very great relief, and on these level paths we felt our energy revive. My traveling companion was not a little proud of the surprise he had so cleverly prepared.

This Alpine meadow was home to the famous Urseren cheese, and the exhilarated youths also did justice to a tolerable wine in order to heighten their pleasure still more and to lend a more fantastic glow to their projects.

On the 22nd at three-thirty we left our inn to go from the smooth Urseren valley into the rocky Leventine valley.[50] Here again, all fertility was suddenly lacking: just bare, seemingly mossy rocks covered with snow, bursts of strong wind bringing clouds up and past, the noise of waterfalls, the ringing bells of packhorses far up in the desolate heights, where neither those coming nor those going were visible. Here it does not overtax the imagination to suppose that dragons nest in the clefts. But still we felt cheered and uplifted by one of the most beautiful of waterfalls, one best suited for a painting, with a grandiose variety in all its terraces. Being opulently supplied with melted snow just at this season, and alternately clouded over and unveiled, it kept us chained to the spot for a considerable time.

Eventually we arrived at some mist lakes, as I should like to call them because they were hardly distinguishable from the streaks in the atmosphere. It was not long before a building emerged from the fog; it was the hospice,[51] and we were greatly content to find immediate shelter under its charitable roof.

Book Nineteen

We were announced by the gentle barking of a little dog who came toward us, and an elderly but robust woman received us at the door in a friendly manner. She made excuses for the good monk, who had gone to Milan but was expected to return that evening. Then, without further ado, she made provision for our needs and comfort. A warm, spacious common room welcomed us. Bread, cheese, and a drinkable wine were set before us, and an adequate supper was promised. Now we went over the day's surprises again, and my friend was more than proud of himself because everything had turned out so well and a day been spent whose impressions far exceeded anything that poetry or prose could express. With the late onset of twilight the portly monk finally entered, greeted his guests with amicable warmth and dignity, and said a few words to the cook about giving us every possible attention. When we did not conceal our amazement that he was willing to spend his life up here, away from all society in this complete wilderness, he declared that he was never without company, and had we not also come to give him the pleasure of our visit? He said the transport back and forth of goods between Germany and Italy was very great, and that this constant exchange of shipments put him in touch with the leading trading companies. He frequently went down to Milan, and more rarely to Lucerne, while the firms there which were in charge of the postal services on this main route often sent him young people that they might acquaint themselves up here on the divide with all the circumstances and eventualities pertaining to such affairs.

The evening passed in such varied conversation as this, and we had a peaceful night's sleep in rather short bunks that were fastened to the wall and were more reminiscent of book shelves than bedsteads.

I got up early and soon found myself under the open sky, but in narrow areas surrounded by lofty mountain tops. I had seated myself on the footpath that led down to Italy and, as dilettantes will, I was drawing what could not be drawn, much less constitute a picture, namely the nearest peaks, whose sides, with their white furrows and black ridges, were exposed by the melting and running snow. Yet this fruitless effort stamped that sight indelibly on my memory.

My companion came up to me in high spirits and began, "What do you say to our clerical host's tales last night? Did you not feel the urge, like me, to go down from this dragon's peak into those delightful regions? The trek down through these gorges must be splendid and effortless, and when they open up near Bellinzona, what a joy that will be! The monk's words made the islands of Lake Maggiore come alive in my mind again. Ever since Keyssler's *Journeys* so much has been heard and said about them that the temptation is too much for me. Surely you feel the same way?" He continued: "You are sitting at the right spot, where I stood once before but lacked the courage to take the leap downward. Just go on ahead and wait for me in Airolo. I shall follow with the porter after I have taken leave of the good monk and settled our account."

"I am uneasy about undertaking such a thing completely on the spur of the moment," I answered. "Why all these misgivings!" he cried. "We have enough money to get to Milan, and we shall find credit. Thanks to our Frankfurt fairs I have more than one business friend there." He became even more insistent. "Go," I said. "Get everything ready for our departure, and then we shall decide."

At such moments, it seems to me, a person feels no inner resolve but instead lets himself be ruled and determined by earlier impressions. Lombardy and Italy lay before me as something entirely foreign, Germany as something familiar, lovable, full of pleasant local prospects. And let it be confessed: the element which had totally encompassed me for such a long time and been the basis for my whole existence remained quite indispensable, and I dared not step outside its confines. A little golden heart, a present from her in our loveliest hours, still hung around my neck, warmed by love, on the same ribbon to which she had tied it. I grasped the heart and kissed it. Let the poem this inspired be inserted here too:

You, my souvenir of joys abated,
Which, here at my throat, I still am wearing,
Are you stronger than the bond our hearts created?
Can you prolong the days of love's brief sharing?

Lili, though I flee you, where'er I go your tether
Holds us together,
In foreign lands, in vales and wood uncharted!
Ah, not so soon could Lili's heart
From heart of mine be parted.

A pet bird that breaks its string will dart
Back up in its tree,
But trails a small piece, all the same,
Of the string, as captivity's shame,
It has no more the old bird's free-born heart,
For it's been someone's property.

I rose quickly to escape this steep perch, not wanting to be pulled into the depths by my friend, who was rushing up with a porter, the latter with a luggage rack on his shoulders. I also took leave of the pious monk and, without saying another word, turned back on the path by which we had come there. Somewhat hesitantly, my friend followed and, despite his love and affection for me, he stayed for a while at some distance behind me, until finally the glorious waterfall brought and kept us together again, and the resolve, once taken, at last was acknowledged to be good and salutary.

I shall say nothing further about our descent except that the snow bridge, over which we had calmly passed a few days ago accompanied by heavily burdened animals, had completely collapsed. And now, being required to make a detour around the opened creek, we could gape in admiration at the colossal ruins of this piece of natural architecture.

My friend could not quite get over the canceled hike to Italy. Apparently he had planned it in advance with affectionate cunning, and had hoped to surprise me with it on the very spot. Therefore our return could not be accomplished so cheerfully. However, on my silent way I was all the more intent on grasping all that vastness, at least in its comprehensible, characteristic details, for after a time it tends to contract in one's mind.

With both new and renewed sensations and thoughts we made our way across Lake Lucerne, with its impressive surrounding heights, to Küssnacht, where we went ashore and continued our journey on foot. We greeted the Tell chapel, which was on our route, and recalled that assassination which is considered, the world over, a praiseworthy act of heroism and patriotism. Likewise we rowed across Lake Zug, which had already caught our eye from a distance as we looked down from the Rigi. In Zug I remember only a few panes of stained glass, not large, but excellent of their kind, that were set into the casement windows of our room at the inn. Then our path led over the Albis into the Sihl valley, where we visited a young man from Hanover named von Lindau,[52] who had chosen to live in solitude. My purpose was to soothe his ruffled feelings about my earlier, not very amicable or courteous refusal of his companionship in Zurich. Actually it was my excellent Passavant's jealous friendship tthat had caused me to reject his dear, but still troublesome presence.

However, before we descend from these splendid heights back to the lake and the attractively located town of Zurich, I must make another comment about my attempt to accomplish something tangible by drawing and sketching the region. From childhood on it had been my custom to see a landscape in terms of a picture, and so, whenever I caught sight of a picturesque natural area, I was enticed into trying to give it a permanent form and thus secure a reliable souvenir of such moments. Having otherwise practiced a bit only on subjects of limited scope, I soon became conscious of my inadequacies in a world like this. Combined stress and haste forced a singular expedient on me: I would choose an interesting subject and suggest it very generally on the paper with a few strokes; then on the side I would describe in words those details that I could neither reach nor convey with my drawing pencil. In this way I kept the view so fresh in my mind that if I afterwards needed any of these localities, perhaps for a poem or a tale, it would at once materialize and be at my command.

On my return to Zurich,[53] the Stolbergs were gone. Their stay had been cut short in a peculiar way.

Let us make the general observation that travelers, having left their domestic limitations behind, tend to think they have entered not only a foreign, but also an entirely free nature. It was all the easier to fall into this error at the time, for there was still no control of passports by the police, no customs duty, or any similar obstacle to remind one at every turn that conditions abroad are even more restricted and unpleasant than at home.

If we first remember the mania at that time for acting out in real life the freedom of nature, then those young hearts can be excused for viewing Switzerland as exactly the right place for indulging their fresh youthfulness in an idyll. After all, they were definitely justified in thinking so on the basis of Gessner's tender poems and most charming etchings.

In actual performance, nothing seems better qualified for the expression of such poetic feelings than bathing in open waters. These nature exercises had already seemed to clash with modern customs on our way to Switzerland, and to some extent we had refrained from them. Once there, however, when we felt the moisture coming from those gushing waters, and saw them running, plunging, gathering in level places, and gradually spreading out into a lake, the temptation was irresistible. I do not deny that I myself joined my comrades for a dip in the clear lake, quite far away from human eyes, or so it seemed. Yet naked bodies gleam afar, and whoever might have seen them took offense.

The good, innocent youths, who found no indecency in seeing each other half naked, like poetic shepherds, or wholly naked, like heathen gods, were urged by friends to desist from doing things like this. It was pointed out to them that they were not disporting themselves in primeval nature, but in a land that considered it good and beneficial to cling to customs and manners dating from the Middle Ages. They were not averse to understanding this, especially since the Middle Ages were involved, which they esteemed as a second nature. So they abandoned the all too bright daylight of the lakeshore, and on their strolls through the mountains found such clear, rushing, refreshing streams that it seemed impossible to them, in the middle of July, to resist such recreation. On one of their wide-ranging expeditions they had reached the gloomy valley where behind the Albis the river Sihl rushes down to pour itself into the Limmat below Zurich. Far from all habitations, even from any busy footpath, they thought it quite unobjectionable to fling off their clothes and boldly challenge the foaming waters of the river. To be sure, this did not take place without some shouting, without wild yelps of pleasure occasioned partly by the cold water and partly by their delight, as they fancied themselves transforming these gloomily wooded cliffs into an idyllic scene.

Now, it is not ascertainable whether they had been secretly followed by previously hostile persons or whether this poetic tumult in the solitude attracted its own enemies. Suffice it to say, they were obliged to experience repeated showers of stones thrown at them from the silent bushes above, not knowing whether by few or by many, whether by chance or on purpose, and therefore they decided that it would be wisest to quit the refreshing element and retrieve their clothes.

No one was hit. The injury they had suffered was the mental one of surprise and anger; and, being happy-go-lucky young men, they were able to shake off the memory of it easily.

But Lavater did not escape the most unpleasant consequences for having welcomed such impudent young people into his home, for having gone out on drives with them, and having otherwise shown them favor, when their wild, uncontrolled, nay, heathenish behavior had caused such a scandal in this well-mannered, well-regulated region.

Our ecclesiastical friend, being expert at smoothing over such events, was nevertheless able to settle this matter too, and everything was restored to normal after these meteoric travelers had departed, and already before we returned.

In the fragment concerning "Werther's Travels,"[54] which has recently been reprinted, with other items, in Volume XVI of my works, I have tried to describe how the nature life demanded by such youthful folly contrasted with laudable Swiss orderliness and legal narrow-mindedness. But whenever a poet makes a frank presentation of something, it immediately tends to be regarded as his definite opinion and a didactic censure. Consequently the Swiss became very upset about this and I discontinued work on the sequel I had intended, which was supposed to give an account of Werther's progress through life up to the epoch where his sorrows are described, and which for this reason would certainly have been welcome to students of human nature.

Once again in Zurich, I made a renewed claim on Lavater's hospitality and devoted my time almost exclusively to him. The *Physiognomy* with all its figures and disfigurements, was an ever weightier burden on this excellent man's shoulders. We discussed everything as thoroughly as possible under the circumstances, and I promised him I would not lose interest after my return home.

I was beguiled into this promise by my boundless youthful confidence in my ability to grasp things quickly, and still more by my consciousness of being most willing and flexible. For actually Lavater's manner of analyzing physiognomies was foreign to my nature. My relationship to an individual was to a certain extent determined by the impression made on me at my first encounter with him, although the general benevolence of my impulses, added to the rashness of youth, was really always the dominant factor and made me see objects in a certain twilight atmosphere.

Lavater's personality was quite imposing. In his vicinity one could not resist his decisive influence, and so I had to agree to look separately at foreheads and noses, eyes and mouths, and to weigh their relationships and affinities. The seer himself had no choice but to do this, so that he could completely explicate what had been shown him so clearly by his intuition. But it always seemed to me like trickiness or spying when I tried to dissect the elements of some person who was present, in order to find a clue to his moral qualities. I preferred to concentrate on the person's conversation, in which he revealed himself at his own discretion. Moreover I cannot deny that Lavater's presence made us slightly nervous. Having mastered our peculiarities by way of physiognomics, he proceeded to become master of our thoughts in conversation, being sharp-witted enough to guess them quite easily from our verbal exchanges.

Whoever feels a synthesis very pregnantly in himself really has the right to analyze because he is testing and legitimizing his inner wholeness on the external detail. Let just one example be given of how Lavater went about this:

Sundays, when the sermon was ended, he, as a clergyman, was charged with the duty of presenting the short-handled velvet pouch to each person on the way out, and to receive the charitable gift with a blessing. One particular Sunday he set himself the task of not looking at the person, but just of paying attention to the hands and interpreting their shape. However, not only the form of the fingers came under his scrutiny, but also their expression while dropping in the gift, and he had a great many disclosures to make to me on this score. Can it be imagined how instructive such conversations were to me, who was, after all, training myself to become a qualified painter of mankind?

At many a period in my later life I have had occasion to think about this man, who must be numbered among the most remarkable persons with whom I have formed a close relationship. Accordingly, the following statements about him have also been written down at various times. Inasmuch as our efforts led us in different directions, we could not help gradually becoming completely estranged, and yet I did not want to let my memories of his remarkable character fade. I frequently called him to mind, and thus these pages came into existence quite independently of each other. Repetitions will be found in them but, I hope, no contradictions.

Lavater was actually a complete realist, and he understood idealism only in the form of morality. If one holds fast to this concept, one has the key to an explanation of this unusual and singular man.

His *Views into Eternity*[55] really presents nothing more than a continuation of our present existence under pleasanter conditions than those endured here. His physiognomy is based on the conviction that the physical being fully coincides with the spiritual one and bears witness to it, indeed even represents it.

It was difficult for him to accept idealized art, because his keen glance recognized all too clearly the impossibility of such entities becoming live organisms, and therefore he banished them to the realm of fable, nay, of monstrosities. His irresistible desire to make the ideal real won him the reputation of being a dreamer, although he was convinced that no one insisted on reality more than he. Consequently he could never discover the fallacy of his way of thought and action.

Not many people have more eagerly sought recognition than he did, and for this very reason he was suited to be a teacher. But even if his efforts were aimed at the improvement of other people's minds and morals, this was by no means the final goal toward which he was working.

His main concern was to give real form to the person of Christ, and this resulted in his near mania for having an endless succession of pictures of Christ drawn, copied, or imitated, naturally without being satisfied with any of them.

His writings have already grown difficult to comprehend, for his real meaning easily escapes one. No one has written like him for and about his own time. His writings are true daily bulletins and require the most factual annotation from the history of the era. They are written in the language of a coterie, with which one must be familiar in order to do them justice, otherwise a great deal will seem, to a sensible reader, quite mad and absurd. Indeed, the man was amply reproached for this already in his lifetime, as well as afterwards.

Thus, for instance, we got him so stirred up and excited with our dramatizing (for we used this form to present every happening and would accept no other) that he took pains to show emphatically in his

Pontius Pilate[56] that no work is more dramatic than the Bible and that Christ's Passion, especially, must be declared the drama of all dramas.

In this chapter of his little book, and indeed throughout the work, Lavater closely resembles Brother Abraham of Santa Clara,[57] for no intelligent man can fail to fall into this tone when his objective is to affect his immediate time. Such a man has to become informed about contemporary trends and enthusiasms, and also language and terminology, so that he may use these to serve his purposes and approach the masses he wants to attract.

His concept of Christ was literally that presented by Scripture and many interpreters of Scripture, and this idea served to supplement his own nature in such a way that, as he continued to incorporate the God-man ideally into his individual humanity, he at last felt entitled to imagine himself actually fused together with Christ, united with Him, indeed to *be* Him.

Thanks to his decidedly literal belief in the Bible he also inevitably became convinced that a person might perform miracles nowadays, just as in Biblical times. Furthermore, by dint of ardent, nay, violent prayer in significant and urgent affairs, he had early succeeded in forcing an immediate favorable reversal of imminent misfortunes, and therefore he was not in the least deterred by coldly rational objections. Moreover he was thoroughly persuaded of mankind's great value, now that it had been redeemed through Christ and destined for a happy eternity. But at the same time he was acquainted with the various requirements of the mind and heart and our insatiable demand for knowledge. Since he himself felt the desire to expand into infinity (for which the starry skies are an invitation even to our senses), he sketched his *Views into Eternity,* which, however, evidently made a very strange impression on most of his contemporaries.

Yet all these efforts, all his wishes, and all his undertakings were subordinated to the physiognomical genius imparted to him by nature. For just as the touchstone, with its blackness and the rough-smooth character of its surface, is best suited to indicate the difference between the metals stroked against it, so he too, with the pure concept of humanity that he nurtured and his gift for sharp but gentle observation (at first employed only superficially and coincidentally, out of a natural impulse, but then reflectively, purposefully, and systematically), was most highly qualified to perceive, know, distinguish, and indeed state the peculiarities of individual persons. Every talent based on a marked natural tendency seems to us to have an element of magic, because we can reduce neither it nor its effects to a concept. And actually his insight into individual persons surpassed all comprehension. It was astonishing when we spoke confidentially about this person or that; indeed it was dreadful to live in proximity to a man who distinctly saw every boundary line that nature has seen fit to draw around us individuals.

Everyone thinks that what he possesses can be transmitted to others, and so Lavater did not want to make use of this great gift only by himself. Instead, it was to be discovered and stimulated in others, and even relayed to people in general. The unenlightened and malicious interpretations, the silly jokes and vile mockery which were abundantly spawned by this striking doctrine are doubtlessly still remembered by some people, and it was to some extent the remarkable man's own fault that they arose. For while the unity of his inner nature was based on a lofty morality, he could not give outward unity to his various endeavors since he had not the slightest talent for either philosophy or art. He was neither a thinker nor a poet, and not even a speaker, in the real sense. By no means capable of attacking some problem in a methodical way, he would confidently take up individual details individually and boldly set them next to each other. His great work on physiognomy is a striking example and testimony of this. No doubt the concept of a moral and physical human being constituted a whole for him personally, but he did not know how to depict it for others except in his old practical way, by means of individual details, as these details had been grasped by him in life.

To our regret, that very work shows us this very intelligent man groping about through the most commonplace data, commissioning every artist and dauber alive, paying incredible sums for characterless drawings and engravings, only to say afterwards in his book that this and that plate is more or less unsuccessful, insignificant, and useless. Of course, by doing so, he refines his own judgment and that of others, but he also proves that he has been more inclined to accumulate data than to bring air and light into it. That was the very reason why he could never concentrate on the results for which I frequently and urgently asked him. What he later confidentially revealed to friends in this regard was unsatisfactory to me, for it consisted of a collection of lines and features, not excluding warts and liver spots, which he considered to be associated with specific moral—and frequently immoral—characteristics. Underneath, he added enough commentary to horrify anyone, but it was all disconnected, with everything put down in disarray, as chance would have it. Instructions were nowhere to be seen, and not a cross-reference was to be found. Nor were authorial method and artistic sense any more prevalent in his other works. Instead, they all contained passionately vehement portrayals of his thoughts and intentions, and invariably substituted the most engaging and ingenious individual details for what they failed to accomplish as a whole.

This might well be the right place to insert the following observations, since they pertain to the same circumstances.

No one is eager to grant other people superior merit, so long as there is some way to deny it. Natural merits of all kinds are the hardest ones to deny, and yet in the common idiom of the day the word "genius" was reserved for the poet alone. But then, suddenly, a different world seemed to open up, and genius was demanded of the physician, the general, the statesman, and soon of every person who was ambitious to excel in the theoretical or practical sphere. It was above all Zimmermann who had enunciated these demands. Lavater in his *Physiognomy,* was obliged to point out that intellectual gifts of all sorts were quite generally distributed. The word "genius" became a universal slogan, and on account of hearing it so often, one assumed that the quality it designated was also widespread. Moreover, since everyone felt justified in requiring genius of others, everyone eventually came to believe that he too must surely possess it. The time was still far in the future when it could be stated that genius consists in the human being's ability to establish law and rule through acting and doing. At that time it only manifested itself by transgressing against existing laws, overturning accepted rules, and declaring itself free of all restraints. Consequently it was easy to be a genius, and nothing could be more natural than for the abuses in word and deed to provoke all orderly people into opposing such scandalous conduct.

When anyone ran about the world on foot, without clearly knowing why or whither, that was called a "genius journey," and when anyone undertook something preposterous, to no purpose or profit, it was a "genius prank." Energetic, often genuinely gifted younger men went astray in their lack of restraint, whereupon their quite manifold misadventures could be very maliciously presented to the public eye as absurd by reasonable older men who, however, were perhaps deficient in talent and spirit.

And so I found myself in the middle, hindered almost more in my development and expression by the false cooperation and influence of those who were of like mind with me than by the opposition of those who were contrary-minded. Words, epithets, and phrases maligning the highest intellectual gifts were propagated in such fashion among the mindlessly imitating crowd that they can still be heard today here and there, in common life, from the mouths of uncultivated people. Indeed they have even made their way into the dictionaries, and the word "genius" suffered such misinterpretation that some argued for the necessity of banishing it altogether from the German language.

And so the Germans, among whom vulgarity has much more opportunity to gain the upper hand than in other nations, might well have deprived themselves of language's loveliest flower, of a word which is only ostensibly foreign and really belongs to all peoples alike. But fortunately a profounder philosophy restored their taste for the highest and best by providing a new foundation for it.

In the foregoing pages we have discussed the youth of two men[58] whose memory will never fade from the history of German literature and manners. However, in the epoch described, we have become acquainted with them only, as it were, in respect to their missteps, into which they were beguiled, along with their companions in age, by a false maxim of the day. But now it is no more than fitting that we present them in their natural form and actual character, with honor and esteem, just as Lavater, in direct contact with them at that time, saw them with his penetrating gaze. Since the heavy and costly volumes of the great physiognomical work may be readily available only to very few of our readers, we do not hesitate to insert here the remarkable passages concerning the two of them in the second part of said work, the thirtieth fragment, page 244.

"The young men whose pictures and silhouettes we have here before us are the first people who sat and stood for me, for physiognomic description, as one sits for a painter to be painted.

"I formerly knew them, these noble persons—and I made the first attempt to observe and describe their characters from nature and with all my other knowledge.—

"Here is the description of the whole individual.—

First, the younger one.

"Behold this youth in the bloom of his 25 years! the lightly hovering, floating, elastic creature! He does not stand, he does not lean, he does not fly; he hovers or floats. Too energetic to rest, too relaxed to stand firmly, too heavy and too soft to fly.

"A hovering object, then, which does not make contact with the earth! In all his contours not a completely slack line, and yet not a straight one, or one that is bowed, or firmly vaulted, or rigidly arched;—no angular indentation; no rocky promontory of a forehead; no hardness, no rigidity; no wrathful coarseness; no threatening superiority; no inflexibility of mind—easily excitable, no doubt, but not inflexible; no determined, searching profundity; no deliberate reflectiveness, or prudent circumspection; nowhere the reasoner with firmly held scales in one hand and a sword in the other, and yet not the least rigidity in observation and judgment either! and yet the most total uprightness of understanding, or, rather, the most immaculate sense of truth! Always the sensitive man of feeling, never the deep analyst; never the discoverer, never the experimenting developer of the truth that has been so quickly seen, quickly recognized, quickly loved, and quickly grasped. . . . Eternal hoverer; observer, idealizer, embellisher. Shaper of all his ideas! Always the half-intoxicated poet who sees what he wants to see;—not the gloomily languishing one—not the cruelly bruising one;—but the sublime, noble, powerful one! who floats back and forth in the regions of the air with moderate 'thirst for the sun,' strives past himself, and then—does not sink to earth! but plunges to earth, dives into the flooding 'cliff stream' and rolls himself about 'in the thunder of resounding rocks'[59]—His glance not the fiery glance of the eagle! His brow and nose not the courage of the lion! his breast—not the firmness of the battle-snorting warhorse! Generally, however, much of the swaying suppleness of the elephant. . . .

"The fact that his protruding upper lip is drawn back toward his unclipped, straight, projecting nose, along with the resoluteness of the mouth, shows much taste and fine sensibility; the lower part of the face shows much sensuousness, indolence, carelessness. The whole outline of the profile shows candor, sincerity, humaneness, but, at the same time, easy susceptibility and a high degree of naive thoughtlessness, which hurts nobody but himself. The central line of the mouth, when in repose, is that of an upright, undesigning, soft-hearted, good person; in motion, that of one who is sensitive, fine-feeling, extremely excitable, kindly, and noble. Homer is not sitting in the arch of the eyelids and the brilliance of the eyes, but someone who is the deepest, most soulful, quickest appreciator and grasper of Homer; not the epic poet, but the writer of odes; genius that gushes up, recreates, ennobles, shapes, hovers, transforms everything into heroic form, deifies everything.—The eyelids, half visible under this arch, are more those of poets with ever-increasingly fine feelings than of planfully creating, deliberately working artists; more those of enamored ones than of stern ones.—In full face, the young man's countenance is much more captivating and attractive than in profile, where it is somewhat too loose, too extended. The slightest movement of the front part of the face bears witness to sensitive, imaginative, innate, inward kindness and gently tremulous vivacity combined with a scorn of injustice and a thirst for freedom. It cannot conceal even the slightest of the many impressions which it receives simultaneously and incessantly.—Everything that comes into close relationship with him makes the blood rush into his cheeks and nose; in matters respecting his honor the most virginal blushes spread lightning-quick over his sensitive skin.

"As for the complexion, it is not the pale one of the all-creating and all-consuming genius; not the savagely flushed one of the scornful trampler; not the milky white one of the shy person, not the sallow one of the tough, hard person; not the brownish one of the deliberate, industrious worker; but the pinkish, violet one, just as expressive and commingled, just as happily mixed as strength and weakness are in his whole character.—The soul of the entire person and of each specific feature is freedom, is nimble activity, which easily sets out and is easily set back. Magnanimity and sincere cheerfulness shine forth from the entire front of the face and the position of the head.—Incorruptible sensibility, delicacy of taste, purity of mind, kindness and nobility of soul, active energy, a feeling of strength and weakness shine through the whole face so pervasively that its other traits of bold self-confidence dissolve into a noble modesty, and the natural pride and youthful vanity are agreeably subdued in this splendidly diverse whole without constraint and artifice.—The very light hair, the elongated, unfleshy figure, the gentle ease of manner, the swaying gait, the flatness of the chest, the white, unwrinkled brow, and various other features besides, dispense a certain feminine quality over the whole person which moderates his inner elastic force and makes his heart forever incapable of any intentional insult and baseness, but at the same time makes it clear that this courageous and fiery poet, in spite of all his unaffected thirst for liberty and liberation, is not destined to become on his own initiative a determined, persevering, plan-executing state official, or to win immortality on the bloody field of battle. And only now at the end do I notice that I have not yet mentioned the most striking things. Nothing about his noble simplicity, which is free of all affectation! Nothing about his childlike heart! Nothing about his total disregard for his outward noble rank! Nothing about the inexpressible bonhomie with which he accepts and tolerates warnings and criticism, even reproaches and injustice.—

"But who can come to an end when it is a question of saying everything that has been perceived or felt about a good person who has so much pure humanity!"

Description of the older one.

"What I have said about the younger brother—how much of the same can also be said of this one! What I can chiefly perceive is this: this figure and this character are more compact and less elongated than the former one. There everything was longer and more even, here everything shorter, broader, more vaulted, more arched; there everything looser, here, more clipped. Thus the forehead; thus the nose; thus the chest; more compressed, livelier, less spread out, more concentrated strength and liveliness! Otherwise the same agreeableness and bonhomie! Not the striking candor; more shrewdness, but the very same honesty at bottom, or, rather, in action. The same uncontrollable horror of injustice and malice; the same inability to reconcile himself with anything resembling intrigue and trickery; the same inexorable hatred of tyranny and despotism; the same pure, incorruptible enthusiasm about everything noble, good, and great; the same need for friendship and freedom, the same sensibility and noble desire for fame; the same universal sympathy with all good, wise, artless, energetic, famous or not famous, appreciated or unappreciated people;—and—the same frivolous thoughtlessness. No! not quite the same. The face is stubbier, tauter, firmer; has more inner, easily developed aptitude for affairs and practical consultations; more spirit for carrying things to conclusion, which is shown especially in the strongly prominent, bluntly rounded-off eye sockets. Not the gushing, abundant, pure, sublime poetic feeling; not the rapid flow of productive energy possessed by the other one. But still lively, true, fervent, although in deeper regions. Not the airy genius of light hovering in the sky at dawn, creating forms.—More inner strength, perhaps less expression! more violent and terrible—less magnificent and rounded, although his brush lacks neither color nor magic.—More wit and mad humors; a comical satyr; forehead, nose, gaze—all of this so downward, so craggy; quite decisive for original, all-enlivening wit, which does not collect from outside but casts abroad from inside. In general, everything about his character is more forward-pressing, sharp-edged, aggressive, ready to attack!—Nowhere dullness, nowhere slackness, except in the eye when the lid is lowered, where, as on the brow and nose, sensuality—springs forth! Otherwise, even on this brow, in this general compactness—even in this gaze—an unmistakable expression of innate greatness; strength, humane impulses; constancy, simplicity, positiveness!—"

Then, after stopping in Darmstadt, where I was obliged to grant Merck his triumph for having foretold the quick dissolution of our merry group, I found myself back in Frankfurt, and well received by everyone, including my father. But silently, if not in so many words, he showed his disapproval of my not having descended to Airolo so that I might send him news of my arrival in Milan. He especially failed to show the slightest interest in those wild cliffs, misty lakes, and dragon nests. He offered no rejoinder, but, when the occasion arose, he did indicate how much I had really missed: if one has not seen Naples, one has not lived.

I did not avoid seeing Lili, indeed I could not, and the relationship between us was tender and considerate. I was apprised that during my absence she had been fully persuaded that she had to break with me, and that this was all the more necessary, and indeed expedient, because I had declared myself clearly enough with my journey and quite arbitrary absence. Yet these same localities both in town and in the country, and these same persons with their knowledge of all the previous happenings, were hardly without effect on the two of us, who were still in love in spite of the curious way we had become separated. It was a bewitched situation, in a certain sense comparable to Hades, where the happy-unhappy departed ones keep company.

These were moments when the bygone days seemed to be recreated, but then would disappear at once, like phosphorescent specters.

Well-meaning friends had confided to me that when all the obstacles to our union were being expounded to Lili, she had stated she was ready, out of love for me, to give up all her present circumstances and conditions and accompany me to America.[60] In those days, perhaps even more than now, America was the Eldorado of those who found their present situation confining.

But the very thing that should have revived my hopes crushed them. My father's fine house, only a few hundred yards from hers, presented, after all, a more tolerably manageable situation than that uncertain environment far across the sea. But I do not deny that in her presence all my hopes, all my wishes, came to the fore again, and new uncertainties awoke in me.

Of course, my sister's commands were very prohibitive and definite. She had not only explained the situation to me with all the sense and feeling of which she was capable, but she also pursued the same text with increasingly forceful arguments in her really painfully vehement letters. "Very well," she said, "if this were an unavoidable situation, you would have to bear it, for it is not something to be *chosen,* but something just to be *tolerated.*" A few months passed in this most wretched of all circumstances. Everyone around us had voiced opposition to our union. In her alone, I thought—I *knew*—lay the strength that would have overcome all obstacles.

Both lovers were aware of their condition and avoided meeting in private, but, as before, we could not escape seeing each other in company. Then I had to undergo the hardest test of all, as every noble-minded soul will agree when I explain in greater detail. Let us make the general observation that a lover prefers to draw a veil over the past when he meets someone new and a new love begins. Love is not interested in antecedents, and, being kindled with the lightning speed of genius, it asks nothing about the past or future. To be sure, my closer intimacy with Lili had been caused by the very fact that she had told me about her childhood: how she, even as a little girl, had excited a great deal of affection and attachment, particularly in strangers who were visitors in her lively house, and how this had delighted her, although there had been no subsequent betrothals.

Genuine lovers regard every previous attachment only as preparation for their present happiness, only as a foundation on which to erect the edifice of their life together. Bygone affections appear to be nocturnal specters that slip away at the break of dawn.

But what happened? The trade fair came round, and then a swarm of those ghosts appeared in the flesh: all the business friends of this notable family eventually arrived, and it soon became clear that not one of them was either willing or able to abandon completely whatever claim he had on the amiable daughter. The younger men, while not importunate, did behave as though they were old friends of hers, while those of middle years, with a certain courteous decorum, seemed to want to ingratiate themselves or, at any rate, emphasize their higher claims. There were some handsome men among them, with the easy manner bestowed by substantial prosperity.

But the still older gentlemen, with their avuncular manners, were quite intolerable. They did not keep their hands in check, and on top of their repulsive fondling they even asked for a kiss, and she did not refuse them her cheek. It was entirely natural for her to respond decorously to such demands. And their conversations as well awakened some dubious memories. There was discussion of some pleasure trips on land and water, of various perilous adventures with happy outcomes, of balls and evening promenades, of tricks paid on ridiculous wooers, and of everything else that could excite jealous anger in the heart of a disconsolate lover like me, who for a while had appropriated for himself, as it were, the sum of those many years. But even in this crowd, in this commotion, she did not neglect her friend, and when she turned to him she could tell him something very tender in just a few words, something which seemed perfectly appropriate to our mutual situation.

However! Let us turn from the still almost unbearable memory of this torment to the poetry that introduced a little solace for heart and mind into these circumstances.

"Lili's Park" may be approximately from this period, but I shall not include this poem here because instead of expressing that tender, sensitive condition it only seeks, with genius-like vehemence, to heighten what was repugnant and to transform renunciation into despair by means of comically angry images.

The following song is better able to express the graceful aspects of the unhappy situation, and therefore let it be inserted here:

Lovely roses, you are jaded,
All my love sustained you naught,
Bloomed, alas, as my hopes faded,
For a soul with grief now fraught.

Of those days I think, lamenting,
When I, angel, clung to you,
Watched for every bud, frequenting
Garden paths in early dew.

All that fruited and that flowered
I was laying at your feet,
As your countenance empowered
Hope within my heart to beat.

Lovely roses, you are jaded,
All my love sustained you naught,
Bloomed, alas, as my hopes faded,
For a soul with grief now fraught.

The opera *Erwin and Elmira*[61] was inspired by the charming ballad included in Goldsmith's *Vicar of Wakefield.* The ballad had given us pleasure in our best times, when we did not suspect that something similar was in the offing for us.

I have already inserted some poetic products of that period earlier, and I only wish that all of them had been preserved. Constant excitement at a time of happy love, further heightened by the approach of care, occasioned songs which expressed absolutely nothing high-flown, but always just my feelings of the moment. Everything from social festival songs to the slightest presentation piece was alive and was shared by a cultivated group. At first these things were happy, then sad, and in the end there was not a peak of happiness or abyss of woe to which a poetic word was not dedicated.

My father had less and less hope of seeing that first daughter-in-law, the one whose charm appealed to him, brought into his house, and all these internal and external events, whenever they could have had an unpleasant effect on him, were most cleverly and emphatically kept from his notice by my mother. But this "grand lady," which was what he always called Lili when speaking privately to his wife, was by no means to his taste.

Meanwhile he let affairs take their course and went on working quite busily in his little chancery. The young devotee of the law, together with the adroit secretary, kept widening the scope of the business they carried on under his direction. Since it is a well-known fact that an absent person is never missed, they granted me my pastimes and tried to establish themselves more and more firmly on ground where I was not destined to thrive.

Fortunately, my father's sentiments and wishes coincided with my inclinations. He had such a high opinion of my poetic talent and took so much personal pleasure in the favor my first works had won that he would often talk to me about my new projects and those I would undertake in the future. On the other hand, I dared not let him become aware of these social jests and passionate poems.

After I had, in my way, mirrored the symbol of a significant world-epoch in *Götz von Berlichingen,* I cast about circumspectly for a similar turning point in the history of nations. The revolt of the Netherlands gained my attention. In *Götz* it had been an excellent man who perished in the delusion that the strong individual of good will has some significance in times of anarchy. In *Egmont* it was a question of firmly based conditions which could not hold out against stern, calculating despotism. I had conversed with my father about it most animatedly—what was to be done, what I wanted to do with this materials—so that he could not contain his desire to see this play, which was already complete in my mind, on paper, in print, and admired.

In earlier times, when I still hoped to win Lili, I had applied my energies wholly to the understanding and practice of business affairs; but just now the terrible gap that separated me from her had to be filled in with matters intellectual and soulful. Therefore I really began to write *Egmont,* but not in logical order like the first version of *Götz von Berlichingen.* Instead, after the first introduction I immediately attacked the main scenes, without being concerned about the eventual connections. I made considerable progress, for I was being spurred on day and night (I do not exaggerate) by my father, who knew my slothful work habits and thought he should be able to see a play so easily conceived also easily completed.

Book Twenty

In these days of passionate unrest and inner discord, I was helped through many a bad hour by the presence of an excellent artist: and here again, as so frequently, I owed my soul's inner peace, at a time when it would otherwise have been unobtainable, to my uncertain quest for some practical training.

Georg Melchior Kraus,[62] born in Frankfurt and educated in Paris, had just returned from a short trip to northern Germany. He looked me up, and I immediately felt a need and desire to become associated with him. He was a cheerful man of the world, and he had found Paris to be the right school for his light, charming talent.

At that time, a pleasant reception awaited any German in Paris: Philipp Hackert lived there, enjoying prosperity and much esteem. His conscientious German method of sketching landscapes from nature and then finishing them successfully in oils or gouache was in welcome contrast to a manneristic expedient the French were devoted to. Wille, greatly respected as an engraver,[63] put German merits on a firm basis. Grimm, already influential, rendered no small service to his countrymen. Pleasant walking tours were undertaken for the purpose of sketching directly from nature, and thus preliminary studies were made for many a good picture.

Boucher and Watteau,[64] truly two born artists, whose works are still considered very respectable despite being whimsical in the spirit and style of the times, were well disposed to the newly arrived Kraus and personally took an active part in his training, although only as a joke and an experiment. Greuze,[65] who lived quietly in the midst of his family circle and liked to depict scenes of private life, was enchanted with his own works and delighted in a delicate, honest brush.

Our Kraus could absorb all this into his talent very well. In society he adapted himself *to* society, and could make very elegant group portraits of friendly gatherings in people's homes. He was no less successful in landscape drawings, which made a very agreeable impression on the eye with their clean outlines, monochromatic areas, and pleasant watercolor palette. A certain naive truthfulness appealed to one's inner sense, and art lovers were particularly pleased with his skill at immediately forming and arranging a picture out of everything he himself sketched from nature.

Personally he was a most pleasant companion. His even-tempered cheerfulness never deserted him. Being obliging but not humble, reserved but not proud, he was at home everywhere, popular everywhere, and was at once the most industrious and most approachable of mortals. Because he was gifted with such talent and character he soon found his way into the favor of higher social circles and was especially well received at the baronial castle vom Stein in Nassau-on-Lahn, where he aided a talented, very amiable daughter of the family[66] in her artistic efforts and at the same time enlivened social affairs in various ways.

After this excellent young lady's marriage to Count von Werthern, the young couple took the artist along with them to their extensive estates in Thuringia, and from there he proceeded to Weimar, where he became known and recognized, and was asked to remain by the local, highly cultured social circle.

He was always eager to help, and so upon his recent return to Frankfurt he advanced me from my former desire merely to collect art to practical exercises in art. It is indispensable for a dilettante to have an artist at hand, for in the latter he sees the complement to his own existence: the amateur's wishes are fulfilled in the artist.

Thanks to practice and a certain natural ability I might succeed in drawing an outline, and also easily formed into a picture what I beheld in nature; but I lacked the true creative power and sturdy determination to lend body to the outline by means of properly blended lights and shadows. My drawings were more like distant presentiments of some form or other, and my figures resembled the light, airy creatures in Dante's Purgatory, who are terrified by the shadows of real bodies because they cast none themselves.

Thanks to Lavater's harassment—for surely that is what one may call his vehement attempts to force everyone not only to contemplate physiognomies but also actually to reproduce facial characteristics, artistically or amateurishly—I had made a practice of drawing my friends' portraits on gray paper in black and white chalk. The likenesses were unmistakable, but my artistic friend's hand was needed to make them stand out from the dark background.

As we paged through and inspected the thick portfolios the good Kraus had brought back from his travels, his favorite topic of conversation, when displaying the drawing of a landscape or person, was the circle at Weimar and its environment. I too was glad to dwell on this subject because it was clearly flattering to a young man to be able to view all these pictures merely as the text of a detailed, repeated sermon: namely, that my presence was desired there. The personages portrayed gave Kraus a very graceful means of enlivening the greetings and invitations he conveyed. One very successful oil painting showed the musical director Wolf[67] at the grand piano with his wife behind him, preparing to sing. In connection with this, the artist expounded very earnestly on how amicably this worthy pair would receive me. Among his sketches were several depicting the hilly, wooded area around Bürgel, where an honest forester, perhaps more to please his charming daughters than himself, had constructed bridges, railings, and gentle pathways to make the roughly contoured rocky sections, underbrush, and wooded stretches suitable for companionable strolls. Young women in white dresses were to be seen on the pleasant trails, with escorts, to be sure. One of the young men was supposed to be Bertuch,[68] who had admittedly serious intentions regarding the eldest girl, and Kraus was not offended when I ventured to connect a second young man with himself and his budding affection for her sister.

Bertuch, who was Wieland's pupil, had made such strides in his education and activities that he had already obtained the post of privy secretary to the duke and showed the very best promise for the future. Wieland's honesty, cheerfulness, and good nature were a prominent topic of discussion. There was detailed allusion to his fine literary and poetic projects, and comment on the influence throughout Germany of his *Mercury*. Special attention was called to numerous names in the context of literature, state affairs, and society, and those of Musäus, Kirms, Berendis, and Ludecus came up in this connection.[69] As to the women, among many others Wolf's wife and a widow Kotzebue,[70] who had an amiable daughter and a lively young son, were singled out for laudable characterization. There was every indication that literary and artistic life was vigorously active.

And so gradually I received a description of the environment where the young duke was to make his influence felt when he returned. The lady high guardian[71] had laid the groundwork for these conditions; however, the execution of important business was to be left to the future regent's best judgment and initiative, as is the duty of such provisional administrations. The dreadful ruins left by the burning of the palace were already being viewed as a stimulus to new enterprises. The idled mine at Ilmenau, whose possible resumption had been insured through the costly maintenance of its deep tunnel; the University of Jena, which had not quite kept pace with the times and was threatened with the loss of some of its best teachers; and many other things as well had aroused a noble public spirit. Persons were being sought who could be called upon to promote the many good efforts stirring in Germany, and so a decidedly fresh prospect was opened, all that any vigorous, lively youth could desire. And if, minus the dignity of an appropriate building, it seemed sad to invite a young princess into a very modest dwelling designed for quite different purposes, still the beautifully situated, well-appointed villas of Ettersburg and Belvedere, and other pleasure seats with many advantages, not only offered present delights but also the hope of finding productive and agreeable activities in this rural life which had become a necessity at the time.

In the course of this biographical recital, we have seen in detail how the child, the boy, and the youth tried to approach the metaphysical by various paths, first affectionately looking to natural religion, then attaching himself lovingly to a positive one, next testing his own abilities by withdrawing into himself, and at last joyously yielding to the universal faith. While meandering in the spaces between these areas, seeking and looking about, he encountered some things that seemed to fit into none of these categories, and he became increasingly convinced that it was better to divert his thoughts from vast and incomprehensible subjects. He believed that he perceived something in nature (whether living or lifeless, animate or inanimate) that manifested itself only in contradictions and therefore could not be expressed in any concept, much less any word. It was not divine, for it seemed irrational; not human, for it had no intelligence; not diabolical, for it was beneficent; and not angelic, for it often betrayed malice. It was like chance, for it lacked continuity, and like Providence, for it suggested context. Everything that limits us seemed penetrable by it, and it appeared to dispose at will over the elements necessary to our existence, to contract time and expand space. It seemed only to accept the impossible and scornfully to reject the possible. This essence, which appeared to infiltrate all the others, separating and combining them, I called daemonic, after the example of the ancients and others who had perceived something similar. I tried to save myself from this fearful thing by taking refuge, as usual, behind an image.

Among the individual parts of world history that I studied more carefully were events that brought such fame to the subsequently united Netherlands. I industriously researched the sources, getting as much direct information as possible, and tried to visualize everything vividly. The situation appeared to me to be extremely dramatic, and Count Egmont struck me as being the chief figure, the one best suited to serve as a focal point for all the others, and his humanely chivalric greatness was very much to my taste. But for my purposes I had to change him into a character with qualities more becoming to a youth than a mature man, to a bachelor than a family father, to an independent person than one who, however liberal-minded, is tied down by various circumstances. Having thus rejuvenated him in my mind and freed him of all restrictions, I gave him a boundless love of life and unlimited self-confidence, the gift of drawing people to him *(attrativa)* and so of winning their favor: the secret affection of a female ruler, the pronounced one of an unsophisticated girl, the sympathy of a clever statesman. Indeed, he even captivates the son of his greatest adversary.

The personal bravery that distinguishes this hero is the foundation on which his character rests, and the soil from which it sprouts. Recognizing no danger, he is blind to the greatest peril threatening him. If need be, we can fight our way through a ring of enemies, but the nets of statecraft are harder to penetrate. The daemonic, which plays a role on both sides of this conflict in which the amiable perishes and the hateful triumphs, and also the prospect of a third force arising from this that will fulfill the wishes of the whole people—probably these are what secured for the play (to be sure, not at the outset, but later, and at the right time) the favor which it still enjoys. And so here, for the sake of my many cherished readers, I shall anticipate myself and, not knowing how soon again I may get the chance to speak, I shall state something I became convinced of only much later.

While the daemonic element can manifest itself in anything corporeal or incorporeal, and indeed is shown very remarkably in animals, its primary, most amazing association is with man, constituting a power not necessarily opposed to the moral world order, but crisscrossing it to the extent that one could be called the warp and the other the woof. There are countless names for the phenomena produced by this, for all philosophies and religions have attempted in prose or poetry to solve this mystery and to settle the matter finally, and may they still remain at liberty to do so! The daemonic principle, however, is at its most fearful when it emerges predominantly in some individual. In the course of my life I have been able to observe several of these, either in proximity or at a distance. They are not always the most excellent men, either in mind or talents, and they seldom have kindness of heart to recommend them. But they radiate an enormous strength and exercise incredible power over all creatures, even over the elements, and who can say just how far such influence does extend? All the moral powers in unison can do nothing against them. In vain the brighter segment of the population tries to make them suspect as deluded men or deluders; still the masses are attracted to them. Seldom or never do contemporaries of this type encounter each other, and they cannot be conquered by anything less than the universe itself, which they have defied. And from such observations may well have arisen that strange but prodigious saying: *Nemo contra deum nisi deus ipse.*[72]

I return from these higher considerations into my own little life, which nevertheless was also moving toward some strange events, events at least suffused in a daemonic glow. From the summit of the Gotthard, turning my back on Italy, I had gone back home, because I could not do without Lili. An affection based on the hope of mutual possession, of a permanent life together, does not immediately wither away; indeed it nourishes itself on contemplation of the legitimate wishes and sincere hopes in one's heart. It is in the nature of the thing that the girl in such cases resigns herself sooner than the young man. As descendants of Pandora, the lovely children are endowed with the desirable gift of being able to charm, entice, and gather men about them, less with affection than by their nature, half deliberately, nay, wantonly. Meanwhile, like the sorcerer's apprentice, they often risk being terrified by the flood of admirers. And then eventually there does have to be a choice, one man must be preferred to the exclusion of others, one must lead his bride home.

And what a role chance plays in determining the choice, in influencing the chooser! It was conviction that made me renounce Lili, but my love made this conviction doubtful. Lili had taken leave of me in the same manner, and I had set out on the beautiful journey which was supposed to distract me but accomplished the very opposite. As long as I was absent I believed in the separation but not in the divorce. All my memories, hopes, and wishes were given free rein. Now I came back, and if the reunion of free and happy lovers is heaven, then the reunion of two persons who have broken up only on practical grounds is a purgatory, a forecourt of hell. When I returned to Lili's world, I was doubly sensitive to all those disharmonies that had disturbed our relationship, and when I again stepped into her presence I was struck to the heart by the realization that she was lost to me. Therefore I resolved on flight a second time, and so nothing could have been more to my liking than the fact that the young ducal pair of Weimar was on its way from Karlsruhe to Frankfurt and that I, according to its earlier and more recent invitations, was to follow it to Weimar. These high personages, for their part, had maintained their gracious, indeed trustful attitude, to which for my part I responded with passionate gratitude. My affection for the duke from the first moment on, my respect for the princess, whom I had known so long, although only by sight, my desire to make some friendly overture personally to Wieland, who had behaved so liberally to me, and to make reparations on the spot for my half-mischievous, half-accidental rudenesses, these were inducements enough to stir up, nay, impel a young man even if he were without passions. But for me there was the additional fact that I had to flee from Lili, on whatever path it might be, whether it be to the south, where my father's stories daily conjured up visions of the most splendid paradise of art and nature, or to the north, where I had been invited by such a notable circle of excellent persons.

Now the young sovereign pair[73] arrived in Frankfurt on its trip back. The ducal court of Meiningen was there at the same time, and I was most amicably received also by it and by the young princes' escort, Privy Councillor von Dürckheim. But, in typically youthful fashion, something odd had to happen, and here it was a misunderstanding that put me into an incredibly, although rather amusingly, embarrassing situation. The lords of Weimar and Meiningen were staying at an inn. I was invited to dine. The court of Weimar so occupied my mind that it did not occur to me to inquire any further, nor was I conceited enough to think that any notice would be taken of me from the Meiningen side.

Dressed in good clothes, I entered the "Roman Emperor," found the rooms of the Weimar lordships empty, and when I was told they were with the Meiningen princes I proceeded there and was amicably received. I thought this was a pre-dinner visit or that perhaps we were eating together, and I waited for the outcome. But suddenly the Weimar party moved out, and I followed them. But they did not go to their rooms, as one might have thought; rather, they went straight down the stairs and into their carriages, leaving me all alone on the street. Instead of being clever and adroit enough to make inquiries about the matter and look for some explanation, I immediately set out for home in my resolute way, and found my parents at dessert. My father shook his head, while my mother tried to make it up to me as well as possible. That evening she confided to me that when I left, my father had said he was most amazed, since I was not stupid otherwise, about my not being able to perceive that those people had simply intended to tease and abash me. But this did not bother me, for I had already encountered Mr. von Dürckheim, who in his kindly manner took me to task with charming, jocular reproaches. Now I awakened from my dream and had occasion to thank very courteously for the unexpected and unhoped-for favor meant for me, and to beg pardon.

Consequently, after I had yielded, for good reasons, to these friendly proposals, the following arrangements were agreed upon: a cavalier, left behind in Karlsruhe to await a landau carriage being manufactured in Strassburg, would arrive in Frankfurt on a specified day, and I was to keep myself in readiness to depart for Weimar with him immediately. The cheerful and gracious farewell spoken to me by their young highnesses, and the friendly behavior of the courtiers, seemed to pave the way for this trip very pleasantly and made it very desirable to me. But at this juncture too, the affair, simple as it was, had to be complicated by chance occurrences, confused by violent emotions, and very nearly ruined altogether. After I had bidden everyone farewell and announced the day of my departure, then hurriedly packed my belongings, not forgetting my unprinted writings, I awaited the hour which was supposed to produce the aforesaid friend in the new carriage and transport me to a new region and into a new situation. The hour passed, the day as well. Since I did not want to say my farewells a second time or, especially, be overwhelmed with crowds of visitors, I had pretended to be absent from that morning on, and so I had to stay quietly at home, nay, in my room, and consequently I found myself in a curious position. But there was invariably something very favorable for me about solitude and confinement, because I felt constrained to use such hours profitably; and so I continued writing at my *Egmont* and almost completed it. I read it aloud to my father, who became particularly fond of this play. His dearest wish was to see it finished and in print, because he hoped that it would add to his son's good repute. And he needed this sort of pacification and new satisfaction, for he was making the most questionable comments about the failure of the carriage to arrive. He again took the whole thing for a fabrication, did not believe there was a landau, and considered the cavalier left behind in Karlsruhe a phantom. To be sure, he only hinted at this to me, but he tormented himself and my mother with it in all the greater detail. He viewed the whole affair as a merry prank of the court which had been concocted as a result of my bad manners, so that I might be insulted and disgraced when now, instead of receiving the hoped-for honor, I was shamefully left sitting. I myself, of course, at first held fast to my belief, was happy about my hours in retirement, which neither friend nor stranger, nor any other social distraction, encroached on, and wrote sturdily away at *Egmont*, though not without inner agitation. And this frame of mind was no doubt of benefit to the play, which was full of so much emotion that it could hardly have been written by someone in a completely unemotional state. Thus a week passed, and perhaps more, and this total incarceration began to be burdensome to me. For several years I had been accustomed to live under an open sky, in the company of friends with whom I had the most sincere, active mutual relationship, in the vicinity of a sweetheart from whom I may have resolved to part but to whom I was irresistibly drawn as long as it was still possible to approach her. All of this began to disturb me so much that the attraction of my tragedy diminished and impatience threatened to halt my poetic activity. On some evenings it had become impossible for me to stay at home. Enveloped in a great cloak I skulked around the town, past the houses of my friends and acquaintances, and did not fail to step up to Lili's window as well. She lived on the ground floor of a corner house, and the green shades were lowered, but I could make out quite well that the lights stood at their usual place. Soon I heard her singing at the piano, and it was the song, "Irresistibly, alas, you draw me!" which had been composed for her not quite a year before. It could not but seem to me that she sang it with more expression than ever, and I could understand it distinctly, word for word. I had pressed my ear as close as the outward-curving grillwork would permit. After she had sung it to the end, I saw by the shadow falling on the shade that she had gotten up. She walked back and forth, but I sought in vain to catch the outline of her lovely person through the heavy texture. Only my firm resolve to go away, not to become burdensome to her by my presence, really to renounce her, and the thought of the strange stir my reappearance would create, could persuade me to leave her dear proximity.

Several more days passed, and my father's hypothesis kept gaining probability, since not even a letter arrived from Karlsruhe to indicate the reasons for the carriage's delay. My literary activity came to a halt, and now my father could easily work on the agitation which inwardly consumed me. He proposed to me that since the matter could not be altered, and my trunk was packed, he would give me the credit documents and cash for going to Italy. However, I had to resolve to start out at once. Though doubtful and hesitant about such an important matter, I finally agreed that, if neither carriage nor news arrived by a certain hour, I would set out and indeed go first to Heidelberg. However, my way from there would not be through Switzerland again but across the Alps via the Grisons or the Tyrol.

Curious things, to be sure, will come to pass when planless youth, which so easily leads itself astray, is also driven onto a false path by an emotional error on the part of age. But that *is* youth, and life in general; we usually perceive the strategy only when the campaign is over. A chance occurrence like this could easily have been explained as part of the normal course of affairs, but we are only too prone to conspire with error against the natural and true, just as we shuffle the cards before dealing them, so as not to infringe on chance's part in the action. And thus is created the very element in which, and upon which, the daemonic so gladly takes effect, playing with us the more wickedly, the more we suspect its presence.

The last day had passed, I was to leave the next morning, and now I felt a boundless urge to see my friend Passavant again, who had just returned from Switzerland. For he really would have had cause to feel resentful if I had violated our deeply felt trust by maintaining complete secrecy. Therefore, through an unknown person, I summoned him to come to a certain place at night, where I, wrapped in my cloak, arrived sooner than he. He came also, and though he had already been amazed at the appointment, he was even more amazed at whom he found in this place. His joy matched his astonishment, and there was no time for discussion and consultation. He wished me happiness on my trip to Italy, we parted, and early the next day I found myself on the mountain road. I had several reasons for going to Heidelberg. One was practical, for I had heard that my friend would come from Karlsruhe via Heidelberg, and as soon as I arrived there I left a note at the post office which was to be given to the cavalier who would be traveling through in the manner I described. The second reason was sentimental and had to do with my former relationship to Lili. That is, Mlle Delph, the confidante of our love, indeed the person who had arranged with our parents for our formal engagement, lived there, and I considered it my greatest good fortune to be able, before leaving Germany, to talk over those happy times once more with a worthy, patient, and indulgent woman friend. I was well received and introduced into many a family, and I particularly enjoyed being in the home of Head Forester von Wrede.[74] The parents were proper but easy-going people, and their only daughter reminded me of Frederica. It was just at the time of the grape harvest, the weather was lovely, and all the feelings I had had in Alsace revived in me here in the beautiful Rhine and Neckar valley. Lately I had experienced strange things in myself and others, but it was all still in a process of development; no lifelong result had come to the fore in me, and my perceptions of the infinite served more to confuse than enlighten me. But in company I was the same as always, indeed perhaps even more obliging and entertaining. Here, under this open sky, among these happy people, I took up the old games again that never lose their charm and novelty for youth. With my former, not yet extinguished love in my heart, I aroused sympathy without wanting to, even though I was silent on the subject, and so also in this circle I soon felt at home, nay, indispensable. I forgot that I had planned to spend only a few evenings chatting and then to continue my journey. Mlle Delph was one of those persons who, although not precisely intriguers, always want to be involved in something, involve others, and carry out some design or other. She had taken a great liking to me and was better able to inveigle me into staying longer since I was her house guest. She could both keep pleasurable things in reserve for my continuing stay and also put all sorts of obstacles in the way of my departure. When I tried to steer the conversation toward Lili, she was not as obliging and sympathetic as I had hoped. Instead, she lauded our mutual resolve to separate, given the existing circumstances, and asserted that one must bow to the inevitable, forget the impossible, and cast about for a new interest in life. Systematic as she was, she was not willing to leave this to chance, and had already conceived a plan to provide for my future. Accordingly I saw that her last invitation to Heidelberg had not been as disinterested as it seemed to be.

That is to say, the Elector Charles Theodore,[75] who had done so much for the arts and sciences, still had his residence in Mannheim, and especially because the court was Catholic while the country was Protestant, the latter party had every reason to strengthen itself with vigorous and promising men. Now I was supposed to go to Italy with God's blessing and develop an expert understanding of art there; in the meantime steps would be taken in my behalf, and upon my return we would see whether my budding affection for Miss von Wrede had grown or faded and if it was advisable to establish me and my fortune in a new fatherland by means of connecting me with a distinguished family.

While I did not reject all of this, my unsystematic nature was unable to mesh completely with the systematic procedure of my friend. I enjoyed the good will of the moment, while Lili's image hovered before me whether I was awake or dreaming and intruded on everything else that might have delighted or distracted me. Then, however, I called to mind the seriousness of my great travel project and resolved to extricate myself in a gentle, courteous manner and to proceed on my way in a few days.

Until late into the night Mlle Delph had described for me in detail what her plans were, and everything that people were willing to do for me. I could not but show gratitude for such sentiments, although it was not altogether unnoticeable that a certain circle was interested in reinforcing itself through me and my potential favor at court. It was nearly one o'clock before we parted. I had not slept long, but deeply, when I was awakened by a postillion's horn as he stopped on horseback in front of the house. Soon afterwards, Mlle Delph appeared holding a candle and a letter, and stepped up to my bed. "There we have it!" she exclaimed. "Read it and tell me what it is. Certainly it is from the Weimar people. If it is an invitation, do not accept it, and remember our conversation." I asked her for the light and a quarter hour of solitude. She left me reluctantly. Without opening the letter, I looked into space for a while. The dispatch rider was from Frankfurt, and I knew the seal and handwriting. So, my friend had arrived there; he was inviting me, and our disbelief and uncertainty had made us overhasty. Why should one not wait quietly in private for a man whose coming has been guaranteed and whose journey could be delayed by so many accidental events? It was as though the scales had fallen from my eyes. All the past kindness, favor, and trust vividly presented themselves to me again, and I was almost ashamed of my curious escapade. Now I opened the letter, and everything had happened understandably. My absent escort had waited day after day, hour after hour, for the new carriage that was supposed to come from Strassburg, as we had waited for him. Then he had gone on business via Mannheim to Frankfurt, and to his horror had not found me there. He immediately sent a dispatch rider with this hurried note in which he presupposed that I, with the error explained, would immediately return and not cause him the disgrace of arriving in Weimar without me.

Although my heart and mind were very much inclined in this direction, still my new orientation did not lack a significant counterweight. My father had worked out a very pretty itinerary for me and given me a little library to take along, so that I could prepare myself and have information right at hand. Up till now this had been my sole entertainment in leisure hours, and even during my last short carriage journey I had thought of nothing else. Those magnificent objects, with which I had become acquainted from childhood on by means of stories and all sorts of pictures, assembled themselves before my mind's eye, and I could think of nothing more desirable than approaching them while resolutely distancing myself from Lili.

Meanwhile I had dressed and was pacing up and down in the living room. My grave hostess entered. "What may I hope?" she cried. "My dear," I said, "do not try to dissuade me, for I have decided to return. I have weighed the reasons in my mind, and it would be useless to repeat them. Finally a decision has to be made, and who is to make it, if not the person actually concerned?" I was upset, she was too, and there was a stormy scene, which I concluded by ordering my servant to arrange for a private coach. In vain I asked my hostess to calm herself and transform my mock farewell to the company yesterday evening into a genuine one. I said she should consider that it was only meant to be a visit, a brief period of attendance at court, and that this would not cancel my Italian journey or prevent my return to Heidelberg. She would not listen to anything and, as agitated as I was, she agitated me still more. The carriage stood before the door laden with my bags, the postillion sounded the customary signal of impatience, I pulled myself free, she still did not want to let me go, and artfully enough summoned up all the arguments in favor of the present situation, so that at last I passionately and enthusiastically exclaimed the words of Egmont:

"Child! child! no more of this! As though whipped on by invisible spirits, the sun-steeds of time run off with the flimsy chariot of our destiny, and nothing is left for us to do except grasp the reins with courage and composure and divert the wheels, now right, now left, from a stone here, or a sudden drop there. Who knows what the destination is? The driver scarcely remembers from whence he has come."

CAMPAIGN IN FRANCE 1792
SIEGE OF MAINZ

Introduction

On 20 April 1792 the French National Assembly declared war on Francis II, King of Hungary and Bohemia, the head of the house of Austria. Francis had just ascended the throne following the sudden death of his father, Leopold II, on 1 March and was totally unprepared for war, although the tensions that led to the French declaration had been building up for the past year. Francis accepted the challenge and was seconded immediately by Frederick William II of Prussia, with whom Austria had negotiated a defensive alliance during the winter of 1791–1792. The war began badly enough for the French: their spring campaign against Austrian forces in the Netherlands was totally unsuccessful and it was only because the Austrians did not have sufficient strength in the region to follow up their advantage that war operations during the spring turned out to be inconclusive.

Prussia and Austria then staked everything on a summer campaign into the heart of France. The invasion was launched from Coblence at the end of July after the issuance of two manifestos by the commander in chief, the Duke of Brunswick, on 25 and 27 July. The Duke of Brunswick, the most respected German military commander after Frederick II's death in 1786, was in an enviable situation: he was leading a confident army consisting of Prussians, Austrians, and French émigrés and containing some of the most illustrious personages of Europe. King Frederick William II himself was with the army, along with several of the Prussian princes. Optimism reigned supreme and all were certain that the march to Paris would be, as the émigré ex-minister Calonne had forecast, nothing but a "military promenade." The émigrés had repeatedly assured the German commanders that French officers and troops would come over en masse to their side and march with them to restore the power of Louis XVI at the first opportunity—there would be no significant opposition.

Unfortunately, the French forces opposing the invaders in the field were not so impressed either with the Duke of Brunswick or with his army. The French armies did not collapse or melt away and Brunswick's manifestos had stirred up a hornet's nest. The campaign which began under such auspicious circumstances rapidly became an unmitigated disaster: with great difficulty the German armies advanced as far as Valmy, just west of the Argonne Forest, where they were confronted by the concentrated French forces. A day-long exchange of cannon fire took place on 20 September. By the next day the French had taken up such strong positions that it was pointless to try to attack. For a week the German armies, all but cut off from their supplies, suffered as their leaders negotiated with the French in the hope of persuading them to join in the march to Paris. On 28 September, after hostilities had been renewed, the Germans began their retreat. Not until a month later were the last units of the Prussian army safely out of France again after having lost thousands of men to hunger and dysentery. As the Prussian army was retreating, a fresh French army invaded the Rhineland from Alsace, capturing Austrian supplies at Speyer and forcing the capitulation of Mainz and Frankfurt before the end of October.

One of the generals who commanded several Prussian regiments was Duke Carl August of Saxe-Weimar, Goethe's sovereign, who had long yearned to reap military glory. Before leaving to take part in what was expected to be a brilliant campaign, Carl August impressed upon Goethe his desire for the pleasure of his company and Goethe finally agreed to take part. He cannot have been very happy about the prospect of being away from Weimar for so long, leaving his mistress, Christiane Vulpius, and a young son behind. He was also in the middle of extensive renovating being done on his newly acquired house (a gift from Carl August, as Goethe does not fail to mention). Goethe put off his departure from Weimar as long as possible, traveling alone with his servant, Paul Götze (who plays a not inconsiderable role in *Campaign in France 1792*), to catch up with the Prussian army after it had already entered French territory. By this time Longwy, the first fortress along the route of the march, had already capitulated and the Germans were to take Verdun almost as easily. Goethe hoped that the campaign would be over quickly and he would be able to return home soon. It is clear from his letters home in August and early September that he was as optimistic about the outcome of the campaign as anyone else. Never having had a taste of the rigors and the unpleasantness of a difficult campaign, he was hardly prepared for the ghastly experiences which awaited him once the army left Verdun to march on towards Paris. The evidence is that even after the German armies had been stopped at Valmy he was at first reluctant to recognize the realities of the military situation, but the privations of the retreat may have opened his eyes more fully to the import of what he had just gone through. At any rate, by the time he reached Luxemburg on his way back to safety he was convinced that he had witnessed the beginning of what he feared would become a new Thirty Years' War that would devastate the whole of Central Europe. This fear, expressed in a letter to one of his Privy Council colleagues, was, as it turned out, more than justified, although the hostilities did not last a full thirty years and ended with Waterloo instead, in 1815.

Campaign in France 1792 and *Siege of Mainz* constitute the third installment of the autobiography which Goethe published under the overall title *From My Life*. It was written from 1820 to 1822 and published in 1822. Goethe *too* was in the Champagne: that is the motto at the beginning of the text. The motto is at once a parallel and a contrast to the motto of the *Italian Journey:* "I too in Arcadia." But the Champagne was far from another Arcadia. The unwritten sense of the motto must be construed: "I *too* was in the Champagne and lived to tell about it." He was also at the siege of Mainz in the spring and summer of 1793, a somewhat less strenuous although on the whole still distasteful affair, with which he ends the volume. Between the end of the French campaign and the siege of Mainz he traveled through Westphalia visiting old friends and new acquaintances in Düsseldorf, Duisburg and Münster and spent what would appear to have been a frustrating winter in Weimar. Although the campaign and the siege take up more than three fourths of the volume, it is not just a military memoir. It is a piece of autobiography, the narrative of what Goethe must have considered a most significant period of his life.

Formally the work consists of two parts, *Campaign in France 1792* and *Siege of Mainz*. In fact, however, it can be viewed as composed of four parts: the campaign in France, August through October, 1792; the journey through Westphalia; the winter in Weimar; and the siege of Mainz. The parts are disproportionate and lacking in external unity, seemingly held together only by the chronology of a year of Goethe's life. They also make use of different poetic and stylistic means. Yet the volume does have one underlying theme: Goethe's feeling of isolation and of being exposed to a hostile and uncomprehending world. Images of isolation and loneliness pervade the military parts of the volume: Goethe alone in his chaise, alone on horseback, alone with his servant in a boat. He tarried as long as possible before traveling alone to catch up with the army for the invasion of France, took the opportunity to detach himself from the main body of the army before it had reached Verdun during the retreat, and finally asked for leave to absent himself altogether after the army had reached Coblence. He terms this departure quite frankly a "flight."

Instead of returning directly to Weimar, however, Goethe journeyed on down the Rhine to visit his old friend Fritz Jacobi in Pempelfort, near Düsseldorf, quite obviously seeking recuperation and compensation for the sufferings of the campaign in the renewed acquaintance with old friends—in Pempelfort he sought to rejoin a circle to which he had previously belonged. The visit in Pempelfort and the stay in Münster with Princess Gallitzin delayed his return to Weimar for a month and a half. If Goethe's account of the campaign is pervaded with images of isolation, from which he hoped to escape by visiting old friends, that isolation becomes the explicit theme of the Pempelfort episode: as Goethe tells it, Jacobi and his circle had no understanding whatsoever for his transformation since the journey to Italy and the awakening of his avid interest in science and nature. The tensions produced by this visit are barely kept under control through the conscious exercise of tact and civility, avoidance of certain subjects, and enlargement of the social circle through visits and activities in Düsseldorf.

The second station of the Westphalian journey—the short stay with Plessing in Duisburg—ostensibly motivates what could be termed a supplement to the first installment of the autobiography, *Poetry and Truth,* by going back in time to Goethe's beginnings in Weimar. He takes recently published speculation about the meaning of his early poem "A Winter Journey in the Harz" as the occasion to recount the origins of the poem and his first meeting in 1777 with the misanthropic Friedrich Victor Lebrecht Plessing, from whom he takes pains to distance himself. But the poem itself unfolds the most splendid image of isolation—the soaring and floating bird surveying the world and spying the misanthrope from on high—and while the Plessing of 1792 is no longer the strict loner or the totally unhappy person Goethe had encountered in 1777, the account of the visit to Duisburg still does nothing to integrate Goethe into a congenial social setting. Paradoxically, it is only in the Münster circle of Princess Gallitzin—strictly Catholic and mystically inclined—that Goethe unexpectedly feels more comfortable and even enjoys the freedom to be himself (as compared with the visit to Jacobi, where he had had to control himself carefully). Yet even here he remains the outsider, tolerated and respected rather than embraced and integrated fully into the circle.

The narrative of the winter spent at home in Weimar chronicles above all his difficulties in writing for the theater and the stagnant state of his poetic genius. All his efforts to come to terms intellectually or poetically with ongoing events in the outside world—the effects of the French Revolution both in France and in the rest of Europe—were destined to failure. Although this time is undoubtedly a part of the gestation period for his renewed work on *Wilhelm Meister's Apprenticeship,* the only poetic success of this winter was ultimately his adaptation of the old Low German animal fable, *Reynard the Fox,* a biting satire on the ways of the world. The final part of the volume, the *Siege of Mainz,* ends on what for Goethe, in spite of the German success in recapturing Mainz, is an uncharacteristically gloomy note, with the uncomprehending encounter with his long-time friend and brother-in-law Georg Schlosser in Heidelberg and the look ahead to the Prussian catastrophe of 1806. The uncomprehending encounter with Schlosser parallels the encounter with Jacobi the previous autumn. Had Goethe ever continued his autobiography down to the year 1794, as he originally planned, he would no doubt have placed the year from August, 1792 to August, 1793 in stark contrast to, and treated it as a psychic preparation for, the encounters with Friedrich Schiller in 1794 which finally led to their enduring friendship and collaboration and ended his period of loneliness and isolation. It is probably safe to say that *Campaign in France 1792* and *Siege of Mainz* appear to be such pessimistic works because they are not followed by any reminiscence of Goethe's friendship with Schiller.

Goethe's *Campaign in France 1792* has come to be considered by the historians as a valuable source for studying the campaign, and his *Siege of Mainz* is probably the most extensive treatment of the siege compiled by any contemporary. Goethe's motto—"I too in the Champagne"—could be taken to mean that he *too* had an account of the campaign to offer. That would, however, be a somewhat misleading inference. At the time when Goethe wrote, there seems to have been little interest in this particular piece of past history. It had been described in considerable detail in the 1790s by a number of writers (most graphically by Christian Friedrich Laukhard in his *Letters of a Prussian Witness* and in his autobiography), but the military men and historians who were to offer "authoritative" accounts of that campaign had not yet begun to publish. The flood of events since 1792, the French occupations of the Rhineland, the Napoleonic conquest of Germany, and the Wars of Liberation had diverted attention from the beginnings of that period of turmoil. Goethe resurrected that interest, perhaps, with his account of the campaign and the meaningful commentary on the cannonade of Valmy which he put into his own mouth in his narrative: "From this time and place a new epoch is beginning, and you will be able to say that you were there." Most of those who had written about the campaign and about Valmy during the 1790s had neither been so prescient, nor had they made so much of that fruitless exchange of cannon balls. In fact, it is unlikely that Goethe himself had been wise enough to make such a comment anytime in September, 1792. Instead, it is most likely that he predated—moving it into a much more dramatic context—the insight which he did indeed later express, in October, 1792, in the letter from Luxemburg, that Europe was now entering a long period of war and social unrest. Hindsight was of considerable benefit when Goethe was working on *Campaign in France 1792* in the early 1820s, and he was able to integrate the purported battlefield aperçu into his narrative structure as its most significant and decisive turning point.

It would be a mistake to take Goethe's account as a primary source for the events of the campaign of 1792. When he began to write he had no personal records to speak of with which to work. Whatever diaries he may have kept during the campaign were long since destroyed and all that Goethe seems to have had in his possession was a map, on the back of which he had jotted dates and short notes about the itinerary of the march. Of course we cannot be certain what memories he retained and reconstructed in the work, but we know that he was highly dependent on other accounts that had been published earlier and on recollections by acquaintances which he solicited for the purpose of composing his narrative. Perhaps his most important and reliable source was a diary kept by Carl August's servant, Johann Conrad Wagner, which was available to him in the ducal library but has still to be published in full. Since shortly after the First World War Goethe scholars have been relatively well informed about Goethe's sources, but the historians have done very little research on the campaign itself and the insights of Goethe scholarship have not yet been put satisfactorily to systematic use.

In spite of the fact that it is in large part demonstrably derivative, Goethe's account is still as intelligible and as unified a narrative as any that was written about the campaign of 1792. It is generally well informed and correct in its broad outlines and can be improved upon—from the point of view of Goethe's own experience and perspective of the campaign—only by the addition of details from other accounts. Most of the time Carl August and Goethe were near headquarters and at the head of the army in the thick of things. Goethe's account deals therefore with the central events of the invasion and retreat. It is, however, the record of a man who makes no claims to any broad overview or perspective on what occurred during the campaign. It offers no real answer to a question which has always vexed the historians, namely the question as to the Duke of Brunswick's true strategic objectives in his conduct of the campaign. In fact, the narrative persona created by Goethe is a surprisingly uninformed and uncomprehending participant in events—surely a piece of narrative strategy rather than a reflection of the true state of affairs. Goethe was, after all, Carl August's confidant and had good contacts with a number of other leaders of the expedition. He surely knew much more about the overall plan of the campaign and the debates among the leaders at the time than his narrative persona ever admits to knowing. What emerges from this narrative strategy is not a text that claims to be an authoritative treatment of the campaign, but a piece of personal experience and depiction of moods, ranging from optimism and exhilaration at the promising beginning to disgust, distaste, and despair during the course of the retreat and relief at finally having reached safety again. Goethe *did* survive this horrible campaign and managed to return home to tell about it in his own way.

When writing *Campaign in France 1792* and *Siege of Mainz* Goethe faced one overriding problem: how to deal with, how to form and give literary shape to such a monstrous amount of unpleasant things. He wanted to produce a literary work, a piece of autobiography, not just a simple memoir, a polemic, or a naturalistic recital of death and suffering. The siege of Mainz must have been easier for him to deal with than the French campaign, for at Mainz it was the enemy who was surrounded, while the besieging forces enjoyed relative comfort, suffered no privations (as opposed to the previous year in the Champagne), and could even afford a diversion or two. Thus the somewhat incongruous account of the garden laid out for Frederick William while he was attending the siege, the gala reception for the Mecklenburg princesses who were betrothed to the royal princes, descriptions of the citizens in their Sunday best who came from Frankfurt and other places in the vicinity to observe the siege. Goethe managed a number of small excursions, and he could choose to accompany the soldiers on their business or not, as he wished. He was not caught in the action as he had been during the French campaign, and he was able, in the end, to describe the siege in a relatively straightforward manner, basically in the form of a day-to-day journal.

Finding the way to give shape to the events of the catastrophic campaign in France was another matter altogether. The story he had to tell of the French campaign was one he could never tell in its entirety. One reason for his reticence was without a doubt the need for delicacy and diplomacy with regard to his sovereign, Carl August, who had been closely related by blood to the Duke of Brunswick and by marriage to the King of Prussia. Whatever disagreements there may have been between the two leaders regarding the conduct of the campaign—the King overruled his commander in chief on more than one crucial occasion—play no part in Goethe's account: Goethe allows himself only two vignettes of their contrary motions and puts most of the direct criticism of the Duke of Brunswick's leadership into the mouth of a retired cavalry officer in Trier. In an encounter with Goethe during the retreat the Duke of Brunswick avers that all right-thinking men will agree on blaming the elements for the catastrophe. True, the weather in August, September, and October of 1792 was abominable and certainly contributed to the disaster, but it was not by any means responsible for the monumental errors committed by the leaders in the planning and conduct of the campaign. Carl August himself plays a stellar role in the narrative and Goethe expresses his heartfelt gratitude to his patron openly—even embarrassingly so, perhaps—in a number of passages.

The second and paramount difficulty facing Goethe was certainly the nature of the experience itself. Here his memories must have tormented him and his remarks in conversation with friends and in his correspondence during the period of composing the work reflect the nightmare quality of the material with which he had to wrestle. In addition, he had in mind to entertain and instruct his readers, a goal which he could not have attained by means of stark realism (which in any case is foreign to all but his earliest works). As a result, the narrative abounds in understatement, euphemism, images, and leitmotifs, that is, in poetic or literary devices. The French émigrés, whom he could have painted in the blackest colors for their role in getting the German Allies into this disastrous situation, are instead viewed predominantly from the ludicrous side. The dysentery that wreaked havoc among the invaders is mentioned only in euphemisms, never by name, does not appear until the turning point of the story at Valmy, and then becomes one of the cast of demons making the retreat from Valmy such a horrible affair—whereas it is clear from other accounts that the Prussian army had been so weakened by the dysentery from the very beginning of the campaign—it had already put in its appearance before the troops had even left Trier territory—that it is questionable whether they would have been any match for the French in a pitched battle. Obtaining food was a continuing problem from beginning to end and contemporaries were horrified at the extent of the plundering that went on—according to Laukhard even in Allied territory, before the army crossed into France. During the advance to Valmy Goethe manages to eat fairly well and only observes the plundering. When he goes out looking for food to take it is "foraging"—but by the time he has reached safety in Luxemburg he has been almost as hungry and as preoccupied with getting food as any of the common soldiers. Likewise, maintaining the thousands of horses necessary for the transport of the army and its baggage was a considerable problem—the horses were already exhausted and dying before the invasion proper ever began. Goethe only reports difficulties in obtaining and keeping horses to pull his own chaise through France: there is no mention of a *dead* horse (aside from the striking death of Carl August's mount, Amaranth, and the account of a mortally wounded horse at Valmy) until he is past Verdun on the way back to safety in Germany. Goethe has formed the narrative in the shape of his own process of realization: the advance as far as Valmy is a study in optimism, encountering no inexorable difficulty in spite of numerous problems with supplies and weather; the real misery begins only in the aftermath of the cannonade, building throughout the retreat to the point where Goethe was able to escape it altogether and flee to visit Jacobi in Pempelfort. Yet, although Goethe feigns lack of expertise and refrains from overt criticism of the campaign and from any final judgment on it, a close reading of the text reveals that he has pinpointed, in his understated manner, practically every element that contributed substantially to the catastrophe. In spite of all his efforts to make it an autobiographical document worthy of his dignity, his text becomes a most devastating assessment of the campaign.

A Note on the Text and Commentary

I have aimed throughout at accuracy in the translation and in most instances faithfully reproduced Goethe's sentence structure and the logic of his periods. The work is highly paratactic and lends itself readily to this type of treatment. I benefited from having available a translation prepared by Heinz Norden for the Chicago Goethe edition that was projected in the 1940s and never came to fruition. I took over a number of parts of sentences and turns of phrase from Norden when his rendering seemed to me more felicitous than my own efforts. On the other hand, the Norden text was only a draft, far from a final version. Its language on the whole was outmoded, it contained numerous errors, and Norden had not translated the *Siege of Mainz*. Work on the translation was begun in my seminar during the fall of 1980 and I wish to thank five of my students—Kathy Brzovic, Kenneth Calhoon, Robert Cowan, Akiko Hitomi, and Clare Peterson—for their work in producing a rough translation of approximately the first third of the text. They will probably no longer recognize their own contributions, but they saved me a considerable amount of the drudgery involved in translating a text whose language is no longer quite the same as that with which we are familiar.

In the Introduction to *Poetry and Truth* I acknowledged my profound indebtedness to Erich Trunz's commentary in volumes 9 and 10 of the Hamburger Ausgabe of Goethe's works, a commentary which has set the standard for modern Goethe editions and has often been taken over with or without acknowledgement by other editors. In my commentary on *Campaign in France 1792* and *Siege of Mainz* I have incorporated many of the results of my own studies of the text and of the campaign of 1792, but I have also made grateful use of the commentary by Waltraud Loos in volume 10 of the Hamburger Ausgabe, by Ilse-Marie Barth in her Reclam edition of the text, and by Reiner Wild in volume 14 of the Hanser Verlag's new Münchener Ausgabe, which appeared in 1986.

Campaign in France
1792

I too in the Champagne!

23 August 1792

Immediately after my arrival in Mainz I visited the elder Herr von Stein,[1] Royal Prussian Chamberlain and Chief Forester, who filled a sort of ambassadorial post and distinguished himself by fierce hatred towards everything revolutionary. In broad strokes he filled me in on the progress of the allied forces up until now, and he provided me with maps from the topographical atlas of Germany which Jäger, the Frankfurt mapmaker, had published under the title "War Theater."

Lunching with Stein I found several French women whom I had cause to observe attentively; one of them (the mistress of the Duke of Orléans,[2] I was told) a stately lady of proud bearing and already somewhat advanced in years, with raven black eyes, eyebrows and hair, who was proper but affable in conversation. A daughter, the very picture of the mother as she must have appeared in younger days, spoke not a word. All the more gay and charming was the Princess of Monaco, a declared friend of the Prince of Condé[3] and the toast of Chantilly in better days. There was no sight more charming than this slim blonde; young, cheerful, jesting: no man whom she wanted to attract could possibly have resisted her. Observing her dispassionately, I was amazed to find myself again in the presence of Philine,[4] whom I had not expected to find here, bright and cheerful, true to her nature. She seemed neither so tense nor so agitated as the rest of the company, who, to be sure, were living alternately in hope, worry, and apprehension. In these very days the allies had forced their way into France. Whether Longwy would surrender immediately or offer resistance, whether the French republican troops would come over to the allies and everyone, as the émigrés had assured us, would declare himself for the good cause and facilitate its progress—all that was still in doubt at this moment. New couriers were awaited any moment: the most recent messengers had reported only the armies' slow advance and the obstacles posed by the muddy roads.

The intense desire of these people became all the more anguished as they could not conceal the fact that they had to wish for the swiftest possible return to their homeland in order to take advantage of their assignats,[5] the invention of their enemies, to live more cheaply and comfortably than here.

I then spent two pleasant evenings with the Sömmerrings,[6] Huber,[7] the Forsters,[8] and other friends; here I felt as if I were at home again. Most of these people were previous acquaintances and fellow scholars, thoroughly familiar with nearby Frankfurt (Sömmerring's wife was from there), all of them well acquainted with my mother, esteeming her genial qualities, quoting many of her bon mots, insisting repeatedly on my great similarity to her in cheerful deportment and energetic conversation. What stimulus and resonance in such a natural, innate, and habitual intimacy! We indulged freely in harmless pleasantries in the areas of science and other intellectual subjects, which put us in the best of spirits. There was no talk of politics, for we felt a mutual need to spare each other's feelings: while they did not altogether deny their republican sentiments, I was for my part clearly making haste to join an army which was intended to put a definite end to such sentiments and their consequences.

Between Mainz and Bingen I experienced a scene which soon offered me further insight into the character of the times. Our light chaise quickly caught up with a heavily laden coach and four; the deep ruts in the road up the mountain forced us to get out, and we asked the coachmen, who had likewise climbed down, who that was ahead of us. The postillion replied with much cursing that it was some French women who thought they were going to pay with their paper money; he was certainly going to overturn them if the opportunity ever arose. We reproached him for his spitefulness without improving his attitude in the least. While the coach was making such slow progress I went up to the lady's coach door and spoke to her in a friendly manner, whereupon a young face, pretty but anxious-looking, brightened somewhat.

She confided immediately that she was following her husband to Trier, from where she hoped to reach France as soon as possible. When I described this step to her as very premature, she admitted that, besides the hope of being reunited with her husband, it was the necessity of again getting by with paper money that drove her to this. Moreover, she demonstrated such confidence in the combined forces of the Prussians, Austrians, and émigrés that one would have been hard put to hold her back, even if the particular time and place had not been so unfavorable.

As we were talking we encountered an unusual obstacle; a wooden millrace had been constructed across the top of the sunken road in which we were confined, to carry the necessary water to a mill on the other side. One would have thought the height of the structure would be gauged to accommodate something at least the size of a hay wagon. Be that as it may, the coach was packed so immoderately high, chests and boxes piled up in a pyramid one atop the other, that the millrace posed an insuperable barrier to any further progress.

Here the postillions really began cursing and shouting, seeing themselves so long delayed; but we gladly volunteered our services, helping to unload and then reload the coach on the other side of the dripping barrier. The good young woman, who had gradually lost her shyness, could not thank us enough, while her hope rose ever higher that we would be able to assist her. She wrote down her husband's name and urged us, since we were certain to reach Trier before her, to leave a note for her at the city gate to inform her of his address. Even with the best will in the world we were dubious about the prospects for such an undertaking because of the great size of the city, but she clung to her hope nevertheless.

Arriving in Trier we found the city full of troops, crammed full with all sorts of vehicles, and nowhere a place to stay; wagons were parked on the squares, people wandered through the streets in confusion; the people in the billeting office, besieged from all sides, were at their wits' end. But such confusion resembles a kind of lottery, the lucky person gets some prize, and thus it was that I ran into Lieutenant von Fritsch,[9] of the Duke's regiment, who greeted me warmly and brought me to a canon, whose large house and extensive courtyard generously and comfortably absorbed me and my compact equipment. I immediately devoted myself to getting some rest. My young military friend, whom I had known and thought highly of since his childhood, had been ordered to remain in Trier with a small detachment to care for the sick who had been left behind, and to receive stragglers, delayed supply wagons, and the like, and expedite them further; in the course of which duties his presence was of benefit to me as well—although he was quite unhappy about remaining in the rear, where such an ambitious young man could expect little opportunity to distinguish himself.

My servant had scarcely finished unpacking the most essential things when he asked permission to look around the city; he returned late, and the next morning the same restlessness drove him again from the house. This strange behavior seemed inexplicable until the riddle was solved: the plight of the pretty Frenchwomen had not left him untouched; he searched carefully and, although unable to find the husband, he had the good fortune to find the women, recognizing their carriage, parked in the main square among a hundred other wagons, by its pyramid of boxes.

On the way from Trier to Luxemburg, I soon had the pleasure of seeing the monument in the vicinity of Igel. Since I knew how felicitous the ancients had been in situating their buildings and monuments, I immediately removed all the huts of the village from my mind's eye, and now the monument stood in the worthiest of settings. The Moselle flows directly past the monument and is joined by the Saar, an imposing river, on the other side; the winding rivers, the rolling countryside, and the lush vegetation lend the spot charm and dignity.

The monument itself could be described as an obelisk with architectural and sculptural embellishments. It rises in several tiers, artistically arranged one above the other, culminating in a point which is ornamented with tile-like scales and crowned by a globe, a snake, and an eagle.

Let us hope that some engineer, brought to this area and perhaps detained here for some time by the present war operations, will not shrink from the task of measuring this monument, and, if he can also sketch passably, preserve and transmit for us the figures on the four sides, as far as they are still recognizable.[10]

How many sad, unadorned obelisks have I not seen erected in my time, without anyone having thought of this particular monument! To be sure, it dates from a later period, but we still see the pleasure and the joy they took in conveying to posterity a view of their own personal surroundings with all the trappings and signs of activity. Here parents and children stand facing one another, families feast together; and in order that the beholder may know the origin of this prosperity, laden pack-horses are shown, and various kinds of trade and commerce are depicted. For actually it was war contractors who erected this monument for themselves and their families as a testimony that then, as now, sufficient wealth can be amassed in a place such as this.

The entire obelisk was built by stacking great sandstone blocks crudely one atop the other and then chiseling out the figures as though from one solid piece of stone. That the monument could withstand so many centuries may well be ascribed to this solid construction.

I could not indulge long in these pleasant and fertile thoughts: for very close by, in Grevenmachern, a most modern spectacle was awaiting me. Here I found the corps of émigrés, comprised entirely of noblemen, most of them chevaliers of the order of St. Louis.[11] They had neither servants nor grooms, so they were caring for themselves and their horses personally. I saw many of them leading their mounts to water or to the smithy. But the thing which evoked the most striking contrast to this humble activity was a large meadow overflowing with coaches and carriages of every description. The émigrés had shown up along with their wives and mistresses, children and relatives, as though to exhibit, for all the world to see, the inner contradiction of their present situation.

As I had to wait several hours out in the open for post-horses, I was able to make another observation as well. I sat in front of the post-house window, not far from the repository for unfranked letters. I have never seen such a crush; letters were dropped through the slot by the hundreds. The boundless endeavor of people striving with body, soul, and spirit to surge through the breach in the dike back into their homeland could not have been demonstrated in a livelier or more pressing manner.

Out of boredom and a desire to discover or invent secrets, I began imagining what might well be contained in this mass of letters. Here I thought I detected a woman in love, who expressed, with pain and passion, the torture of longing involved in such separation; or someone in dire straits, asking a friend for money; exiled women with children and servants, whose financial reserves had shrunk to a few coins; fervent supporters of the Princes,[12] encouraging and cheering each other on, hoping for the best; others who already sensed the catastrophe in the offing and bitterly lamented the impending loss of their estates—and I do not think my guessing was very wide of the mark.

The postmaster, who sought to entertain me and thereby to relieve my impatience at having to wait so long for my horses, enlightened me on a number of things. He showed me several letters with postmarks from distant places which would now have to be forwarded to addressees who had advanced and were still advancing into France. According to him France was beleaguered by such unfortunates on all its borders from Antwerp to Nice; facing them were the French armies, ready to defend themselves and to go over to the counteroffensive. Many things he said gave me pause, and in his opinion the current situation was quite uncertain.

Since I did not seem to be as fanatical as others who were then storming into France, he soon took me for a republican and became more confiding; he told me about the misery which the Prussians had suffered due to weather and road conditions on their march by way of Coblence and Trier and provided a terrifying description of what awaited me in the encampment at Longwy; he was well informed about everything that was happening and was not averse to passing on his information to others; in conclusion he called my attention to the way in which the invading Prussians had plundered quiet, innocent villages, although there was some uncertainty as to whether it had been the regular troops themselves or the baggage train and stragglers who had done the plundering; these acts had been punished for the sake of appearances, but they had aroused great resentment among the inhabitants.

Here I could not help thinking of a certain general during the Thirty Years' War who, hearing strong complaints about the behavior of his troops in friendly territory, replied: "I can't transport my army in a sack." But I could tell nevertheless that our rear was not going to be very secure.

Longwy, the capture of which had been announced triumphantly to me while I was still en route, lay at some distance to my right as I passed by, and I arrived at the encampment at Praucourt on the afternoon of 27 August. Pitched as it was on a plain, it was possible to oversee all of it, but it could not be reached without some difficulty. The muddy, churned-up ground was an obstacle to horses and vehicles, and in addition it was surprising that we met neither guards nor sentries, nor anyone else to inspect our passes and from whom in turn we might have gotten some information. We drove through a wilderness of tents, for everyone had crawled into hiding to find whatever miserable shelter he could from the horrible weather. It was only with difficulty that we got people to tell us where to find the Duke of Weimar's regiment, but we eventually reached the spot, saw familiar faces, and were warmly received by our comrades in suffering. The Duke's man Wagner[13] and his black poodle were the first to greet us; both of them recognized an old comrade, who was once again destined to endure a critical epoch with them. At the same time I learned of an unpleasant incident. The Duke's favorite horse, Amaranth, had collapsed yesterday with a hideous scream and died on the spot.

Now I had occasion to observe and hear much worse things about the situation than the postmaster had predicted. The camp was pitched at the foot of a gently rising hill, at the bottom of which there was an old culvert designed to prevent water from rushing down over the fields and meadows. But this ditch had very quickly been turned into a receptacle for all the camp's refuse and garbage; it had become stopped up and in the night violent torrents of rain had broken through the dike and brought the most disgusting calamity down upon the tents. Entrails, bones, and everything else the butchers had discarded had been carried down into the already damp and unhealthy sleeping quarters.

I too was to be provided with a tent, but I preferred to spend the days with friends and acquaintances and to sleep at night in the large sleeping carriage, whose comforts were already familiar to me from previous occasions. But it seemed very strange that the carriage, though only thirty paces from the tents, was still so inaccessible that I had to have someone carry me there in the evening and back in the morning.

28 August

It was in this strange situation that my birthday came around this year. We mounted our horses and rode into the captured fortress; the well-built and fortified town lies upon a knoll. I had the intention of buying some large woolen blankets, and we proceeded at once to a shop where we found a mother and her daughters, pretty and charming. We did not haggle a lot and we paid a good price, and were as well-mannered as any Germans can possibly be, who, after all, are totally lacking in polished French elegance.

The fortunes of this house during the bombardment had been quite miraculous. Several shells had fallen one after the other into the family quarters, sending the inhabitants fleeing; the mother snatched a child from his cradle and hurried away, and in that moment another shell had gone through the pillows where the little boy had lain. Fortunately none of the shells had exploded, and though they had destroyed some furniture and singed some paneling there had been no further damage—no shells had fallen in the shop.

That the patriotism of the inhabitants of Longwy must not have been terribly ardent was evidenced by the fact that the populace had forced the military commander to surrender the fortress very quickly; and we had hardly left the shop when the internal discord among the citizens was amply illustrated. Some royalist sympathizers, hence our friends who had brought about the quick capitulation, expressed their regret that we had happened on this particular establishment and had spent so much money with this worst of all Jacobins, who, along with his entire family, was good for nothing. Likewise we were warned about a certain prominent tavern, in such a way as to make us wonder whether the food were not to be trusted; a less pretentious place was recommended to us as reliable, where indeed we found ourselves warmly received and reasonably well served.

There we found ourselves now, old comrades in field and garrison, happy to be reunited; there were officers from the regiment, as well as members of the Duke's court, house, and chancellery. We discussed recent events, how momentous and stirring it had been at the beginning of May in Aschersleben,[14] when the regiments had received orders to prepare to march, the Duke of Brunswick[15] and other high personages had paid visits there, among whom we did not neglect to mention the Marquis de Bouillé,[16] an important foreigner who had played a significant role in this operation. No sooner had the eavesdropping innkeeper heard this name than he eagerly inquired whether we knew the gentleman. Most of us were able to answer in the affirmative, whereupon he showed us great respect and expressed a strong hope that this worthy and active man might contribute greatly to the campaign—it even seemed as though we received better service from this moment on.

Since all of us gathered here professed loyalty, with body and soul, to a sovereign who had developed such great virtues during his reign and who now was to prove himself at waging war, a craft to which he had been inclined since youth and which he had now practiced for some time, we drank to his health and that of his family in the good old German manner, and especially to Prince Bernhard,[17] at whose baptism Colonel von Weyrach, representing the regiment, had stood godfather shortly before the departure.

Everyone had some tale to tell about the march itself; how, skirting the Harz Mountains on the left, they had passed by Goslar, reaching Northeim by way of Göttingen. We heard of billets both excellent and poor, of hosts who were rustically unfriendly, cultivatedly ill-humored, and hypochondriacally pandering, of convents and of the vicissitudes of roads and weather. They had then marched along the eastern border of Westphalia to Coblence, had many a pretty lady to remember, reported on various eccentric clergymen, unexpected encounters with friends, broken wheels, and overturned vehicles.

From Coblence on they had much to complain about regarding mountainous regions, difficult roads, and all sorts of scarcities, and after these reminiscences of the past they drew nearer to the present; they described their crossing into France in the worst possible weather as extremely unpleasant and a fitting prelude to the situation which we could foresee upon returning to camp. But in such company each fires the other's courage, and I for my part was soothed by the sight of the precious woolen blankets which the groom had strapped to my saddle.

In camp that evening I found the finest company in the great tent; everyone had stayed there, as it was not possible to venture out; everyone was in good humor and full of confidence. The quick surrender of Longwy bore out the assurances of the émigrés that we would be welcomed everywhere with open arms, and it seemed as though only the weather was opposed to our great enterprise. Prussians, Austrians, and émigrés, without exception, displayed the same hatred and contempt for revolutionary France as had been enunciated in the manifestos of the Duke of Brunswick.[18]

And in truth, from what was known of the situation in France, it seemed apparent that a people which was not simply divided into parties, but demoralized to its very core, split into its smallest constituent parts, would not be able to resist the high sense of purpose of the noble allies.

There were also military deeds to be recounted; just after entering France five squadrons of hussars from the von Wolfradt regiment out on reconnaisance had come across a thousand French chasseurs who had been sent out from Sedan to observe our progress. Ably commanded, our troops attacked, and since the enemy defended themselves bravely and would accept no quarter, there was a great slaughter in which we were the victors, made prisoners, and captured horses, carbines, and sabers, through which prelude our fighting spirit was heightened, and hope and confidence were reinforced.

On 29 August we pulled out of this mass of mud and water, slowly and not without difficulty: for how was one to keep tents and baggage, uniforms and the like even halfway clean when there was not even a dry spot to be found where they could be spread out and put in order?

The attention, however, which the highest commanders devoted to this decampment gave us fresh confidence. All vehicles were given the strictest orders to follow behind the columns, the only exception being that regimental commanders were each authorized to have one chaise preceding their troops; I thus had the great fortune for now of leading the whole army in a light open carriage. The two leaders, the King and the Duke of Brunswick, had positioned themselves with their respective entourages so that everyone had to pass before them. I saw them from afar, and as we approached the spot, His Majesty rode up to my carriage and asked in his laconic manner: to whom did the vehicle belong? I answered loudly "The Duke of Weimar," and we marched on. It is not likely that anyone has ever been stopped by a nobler inspector.

Further on we found the road rather better in places. In a curious region where hill and dale alternated continually, there was enough dry ground to enable those who were on horseback to advance comfortably. I mounted my own horse and thus proceeded more freely and cheerfully; our regiment was leading the army, so we could always be out in front and thus free ourselves completely from the cumbersome movement of the main body of troops.

The march left the main road and we proceeded by a route which took us to Arrancy, and thence on through Châtillon l'Abbaye, where we came upon the first effects of the revolution, a church property that had been sold, its walls partially broken down and destroyed.

Now, however, we saw the King's Majesty, racing across hill and dale on horseback, like the core of a comet followed by a long, tail-like retinue. Scarcely had this phenomenon receded with lightning speed when a second appeared from another side, crowning hills and filling valleys. It was the Duke of Brunswick, who was attracting similar elements and trailing them behind him. Though we were more given to simple observation than to passing judgment, we could nevertheless hardly help wondering which of the two powers was in fact supreme. Which would make the decisions at critical junctures? Unanswered questions which left behind only uncertainty and apprehension.

What gave even greater cause for thought on this occasion was the sight of the two commanders riding openly and without precautions into a territory where a mortal enemy could easily be lurking behind every bush. But we had to admit that it was just such personal daring and abandon which had won victories and established dominions from time immemorial.

The sun was very hot through an overcast sky; the wagons made slow progress in the mud. Broken wheels on wagons and cannon caused frequent delays, and here and there we saw exhausted infantrymen who could not drag themselves any further.

We heard the sound of cannon coming from Thionville and wished the Austrians success.[19]

That evening we rested in a camp near Pillon. We were in a pleasant forest clearing, the shade itself was refreshing, and there was enough brush for kitchen fires; there was a stream flowing past which formed two clear pools, both of which seemed destined immediately to be muddied by men and animals. I left one of them to its fate, but defended the other staunchly and had it cordoned off with ropes and poles. This could not be done without much scolding. One of our troopers asked another, while they were calmly cleaning their equipment, "Who's that fellow acting like such a big man?"—"I don't know," answered the other, "but he is right."

In this wise Prussians, Austrians, and a part of France were coming to wage war in France. By what power and authority were they doing this? They could perfectly well act in their own names; after all, war had been declared on one of them, and their alliance was no secret. But now another pretext was invented: they were acting in the name of Louis XVI, they didn't levy requisitions, but they borrowed by force. Coupons had been printed up, which were signed by the commanding officer, but whoever had them in hand could fill them in as he saw fit and Louis XVI was supposed to redeem them. With the exception of the manifesto itself, there was probably nothing which so aroused the people against the monarchy as this kind of treatment. I myself was present at one such scene which I remember as having been quite tragic. A number of shepherds had apparently combined their flocks so as to hide them in the forest or in other out-of-the-way places; when found and led off to the army by our patrols, they were at first received in a friendly manner. Inquiries were made as to the respective owners, the sheep were sorted into individual flocks and counted. The faces of these good men showed traces of worry and fear, though mixed with some hope. But this procedure was only the necessary preamble to dividing up the flocks among the regiments and companies, in exchange for which the owners were politely given the coupons drawn on Louis XVI while their woolly charges were murdered at their feet by impatient, meat-craving soldiers. I must admit that my eyes and soul have never witnessed a crueler scene or more profound sorrow. Only Greek tragedies have the power to move the spectator so simply and deeply.

30 August

On this day, which was to bring us close to Verdun, we were expecting some adventures, and we were not disappointed. The road, which wound up and down the hills, was much drier, the vehicles were able to make better progress, and riders found the going easier and more pleasant.

A cheerful group of us, on good mounts, advanced ahead of the troops until we met up with a detachment of hussars which formed the actual advance guard of the main army. Their commander, a serious man past his middle years, did not seem pleased at our arrival. He had been ordered to exercise the strictest caution and prudence and to prevent, as discreetly as possible, the occurrence of any unpleasant incidents. He had distributed his troops precisely, they were advancing in single file, and everything was proceeding in a calm and orderly fashion. The countryside was deserted, the extreme solitude ominous. In this wise we had advanced up and down the hills past Mangiennes, Damvillers, Wawrille and Ormont, when, at the top of a hill which offered a beautiful view of the landscape, there was a shot from the vineyards to our right. The hussars immediately went off to investigate the area. They proceeded to bring back a bearded black-haired man who looked quite uncouth, in whose possession they had found a cheap pistol. He claimed defiantly that he was only scaring off the birds from his vineyard and was not doing anyone any harm. The commander, deliberating coolly, decided this case in the light of his explicit orders and let the threatened prisoner off with a few blows, which sent the chap on his way so quickly that our soldiers lustily threw his hat after him. But he seemed to feel no urge to stop and pick it up.

We proceeded on, conversing about things that had happened and about things that might yet occur. It should be observed that our small company, which had imposed itself on the detachment of hussars, was composed of widely differing elements which had come together more or less by accident; for the most part its members were upright men, each in his way totally dedicated to satisfying the demands of the present moment. But I must mention one in particular, a serious man who inspired respect, a type which one came across often in the Prussian army in those days, more aesthetically than philosophically inclined, serious, with a certain hypochondriacal character, quiet and reserved and yet with a delicate passion for doing good.

While advancing in this fashion we came across a phenomenon as unusual as it was pleasant, one which aroused general sympathy. Two hussars were accompanying a two-wheeled, one-horse cart up the hill, and when we investigated what was under the canvas top, we found a boy, perhaps twelve years old, who was driving the horse, and a girl or young woman, pretty as she could be, who leaned out of the corner to survey the riders surrounding her two-wheeled shelter. None of us was untouched by the sight, but it was our compassionate friend who felt called upon to lend active assistance to the young beauty; from the moment when he first observed the flimsy vehicle he felt the irresistible urge to effect her salvation. We clustered in the background while he asked in detail about her circumstances, and it turned out that the young woman, who lived in Samogneux, seeking to escape the impending danger by going to join friends who were farther removed from the line of march, had fled straight into its jaws, as often happens in such trying situations when a person thinks things are better anywhere else than where he is at the moment. We all did everything we could to make her understand, in as friendly a way as possible, that she had to go back home. Even our leader, the hussar commander, who at first had suspected attempted espionage, was convinced by the warm eloquence of the decent man who finally, accompanied by two hussars, brought her back to her home, more or less reassured, where, a little while later, as we passed through the town in an orderly and disciplined fashion, she greeted us in a friendly manner, standing among her relatives on a low wall and full of hope because her first adventure had ended so well.

It is at moments like this in the midst of military campaigns that men seek to gain credit by instant discipline and bring about a kind of legal peace in the midst of confusion. Such moments are precious to peasants and townsfolk alike and to anyone who has not yet been deprived of all faith in humanity by the unabated horrors of war.

Camp was pitched this side of Verdun and we counted on a few days' rest.

The morning of the thirty-first I lay half awake in the sleeping-carriage—surely the driest, warmest and most pleasant of resting places—when I heard something brush against the leather curtains and, upon opening them, found the Duke of Weimar, who had brought an unexpected visitor. I immediately recognized the adventurous Grothaus[20] who, prepared to play his accustomed role as intermediary again here, had arrived to take charge of the hazardous mission of calling on Verdun to surrender. In this capacity he had come to ask our sovereign for a staff trumpeter; the trumpeter, proud of such a distinction, was immediately ordered to participate in the mission. We greeted each other happily, recalling our previous strange experiences together, and Grothaus hurried off on his business, about which mission there was a good bit of joking afterward. It was recounted how he had ridden down the road, preceded by the trumpeter and followed by hussars, and how the Verduners, veritable sansculottes who either knew nothing of international law or disregarded it totally, had fired off cannon at him when he attached a white flag to the trumpet and ordered the trumpeter to play ever louder; also how he had been led by a detachment of French soldiers into the fortress, blindfolded and alone, and how he had spoken impressively there, but achieved nothing, and more such things, by the mention of which it is customary to belittle services rendered and besmirch the honor of such enterprising men.

When the fortress rejected the first call to surrender, as was only to be expected, we had to proceed with preparations for a bombardment. The day passed thus, while I took care of a small piece of business whose results have benefited me down to the present day. In Mainz, as will be recalled, Herr von Stein had provided me with Jäger's atlas which portrayed on several pages the present and, it was to be hoped, the next areas of the war theater as well. I took out one page, number forty-eight, which depicted the area I had traversed from Longwy on, and, as there just happened to be an embosser among the Duke's retinue, I had it cut out and mounted, and it still serves me as a means of recollecting those days which were so important both for the world and for myself.

Having thus taken care of my future needs and present convenience, I surveyed the meadow where we were encamped and the tents stretching far up the hillsides. On this expansive green carpet a strange spectacle attracted my attention: a number of soldiers had sat down in a circle and were occupied with something inside that circle. When I looked more closely I found them gathered around a funnel-shaped sinkhole which must have been thirty feet in diameter at the top and was filled with the purest spring water imaginable. There were innumerable small fish which the soldiers were trying to catch with gear they had brought along in their packs. The water was the clearest in the world and this pursuit of the fish amusing enough to observe. Nevertheless I had not watched this game very long before I noticed that the small fish flashed different colors as they moved about. At first I took this phenomenon to be due to the irridescence of the moving bodies themselves; however, a more satisfactory explanation soon occurred to me. A piece of earthenware had fallen into the pool, which, as it lay there in the depths, was providing me with a display of the loveliest prismatic colors. Lighter in color than the bottom and easily visible, this fragment displayed blue and violet colors on the edge farthest from me, and reds and yellows on the side nearest me. When I then moved around the pool, the phenomenon followed me, as is natural in such subjective experiments, and the colors always appeared the same in relation to my position.

Since I was passionately concerned with such phenomena anyway, I was overjoyed to see, out here in the wide world, fresh and natural, the same thing which physics teachers for almost a hundred years had sought by shutting themselves and their students up in a dark room. I got hold of a few more pieces of pottery which I threw into the water, and could observe quite well that the phenomenon began just below the water's surface and grew more intense as the shard descended, until finally a small white body, completely enveloped in color, reached the bottom looking like a little flame. In the course of this experiment I remembered that Agricola[21] had already mentioned this phenomenon and had been moved to class it among the so-called fiery phenomena.

After dinner we rode up the hill which lay between Verdun and our tents; we found the location of the city itself quite pleasant, surrounded as it was by meadows and gardens in a sunny plain through which flowed several arms of the Meuse, with nearer and more distant hills as a backdrop. As a fortress, to be sure, it was vulnerable to bombardment from all sides. Since the city had refused to capitulate, the afternoon was spent setting up our batteries. We observed the city meanwhile through good spyglasses and could make out very clearly what was going on on the rampart directly opposite us, numerous people moving back and forth who seemed to be especially busy at one particular spot.

The bombardment began at midnight from the battery on our right flank and from another battery on our left which, being closer to its target and firing incendiary rockets, had quite a considerable effect. We had only to watch calmly as these fiery meteors flew through the air and then we could see soon afterward a section of the city in flames. Our spyglasses, trained in that direction, permitted us to see this damage in detail; we could make out the people on top of the walls trying hard to stop the fires, and we could see and distinguish the collapsing beams. All this was observed in the company of both friends and strangers, who made indescribable, often contradictory comments and expressed widely divergent sentiments. I had walked into the midst of a battery that was working away vigorously, but the terrible booming sound of the howitzers proved unbearable to my peace-loving ears and I soon had to move away. Then I ran into Prince Reuss XI,[22] who had always been a friendly and gracious lord to me. We paced back and forth behind vineyard walls, protected from the cannon balls which the besieged forces were firing vigorously at us. After various political discussions, which, to be sure, only entangled us in a labyrinth of hopes and anxiety, the prince asked me what I was presently engaged in and was greatly surprised when, instead of telling him about this or that tragedy or novel, I began, stimulated by the refraction phenomena I had observed that afternoon, to speak animatedly about the theory of colors. For with me, a discourse on natural phenomena was the same as the writing of poems, I did not make them, but rather they made me. My interest, once aroused, asserted itself and ran its course without being in the least bit disturbed by cannon balls and incendiaries. The prince wanted me very much to explain how I had got interested in this matter. What had happened today came in very handy for the purpose.

It did not take long to convince such a man that a nature lover who spends much of his life outdoors, in the garden, on the hunt, traveling, or on military campaigns, was bound to find opportunity and leisure enough to observe nature as a whole and to become familiar with individual phenomena of all kinds. For example: the air, vapors, rain, water, and soil constantly present us with changing color phenomena and, indeed, under such differing conditions that one has the urge to become acquainted with them more intimately, to differentiate them from each other, and to organize them under certain rubrics in order to determine the relationships between them. In this way one would win new insights in every area of study, as opposed to the dogmatic teachings of the schools and what we read in books. Our ancestors, I said, endowed with magnificent sensory perception, had made splendid observations, but they had not continued or followed through on them; they had been least successful at ordering phenomena and putting them under the proper rubrics.

Such were the topics of our conversation as we paced back and forth through the damp grass; stimulated by his questions and remarks, I continued to hold forth until the chill of the breaking day drove us to an Austrian bivouac which offered a huge, attractive circle of glowing coals that had been kept burning throughout the night. Absorbed by my subject matter, with which I had busied myself only for the past two years, so that it was still quite fresh and only roughly thought out, I would hardly have been able to know whether the prince was still listening to me, had he not interposed perceptive comments here and there and, at the end, picked up my train of thought anew and offered approval and encouragement.

I have always observed, when it comes to scientific matters, that it is better to deal with men of affairs, men of the world, who have to listen to many impromptu oral reports and therefore must always be on their toes, because they keep an open mind and pay close attention to the speaker, with no other interest than their own enlightenment; whereas scholars, by contrast, normally hear nothing but what they themselves have learned and taught and about which they are in agreement with their fellow scholars. In place of the object itself there is created a word-credo to which it is as reassuring to remain faithful as to any other.

The morning was cool, but dry; we were pacing back and forth again before the fire, half roasted, half frozen, when suddenly we saw something moving at the vineyard wall. It was a squad of riflemen who had spent the night there, but now were taking up their rifles and knapsacks again and moving down into the burned-out suburbs of the city in order to harass the ramparts from there. Advancing toward almost certain death, they were singing very bawdy songs, which was perhaps pardonable under the circumstances.

Hardly had they left the spot when I thought I perceived a very striking geological phenomenon where they had been resting. On the low limestone wall there was a layer of light green stones, exactly the color of jasper, and I was totally at a loss to explain how such a remarkable mineral could be found in such quantity in the midst of these limestone deposits. Great was my disappointment, however, when, on approaching this fantastic sight, I immediately observed that it was the insides of moldy loaves of bread which the riflemen, unable to stomach, had jocularly cut up and arranged on the wall as decoration.

This incident gave us immediate cause to talk about the possibility of poisoning, a topic which had been constantly under discussion since we had entered enemy territory. This, quite understandably, fills a fighting army with panic, because one suspects not only every dish offered by one's host, but even the bread baked by one's own army. But the quickly developing inner mold was attributable to quite natural causes.

It was eight o'clock on the morning of 1 September when the bombardment ceased, although there was still some exchange of fire. Especially worthy of mention was a 24-pounder that the besieged had directed at us, whose infrequent rounds they seemed to fire more in jest than in earnest.

On the open summit, to the side of the vineyards and directly in the line of fire of this largest cannon, two hussars had been posted on horseback to keep close watch on the city and the area between it and us. They remained unmolested the whole time they were posted there. The Verdun cannoneers were holding their gun in readiness, however, for while these lookouts were being relieved the number of soldiers on the spot increased, some spectators also ran up, and a large mass of people came together. At this moment I was speaking with a friend, with my back turned to the crowd of people, when suddenly there was a fierce, whistling, crashing sound behind me so that I turned around immediately, without being able to say whether this about-face had been caused by the sound, the rushing air, or an inner psychic, moral stimulus. I still was able to see the cannon ball ricochet through a number of fences far behind the scattering crowd. Once the danger was past they ran after the cannon ball with a great shout; no one had been hit and the lucky people who had taken possession of this round iron mass carried it around triumphantly.

Toward noon the city was called upon a second time to capitulate and requested twenty-four hours to consider. We too used this time, to establish ourselves more comfortably, lay in provisions, and ride around the area. I did not fail to return more than once to the instructive sinkhole, where I could pursue my observations more calmly and deliberately; for the water had been completely emptied of fish by the soldiers and had returned to a completely clear and undisturbed state, so it was possible to repeat at will the game of the sinking little flames and I found myself in a most agreeable state of mind.

Several misfortunes, however, soon put us back on a war footing. An artillery officer had been trying to water his horse; there was not much water in the area; the water in my sinkhole, although he passed by it, was too far below the rim, so he went down to the Meuse, which flowed nearby, where he and the horse fell in because of the steep bank. The horse was able to reach safety but the officer was pulled out dead.

Shortly after that we saw and heard a strong explosion in the Austrian camp, which was on a hill within our view; explosions went off more than once and each time we could see smoke. Through carelessness a fire had broken out while they were loading bombs, and there was grave danger; the fire spread to bombs that had already been loaded and there was fear that the whole supply of munitions might go up in smoke. But quickly the fear was allayed by the commendable action of the imperial soldiers, who, disregarding the danger that threatened, hastened to carry the powder supplies and the loaded bombs out of the tent.

And so this day too passed; the next morning the city capitulated and was occupied, but we immediately learned of an act that was typically republican in character. The commandant, Beaurepaire, under great pressure from the anguished citizenry who feared the whole city might be burned and destroyed if the bombardment continued, had not been able to put them off any longer; but after he had given his assent to the capitulation at the meeting in the city hall he pulled out his pistol and shot himself, and thus provided yet another example of the highest patriotic sacrifice.[23]

After such a quick conquest of Verdun no one doubted any longer that we would soon move on and recover splendidly from our previous hardships with the help of the good wines of Châlons and Epernay. Therefore I lost no time in having the Jäger maps showing the route all the way to Paris cut out and mounted carefully, and I had white paper pasted on the back, as with the first map, so that I could make brief daily notations.

3 September

Early in the morning a party assembled to ride into the city, and I joined them. Immediately upon entering the city we found evidence of extensive preparations indicating that originally a much lengthier resistance had been contemplated; the paving stones had been taken out of the middle of the streets and piled up against the houses, which made it rather unpleasant to walk around in the wet weather. But we went straight to the especially famous shops where the best liqueurs of all kinds could be had. We sampled them all and bought a number of different ones. Among them was one with the name "Baume humain," which was less sweet, but stronger, and especially refreshing. We also didn't pass up the "dragées," sugar-coated spicy morsels packed in neat cylindrical paper tubes. In the midst of so many good things we naturally did not forget the dear people at home who would know how to appreciate them on the peaceful banks of the Ilm. Little boxes were packed and it was not hard to persuade obliging couriers, who had been assigned to take news back to Germany of our successes so far, to load themselves down with some of this kind of baggage by which we could convince the ladies at home that we were pilgrims in a land where spirits and sweets would never run out.

After that, when we took in the partially damaged and devastated city, we repeated an observation which had been made before us, that in the midst of such tragedies which men inflict on their fellows, as in those which nature inflicts upon us, there are occurrences which seem to point toward the existence of a favorable Providence. The bottom floor of a corner house on the marketplace contained a porcelain shop, well lighted by many windows; we were informed that a bomb which struck the square had bounced against the stone doorpost of this shop, only to be diverted and bounce off in another direction. And the doorpost had indeed been damaged, but it had done its duty well: behind the clear polished windows the splendid array of gleaming porcelain still stood in all its reflecting glory.

At our noonday meal in a tavern we were regaled with good leg of mutton and wine from Bar, a wine which doesn't travel well and must be enjoyed where it is grown. It is customary at these places to provide spoons, but neither knives nor forks, so the diner must bring his own. Informed in advance about this custom we had bought flat and nicely worked knives and forks for ourselves, of a kind which are produced in Verdun. Resolute and good-natured girls waited on us just as they had waited on the garrison only a few days before.

During the occupation of Verdun there was one incident which, though only an isolated case, created a great stir and aroused general interest. As the Prussians were marching in a shot fell from out of the crowd. It injured no one, but the French grenadier who had fired it could not deny, in fact had no intention of denying, his daring act. I saw him myself at the main guardhouse where he was taken: he was a very handsome, well-built young man with a firm gaze, and bore himself calmly. He wasn't watched very carefully while his fate was being deliberated. Next to the guardhouse was a bridge over one of the arms of the Meuse; he sat down on the low wall, remained still for a while, then threw himself over backwards into the water and was dead by the time he was brought out again.

This second heroic and ominous act aroused violent hatred among the new arrivals, and I heard otherwise reasonable persons insisting that neither the grenadier nor the commandant should be given a decent burial.[24] It is true that we had expected completely different sentiments on the part of the French army, and as yet we saw not the slightest sign that the French troops would come over to our side.

We took greater pleasure, however, in the story of the King's good reception in Verdun; fourteen of the fairest and most refined maidens had welcomed His Majesty with pleasant speeches, flowers, and fruit. His intimates had counseled against eating the fruit, for fear that it might be poisoned, but the magnanimous monarch did not hesitate to accept these choice gifts with a gallant flourish and to taste them confidently. These charming girls seemed also to have inspired some confidence among our young officers; certainly those individuals who had the good fortune to attend the ball could not say enough in praise of their grace and good manners.

But more solid pleasures were also provided here: for as we had hoped and anticipated, the fortress was plentifully stocked with the finest provisions, and everyone hurried—perhaps too precipitously—to recuperate from the sufferings of the march. I could not but observe that people were wasting the smoked bacon and meat, the rice and lentils, and other good and necessary foodstuffs, which seemed a poor policy in our situation. On the other hand it was amusing to see how an arsenal, or rather a weapons collection, was coolly and calmly plundered. All sorts of guns, mostly old ones, had been collected in a monastery, along with any number of other curious things with which a man who wants to defend himself can hold off his opponent or even kill him.

That leisurely plundering went as follows: when the high military officials undertook, after the occupation of the city, to survey the supplies of all kinds which they had captured, they also came upon this collection of weapons, and while they were laying claim to it for military purposes they also found many a particular item which any individual would have liked to possess, and it was not easy for anyone to inventory these weapons without wanting to take something for himself as well. This went on down through the ranks until in the end this treasure came to be fair game. Now almost anyone could give the guard a small tip, get into the collection, and take along whatever might suit him. In this way my servant acquired a long flat cane which was skillfully and sturdily wound with twine and at first glance hardly seemed unusual; but its weight suggested that it might contain something dangerous, and in fact the cane concealed a broad sword-blade, some four feet long, with which a powerful hand could have done wonders.

Thus we continued between order and disorder, between conserving and destroying, between robbing and paying, and this is what it must actually be that makes war so corrupting for the soul. One plays first the part of the bold soldier, the destroyer, and then that of the gentle person, the giver of life; one accustoms oneself to phrases which, in the most desperate situation, arouse and strengthen hope; in this way a type of hypocrisy is born, a type which has its own special character and is quite different from priestly hypocrisy or courtly hypocrisy, or whatever the other kinds may be called.

I must mention still another notable person whom I saw, to be sure at some distance, behind jail bars: the postmaster of Ste.-Menehould, who had quite clumsily allowed himself to be caught by the Prussians.[25] He was in no way bothered by the stares of the curious and seemed quite calm about his uncertain fate. The émigrés claimed that he deserved to be put to death a thousand times over and they agitated accordingly with the authorities, to whose credit it must be said, however, that they behaved with becoming dignity and decency here, as well as in a number of other cases.

4 September

We had a steady stream of visitors in our tents throughout the day; many things were related, discussed, and deliberated upon and the situation became clearer than before. Everyone agreed that we had to get to Paris as soon as possible. We had bypassed the unconquered fortresses of Montmédy and Sedan and seemed to have little to fear from the army stationed in that area.

Lafayette, who had had the confidence of the common soldiers, had been obliged to withdraw from the war; he had found himself forced to go over to the other side and yet was treated as an enemy by them.[26] Dumouriez,[27] although he had shown insight into military affairs while minister of war, had not distinguished himself in any previous campaign and now, ordered straight from the ministry to take command of the French armies in the field, he seemed to display just the same inconsistencies and hesitation as his predecessors. News of the unhappy events of mid-August trickled through; in defiance of the Duke of Brunswick's manifesto the King had been imprisoned, dethroned, and treated as a criminal. The topic discussed most intensely, however, was the problems related to our future operations.

The Argonne Forest, that thickly wooded mountain range which causes the Aire river to flow from south to north, lay immediately ahead of us and blocked our advance. There was much talk of Les Islettes, the important pass between Verdun and Ste.-Menehould. We could not agree as to why the pass had not already been occupied, and was not being occupied even now. The émigrés were said to have made a surprise attack on it, but to have been unable to hold it. This much was known: the garrison that withdrew from Verdun had gone there, and while we were on the march to Verdun and bombarding the city Dumouriez had also sent troops straight across country to reinforce the post and to cover the right flank of his position behind Grandpré, thus confronting the Prussians, Austrians and émigrés with a second Thermopylae.

We admitted that our position was extremely disadvantageous and we had to resign ourselves to a plan of operations whereby the army, which should have forced its way straight ahead without stopping, would instead march north along the Aire to try its luck at one of the other fortified mountain passes. It was a stroke of good fortune that the Hessians had at least been able to take Clermont from the French and use the city as a base for staging attacks on Les Islettes:[28] if they could not take the pass, they could at least harass it.

6 September

In line with this strategy the camp was moved beyond Verdun; the names of the King's and the Duke's respective headquarters, Glorieux and Regret, were cause for a number of strange reflections. I myself chanced upon the former as the result of an annoying incident. The Duke of Weimar's regiment was to be stationed at Jardin Fontaine, close to the city and the Meuse. We managed to get out of the city gates easily enough by squeezing into the wagon train of an unfamiliar regiment which carried us along with it, although we could see that we were going too far; also it would not even have been possible to get out of the column, as the road was so narrow we would have ended up helplessly in the ditch. We looked right and left without seeing any escape, we also inquired but got no answer, because everyone was a stranger here and very vexed at the situation. Finally, as we came to the top of a low hill, I looked down into a valley on my left, which must have been quite nice in good weather, and saw an attractive settlement with a castle and other buildings. A gently sloping green embankment promised to make it easy for us to get down there, and I was all the more inclined to bolt sideways out of this awful marching column, as I saw officers and grooms down below on their horses, and carriages and wagons standing there. I had an idea this was one of the headquarters, which turned out to be true: it was Glorieux, where the King was staying. But there too my inquiries as to the location of Jardin

Fontaine were totally fruitless. Finally I ran into Count von Alvensleben,[29] who had always been friendly toward me, and now he was like an angel from heaven; he told me to follow the village road, which was quite free of traffic, down the valley and toward the city, but to turn off to the left before reaching Verdun, and I would soon discover Jardin Fontaine.

I followed his directions and found our tents already pitched, but in the most terrible condition. The campground was a sea of mud, the rotting tent ropes snapped one after the other, and the canvas collapsed around the head and shoulders of anyone who had in mind to shelter there. We put up with it for a little while but finally decided to move into the village itself. We found a well-furnished house whose owner, a good man who liked to tease us, had once been a cook in Germany; he took us in without complaint and we got nice bright rooms on the ground floor with a good fireplace and everything else we needed.

The Duke's retinue was fed from the ducal kitchen but our host entreated me to let him cook for me, at least just once. And he really did prepare a very fine meal, but it didn't agree with me at all; I might well have suspected poison, had I not remembered the garlic which had been necessary to make those dishes so tasty, but which usually had a very powerful effect on me, even in the smallest doses. My indisposition was soon past and I preferred to stick with German cuisine as before, as long as it could provide me with anything at all.

When we said goodby our good-humored host gave my servant the letter of introduction he had promised him to a sister in Paris; but after a few words he added good-naturedly: "I doubt you will get there."

11 September

After a few days of being well cared for, we were thus thrust back out into the most awful weather; our route followed the mountain ridge that marked the watershed between the Meuse and the Aire and forced both to flow northward. After severe hardships we reached Malancourt, where we found empty wine cellars and deserted kitchens, and had to be satisfied with eating on a bench under a roof the little bit we had brought with us. I liked the way the homes were furnished, reflecting a quiet domestic contentment; everything was simple and natural, adequate to satisfy basic needs. We had disturbed all this, this is what we were destroying, for in the neighborhood there arose anguished cries for help against plunderers; we rushed there and were able, not without some danger to ourselves, to put a stop to the marauding for the moment. It was strange indeed to hear the poor unclad wretches from whom we wrested coats and shirts accuse us of the most extreme cruelty for not allowing them to cover their nakedness at the expense of the enemy.

But we were yet to hear an even more curious reproach. Returning to our quarters we found a distinguished émigré, with whom we were already acquainted. We greeted him warmly and he did not scorn to share our frugal meal, but it was quite obvious that he was very upset, exclaiming under his breath about something which he was trying to get off his chest. When, in accordance with our previous friendship, we tried to win his confidence somewhat, he bemoaned the cruel way in which the King of Prussia had treated the French princes. Surprised and utterly baffled, we asked him what he meant. We heard from him then that the King, totally disregarding the wretched weather during the departure from Glorieux, had not worn any coat, whereupon the royal princes had felt it incumbent upon themselves also to go without any such weatherproof garments. The sight of these most distinguished personages in their light clothing, soaked to the skin and dripping, had caused our marquis the greatest distress, and indeed, had it been of any avail, he would gladly have given his life to provide a dry carriage for those princes, on whom rested the hope and salvation of the entire fatherland, and who were accustomed to a completely different manner of living.

To be sure we had nothing to say in reply, since he would scarcely have been reassured by the reflection that war, which is a kind of foretaste of death, makes all men equal, cancels all rights of ownership, and threatens even the most illustrious with suffering and danger.

12 September

The next morning, however, I decided, considering I had such lofty examples, to leave my chaise—which, though light, was drawn by four requisitioned horses—under the protection of the dependable Wagner, who had been entrusted with bringing the equipment and our quite indispensable coin in the baggage train. I sprang into the saddle and set off on the march to Landres with a few good companions. Halfway there we found logs and brush from a small birch grove that had been cut down; the wood's inner dryness quickly overcame its outer wetness and we soon had a blazing fire and hot coals, enough to warm us up as well as enable us to cook. But our accustomed regimental dining service was incomplete. Tables, chairs, and benches failed to arrive and we had to get along as best we could, standing up or leaning against whatever we could find. But we reached the encampment towards evening without mishap; we were camped close to Landres, directly opposite Grandpré, knowing full well how strongly the pass was defended.

It rained incessantly, with blasts of wind, and the tent afforded little shelter.

But blessed is he whose heart is filled with a higher passion; these past days the thought of the color phenomenon in the pool had not left me for a moment. I kept going over it in my mind in order to devise suitable experiments. Then I dictated a draft to Vogel[30]—who proved himself, here as ever, a faithful secretary—and later drew in the figures. I still possess those papers, with all the traces of the rainy weather, as testimony to faithful endeavors along the doubtful path I had taken. But the road to truth has this advantage: that it is pleasant to think back on unsure steps, a detour, even a mistake.

The weather got worse and became so bad in the night that it had to be reckoned a great good fortune that we were able to spend it under cover of the regimental wagon. What a horrible situation it was, considering we were camped in the face of the enemy and had to be apprehensive that he might take it into his head to swoop down on us somewhere from his mountain and forest fortifications.

From 13 to 17 September

Wagner arrived in good time, carriage, poodle, and all; he had spent a terrible night. After overcoming a thousand obstacles, he had strayed from the army in the dark, misled by a general's servants, drunk with wine and sleepiness, whom he had followed. They had reached a village and suspected that the French were in the immediate vicinity. Made fearful by all the commotion and left in the lurch by horses that didn't come back from watering, he nevertheless had managed to get out of the wretched village and we finally found ourselves again in possession of our belongings.

Finally there was a current of excitement and hope. We heard heavy cannon fire on our right flank and it was said that General Clerfait[31] had arrived from the Netherlands and attacked the French on their left flank. Everyone was very anxious to learn the outcome.

I rode to headquarters to get a better idea what the cannon fire was all about and what we should expect. There they did not know anything yet for certain, except that General Clerfayt must have engaged the French. I ran into Major von Weyrach, who—from impatience and boredom—was just mounting to ride to the outposts. I accompanied him, and soon we reached a hill where we could get a good view. We came upon a hussar post and spoke with the officer, a handsome young man. The cannon fire was far beyond Grandpré and he was under orders not to advance, for fear of causing unnecessary troop movements. We hadn't been talking long when Prince Louis Ferdinand[32] arrived with a small retinue and, after a short exchange, demanded of the officer that he advance. The prince, paying no attention to the officer's urgent objections, rode forward, and we all had to follow. We had not gone very far when a French sharpshooter was seen in the distance. He advanced quickly until he was in range, and then turning around disappeared again just as quickly. After him followed a second and a third, who likewise disappeared. But the fourth one—probably the first again—shot at us in earnest, for we could distinctly hear the bullet whistling. The prince did not let this deter him, and the French also stuck to their business, so that several more shots were fired as we continued advancing. I looked at the officer several times, who was in a very embarrassing position, torn as he was between his duty and his respect for a royal prince. Probably thinking he had caught a look of sympathy in my eye, he rode up to me and said: "If you have any influence with the Prince, try to get him to go back, as he is placing me in a position of grave responsibility. I have the strictest orders not to leave my assigned post, and there would be nothing more foolhardy than to provoke the enemy, who is encamped in a secure position behind Grandpré. If the Prince doesn't go back, the whole chain of outposts will sound the alarm, headquarters won't know what to make of it, and I will be the one who gets the blame, through no fault of my own." I rode up to the Prince and said: "Someone has just paid me the honor of assuming that I possess some influence with Your Highness, and therefore I respectfully ask to be heard." I then put the situation to him clearly, which was hardly necessary, since he saw it all by himself and was gracious enough to turn around at once with a few kind words, whereupon the sharpshooters also stopped shooting and disappeared. The officer thanked me most sincerely, and one can see from this that a mediator is always welcome.

The situation gradually became clear. Dumouriez' position at Grandpré was an advantageous one and well secured, and we knew quite well that he could not be attacked on the right flank. To his left there were two major passes, La Croix aux Bois and Le Chesne Populeux, both well fortified and considered to be impregnable. The latter, however, had been put in the charge of an officer who was either negligent or not equal to such a task. The Austrians attacked. Prince von Ligne,[33] the son, was killed in the first charge, but then they were successful, the post was overpowered, and Dumouriez' grand plan was ruined: he had to abandon his position and march up the Aisne river, and Prussian hussars were able to force their way through the pass and pursue the French past the Argonne Forest. They caused such fearful panic among the French forces that ten thousand men fled in the face of five hundred, and it was only with great difficulty that they could be halted and regrouped; here the Chamborant regiment distinguished itself particularly and kept our troops from advancing further. Since they had been dispatched more or less only for reconnaissance purposes anyway, they returned triumphantly, full of joy, and they let it be known that they had captured several wagons of good booty. They divided up among themselves whatever was of some immediate use—money and clothing—and I received what I had coming to me as a chancellery official, namely the papers, among which I found some of Lafayette's old orders and several very neatly written lists. What surprised me most, however, was a fairly recent *Moniteur*.[34] This type, this format, with which we had been familiar for several years, and which we had not seen for several weeks now, greeted me in a rather unfriendly manner with a laconic article dated 3 September which threatened ominously: "Les Prussiens pourront venir à Paris, mais ils n'en sortiront pas."[35] So in Paris it was considered possible that we might get there after all; but some higher power would have to take care of our return!

The horrible situation we were in, dangling so to speak between heaven and earth, was relieved to some extent when we saw the army approaching and one detachment after another of the vanguard moving forward. Finally it was our turn too; we passed over hills, through valleys, by vineyards where many found some refreshment. As it grew lighter we came to a more open region and saw the castle at Grandpré, well situated on a hill in a pleasant valley of the Aire, just at the point where the Aire forces its way west between the hills to join with the Aisne on the other side of the mountains, whose waters then, always flowing toward the sunset, reach the Seine by way of the Oise; from which it is apparent that the mountain range which separated us from the Meuse, though not particularly high, but with a decisive influence on the watercourse, was sufficient to bring us into a different watershed.

During this march I found myself by chance first in the suite of the King, then of the Duke of Brunswick; I conversed with Prince Reuss and other diplomatic and military acquaintances. The lines upon lines of horsemen made a handsome picture against the pleasant landscape, one would have wished for a van der Meulen[36] to be there to immortalize such a procession; everyone was bright and cheerful, heroic and full of confidence. To be sure, several villages were on fire ahead of us, but smoke can hardly detract from a war scene. Supposedly people had shot at our vanguard from the houses, and in accordance with the laws of war the soldiers had immediately taken their revenge. This action drew a reprimand, but it could no longer be changed; the vineyards, on the other hand, were protected carefully, though their owners could hardly expect any very large harvest, and thus we advanced, behaving now like friends and now like foes.

Leaving Grandpré behind, we reached and crossed the Aisne and camped at Vaux les Mouron; we were now in the notorious Champagne, but it didn't seem so forbidding as yet. Well-kept vineyards stretched up the slopes on the sunny side of the river; and where we foraged in villages and barns we found enough provisions for man and beast. Unfortunately the wheat was not yet threshed, nor were there enough mills to grind it, baking ovens were quite scarce, and thus in truth we were approaching a situation closely resembling the predicament of Tantalus.

18 September

A large group gathered to meditate on such things, a group which in fact came together with some degree of intimacy whenever there was a halt, especially at afternoon coffee; the group consisted of curiously mixed elements, Germans and Frenchmen, officers and diplomats, all of them people of note, experienced, intelligent, witty, aroused by the urgency of the moment, all of them men of merit and dignity, but not actually participants in the inner councils and therefore all the more eager to figure out what decisions might be taken and what would happen.

When he could no longer hold the pass of Grandpré, Dumouriez had retired up the Aisne. Since his rear was secured by Les Islettes, he had taken up a position on the heights of Ste.-Menehould, his front line facing toward France. We had penetrated the narrow pass and had left enemy strongholds behind us and on the side, at Sedan, Montmédy, and Stenay, which could harass our supply line at will. In the worst kind of weather we had set foot in a strange land whose thankless limestone soil could support only wretchedly scattered settlements.

Of course Rheims, Châlons, and their fertile environs lay not far off and we could hope to recuperate there; therefore the group was almost unanimous in the conviction that we had to march toward Rheims and take possession of Châlons; in that case Dumouriez could not remain inactive in his advantageous position, a battle would be inevitable, wherever it might take place, and we considered that battle to be already as good as won.

19 September

There were therefore some misgivings on the 19th when we were ordered to march toward Massiges, up the Aisne, and to keep the river and the forested slopes to our left, whether close by or farther away.

Along the way, however, we forgot our reservations by focusing on numerous incidents and happenings; and one quite peculiar phenomenon attracted my own full attention. In order to advance several columns side by side, one column had been led across country over some low hills, but when descending back into the valley it encountered a steep slope; the slope was leveled off as far as possible, but still remained fairly steep. Just at noon the sun appeared and its light was reflected on all the rifles. I paused on a hill and watched this gleaming river of weapons approach in impeccable order; but it was an astonishing sight when the column reached the steep drop, where the formations, until now closed up, dissolved suddenly and every individual tried as best he could to get to the bottom. This disarray distinctly resembled a waterfall: a huge number of bayonets glittering now and then in the confusion indicated lively motion. And when they finally got back into formation at the bottom of the slope and marched on in the valley in the same way as they had when they arrived on the slope above it, the impression of a river became ever more vivid; and the whole scene was quite pleasant, as it was brightened continually by rays of sunlight, the value of which one learned to appreciate properly in those uncertain hours only after going without it so long.

In the afternoon we finally reached Massiges and were now only a few hours from the enemy; the camp had been marked out and we occupied the area assigned to us. Posts had already been set in the ground, the horses tethered, fires started, and the mess wagon opened up. Therefore it came as a complete surprise when we heard that we would not camp there after all. There was a report that the French army was moving from Ste.-Menehould to Châlons; supposedly the King did not wish to let the enemy get away so easily and had therefore given the order to march. I went straight to the top to get the facts but was told again what I had already heard, with one addition: acting on this uncertain and improbable intelligence, the Duke of Weimar and General Heymann had gone out to reconnoiter with the very same hussars who had caused all the stir in the first place. After a time these generals returned and assured us there was not the slightest movement to be detected, and the patrols that had originally reported the movement had to admit that they had deduced, rather than actually seen, what they had reported.

But now we had been set in motion, and the command came down for the army to advance, leaving all its baggage behind; the vehicles were to return to Maison-Champagne, form themselves into a circle, and await what was expected to be the favorable outcome of the battle.

Not hesitating for a moment, I entrusted my horses, carriage, and belongings to my resolute and trustworthy servant and immediately mounted with my comrades. We had already discussed such situations several times and concluded that anyone who embarks on such a military expedition should remain with regular troops, no matter what detachment, through thick and thin and not shrink from any danger: for whatever might befall us would be honorable, whereas to remain behind with the baggage or the campfollowers or wherever would be dangerous, and dishonorable as well. Accordingly I had agreed with the officers of the regiment that I would always stay with them—and if possible, among the Duke's personal guard—for this would further strengthen our close relationship.

Our route was along a small river, the Tourbe, through the most dismal valley in the world between low hills where there was neither a tree nor a bush. We were under strict orders to march in complete silence, as though we meant to surprise the enemy, although in his position he could scarcely fail to discover the approach of an army of fifty thousand men. Night fell, neither moon nor stars lightened the sky, a savage wind was whistling, the silent movement of such a long column of men in deep darkness made a weird impression.

Riding beside the column, I encountered a number of officers whom I knew, galloping up and down the line, now to hasten the march, now to slow it down. We exchanged a few words, we paused, and before long a group of some twelve men, both friends and strangers, had gathered. We asked each other questions, complained, marveled, cursed, and reasoned together, and above all we couldn't forgive our commander for interrupting our noonday meal. One cheerful fellow would have settled for simple fried sausages and bread; another immediately raised the level of desire, longing for roast venison and herring salad; and since all this was free of charge, there was no lack of pastries and other such delicacies, or of the finest wines, and we finally had such a perfect banquet set out that one man, whose appetite had become inordinately aroused, wished the whole company to the devil and cursed the unbearable agony of having such excitable imaginations in the face of such scarcity. We dispersed and lost sight of each other, and each of us alone was no better off than when we had all been together.

Night of 19 September

And so we got as far as Somme-Tourbe, where we stopped; the King had put up at an inn, while the Duke of Brunswick set up headquarters and chancellery in a kind of arbor outside the door. The grounds were large and a number of fires burned, fed by great bundles of vine stakes. On several occasions the princely field marshal personally criticized the fact that the fires were allowed to blaze so brightly. We discussed the matter among ourselves, and no one was prepared to believe that our presence there had remained a secret from the French.

I had arrived too late, and however much I looked around, everything edible had already been claimed, if not yet eaten up. While I was foraging, the émigrés put on a clever cooking demonstration; they sat around a large circular mound of glowing embers to which many a crackling vine stake had contributed. Quickly and shrewdly they had laid hold of all the eggs in the village, and it was truly appetizing to see the eggs standing side by side in the embers, to be taken out greedily one after the other as they got done. I didn't know any of this company of noble cooks, and as a stranger I didn't want to try to approach them; but then I encountered a good acquaintance who was suffering from hunger and thirst as much as I, and I thought of a stratagem based on an observation I had already had occasion to make during my brief military career. I had noticed that when foraging in and around villages soldiers proceeded in the clumsiest manner imaginable; the first to arrive broke in, grabbing some things, ruining and destroying others. Those who came later found less and less, and what was lost in this way benefited no one. It had already occurred to me that in such a case one ought to proceed strategically: if the mass of foragers were storming the front, one should do one's own searching from the opposite side. Such methods were hardly applicable here, for the place was already flooded with foragers, but the village extended a long way from the road by which we had entered it. I invited my friend to walk with me down the long street. A soldier came out of the next-to-last house, cursing because everything had already been eaten up and there was nothing to be had anywhere. We looked in at the window and saw a couple of sharpshooters sitting there quietly; we went inside, in order at least to be able to sit on a bench under a roof, greeted them as comrades, and of course lamented the general lack of provisions. After a few words they wanted us to promise to keep their secret, and we shook hands on it. They now disclosed that they had found a fine, well-stocked cellar in the house. They had of course concealed the entrance, but would not mind giving us a share of its stocks. One of them pulled out a key, and after various obstacles had been cleared away, a cellar door came in view and was opened. Having climbed down, we found a number of rather large casks, each about two buckets in size, and—what was even more interesting to us—various clusters of full bottles laid away in sand. Our good-natured comrade, who of course had already tried them all, pointed out the best ones. I took two bottles in each hand and held them under my coat, my friend did the same, and so we strode back up the street savoring the refreshment we were about to enjoy.

Close by the big campfire I found a strong heavy harrow, sat down on it, and, under my coat, shoved the bottles in between the tines. Soon I brought out one bottle. Immediately my neighbors hailed me and asked for a sip, and I quickly offered to share with them. They all took a good swig except for the last man, who was more moderate because he saw that he was leaving only a little for me. I hid the bottle beside me, brought out the second one soon afterwards, and drank to my friends, who didn't mind sharing with me again, not noticing the miracle involved; but by the third bottle they were cheering the magician loudly, and in such miserable circumstances the merriment was extremely welcome.

Among those whose forms and faces were illuminated by the fire I caught sight of an older man whom I thought I knew. After I had inquired and drawn closer, he was more than a little astonished to see me here. It was the Marquis de Bombelles,[37] whom I had visited two years before in Venice while attending the Duchess Amalia.[38] Residing there as the French envoy, he had gone to great lengths to make the stay of this estimable duchess as pleasant as possible. Mutual wonderment at seeing each other here, the joy of our reunion and memories of the past brightened this solemn moment. We talked about his splendid residence on the Grand Canal; I praised the manner in which, arriving in gondolas, we had been honorably received and graciously entertained there; how he had regaled the Duchess and her entourage with various small fêtes which accorded so perfectly with the tastes of this lady, who loved the conjunction of nature and art, merriment and decorum, and how, through his influence, he had made it possible for her to enjoy many other good things that were ordinarily inaccessible to foreigners in Venice.

Having meant to please the Marquis with these words of praise, I was quite taken aback when I heard him exclaim in melancholy tones: "Let us not talk of those things. That time belongs to the all too distant past, and even then, while I was entertaining my high-born guests with apparent light-heartedness, there was pain gnawing at my heart, I foresaw the consequences of what was happening in my homeland. I was amazed by the carefree spirit that kept you from sensing the danger awaiting you in Germany as well. I was already quietly preparing to change my situation, and not long afterward I had to leave my honorable post and my beloved Venice and embark on an odyssey which has finally led me here."

The air of secrecy with which our commanders had sought from time to time to shroud this open advance led us to assume that we would break camp and march again this same night; but the day was already breaking, and with it came a light drizzle; it was already completely light when we set out. Since the Duke of Weimar's regiment formed the vanguard, his personal guard, which led the whole column, was strengthened by the addition of hussars who supposedly knew the way. Now we went, occasionally at a quick trot, over fields and hills that had no trees or shrubs; on our left we could see the Argonne Forest at a distance. The drizzle came down harder in our faces; soon, however, we caught sight of a row of poplars, quite beautiful and well maintained, which intersected our line of march. It was the road from Châlons to Ste.-Menehould, the route from Paris to Germany; we crossed it and pressed on toward the gray horizon.

We had already observed the enemy encamped and drawn up at the edge of the woods, and it was also clear that new troops were arriving; it was Kellermann,[39] who was joining up with Dumouriez to form his left wing. Our troops burned with desire to get a chance at the French. Officers and men alike hoped eagerly that the commander would attack this very minute; our vigorous advance also seemed to indicate this would be the case. But Kellermann had been able to take up too strong a position, and now began the cannonade which has become famous, the ferocity of which cannot be described or even recalled to the imagination.

The road already lay far behind us, we were storming on toward the west, when suddenly an adjutant galloped up and ordered us back; we had gone too far, and now we received orders to go back across the road and anchor our right wing there. We complied and so formed our front toward the outworks at La Lune, which was visible on a height just down the road. Our commander approached; he had just brought up half a mounted battery. We were ordered to advance under cover of this battery and found along the way an old cavalry sergeant lying stretched out on the field, the first casualty of the day. We rode on confidently and drew nearer to the outwork. The battery there was firing vigorously.

But soon we found ourselves in a strange predicament, cannon balls flying wildly at us without our being able to understand where they could be coming from. After all, we were advancing behind a friendly battery and the enemy guns on the hills opposite us were much too far away to reach us. I paused somewhat to the side of our front line, and saw a most extraordinary thing: cannon balls were coming down by the dozens ahead of the squadron. Luckily they were not ricocheting and were digging themselves into the soft ground instead; men and horses were being spattered with mud and filth; the black horses, kept in formation as well as possible by skillful riders, reared and snorted. The whole mass was in surging motion, without becoming separated or confused. A remarkable sight reminded me of other times. In the first rank of the squadron the standard swayed to and fro in the hands of a handsome young lad; he held it firmly, but was swung back and forth against his will by his excited horse; his charming face called to mind—strange, but natural enough in this frightful moment—his even more charming mother, and I remembered the peaceful moments spent in her company.[40]

At last came the command to turn back, and all the cavalry regiments complied calmly and in good order, only one single horse from the Lottum regiment was lost, whereas all of us, especially those on the extreme right flank, should really have perished.

After we had pulled back out of range of this mysterious cannon fire and had recovered from our surprise and astonishment, the riddle was solved; we found the half-battery, which we had assumed to be covering our advance, at the very bottom of one of the many hollows characteristic of this terrain. It had been driven out of its position on the high ground and had gone down into a ravine on the other side of the road, so that we had been unable to observe its withdrawal; enemy cannon had taken its place and what was to have protected us almost became the death of us. When we reproached them the fellows only laughed and assured us jokingly that it was much better down there under cover.

But afterwards, when we could see for ourselves how such a mounted battery had to drag itself agonizingly up and down the dismal, muddy hills, we again had cause to ponder the serious situation into which we had gotten ourselves.

Meanwhile the cannonade was still going on; Kellermann held a threatening position next to the mill in Valmy, which is what we were actually firing at. A powder wagon there blew sky high and we were happy about the damage it had probably done the enemy. And thus in fact we remained only spectators and listeners, whether under fire or not. We paused on the road from Châlons at a signpost which pointed towards Paris.

The French capital was thus at our backs, and the French army was between us and our fatherland. There had perhaps never been more formidable barriers placed in our way, particularly alarming to someone like myself who had been studying the detailed map of the war theater for four weeks on end.

Nevertheless, the need of the moment makes good its claim even against the immediate future. Our hussars had captured a number of bread wagons on their way from Châlons to the French army, and escorted them down the highway to us. Just as it seemed strange to us to find ourselves positioned between Paris and Ste.-Menehould, the people from Châlons could hardly have expected to run into the enemy on the way to their own army. For a consideration the hussars let us have some of the bread; it was the finest white bread, the Frenchman recoils in horror from so much as a crumb of black bread. I shared more than one loaf among my closest acquaintances on the condition that they save some of it for me for the next few days. I found the opportunity also to take another precaution; a sharpshooter in the company had bargained with these hussars for a good woolen blanket and I offered to rent it from him for the next three nights at eight groschen a night, provided that he would take care of the blanket during the day.

He considered this a very advantageous arrangement; the blanket had cost him one guilder and after a very short time he was getting it back with a profit. But I too had reason to be content: my precious blankets from Longwy had been left behind with the baggage, but I had now obtained, in the absence of any other kind of shelter, a second protective layer in addition to my coat.

All this went on to the continual accompaniment of thundering cannon. Each side squandered ten thousand rounds that day, resulting in the loss of two hundred men on our side, and even these to no avail. The sky cleared as a result of this terrible convulsion: for the cannon were shot off just like volleys of muskets, somewhat unevenly, to be sure, now increasing, now decreasing in volume. The heaviest firing took place at one in the afternoon, after a pause. The earth literally shook, and yet one could not see the slightest change in the respective positions. No one knew what was to come of all this.

I had heard a lot about cannon fever and wanted to find out exactly what it was like. Boredom, and a spirit which is provoked to audacity, even to temerity, by every danger, lured me into riding up quite calmly toward the La Lune outwork. This position had been taken again by our forces; it presented, however, quite a wild sight, with the shot-up roofs, the sheaves of grain strewn about, the mortally wounded soldiers stretched out on them here and there and in the midst of this an occasional stray cannon ball landing and rattling the remains of the tile roofs.

All alone, left to myself, I rode away to the left on the ridge and had a clear view of the good position held by the French; they were emplaced in the form of an amphitheater, solid and secure, though Kellermann, on the left wing, was somewhat more exposed than the rest.

I met up with good company, officers I knew from the general staff and from the regiment, who were quite astonished to find me here. They wanted to take me back with them, but I told them I had my own reasons for being there and without further ado they left me to my well-known eccentric obstinacy.

I had now reached the area where the cannon balls were landing; the sound is strange enough, as though composed of the hum of a top, the bubbling of water, and the whistling of a bird. They were less dangerous because of the wet ground; they stuck where they landed, and so my foolish ride tempting fate was at least safe against the danger of ricochets.

Even under these circumstances, however, I could soon tell that something unusual was happening inside me; I paid careful attention to this, and yet I can only describe this feeling in the form of a simile. It seemed as though I were in a very hot place, and thoroughly permeated by that same heat, so that I felt completely at one with the element in which I found myself. My eyes lost nothing of their strength or clarity of vision, yet it was as though the world had a certain reddish brown tone, which made my own condition, as well as the objects around me, still more ominous. I did not notice any quickening of the blood, everything seemed rather to be caught up in this intense burning. From this it became apparent to me in what sense this condition could be called a "fever." Nonetheless it is still remarkable how whatever causes such terrible anxiety is conveyed to us solely through our sense of hearing; for it is the thunder of the cannon, and the howling, whistling and blasting of cannon balls through the air that is actually the cause of these sensations.

When I had ridden back and was out of danger, I found it remarkable that all that burning had been instantly extinguished and not the slightest trace of feverish agitation remained. This state, incidentally, is one of the least desirable and I found among my dear and noble companions in arms hardly anyone who would have expressed any really ardent desire to experience it.

And so the day passed; the French stood immovable, Kellermann had taken up a more comfortable position; our people were pulled back out of the cannon fire, and it was just as though nothing had happened. The greatest consternation spread through the army. Only that morning we had fully expected to roast all the Frenchmen on a spit and devour them, it had been my own absolute faith in such an army and in the Duke of Brunswick which had enticed me to participate in this dangerous expedition; now, however, everyone kept to himself, we didn't look at each other—or if we did, it was only to curse and swear. Just as night was falling we happened to form a circle, in the center of which we could not even light our customary fire, most of us silent, a few conversing among themselves. In reality, every one of us was unable to think or to judge what had happened. Finally I was called upon to say what I thought, since I usually cheered and refreshed the company with my remarks, and this time I said: "From this time and place a new epoch is beginning, and you will be able to say that you were there."

In these moments, when no one had anything to eat, I reclaimed a bit of the bread I had acquired that morning. Of the wine I had shared so liberally the evening before there was only enough left to fill a small brandy flask, and so I had to forego completely the role of the welcome miracle worker I had played so daringly yesterday by the fire.

The cannonade had hardly ended when the storm and rain set in again and made our situation out in the open and on the sticky clay soil most unpleasant. And yet, after having been awake so long, and after such physical and emotional exertions, sleep came of its own accord after night had fallen. We had settled as well as we could behind a rise which warded off the piercing wind, when someone got the idea that tonight we should dig ourselves into the ground and cover ourselves with our coats. We began doing this right away, and a number of graves were hewn out with tools loaned us by the mounted artillery. Even the Duke of Weimar did not disdain such premature interment.

Now, in return for my eight groschen, I demanded the aforesaid blanket, wrapped myself in it, and spread my coat out over the blanket, not feeling very much of its dampness. Ulysses cannot have rested with more comfort and self-satisfaction under the coat he had acquired in similar fashion.[41]

All this had been done against the wish of our colonel, who pointed out to us that the French had a battery stationed behind bushes on the hill opposite us and could bury us in earnest and annihilate us at will. But we had no desire to give up this spot where we had found shelter from the wind, or the comfort we had so cleverly contrived—and this wasn't the last time I noted that one often disregards danger for the sake of avoiding discomfort.

21 September

There were no cheerful greetings upon awakening, for we found ourselves in a shameful and hopeless situation. We were positioned on the rim of a huge amphitheater. Opposite us the enemy formed a vast semicircle on the heights with rivers, ponds, streams, and marshes between us. On our side we were standing just where we had been yesterday—lighter by 10,000 cannon balls but no better situated for an attack. We looked down into a broad arena where the hussars from both sides maneuvered among the cottages and garden plots and held the attention of spectators for hours with their shadow-boxing backwards and forwards. But the only result of all this charging up and down and shooting back and forth was that one of our men, who had ventured out too far between the hedgerows, was surrounded and shot down when he refused to surrender.

This was the only battle casualty of the day; but the disease which had befallen us made the uncomfortable, oppressive and helpless situation all the more dreadful and dismal.

However prepared and eager for battle we had been the day before, it had to be admitted now that a truce was desirable; it took little reflection for even the boldest and most passionate among us to see that to attack would be the rashest undertaking in the world. Opinions still wavered throughout the day, while for the sake of maintaining our honor we held the same positions as during the cannonade; toward evening, however, we changed them somewhat, finally the headquarters was moved to Hans and the baggage arrived. Now we heard accounts of fear and danger, and how we had nearly lost both our servants and our belongings.

The Argonne Forest from Ste.-Menehould to Grandpré was occupied by the French; from that base the French hussars were carrying out daring and unpredictable small-scale actions. We had learned yesterday that a secretary of the Duke of Brunswick[42] and several other members of that entourage had been captured between the army and the so-called wagon fortress, which hardly deserved to be called a fortress because it was badly situated, not properly drawn together, and inadequately guarded. They had been thrown into a panic by one false alarm after another and by the cannonade in close proximity to them. Afterwards it was rumored—or perhaps this was the truth—that the French had come down out of the mountainous forest in order to capture all our equipment; General Kalckreuth's[43] messenger, who had been captured and then released, took credit for averting an enemy attack by successfully lying to them about there being a strong guard, mobile batteries, and the like at the baggage camp. Quite possible! Everyone does, or has done, his share in such moments.

Now we had our tents, vehicles, and horses, but no food for man or beast. In the midst of all that rain we even lacked drinking water, and some of the ponds were already dirtied by horses that had fallen in. All in all, it was a dreadful situation. I was puzzled when I saw Paul Goetze, my loyal pupil, servant, and companion, diligently collecting the accumulated water from the leather of the carriage; he informed me that it was for making chocolate, a supply of which he had fortunately brought along. I even saw men quench their intolerable thirst by scooping water from the hoof-prints of horses. Veteran soldiers, used to deprivations, sold us their bread in order to save up to buy brandy whenever it became available again.

22 September

We heard that Generals Manstein[44] and Heymann[45] had gone to Kellermann's headquarters in Dampierre, where Dumouriez was also expected to turn up. Ostensibly they were to talk about exchanging prisoners and caring for the sick and wounded; on the whole, however, there was some hope of effecting a reversal of the situation. Since the tenth of August Louis XVI had been under arrest; and atrocious murders had taken place in September. It was known that Dumouriez had been sympathetic to the king and to the constitution; for his own safety and well-being he was obliged to oppose the present state of affairs, and it would have been a momentous event had he made common cause with the Allies and marched with them on Paris.

Since the arrival of the baggage the situation of those of us who were with the Duke of Weimar was greatly improved, for it must be said of the steward, the cook, and the other household officials that they were never without provisions, and even in the midst of the worst shortages they were always able to provide something in the way of a hot meal. Refreshed by this, I rode around in order to acquaint myself better with the area, but this was fruitless: these flat hills had no character, no one object stood out from the rest. To orient myself I searched for the long avenue of tall poplars which had been so conspicuous the day before, and when I couldn't find it I believed I had become badly lost, but on closer observation I discovered that the trees had been cut down, carried away, and were probably already burned up.

In the places where the cannonade had taken its toll there was great misery: people lay unburied, and the badly injured animals could not die in peace. I saw a horse that was stumbling around wretchedly, its front feet entangled in its own entrails, which were hanging out of its belly.

On the ride back I met Prince Louis Ferdinand in an open field, sitting on a wooden chair someone had brought up from a village; some of his people had just dragged up a heavy, locked kitchen cabinet; they had said there was something rattling inside and they hoped they had found something good. They greedily broke into the cupboard but found only a very fat cookbook, and now, while the broken-up cupboard was burning, they were reading aloud the most delicious recipes, thus again intensifying hunger and desire to the point of despair by exciting the imagination.

24 September

The most terrible weather in the world was made somewhat more bearable by the news that an armistice had been agreed upon, and that we therefore at least had the prospect of being able to suffer and starve with some tranquility of mind; but even this turned out to be only half a consolation, for we soon learned that it was in reality only an agreement that the outposts would leave each other in peace, and that both sides reserved the right to resume operations as they saw fit, with that one exception. This condition was actually favorable only to the French, who could change their positions all around us and close us in better, whereas we had to stay quietly in the middle and remain in our state of paralysis. The sentries, however, eagerly seized on this opportunity; first they agreed among themselves that whichever of the two sides had the wind and rain in its face should have the right to turn around, bundle up in its overcoats and have nothing to fear from the other side. They even went further: the French still had a little something to eat, whereas the Germans were short of everything; so the French shared some of what they had and they all became more and more friendly with one another. Finally, the French went so far as to distribute, in all friendliness, printed leaflets which preached the gospel of freedom and equality to the good Germans in both languages. The French thus were imitating the manifesto of the Duke of Brunswick in reverse and offered good will and friendship. Although on their side more people had already been mobilized than they knew how to absorb into their command structure, they still made this appeal, at this moment at least, more in order to weaken us than to strengthen themselves.[46]

Addendum to 24 September

At this time I took pity on two fellow sufferers, handsome young lads between fourteen and fifteen years old. Requisitioned along with their four weak horses, they had barely been able to pull my light chaise this far. They suffered quietly, more for the sake of their animals than for themselves, and yet they could not be helped any more than the rest of us. Since they were enduring all this misfortune on my account, I felt obliged to do something for them and offered to share my army bread with them; but they refused it, saying they could not eat anything like that, and when I asked what they usually got to eat at home they answered: "Du bon pain, de la bonne soupe, de la bonne viande, de la bonne bière."[47] Since they had it so good at home and things were going so badly with us, I readily forgave them a short time afterward when they deserted and left their horses behind. They had had much to endure, but I believe it was the army bread I offered them that, like some dread ghost, moved them to take this decisive step. White and black bread is really the shibboleth, the battle cry between Germans and French.

I should make one observation at this point: we came, to be sure, at the worst time of year to a land which, while not blessed by nature, at least provides sufficient nourishment for its few hardworking, orderly and frugal inhabitants. Richer and nobler regions may well treat an area such as the Champagne with contempt; but nowhere did I come upon any vermin or beggars' hovels there. The houses are built of masonry with tile roofs, and everywhere there is sufficient work. And also, the really bad stretch is at the most a few miles across, and the land is much better in the area of the Argonne Forest as well as in the area of Rheims and Châlons. Children who had been taken at random from a village, such as my two youths, spoke contentedly of the food they got at home, and I had only to think of the cellar at Somme Tourbe and the fresh white bread that had fallen into our hands on its way from Châlons to the French army to believe that in times of peace hunger and vermin would not exactly be at home here.

25 September

It was only to be expected, and it was now confirmed, that the French would not be idle during the truce. They sought to reestablish their communication with Châlons and to displace the émigrés at our rear, or rather to drive them in upon us; but, for the time being, the most damaging thing for us was that they could disrupt, if not totally destroy, our supply line, attacking it from the Argonne Forest as well as from Sedan and Montmédy.

26 September

Since I had the reputation of being interested in various things, the men brought me everything that seemed to be somewhat out of the ordinary; among other things I was brought a cannon ball which looked almost like a four-pounder. The peculiar thing about it was that one could see a crystallized pyramid pattern over its entire surface. So many cannon balls had been fired that day that one could very well have found its way over here. I thought up all sorts of hypotheses to explain how the metal might have taken on this shape, whether during casting or afterwards; I learned the truth quite by accident. Returning to my tent later after a short absence, I asked about the ball because I couldn't find it. When I persisted, they confessed that they had been fooling around with it and it had shattered. I demanded to see the pieces and found, to my great astonishment, a crystallization that radiated out from the center toward the surface. It was iron pyrites, which must have formed into layers around the center. This discovery led me further. There were more such pyrites to be found, although smaller, in spherical and kidney shapes, as well as in other less regular forms, all of them, however, alike in the fact that they had never been part of a greater mass and that their crystallization was always around a center; they were also not rounded at the edges, but had sharp and typically crystalline contours. Is it possible that they were formed in the ground, and are there more such things to be found in the fields?

But I was not the only one interested in the minerals of the area; the beautiful chalk which could be found everywhere seemed definitely to be of some value. It is literally true that a soldier had only to dig out a cooking hole and he would invariably hit upon the clearest white chalk, which he normally needed so badly to clean and polish his gear. An order was actually issued that the soldiers should provide themselves with as much as possible of this necessary commodity, which was to be had here for free. This of course gave rise to a certain amount of ridicule: mired in this most awful filth, the men were to load themselves down with a cleaning and polishing agent; where the men were groaning for bread they were to content themselves with dust. The officers too were more than a little taken aback when they were reprimanded at headquarters for not appearing as clean and elegant as on the parade-ground in Berlin or Potsdam. Since the commanding officers couldn't help, it was the general view that they should at least not have handed out reprimands.

27 September

A somewhat curious expedient for alleviating the pressing hunger was publicized in the army: the men were to thresh all available sheaves of barley as well as possible, boil the grain in water until it burst, and seek to satisfy their hunger with this food.

Fate, however, had destined a better relief than this for our immediate company. We saw two wagons in the distance, mired in the mud. Because they were laden with provisions and other supplies, we gladly came to their aid. Von Seebach, the equerry, sent horses out at once, the wagons were got loose and brought directly to the Duke's regiment; the drivers protested that their wagons were intended for the Austrian army, which was in truth the destination written in their passes. But we had acquired a benevolent interest in them; the drivers were assigned a guard in order to keep the crowd away and hold on to them at the same time, and since we also paid them what they demanded, they had to be satisfied with finding their true destiny here.

First of all the stewards, the cooks, and their assistants hurried up and took possession of the cases of butter, the hams and the other good things. The crowd multiplied, most of them demanding tobacco, a lot of which was then sold at a high price. The throng pressed so tightly around the wagons, however, that finally no one else could get close, so some of our staff and troopers appealed to me and begged me to get them some of this most urgent necessity.

I had soldiers clear the way for me and immediately climbed up on the closest wagon, so as not to get lost in the crowd; there, for a goodly sum of money, I loaded myself with as much tobacco as my pockets would hold, and when I got down again and worked my way through the crowd, passing it out freely, I was praised as the greatest benefactor ever to take pity on suffering mankind. Brandy had also arrived. The men bought it eagerly and were happy to pay a Laubtaler[48] for a bottle.

27 September

We tried to find out about the state of things, not only at headquarters itself, which we got to visit once in a while, but also from everyone who came from there; the situation could not have been more critical.

We heard more and more about the awful things going on in Paris, and what at first we had taken to be a fable seemed in the end, when it turned out to be true, horrible beyond belief. The King and the royal family were being held captive, there had already been talk of deposing the monarch, hatred was spreading against the monarchy in any form, indeed, it was to be expected that legal proceedings would soon be initiated against the unhappy ruler. Our immediate military opponents had reestablished their communications with Châlons; there Luckner[49] was supposed to be turning the volunteers streaming from Paris into an army; but these volunteers, who had poured out of the capital through the torrents of blood that were flowing in those horrible early September days, brought with them more of a lust to rob and murder than to wage legitimate war. Following the example of the horrible Paris mobs they arbitrarily chose victims whom they could rob of all authority, possessions, and even life itself as the case might be. They had only to be turned loose without any discipline and they would be the death of us.

The émigrés had been forced in close upon us and we heard about many a catastrophe threatening us in the rear and on the flanks. In the area of Rheims twenty thousand peasants were said to have banded together, armed with farm tools and other crude weapons; there was a great fear that these people too might break loose upon us.

Such things as these were discussed during the evening in the Duke's tent with a number of veteran colonels present; everyone brought his news, his conjectures, and his worries as his contribution to this council without counsel, for it really looked as though we could be saved only by a miracle. At this moment it seemed to me, however, that in such precarious situations we usually like to compare ourselves with great men, especially those who have been in even worse circumstances than we; here I felt the urge to relate some of the most harrowing incidents from the history of St. Louis,[50] if not to cheer up the company, then at least to divert them. On his crusade the King wants first to humble the Sultan of Egypt, because at this time the Sultan is in control of the Holy Land. Damietta falls to the Christians without a siege. Urged on by Count Artois, his brother, the King undertakes an expedition up the right bank of the Nile towards Babylon-Cairo. The Christians succeed in filling in and crossing a canal that draws water from the Nile. But now they find themselves hemmed in between the Nile and its main and secondary canals, whereas the Saracens are well positioned on both banks of the river. It is difficult to get across the major waterways. They build blockhouses to counter those of the enemy, but the Saracens have the advantage of Greek fire, with which they inflict damage upon the wooden bulwarks and buildings and upon the soldiers. What good does it do the Christians to have an impressive order of battle when they are constantly being provoked, taunted, and attacked by the Saracens, sometimes even engaged in skirmishes. Individual deeds of daring and hand-to-hand combats are impressive and uplifting, but the heroes and even the King himself are cut off. To be sure, the bravest ones break through, but the confusion grows. The Count of Artois is already dead, the catastrophe grows to extreme proportions. On this hot day everything depends on defending the bridge over one of the side canals in order to keep the Saracens from falling upon them in the rear of the main battle. The small band of warriors positioned there is attacked in every way imaginable, it is fired upon by the enemy soldiers, pelted with stones and filth by the campfollowers. In the middle of this disaster the Count of Soissons says jokingly to Sir Joinville: "Seneschal, let that pack of dogs bark and growl! By God's throne" (for such was his customary oath) "we will live to tell of this day back home in front of the ladies."

My listeners smiled, considered this a good omen, talked about what might happen, emphasizing especially the reasons why the French were bound to spare rather than destroy us; the long-preserved truce and the enemy's restrained behavior up to now gave us some hope. To encourage this hope I made bold to deliver another historical discourse and reminded them, using maps of the area, that only some five miles to the west lay the notorious Catalaunian Fields, the farthest point reached in the year 452[51] by Attila, King of the Huns, and his vast horde, before they were defeated by the Burgundian princes with the support of the Roman general Aetius. Had they followed up their victory, I reminded my listeners, Attila himself and all his followers would have been destroyed. But the Roman general, loath to relieve the Burgundians completely of their fear of this powerful enemy, because they then would have turned against the Romans, convinced the princes, one by one, to go home; and so the King of the Huns escaped with the remnants of his vast horde.

At this very moment we received news that the expected bread transport had arrived from Grandpré; this too enlivened our spirits two or threefold. We parted in a more hopeful frame of mind and I read aloud to the Duke until almost morning from an amusing French book which, curiously enough, had fallen into my hands. Reading its outrageous and audacious jests, which even in our dire circumstances could still make us laugh, I remembered those frivolous sharpshooters at Verdun who went to their deaths singing bawdy songs. When one wishes to dispel the bitterness of death, it is not good to be too fastidious about the means.

28 September

The bread had arrived, though not without some difficulty and loss; some of the wagons had got stuck on the terrible roads between Grandpré, where the bakery was located, and our camp, others had fallen into the enemy's hands. In addition a part of what we received was inedible; the hastily baked bread was damp, the crust separated from the inside and mold was growing in between. Once again fearing poison, people brought me such loaves, this time bright orange on the inside, hinting at the possibility of arsenic or sulphur, as the green bread at Verdun had evoked a fear of verdigris. Even though it was not poisoned, the mere sight of it aroused loathing and disgust, and disappointed expectations sharpened our hunger; sickness, misery, despondence thus weighed heavily on such a great mass of good people.

In the midst of such afflictions we were greatly surprised and disturbed by the incredible news that the Duke of Brunswick had sent his previous manifesto[52] to Dumouriez, who, absolutely astonished and outraged by this, had immediately called off the truce and ordered the resumption of hostilities. Great as was our danger already, and though we now foresaw even greater, we still could not keep ourselves from sneering and making jokes, remarking what a catastrophe it was to be an author! Every poet and other kind of writer was always happy to recite from his work to anyone who would listen, without ever asking whether it was the proper time or place; and now the same thing was happening to the Duke of Brunswick, who, savoring the joys of authorship, was pulling out his unfortunate manifesto again at precisely the worst possible time.

We now expected to hear the sentries shooting at each other again and we looked around at the hills to see whether or not some enemy might appear. But everything was peaceful and quiet as though nothing had happened. Meanwhile we lived in the most painful uncertainty and insecurity because anyone could easily see that we were strategically lost if the enemy should ever take it into his head to harass and pressure us. In this state of uncertainty there were nevertheless some indications of more peaceful intentions and agreement between the two sides; for example we had freed the postmaster of Ste.-Menehould in exchange for the members of the royal entourage who had been captured on the twentieth between the army and the wagon train.

29 September

The baggage train got under way towards evening in accordance with the orders that had been given; no longer protected by the Duke of Brunswick's regiment, it was supposed to precede us, the army itself following at midnight. Everyone was in motion, but slowly and in a bad humor; for even the best will in the world faltered on that muddy ground and sank before it knew what was happening. But these hours passed too: time runs its course, even on the worst day!

Night had come, this one too to be spent without sleep; the sky was not unfavorable, the full moon shone but had nothing to illuminate. The tents had disappeared, baggage and wagons and horses were all gone, and our small group in particular was in a strange situation. We were supposed to be brought horses on the spot where we were, but they had failed to appear. Everything seemed bleak and empty as far as we could see in the pale light. We listened in vain, there was neither shape nor sound to be made out. We could not make up our minds what to do; we preferred to remain at the appointed place rather than put our people in the same predicament and miss them completely. Yet it was horrible, seeming—if not actually—for the moment to be abandoned in enemy country after all that we had experienced. We were on guard to see if the enemy might appear, but nothing was stirring or moving, neither friend nor foe.

Little by little we gathered together all the straw that was left from the tents and burned it, not without some concern. Attracted by the flame, an old woman, a canteen keeper, drew near; apparently she had not tarried idly during this retreat, for she had substantial bundles under her arms. After greeting us and warming herself at the fire, she first praised Frederick the Great to the skies and glorified the Seven Years' War, in which she claimed to have taken part as a child; then she scolded present-day princes and military leaders furiously for bringing such a large army into a country where a canteen keeper could not ply her trade, which was, after all, the real purpose of such an undertaking as waging war. Her way of looking at things was quite amusing and momentarily diverting, but the horses were extremely welcome when they arrived; whereupon we set out with the Duke's regiment on our ominous retreat.

Certain precautionary measures and significant orders given us led us to fear that the enemy would not simply stand by passively and watch our departure. During the day it had already been a cause of great anxiety to see how faltering was the progress of all our vehicles, especially the artillery sinking into the muddy earth; what were we to expect now that it was night? With sorrow we saw overturned, broken wagons lying in the streaming water, with laments we left our helpless sick behind. Now that we were fairly well acquainted with the area we had to admit that, whichever way we looked, there was no hope for us if ever the enemy, whom we knew to be behind and on both sides of us, should choose to attack; since, however, this did not happen in the first few hours, human nature, which cannot survive without hope, quickly reasserted itself, and that spirit in man which desires to impose some reason and understanding on everything that occurs reassured itself with the thought that the negotiations between the two headquarters in Hans and Ste.-Menehould had been concluded propitiously and in our favor. This belief grew from hour to hour, and when I saw all the vehicles driving up in good order to make a halt beyond the village of St. Jean, I was already absolutely certain that we would get home again and be able to speak in polite company (devant les dames) and tell of the sufferings we had endured. This time too I communicated my conviction to friends and acquaintances and we bore the present misery quite cheerfully.

No camp was pitched, but our people put up a large tent, with the thickest, most wonderful sheaves of grain spread inside and out to sleep on. The moon shone brightly through the calm air, only delicate light clouds were to be seen, the whole area was visible and distinct, almost as if it were day. The moon illuminated the sleeping men and the horses, still awake from hunger, among them many white ones which reflected the light strongly; the white wagon tops, even the white sheaves that served the night's sleep, everything spread brightness and serenity over this memorable scene. In truth, the greatest artist would have considered himself fortunate to paint such a picture.

It was quite late when I lay down in the tent, hoping to enjoy the deepest sleep; but nature has mixed in many a disagreeable thing among her most beautiful gifts, and thus it is one of man's most unsociable traits that in his sleep, just when he himself is most completely at rest, he is in the habit of keeping his fellows awake by loud snoring. I lay head to head, I on the inside, he outside the tent, with a man who disturbed my so badly needed rest by his horrible groaning. I unfastened the cord from the tent stake in order to acquaint myself with my adversary; it was a good and worthy man, one of the servants, who lay, illuminated by the moon, in such a deep sleep that he might have been Endymion himself. The impossibility of getting any rest in such company aroused the rogue in me; I took a wheat stalk and held it so that it swayed to and fro over the sleeper's forehead and nose. Disturbed in his deep slumber, he brushed his hand over his face several times, and as soon as he sank back into sleep I repeated my game without his ever being able to figure out where a horsefly could come from at this time of year. Finally I got him to the point where he was wide awake and decided to get up. Meanwhile, I too had lost all desire to sleep; I stepped outside the tent and admired in the now only slightly altered picture the endless peace alongside the greatest, still imaginable danger. And as in such moments we alternate between fear and hope, anxiety and confidence, I once more became alarmed when I realized that if the enemy were to attack us at this moment not a single wagon spoke nor a human limb would survive the attack.

The dawning day soon dispersed such thoughts, for a number of peculiar things could then be seen. Two old canteen keepers had put on a number of silk skirts, without any visible order, one on top of the other, around their hips and chests, with the topmost skirt around the neck, and on top of that a cloak as well. They strutted around quite comically in this finery and claimed they had acquired it by purchase and barter.

30 September

Although all the wagons got under way at daybreak, we covered only a short distance, for at nine o'clock we already stopped, between Laval and Wargemoulin. Men and animals sought to rest, but no camp was set up. Then the main army arrived and took up a position on a hill; the greatest peace and order prevailed throughout. To be sure we noted well from the precautions taken that all danger was not yet past; men were sent out to reconnoiter, there were furtive conversations with unknown persons, and there were preparations for continuing the march.

1 October

The Duke of Weimar was simultaneously leading the vanguard and guarding the baggage. Order and calm reigned this night, and we were reassured by this calm until the order came at midnight to move on. It was apparent that the impending march was not regarded as entirely safe because of raiding parties, which, it was feared, might come down out of the Argonne Forest. Even if there had been an agreement made with Dumouriez and the highest authorities—which could not even be assumed as entirely certain—in those days one man did not readily obey the other and the troops in the mountain forests had merely to declare themselves independent and make an attempt at destroying us, something of which no one at that time could have disapproved.

Today's march too did not go very far: it was intended that the baggage and army should keep pace with the Austrians and the émigrés, who were retreating parallel to us on the left.

We halted shortly before eight o'clock, soon after we had passed Rouvroy; some tents were pitched, it was a beautiful day and nothing disturbed the calm.

I would also like at this point to mention that in the midst of all this misery I made the oddest vow: that should we be saved and I ever find my way home, no one should ever again hear me complain about the neighbor's gable that obstructs the view from my room—that gable which, on the contrary, I now very much yearned to see; my second vow was never again to complain of boredom and discomfort in the German theater, where one could at least thank God for being under a roof, no matter what was happening on stage. And I even made a third vow which, however, I can no longer think of.

For the moment it was enough that everyone took care of himself as well as he did and that horses and wagons, men and horses stayed together in orderly fashion in their units so that we too always found tables set and benches and chairs as soon as we halted or pitched camp, although it seemed to us as though we were still being put off with too slender fare; yet we immediately resigned ourselves modestly to such treatment in view of the well-known overall shortage.

Meanwhile good fortune afforded me the opportunity of attending a better feast. Night had fallen and everyone had immediately lain down on the straw; I too had fallen asleep, but I was awakened by a vivid, pleasant dream: it was as though I could smell and taste the finest morsels, and when I awoke from this dream and sat up, my tent was filled with the most divine smell of frying pork fat, which made me quite ravenous. Completely at the mercy of nature as we were, we had to be forgiven for regarding a swineherd as a divinity and a pork roast as an invaluable treasure. I stood up and saw a fire some distance away, fortunately upwind of me: that was the source of the aroma. Without hesitation I followed the glow and found all the servants busy around a large fire that was quickly turning to embers, the back of the hog almost done, the rest already in pieces ready to be packed, everyone hard at work to finish the sausages quickly. Not far from the fire lay several large logs; after greeting the company I sat down there, and silently watched this activity with great pleasure. In part because these good people wanted to be nice to me, in part because they could not very well exclude the unexpected guest without being rude, I indeed received a tasty piece when it came time to share out the meat; there was bread as well, and a sip of brandy to go with it; in short, nothing was lacking.

In addition I received a good-sized piece of sausage when we mounted again in the dark and mist; I put it in my pistol holster, and so I had profited from a favorable night wind.

2 October

Although I had been fortified by food and drink and my spirits were solaced by moral reflections, hope and anxiety, chagrin and shame continued to alternate in my unsteady soul; happy to be alive, one nevertheless cursed the necessity of living under such conditions. We decamped at two o'clock in the morning, cautiously skirted a forest, passed our recent campsite at Vaux, and soon reached the Aisne. Here we found that two bridges had been thrown across to take us to the right bank. After crossing, we halted on a sandy promontory covered with willows where we could oversee both bridges, and immediately built a roaring cook-fire. Soon we had prepared long red, very delicious potatoes, and the tenderest lentils I have ever tasted. When we had finished cooking the hams that we had commandeered from the Austrian drivers and kept strictly secret until now, we were finally completely restored.

The baggage train was already across, but there soon followed a spectacle which was both majestic and sad. The infantry and artillery marched across the bridges while the cavalry used a ford, every face gloomy, lips sealed tight, communicating a grim state of mind. When regiments arrived in which we knew people, we ran to meet them, embraced them, spoke with them—but what questions! what laments! what humiliation!—and not without tears.

Meanwhile we were happy to be in a position, like canteen keepers, to offer refreshment to one and all, high and low alike. At first we made do with using a drum for a table, then chairs and tables were fetched from neighboring villages and we made ourselves and a wide variety of guests as comfortable as possible. The Crown Prince[53] and Prince Louis[54] savored the lentils, and a number of generals were attracted by our smoke. To be sure, how were we to feed so many, no matter how great a supply we had? We had to cook a second and a third batch and our reserves dwindled.

Our Duke had always shared everything gladly, and now so did his servants. And there's no telling how many of the unfortunate sick who passed by were refreshed by the steward and the cook.

So it went the whole day! and I saw the retreat portrayed not only in exempla and images, but in full reality, and the pain was renewed and multiplied by each new uniform. It was ordained that such a dreadful spectacle should also end fittingly; the King and his general staff rode up from afar, paused for a while at the bridge as though to survey and reflect upon the situation once more; finally, however, in the end, he took the same path as all his men and crossed over. Likewise, the Duke of Brunswick appeared at the other bridge, hesitated, and rode across.

The night came, windy but dry, and was spent, mostly without sleep, on the miserable gravel here under the willows.

3 October

We left this site at six o'clock in the morning, marched over a hill toward Grandpré, and found the army encamped. There we discovered new miseries and new worries; the castle had been converted into a hospital and it was crowded with several hundred unfortunate sufferers who could neither be helped nor relieved. We passed by with dread and were forced to abandon them to the compassion of the enemy.

Another fearful rain came down upon us here, paralyzing all movement.

4 October

Our progress became ever more difficult; in order to escape from the impassable main road we tried to make our way across the fields. The reddish soil, even stickier than the chalky ground we had had to cope with up to now, hindered every movement. The four small horses could scarcely pull my chaise, so I thought I would at least relieve them of the weight of my own body. The saddle horses were nowhere to be seen; the large kitchen wagon, drawn by six strong horses, came by. I climbed up on it; it was not completely empty of provisions, but the kitchen girl was sitting very cross in a corner. I immersed myself in my studies. I had taken the third volume of Fischer's lexicon of physics[55] out of my trunk: in such situations, where there is some interruption every moment, a dictionary is the most welcome company. It also affords the best diversion by leading us from one subject to the other.

Out of necessity we had ventured out incautiously onto the sticky red clay fields; in such a terrain even the powerful horses pulling the kitchen wagon were bound to tire. In my wagon I felt like a parody of Pharaoh in the Red sea, for all around me too there were riders and footsoldiers of the same color, also sinking in the mire. With longing I looked up at all the surrounding hills, and then I finally caught sight of the saddle horses, among them the gray that was assigned to me; I waved them over excitedly, and after entrusting my physics lexicon to the poor, sick, ill-humored kitchen girl and asking her to take good care of it, I swung myself up on the horse with the firm intention of not riding in a wagon again any time soon. Now, to be sure, I was able to travel more independently, but neither better nor faster than before.

We were glad to leave Grandpré behind, which had been depicted to us as a place of pestilence and death. A number of comrades came together and formed a circle around a fire, holding the reins of their horses behind them. They say this is the only time I wore an unhappy face and neither fortified them with my seriousness nor cheered them by my jesting.

4 October

The route the army had taken led towards Buzancy because we intended to cross the Meuse upstream from Dun. We pitched camp close to Sivry and found that there was still something to eat in the neighborhood. The soldiers burst into the first gardens they came to and ruined things that others would have been able to enjoy. I encouraged our cook and his helpers to undertake a strategic type of foraging, we went around the entire village and found a garden that was as yet completely untouched and a rich harvest all for ourselves. Here was an abundance of cabbages and onions, roots and other good vegetables; we were considerate and moderate, taking no more than we needed. The garden was not large, but quite neatly kept, and before we crawled out through the fence again I wondered a little why, since the garden belonged to a house, there was no trace of a door through which one could enter the adjacent building. As we were returning, heavily laden with our booty for the kitchen, we heard a great commotion going on in the regiment. A horse that had been requisitioned in this area some twenty days before had escaped from its rider, pulling up the stake to which it had been tied, the cavalryman was faced by a withering stare, threatened, and ordered to get the animal back.

Since it had been decided that we should rest in this vicinity on the fifth, we were billeted in Sivry; after so many hardships we found this domesticity quite delightful. To our great entertainment and diversion, we were again in a position to observe more closely these rural French, idyllic Homeric conditions. One did not enter the house directly from the street, but found oneself first in a small, open, rectangular vestibule, the size of which was determined by the door; from there, passing through the actual house door, one entered a spacious, high room that was reserved for family activities; it was paved with bricks, and to the left, on the long wall, at floor level, was the hearth; the chimney which drew off the smoke was above it. After greeting our hosts, we gladly took a place at the fire, where we observed that there was a definite hierarchy of place. On the right, next to the fire, stood a high box which also served as a chair; it contained the salt, which, procured in quantity, had to be kept in a dry place. This was the seat of honor, which was immediately assigned to the most distinguished visitor; the other newcomers sat down with other members of the household on a number of wooden chairs. Here, for the first time, I was able to observe closely the traditional French cooking apparatus, the "pot au feu." A large iron kettle hung over the fire from a hook which could be raised and lowered by means of a series of notches; there was already a good piece of beef in the pot with water and salt, turnips and carrots, leeks, cabbage, and other vegetable ingredients.

While we engaged in friendly conversation with these good people I noticed for the first time how cleverly the sideboard, the sink, and the shelves for pots and dishes were arranged. These completely filled the longish narrow space left by that rectangular open vestibule. All the kitchen utensils were arranged neatly with everything in its proper place; a maid, or perhaps the sister of one of our hosts, took care of everything very graciously. The mistress of the house sat by the fire, a little boy was standing at her knee, two small daughters pressed toward her. The table was set, a great earthenware bowl placed on it, beautiful white bread sliced into it, the hot broth poured over it, and everyone was wished a good appetite. Those two boys who so disdained my army bread could have pointed to this as the perfect example of "bon pain" and "bonne soupe." This course was followed by the vegetables and meat which had been cooked in the broth, and anyone could have been content with this simple culinary display.

We inquired about their circumstances; they had already suffered a great deal earlier, when we stayed so long at Landres, and now, scarcely recovered, they feared total ruin at the hands of a retreating enemy army. We showed ourselves sympathetic and friendly, consoled them by saying this would not last much longer, since we were the last detachments except for the rear guard, and gave them advice and rules as to how they should behave towards stragglers.

Because of constantly alternating storms and showers we spent most of the day inside by the fire, thinking about the past and considering, not without some apprehension, the immediate future. Since Grandpré I had seen neither my chaise nor my trunk nor my servant again, and consequently I was torn every moment between hope and anxiety. Night came and the children were supposed to go to bed; they approached father and mother respectfully, kissed their hands, and said "bon soir Papa, bon soir Maman," with delightful charm. Soon afterward we learned the Prince of Brunswick[56] was in the vicinity, lying dangerously ill, and made inquiries about him. His entourage would not allow us to visit him and assured us that he was now much better, so that he intended to depart the next morning without delay.

Scarcely had we escaped the terrible rain and made it back to the fireplace when a young man entered. Because of a distinct similarity we immediately took him to be the younger brother of our host, as in fact turned out to be the case. A handsome young man, he made his entrance dressed in French peasant costume, a sturdy staff in his hand. Very severe, in fact aggrieved and fierce, he sat next to us by the fire without speaking; yet he had hardly warmed himself when he started pacing back and forth with his brother and then they went into the next room. They spoke together very intimately and animatedly. He went out into the terrible rain again without our hosts attempting to stop him.

But we too were called out into the stormy night by fearful screams for assistance. Under pretext of foraging in lofts and attics, our soldiers had begun to plunder, and indeed in a rather clumsy fashion, by taking away a weaver's tools, which of course were totally useless to them. We settled the matter by being stern with the soldiers and diplomatic with the victims; it was only a few of the soldiers who had dared to do such things. But this behavior might easily have become contagious and created a state of chaos.

After a number of people had gathered there, a Weimar hussar, a butcher by profession, approached me and confided that he had discovered a fattened hog in a neighboring house; he was bargaining for the hog but couldn't get the owner to let him have it, and we should do what we could to help out: for in the next few days we were going to be running out of everything. It was of course somewhat odd that we, who had just put an end to plundering, should be called upon to engage in much the same kind of thing ourselves. However, since hunger knows no law, we went with the hussar to the house, found there too a great fire burning on the hearth, greeted the people, and sat down with them. A second Weimar hussar by the name of Liseur had joined us, and we entrusted the matter to his adroitness. In fluent French he began extolling the virtues of the regular troops, praising such people who asked only for the most necessary victuals in return for cash payment; by contrast he had only harsh words for the stragglers, camp-followers, and canteen keepers, who were in the habit of taking everything, down to the last crumb, by force and violence. He would therefore advise everyone to consider selling their goods, because money was always easier to hide than the animals, which would probably be discovered and requisitioned. His arguments, however, didn't seem to be making any great impression, and then his negotiations were interrupted in a curious manner.

Suddenly there was a loud knocking at the firmly locked front door. No one paid any attention because there was no desire to let in any more visitors; the knocking continued, a most pitiable voice cried out between knocks, a woman's voice pleading in good German for us to open the door. Resistance softened at last, the door was opened, an old canteen keeper pushed in, carrying in her arms something wrapped in a cloth; behind her a young woman, not ugly, but pale and so weakened she could barely stay on her feet. The old woman explained the situation in a few blunt words by showing us a naked baby, to which the young woman had given birth while in flight. Having been delayed by the birth, and mistreated by the peasants, they had finally arrived at our door tonight. The mother had not been able to feed the baby since its birth, because she had no milk. Now the old woman vehemently demanded flour, milk, a saucepan, and also linen to wrap the baby in. Since she knew no French we had to make the demands in her name, but her domineering personality, her vehemence gave our words enough pantomimic weight and urgency: it was impossible to fetch the things she demanded quickly enough, and what was brought was not good enough to suit her. On the other hand it was quite a sight to see how deftly she could operate. She had pushed us away quickly from the fire, the best seat was taken over immediately for the new mother, she herself was as comfortably settled on her stool as though she were the only person in the house. In no time at all the baby was washed and swaddled, the pap cooked, she fed the little creature, then the mother, hardly thinking of herself. Then she demanded fresh clothes for the mother while the old ones were drying. We watched her with amazement, for she really understood the art of requisitioning!

The rain subsided, we returned to our earlier quarters, and shortly afterward the hussars brought the hog. We paid a fair price for it; then it was slaughtered, and no sooner had we discovered a pulley screwed into the main ceiling beam of the adjoining room than we had the hog hanging from it so that it could be cut up and prepared in a professional manner.

We were somewhat surprised that our hosts did not seem to be annoyed by this business, but were rather helpful and accommodating, since they would have had grounds enough to find our behavior rude and inconsiderate. In the same room where we undertook the butchering operations the children were lying in clean beds, and, awakened by our noise, they peeped timidly from underneath their covers. The hog hung close to a great double bed which was carefully enclosed by green serge curtains, so that the curtains made a picturesque background to the illuminated carcass. It was a night scene without equal. But the inhabitants of the house could not yield to such aesthetic musings; we noticed, on the contrary, that they were not on particularly friendly terms with the family from which we had obtained the hog and that consequently our success afforded them a certain malicious glee. Earlier we had also generously promised them some of the meat and sausage, and this helped in carrying out the operation, which was to be completed in a few hours. Our hussar proved to be as industrious and dextrous in his field as the gypsy woman in the other house in hers, and we were already looking forward to the good sausages and roasts that were to be our share of this semi-booty. With this expectation we lay down in our host's smithy on the most beautiful sheaves of grain and slept peacefully until daylight. Meanwhile our hussar had finished his work in the house, some of the meat was ready for breakfast, and the rest had already been packed up after the hosts had been given their share—not without some annoyance on the part of our fellows, who claimed that generosity was wasted on these people; without a doubt they had hidden away even more meat and other good things that we had simply not yet learned to ferret out properly.

As I was looking around in the inner room, I finally discovered a locked door which, judging from its location, had to open into a garden. Through a small window on the side I was able to confirm this; the garden lay somewhat higher than the house, and I clearly recognized it as the same garden where we had earlier provided ourselves with things for our kitchen. The door was barricaded and so skillfully covered from the outside that I now clearly understood why I had looked for it this morning[57] in vain. And so it was written in the stars that we were to manage to get into the house in spite of all the precautions taken against us.

6 October, early morning

In such an environment one should not expect even a single moment of calm, or that anything will remain the same even for an instant. At daybreak the whole village was suddenly in a great commotion; the story of the runaway horse came up again. The worried rider, who had to get the horse back or be punished and have to march on foot, had chased around the neighboring villages, where finally, in order to be rid of the nuisance, people had assured him that the horse had to be in Sivry: it was there that a black horse such as he described had been requisitioned several weeks ago, the horse had run away precisely at Sivry, and so on. Now he came, accompanied by a stern noncommissioned officer, who finally solved the mystery by threatening everyone in the place. The horse had in truth returned to Sivry to its former master; they say the family's joy at seeing their house- and stable-mate again was boundless, and all the neighbors had shared in their rejoicing. With a great deal of ingenuity they had managed to get the horse upstairs into the loft and hidden it behind some hay, and everyone kept the secret. Now, however, the horse was hauled out again amidst general wailing and lamentations, and grief afflicted the entire community as the rider mounted and followed the sergeant. No one thought either of his own burdens or of the fate of the village as a whole: the horse and its owner, who was now bereft for the second time, were the main interest of the crowd that had collected.

A momentary hope presented itself; the Crown Prince of Prussia came up on horseback, and when he began to inquire why this crowd had gathered, the good people approached him with pleas that he should give them back their horse. But that was not in his power, the fortunes of war being more powerful than kings; and so he rode off without a word and left them disconsolate.

We repeatedly discussed with our kind hosts how they should act with regard to stragglers, for this rabble was already showing up here and there. Our advice was that man and wife, maid and hired hand should position themselves in the doorway inside the small vestibule, and if need be pass out a piece of bread or a sip of wine if it were demanded, but that they should firmly resist any attempt to enter the house. We told them that such people would not easily take a house by force, but once they were inside, no one would be able to control them. The good people asked us to stay a while longer, but we really had to think of ourselves; the Duke's regiment had already marched on and the Crown Prince had left; this was enough to determine our own departure.

It became even clearer to us what a wise decision this had been when we heard, after catching up with the column, that yesterday the vanguard of the French princes had been attacked by peasants between Les Grandes and Les Petites Armoises just after it had left the pass of Chesne Le Populeux and crossed the Aisne; one officer's horse was said to have been shot from under him, and a bullet had passed through the hat of the commander's servant. Now it weighed on me that the night before I had not been able to ward off premonitions of such occurrences when the surly brother-in-law entered the house.

Addendum to 6 October

We were now out of the worst danger, but our withdrawal was still difficult and hazardous; the transport of our household became more burdensome day by day, for in truth we were carrying complete furnishings; aside from kitchen equipment we had tables and benches, chests, boxes and chairs, even a few metal stoves. How were we supposed to move these numerous wagons when the number of horses dwindled each day? Some of them fell in their tracks and others had no strength left. There was nothing else to do but leave one wagon behind in order to keep the others moving. We held deliberations as to which things we could most easily do without, and as a result we abandoned one wagon loaded with all sorts of equipment in order to save the rest. This operation was repeated several times and our train became considerably more compact, and yet we faced the need for lightening our load once again while we were dragging ourselves along the low banks of the Meuse in the greatest discomfort.

What worried and oppressed me the most during those hours, however, was that my chaise had been missing now for several days. I could only conjecture that my servant—normally quite a determined fellow—had had some trouble, lost his horses perhaps and not been able to requisition new ones. At this point I pictured to my sorrow my fine Bohemian chaise, a gift from my sovereign which had already carried me so far in the world, sunk in the mire, perhaps even overturned, in which case all that I owned was what I had with me on horseback. The trunk with my clothing, manuscripts of all kinds, and other things that were of value simply because I was accustomed to them—I feared that all was lost and already scattered to the four winds.

What had become of the wallet with money and important papers? What of other objects that one carries about? But when I thought it through carefully and in detail, my spirits soon recovered from this intolerable situation. My faith in my servant began to revive, and whereas I had earlier bewailed my losses, I now imagined how everything had been preserved by his actions and delighted in my possessions as though they were right before my eyes.

7 October

While marching upstream along the left bank of the Meuse to reach the place where we were supposed to cross and get to the main road on the other side, just when we were in the swampiest patch of pastureland, we heard that the Duke of Brunswick was coming up behind us. We halted and greeted him with all due respect; he also stopped, very close to us, and said to me: "I am indeed sorry to see you in this unpleasant situation, yet I welcome your presence as one more judicious and credible witness who can testify that we have not been conquered by the enemy, but rather by the elements."

He had seen me in passing at the headquarters in Hans, and he knew in fact that I had been present throughout the whole wretched expedition. I made a fitting reply and finally expressed my regrets that, after so much suffering and exertions, he had new cause for worry in the illness of his princely son, which, I told him, had caused us great concern the previous night in Sivry. He listened to me graciously, for this Prince was his favorite; then he pointed him out, for he was standing close by, and we made our bow to him as well. The Duke wished all of us fortitude and endurance, and in return I wished him continued good health, for there was nothing else he needed in order to save us and our righteous cause. He had never actually liked me—I had to accept that. He had made no secret of it and I could forgive him that; now, however, misfortune had become a gentle mediator and brought us together in a manner that allowed us to sympathize with one another.

7 and 8 October

We had crossed the Meuse and taken the road leading from the Netherlands to Verdun; the weather was more horrible than ever and we camped near Consenvoye. The discomfort, or rather the catastrophe reached its peak, the tents were soaked and there was no other protection or shelter; I didn't know where to turn; my chaise was still missing and I lacked even the bare necessities. Even if one could shelter under a tent, still it was impossible to find a place really to rest. How we longed for some straw, or even for some boards, and yet in the end there was nothing else to do but lie down on the cold wet ground.

In previous cases such as this I had already thought out a practical expedient for enduring such misery; namely, I stayed on my feet until my knees gave way, then I sat down on a campstool, where I remained, in spite of everything, until I thought I was about to drop, at which point any place was very welcome where it was possible to stretch out horizontally. And just as hunger is always the best spice, exhaustion is the finest sleeping potion.

We had passed two days and two nights in this way when the sad state of a number of sick men brought some benefit to the healthy. The Duke's valet was stricken by the general malady, and our sovereign had also rescued a junker of our regiment from the field hospital at Grandpré; now the Duke decided to send the two of them to Verdun, which lay about five miles away. Wagner was sent along to care for them, and in response to the benevolent urging of the Duke I wasted no time in taking the fourth seat. We were sent off with letters of introduction to the commandant at Verdun, and since the poodle would not allow himself to be left behind, the otherwise so treasured sleeping-carriage was turned into half a hospital and also something resembling a menagerie.

As our escort, quartermaster, and forager, we were fortunate in having the hussar Liseur, who, coming from Luxemburg, knew the area well and possessed skill, cleverness, and the daring of a buccaneer; he rode ahead of us in high spirits, cut a good figure, and lent an impressive air to our carriage which was pulled along by six strong gray horses.

Packed between contagious patients, I was not at all apprehensive. As long as he remains true to himself a man finds a helpful maxim for any situation; whenever the danger became great I was always aided by the strictest fatalism, and I have noticed that people who are engaged in very dangerous professions feel themselves steeled and strengthened by this same belief. The religion of Islam affords the best proof of this.

9 October

Our unhappy hospital journey progressed slowly and occasioned solemn reflections, since we were traveling along the very same road by which we had invaded the country with such high hope and courage. Here we passed again through the same region where the first shot had been fired from the vineyard, the same stretch where the pretty young woman had fallen into our hands and been escorted home, the low wall from which she and her family had greeted us in such a friendly manner and with such newly inspired hope. How different it all looked now! and how doubly depressing appeared the aftermath of a fruitless campaign through the clouded veil of continual rainy weather!

But in the midst of all this gloom I was to find what I desired most in all the world. We caught up with a vehicle driving along with four small nondescript horses; there was a scene of joy and recognition, for it was my chaise, my servant. "Paul!" I cried out, "you rascal, is it really you? How did you get here?" The trunk stood strapped to its accustomed place, undisturbed; what a welcome sight! And while I was inquiring in haste after my wallet and other things, two friends sprang out of the chaise, Private Secretary Weyland and Captain Vent. That was a really joyful reunion and I learned what had happened up to now.

After the flight of the peasant boys my servant had managed to get himself and the four horses through everything, not only from Hans to Grandpré, but also from there on, after he had lost sight of me, across the Aisne and ever further, by demanding, asking, foraging, and requisitioning, until finally we met up happily with one another again and now, reunited and very contented, traveled on to Verdun, where we hoped to find all the rest and refreshment one could desire. Our hussar had also made the best possible arrangements for this in his wise and clever way; he had preceded us into the city and quickly became convinced that in view of the crush, there was no hope of obtaining anything through regular channels, through even the best efforts of the billeting office; by good luck he happened to see people in the courtyard of a fine house preparing to depart, and galloped back and gave us directions for finding the place. Then he hastened to cover the courtyard gate as soon as the other people had left to prevent its being locked, and to receive us in proper fashion. We drove in and alighted, despite the protests of an aged housekeeper who had just got rid of one party of billetted guests and felt no desire to take on another, especially without official orders. But meanwhile the horses were already unharnessed and in the stable, while we had divided the upstairs rooms among ourselves; the owner of the house, a nobleman, elderly, a chevalier of St. Louis, shut his eyes to it; neither he nor his family wanted anything more to do with guests, least of all this time retreating Prussians.

10 October

A youth who guided us around the desolated city asked us meaningfully whether we had ever tasted the incomparable Verdun pastries. He then took us to the most famous master of this art. We stepped into a large hall in which there were ovens, large and small, ranged around the walls, and tables and benches in the middle for customers to enjoy the freshly baked goods. The master appeared, despairing that he would not be able to serve us, since there was no butter at all. He showed us his beautiful supplies of the finest wheat flour; but what good was this without milk and butter? He boasted of his skill, of the praise he had garnered from Verdun citizens and travelers alike, and lamented the fact that precisely at this moment, when he had the chance to perform for such distinguished foreigners and broaden his reputation, he lacked exactly the things most necessary to his craft. He begged us therefore to get him some butter, hinting that if we would only set ourselves to the task in earnest we would surely be able to find some somewhere. We satisfied him for the moment by promising to bring him some from Jardin Fontaine, in case we stayed long enough.

Our young guide accompanied us on through the city and seemed to be as much of an authority on pretty girls as on pastries. We asked him about a particularly lovely girl who happened to be leaning out of the window of a solid bourgeois house. "Aye!" he exclaimed, after having told us her name, "may her pretty little head remain firmly on her shoulders. She is another of those who gave fruit and flowers to the King of Prussia. Her house and family thought at the time that they were on top again, but now the tables are turned; right now I wouldn't want to be in her place."[58] He spoke matter-of-factly, as though this were totally in accord with the nature of things and could not and would not turn out otherwise.

My servant had returned from Jardin Fontaine, where he had gone in order to greet our old host and return the letter to the sister in Paris. The droll fellow received him well enough, entertained him in his best manner and invited the rest of us to come, promising us the same hospitality.

But we were not destined to fare so well, for hardly had we hung the kettle over the fire with the traditional ingredients and ceremonies, when an orderly arrived and informed us respectfully, in the name of the commandant, Herr von Courbière,[59] that we should arrange to leave Verdun at eight o'clock the next morning. Deeply distressed that we should be expected to leave shelter and hearth so quickly, before we had even had a chance to recuperate somewhat, and be thrown out again into the chaotic and filthy world, we drew attention to the sickness of the junker and the valet; whereupon the orderly advised us to try to get them away from here as soon as possible, because during the night the hospitals would be emptied and only those sick soldiers would be left behind who could not stand being transported at all. We were overcome by fear and horror, for up until now no one had doubted that the Allies would hold on to Longwy and Verdun, perhaps even capture some other fortresses, and take up secure winter quarters in France. We could not bring ourselves to abandon these hopes all at once; we chose rather to believe that the intention was merely to rid the fortress of the countless sick and the unbelievable crowd of campfollowers, so as to be able to station the necessary garrison there. Wagner, however, who had delivered the Duke's letter to the commandant, interpreted these measures in the most alarming light. However the situation might turn out in the end, we had no choice for now but to resign ourselves to our fate and were dining calmly on the various courses of our simple fare when another orderly arrived and informed us that we should try to get out of Verdun, without delay or further sojourn, by three o'clock the next morning. Wagner, who believed he knew the contents of the letter to the commandant, saw in this a clear admission that the fortress was going to be returned to the French immediately.[60] Now we recalled the implied threat of our guide, the beautiful girls in their finery, the fruit and flowers, and for the first time we lamented sincerely and thoroughly the great enterprise which had miscarried so completely.

Although I have real friends among the diplomatic corps whom I respect very highly, I still could not refrain from certain comical thoughts whenever I saw them acting amidst such momentous events: they seemed to me like theater directors who choose the plays, assign the roles, and themselves walk around in unpretentious garb, while the troupe of actors, decked out in the fanciest costumes, must do as well as they can and leave the final judgment on their efforts to fortune and the whims of the public.

Baron Breteuil[61] lived across from us. I had never stopped thinking about him since the diamond necklace affair. His hatred for Cardinal Rohan[62] led him to the most precipitous action; the shock waves loosed by that trial shook the state to its foundations, destroyed all respect for the Queen and for the privileged classes as a whole: for alas, all that came out in the course of it merely served to put the spotlight on the dreadful depravity which prevailed at court and among the aristocracy.[63]

It was now believed that he had negotiated the remarkable agreement which obliged us to withdraw, which could be excused only under the presupposition that it contained some highly favorable terms; we were assured that the King, the Queen, and their family were to be set free, and in addition a number of other desirable conditions were to be fulfilled. But the question of how these great diplomatic triumphs were to be reconciled with everything else we knew raised doubt upon doubt in our minds.

Our rooms were well furnished; my attention was drawn to a bookcase on the wall, through whose glass doors I saw a large number of volumes in quarto, carefully cut so that they all looked alike. To my surprise, I learned from these volumes that our host had been in Paris in 1787 as one of the Notables[64]; in these volumes were printed all their briefs. The moderation of the demands made at that time, the modesty with which they were set forth, were in complete contrast to the brute force, arrogance, and despair that characterized the present state of affairs. I was deeply moved as I read these pages and I took a few copies for myself.

11 October

At three o'clock in the morning, having gone without sleep, we were just about to climb into our carriage at the courtyard gate when we became aware of an insurmountable obstacle; for there was already an unbroken column of ambulance wagons passing between the heaped-up paving stones down the street, which had become a morass of ruts. While we were standing there, waiting to see what could be done, our host, the Chevalier of St. Louis, brushed past us without greeting us at all. But our astonishment at his early appearance and unfriendly behavior soon turned to pity, for his servant followed him, carrying a little bundle on a stick, and so it became all too clear that he was once again having to leave the house and home he had regained only four weeks before, just as we for our part were having to abandon our conquests.

My attention was then drawn to the better horses harnessed to my chaise; my dear servants confessed that they had traded the former weak and useless horses for sugar and coffee, whereupon they had immediately been successful in requisitioning new ones. The hand of the skillful Liseur in this business was unmistakable, and it was also he who managed to get us moving, for he rushed into a gap in the ambulance procession and held back the next wagon long enough for us to swing our four- and six-horse teams into the line. Now I was able once more to enjoy the fresh air in my light chaise.

We moved at a funereal pace, but at least we were moving; the day dawned and we found ourselves on the outskirts of the city in the midst of the greatest possible chaos and confusion. All kinds of vehicles, a few horsemen, and countless people on foot were milling about the great square before the city gate. We bore to the right with our column in the direction of Etain, on a narrow roadway with ditches on either side. The instinct of self-preservation in such an immense throng no longer allowed for pity or consideration; not far ahead of us a horse pulling a baggage wagon collapsed, the traces were cut and the horse left lying there. When the three remaining horses were unable to move the load they too were cut loose, the heavily laden wagon was shoved into the ditch, and after only a short delay we drove on, right over the first horse, which was just struggling to get back on its feet, and I could see plainly how its bones crunched and quivered under the wheels.

Riders and walkers tried to escape from the narrow rutted road into the fields; but the fields too were made impassable by the rains, flooded from overflowing ditches and the network of foot-paths constantly interrupted. Four fine-looking, handsome, impeccably dressed French soldiers waded for a while alongside our carriages, thoroughly neat and clean; they knew how to pick their way so nimbly that their shoes showed only up to the ankles the traces of the muddy pilgrimage these good fellows were enduring.

It was only natural under these circumstances that we should catch sight of many dead horses in the ditches and on the pastures, fields, and meadows; soon, however, we came across some that had been flayed as well, with the fleshy portions cut out—sad testimony to the general want!

And so we proceeded, every moment in danger of being pushed into the ditch ourselves, should we so much as falter in the least; indeed, under these circumstances the attentiveness of our escort, Liseur, could not be praised and commended highly enough. The same attentiveness and conscientiousness also came into play at Etain, where we arrived toward noon, only to discover, in the pretty, well-built little city, a confusing tumult in all the streets and squares. A mass of people was swinging to and fro, and because everyone was trying to push his way forward the result was that each only got in the way of his fellows. Our guide unexpectedly had the carriages draw up before an imposing house on the marketplace; we went in and the master and mistress greeted us at a respectful distance.

We were escorted into a paneled room on the ground floor, where an inviting fire was burning in the black marble fireplace. We were not happy about the picture we saw of ourselves in the large mirror above the fire, for I had as yet not been able to bring myself to have my long hair cut short, and it was now as disheveled as a distaff tangled with hemp fibers. Our stubbles of beard added to our wild appearance.

Now, however, surveying the marketplace from the low windows of the room, we could practically reach out with our hands and grasp the teeming confusion. All kinds of people on foot—uniformed personnel, tired, sound but saddened civilians, women and children—jostled and squeezed each other between vehicles of all descriptions; baggage wagons and open wagons, carriages drawn by teams of all sizes, countless lawfully owned or requisitioned horses, now yielding, now colliding, obstructed each other on all sides. There were droves of cattle, too, probably herds that had been commandeered and taken along on the retreat. There were few horsemen to be seen, but the elegant carriages of the émigrés were quite conspicuous, lacquered in many colors with gilt and silverwork, carriages which I had probably already admired in Grevenmachern. The worst crush occurred where the crowd filling the marketplace was trying to turn off into a street which was, to be sure, straight and wellpaved, but much too narrow. I have never seen anything like it in my life; the sight could be compared to a river which has risen over its banks and now is forced to flow off between the piles of a narrow bridge and keep to a narrowly confined channel.

The strangest tide swept irresistibly down the long stretch of street that we could see from our window; a high two-seater traveling-carriage loomed above the crowd. It reminded us of the beautiful French women, it was not they, however, but Count Haugwitz, whose slow and teetering advance I watched, not without a certain malicious pleasure.[65]

Addendum to 11 October

A fine meal had been prepared for us, the very delicious leg of mutton was particularly welcome; there was no lack of good bread and wine and so, alongside the greatest tumult, we enjoyed the sweetest calm: just as one can sit on the stone mole at the foot of a lighthouse and watch the stormy sea, the wild waves breaking, and see once in a while a ship that falls victim to the water's whim. But a truly heartrending family scene still awaited us in this hospitable house.

The son of the house, a handsome young man, carried away by the general enthusiasm for the revolution, had served in the National Guard in Paris for a while and distinguished himself there. But when the Prussians invaded and the émigrés arrived here with their proud expectations of certain victory, the parents, full of renewed confidence, had implored their son ever more urgently to give up his position in Paris, which must by now have become abhorrent to him, as quickly as possible, return home, and fight for the good cause. The son, against his will, returns, out of filial piety, at the very moment when Prussians, Austrians, and émigrés are retreating, and hurries full of desperation through the throng to the house of his fathers. What should he do now and how should they receive him? Joy at seeing him was mingled with grief at losing him again in the same moment and doubt as to whether house and home could be preserved in such a storm. As a young man favorably disposed to the new system, he returns under duress to the party which he abhors, and just as he has resigned himself to his fate he sees that party doomed. A deserter from Paris, he knows his name is already entered in the crime- and death-rolls, and now in a flash he is to be banished from his fatherland, cast out of his father's house. His parents, who would so eagerly like to bask in his presence, must cast him out themselves and he, in the painful bliss of reunion, does not know how to tear himself away; their embraces are so many reproaches, and the leavetaking, which took place before our eyes, was awful to behold.

All this happened in the hall immediately outside our door. The parents had just gone away in tears and all was quiet again when we ourselves became involved in a scene which was almost even more curious, notable, embarrassing, but touching as well, which made us smile in the end. A group of peasant people, men, women, and children, burst into our room and threw themselves lamenting and crying at my feet. With all the eloquence of grief they claimed that their fine cattle were being driven off. They seemed to be the tenants of a good-sized farm. They said all I had to do was look out the window, where they were being herded past right at that moment. It was the Prussians who had seized them. I should give orders, find some way of helping them. Hereupon I stepped to the window to consider the situation; the unscrupulous hussar came up behind me and said: "I beg your pardon, sir! in order to make sure of a good reception and hospitality I said you were the brother-in-law of the King of Prussia. The peasants shouldn't have come in here, to be sure; but you can say a kind word, refer them to me, and pretend to be convinced by my proposals."

What was I to do? Surprised and irritated, I pulled myself together and reflected on the situation. "Guile and cunning," I said to myself, "are praised in time of war! Whoever has rogues for servants runs the risk of being led astray by them. A big uproar, which would be humiliating and serve no purpose, should be avoided at all costs." And just as a physician in the most desperate cases writes out a prescription which represents only a last hope, I dismissed the good people, rather more with gestures than with words; and then I said to myself for reassurance: "If the genuine Crown Prince was unable to restore a horse to its anguished owners at Sivry, then the pretended brother-in-law of the King can be forgiven for seeking to turn away petitioners with some clever phrase or other that has been whispered in his ear."

In the dead of night we reached Sebincourt; all the windows were lit as a sign that all the rooms had been taken. We met with protests at every door, both from the inhabitants, who did not want to take in any more guests, and from those already billeted there, who did not want to take in any more companions. Without much ado, however, our hussar shouldered his way into a house, and when he found some French soldiers at the fire in the hall he requested forcefully that they make room by the fireplace for the high-born gentlemen he was escorting. We came in immediately after, they were friendly and moved closer together, but soon took up again their curious posture with feet raised toward the fire. Now and then they would walk up and down in the hall, only to return to their former position, and finally I realized that they were intent on drying the lower part of their leggings.

Soon enough I recognized them; they were the same men who had marched along so neatly in the mud this morning alongside our carriage. Now, having arrived before us, they had already washed and brushed their lower footwear at the fountain, and now they were drying it, in gallant preparation for the encounter with more mud and filth tomorrow. This was exemplary conduct, which might well be remembered on certain occasions in one's life! I also thought in this connection of my own dear comrades in arms, who had grumbled so at receiving orders to keep themselves clean.

But the shrewd and obliging Liseur was not content with having thus provided us shelter; the fiction of this past noon, which had led to such fortunate results, was repeated with great daring; the high-born general, the brother-in-law of the King, had a powerful effect and drove a whole crowd of émigrés out of a room that had two beds in it. In return we took in two officers from the Köhler regiment to share our room. I myself went outside to the trusty old sleeping-carriage, whose shafts, pointing this time toward Germany, aroused quite peculiar thoughts in me, reveries, however, which ended when sleep overcame me quickly.

12 October

Today's journey seemed to be even drearier than yesterday's; exhausted horses had fallen more frequently by the wayside and often lay in the meadows beside their overturned vehicles. Quite elegant valises, belonging to a corps of émigrés, had fallen through the bursting covers of some baggage wagons; the colorful inviting sight of this ownerless and abandoned property aroused desire in those who saw it, and many a passerby weighed himself down with a burden which he soon was to cast aside. This may well have been the source of the rumor that the émigrés had been plundered by the Prussians during the retreat.

Many such incidents were related, some not without an element of humor; a heavily laden émigré wagon had become mired down and was abandoned on a hill. The troops following behind search the contents, find moderate-sized chests of considerable weight, join together to shoulder the burden and drag the chests with indescribable labor to the top of the next hill. Here they start to share out the burden and the treasure, but what a sight! Decks of playing cards spill out in profusion from every smashed chest, and the gold-hunters console themselves with jokes and laughter at each other's expense.

We ourselves moved on through Longuyon to Longwy; and here we must consider it fortunate that although the memory of great joys tends to fade from the mind, pictures of frightful suffering also become dulled in the imagination. There is no need for me to repeat that the roads got no better, and that now as before we were repelled over and over again by the sight, to right and left, of flayed and butchered horses between overturned wagons. We also began to notice quite often plundered and stripped human bodies only poorly concealed in the bushes, and in the end they were lying in plain view next to the road.

We were again, however, to find relief and refreshment off the beaten path, but also to find further occasion for sad reflections on the situation of prosperous contented citizens confronted by the terrible and totally unexpected horrors of war.

13 October

Our guide was determined not to have boasted in vain about his hospitable and well-to-do relatives in this region; he therefore made us take a detour by way of Arlon, a nice little town where, at his instigation, we were received very warmly by respectable and solid people in a well-built and well-furnished house. The good people were delighted to see their cousin, judging it to be an indication of advancement and impending promotion that he had been honored with the task of leading us, with two carriages, so many horses and, as he led them to believe, with much money and precious things, out of this most dangerous entanglement. We for our part had nothing but praise for his services up to now, and although we couldn't lend any special credence to the conversion of the prodigal son, we were so deeply in his debt now that we could not completely refuse to repose some faith in his future behavior as well. The rogue did not fail to use some flattery of his own and the good people in fact secretly presented him with a nice gift of gold. We, for our part, heartily enjoyed a fine cold breakfast and vintage wine, answering as charily as possible the questions put to us by these good people about what was probably going to happen in the near future.

We had noticed several curious wagons in front of the house, longer and in part higher than ordinary baggage wagons, and with strange attachments on the sides; my curiosity aroused, I inquired about these odd vehicles. They confided in me, but with some caution: that was the émigrés' printing plant for making counterfeit assignats, and they went on to relate what untold misfortune this counterfeiting had brought to their region. For some time past it had been practically impossible to cope with the genuine assignats, and now, since the allied invasion, these counterfeits had likewise been forced into circulation. Immediately sharp-eyed tradesmen, in order to protect themselves, had found a way to send this suspicious paper money to Paris and obtain official certification that it was counterfeit, but it was confusing trade and commerce immensely: with the genuine assignats one's investment was only partially endangered whereas with the counterfeits one could lose everything at once, and since at first glance it was impossible to differentiate between the two no one knew any more what to pay or demand in payment, and this was spreading such uncertainty, distrust and anxiety all the way to Luxemburg and Trier that the situation could not possibly become any worse than it was already.

Despite all the hardships these people had either already suffered or still had to anticipate, they maintained, to our amazement, a simple dignity, friendliness, and good manners of a type which we see reflected in serious French dramas both of the past and present. Neither the actual reality of our own fatherland nor its projection on the stage is able to give us any conception of such a society. The *Petite Ville* may be comical, *Die deutschen Kleinstädter* on the other hand is simply absurd.[66]

14 October

We were very pleasantly surprised to travel from Arlon to Luxemburg on a fine paved road and we were admitted into this important and otherwise well-defended fortress with no more to-do than if it were just a little village. Without once being stopped or questioned we soon found ourselves first within the outworks, then on the ramparts, moats, drawbridges, walls, and gates, entrusting everything to our guide, who claimed he would find his parents here. The city was crowded with sick and wounded, and with busy people getting themselves, their horses, and their vehicles back into shape again.

Our party, which had remained together until now, had to separate; our clever guide managed to get me a nice room whose high windows let in sufficient light, though the room looked out onto a tiny courtyard that was more like a chimney. He got me settled comfortably with my luggage and other things, and attended to my other needs; and he told me all I needed to know about the owner and tenants in the house, assuring me that for a small consideration I would be well treated and safe from being evicted.

Here, for the first time, I was again able to open up my trunk and check on my travel gear, my money, and my manuscripts. First of all I put my papers on the theory of color in order, always bearing in mind my earliest maxim: to broaden my experience and refine my method. I couldn't bring myself to touch my war and travel diary. The hapless course of the undertaking, which made us fear that even worse was still to come, gave frequent occasion for brooding about our past misfortunes and stimulated new anxiety. My quiet room, far away from all noise, was like a monk's cell, giving me a perfect space for the most tranquil contemplation; whereas any time I set foot outside the door I found myself immediately back in the liveliest turmoil of war and could stroll at will through what was perhaps the strangest place in the world.

15 October

Anyone who has never seen Luxemburg can have no idea of the intricate and complicated structure of this citadel. The imagination becomes confused when one seeks to recall the curious diversity which was so baffling to the eye of the visitor walking around the city. It will be necessary for the reader to consult a map of the city in order to make any sense of the following account.

A brook, named the Pétrusse, first by itself, and then together with the river which meets it, the Alzette, meanders between cliffs through and around the city, sometimes following a natural course, sometimes an artificial channel. The old city, lying on high level ground on the left bank, has fortifications facing toward the open country and is similar to other fortified cities. But once the city had been firmly secured from the west, the citizens must have realized that it was also necessary to safeguard it along the steep slopes leading down to the river; and as the art of warfare progressed, that too was not enough; it was necessary to build new redoubts on the right bank toward the south, east, and north, extending them on the irregular crags which jut out at various angles, the one redoubt always essential for the protection of the other. The result of all this is a vast network of bastions, redoubts and demi-lunes, and a jumble of nooks and crannies such as the art of fortification has seldom been called upon to produce.

There is therefore no more curious sight than the narrow valley of the river winding its way through all these fortifications; all the level spaces, as well as the gentle and even the steeper slopes, have been turned into gardens and terraced, dotted with summer houses from which one looks up at the steep crags and the high walls left and right. Here there is so much grandeur combined with grace, gravity with charm, that one could wish that Poussin[67] had exercised his glorious talent here.

The parents of our free and easy guide owned a fine sloping garden in the Pfaffental[68] and they were kind enough to allow me the pleasure of using it. The church and cloister close by gave this paradise its name and in this spiritual environment even the secular inhabitants seemed assured of peace and quiet, although every time they turned their eyes upward they were reminded of war, violence, and destruction.

It was highly beneficial now to escape into such tranquility from the city, where the sorry epilogue of war was being enacted, with its hospitals, tattered soldiers, broken weapons, wheels and caissons in need of repair, along with other remnants of all kinds; it was a comfort to flee the streets where wheelwrights, blacksmiths, and other artisans plied their trade in public, tirelessly and noisily, and to steal away into the little garden in the spiritual valley. Here a man in need of rest and composure could find welcome asylum.

16 October

The unimaginable diversity of the ramparts, piled next to and atop each other, which presented a different perspective with each step one took, forwards or backwards, up or down, aroused the desire to catch at least something of this on paper. And indeed, my artistic inclination was bound to be awakened again, since it had been so many weeks since I had laid eyes on anything which inspired me. Among other things it was extraordinary to see how many cliffs, walls, and defense works that stood across from each other were joined together high up by drawbridges, galleries, and certain other strange contrivances. An expert would have looked upon all this with trained eyes, delighting in the secure bastions from a soldier's point of view; as for me, I could appreciate only the picturesque effect and would gladly have tried my hand at sketching it, had not all drawing in and around the fortification been strictly prohibited.

19 October

For several days, alone and lost in contemplation, I clambered about this labyrinth, where natural cliff vied with man-made battlement in creating weird, steep canyons, yet still leaving space for gardens, orchards, and parks. Coming home, I began to put down on paper the images as they had impressed themselves gradually on my imagination, imperfectly, to be sure, but well enough to preserve the memory of these fantastic sights.

20 October

I had gained time to think over the events of the recent past, but the longer I thought, the more confused and uncertain everything appeared to the mind's eye. I also saw that the most necessary thing to do was to prepare myself for what lay immediately ahead. The few remaining miles to Trier still had to be traversed; but what would we find there, now that the rulers themselves were rushing to leave with the other refugees?[69]

The most painful thing, which filled all of us with rage and fury even though we were more or less resigned to everything, was the news, which could no longer be concealed, that our highest-ranking leaders had been forced to reach an agreement with the accursed rebels, with the very men who had been threatened with destruction by the Duke of Brunswick's manifesto and been damned by their frightful deeds before all the world, to give back the fortresses we had captured, merely in order to withdraw safely with their forces. I saw some who were in danger of going crazy over this.

22 October

On the way to Trier there was nothing left of that gallant assemblage of carriages at Grevenmachern; the meadows were now deserted, ravaged and rutted and only those tracks everywhere still bore witness to that earlier lively scene. This time I drove quietly past the posthouse with my requisitioned horses, the letter box was still in its place, but there was no crowd around; it was impossible to keep from having very strange thoughts.

But brilliant sunlight was just brightening the countryside when the monument of Igel shone forth ahead of me, appearing like a lighthouse to the sailor at night.

Perhaps the power of antiquity has never been felt so strongly as in this contrast: a monument, to be sure a monument of warlike times, but of fortunate and victorious days and the continuing well-being of bustling, active people in this region.

Although built at a late period, under the Antonines, it still possesses so many of the characteristics of great art that on the whole its graceful seriousness is appealing, and its members, although some are very much damaged, communicate to us a feeling of joyful and active life. The monument held me spellbound for a long time; I noted down a number of things and departed with regret, since I felt all the more uncomfortable in my wretched state.

But once again this feeling was superseded by joyful anticipation which soon afterward became reality.

23 October

We brought our friend Lieutenant von Fritsch, whom we had left behind earlier unhappy with his assignment, the welcome news that he had been awarded the Military Order of Merit; he had more than earned it by a valorous exploit, and was fortunate not to have had to share our misery. This is what had happened:

The French, because they knew we had advanced deep into their country and were quite far away in great difficulties, attempted to strike at us unexpectedly in the rear; they approached Trier in some force, even armed with cannon. Lieutenant von Fritsch learns of it and with a small detachment he goes out to meet the enemy; the enemy, surprised at such vigilance and fearing that still more troops might be on the way, retreats as far as Merzig after a short engagement and does not appear again. Our friend's horse has been wounded and the same bullet has grazed his boot, but on his return he is acclaimed as the victor with honors. The magistrates and the citizens show him all possible respect; the women too who had known him previously as a handsome young man, are doubly proud now that he is a hero.

He reports the incident at once to his commanding officer, and it is quite properly brought before the king, with the result that the blue cross is bestowed upon him. It was an uncommon pleasure to share the joy and happiness of the brave young man; fortune, which had eluded us, had sought him out in our rear, and he saw himself rewarded for this act of military obedience which had seemed to condemn him to inactivity.

24 October

My young friend had billeted me again with the canon. I too had not remained altogether free from the general sickness and therefore needed some medication and rest.

In these quiet hours I immediately took out the brief notes I had made at the Igel monument.

Put in the most general terms, life is placed here opposite to death and the present to the past, and the two pairs are reconciled with each other aesthetically. This splendid style and manner of the ancients was preserved in the world of art for a long time.

The height of the monument would be about seventy feet. It rises in several tiers in the shape of an obelisk; first the foundation, then a pedestal, followed by the main section surmounted by an architrave and then a gable, finally a curiously twisting pinnacle on which can be seen the remnants of a sphere and an eagle. Each of these sections, and its parts, is embellished throughout with figures and ornaments.

This feature indicates that the monument is of a later period: for this type of ornamentation appears as soon as purity of proportion in the structure as a whole is lost, and indeed there is considerable evidence of that here.

Nevertheless it must be admitted that this particular work is derived from a higher art which had been flourishing until just before this time. The whole is pervaded with the spirit of antiquity, in which real life is represented with some allegorical seasoning by way of mythological allusions. The main section shows a man and woman of colossal proportions reaching out toward each other, their hands joined together by a third figure, now obliterated, which blesses them. They stand between two highly ornamented pilasters which are embellished with dancing children, one above the other.

All the other groups of figures indicate happy family relationships, depicting kinsmen who work together and think alike, and to honest and pleasant community life.

It is this sense of industry that seems to predominate everywhere, though I am not confident I can interpret everything. In one section merchants seem to have gathered to discuss business: one can see plainly ships laden with goods, ornamental dolphins, transport on packhorses, the arrival and inspection of merchandise, and a number of other human and natural things.

Then in the zodiac there is a running horse which perhaps at one time pulled a chariot and driver; in friezes and in other spaces there are figures of Bacchus, fauns, the sun and the moon and whatever else in the way of miraculous beings decorates or may once have decorated the top.

The monument as a whole is very pleasing, and it would be quite possible to erect, in the same spirit, at the level which architecture and sculpture have attained in the present age, a glorious monument to the worthiest men, their pleasures and achievements. And thus it was quite pleasant for me, occupied with such thoughts, to celebrate quietly the birthday of our revered Duchess Amalia and to think back in detail on her life, her noble works and benevolent acts; quite naturally this inspired me to dedicate a similar obelisk to her in my mind, embellishing all the spaces on it with her virtues and with scenes from her life.

Trier, 25 October

I made further use of the rest and comfort I was finally enjoying to write down and put in order a number of things that I had worked out in those chaotic days. I went over and revised my files on the theory of color, drawing a number of figures to the color tables, which I changed quite frequently in order to make my exposition and my hypothesis ever more plausible. At this point it occurred to me to try to get back my third volume of Fischer's physics lexicon. After some inquiries I finally found the kitchen girl in a hospital which had been set up in a convent. She was suffering from the prevalent sickness, yet the rooms were airy and clean. She recognized me, although she couldn't speak, took the volume from under her head and returned it to me quite as clean and well preserved as it had been when I entrusted it to her, and I only hope that the good care I urged on her behalf will have benefited her.

A young school teacher who visited me and brought me several of the latest journals gave me the opportunity for pleasant conversations. Like many others he was amazed that I didn't want to discuss poetry and that I seemed on the contrary to have thrown myself into scientific observations with all my soul. He was versed in the philosophy of Kant, and I was therefore able to give him some idea of the path on which I had embarked. When, in the *Critique of Judgment,* Kant puts teleological judgment on a par with aesthetic judgment, one can surmise that he wanted to indicate that a work of art should be treated like a work of nature, a work of nature like a work of art, and that the evaluation of each must be developed according to its own peculiar laws and from observation of the individual object. I could become quite eloquent about such things and I believe I was of some service to this good young man. It is curious how every period carries and drags along with it truth and error from both the recent and the more remote past, whereas enterprising spirits strike out on a new path, where, to be sure, they have to be willing either to go it alone for the most part or to tug a companion along for a short distance.

Trier, 26 October

It was not possible to leave such a tranquil environment without finding oneself as though in the Middle Ages, where cloister walls and the most insane and confusing state of war existed in sharpest contrast to one another. Citizens of the city as well as returning émigrés complained most about the terrible misfortune that had come over town and country in the form of counterfeit assignats. Merchants had already managed to send some of them to Paris and had been informed that these were false, totally invalid, and that they would run a great risk if they were to have anything at all to do with them. Everyone knew the genuine assignats would also be discredited as a result, and that, were the tables to be turned completely, they could expect the value of all this paper to evaporate. This incalculable evil was now added to all the others, so that imagination and feeling perceived it as quite boundless—a situation full of desperation, similar to what one experiences when one sees a city burn down.

Trier, 28 October

The table at the tavern, where one was very well served, also presented a bewildering spectacle; soldiers and officials, all kinds of uniforms, colors, and costumes, were there, in moody silence, sometimes also given to violent outbursts, but all as though gathered together in one common hell.

There I had a truly moving encounter; an old hussar officer of medium height, with gray beard and hair and flashing eyes, came up to me after dinner, grasped my hand, and asked me whether I too had endured all that? I was able to tell him a little bit about Valmy and Hans, enough to let him imagine the rest with no difficulty. Hereupon he began to speak with warmth and enthusiasm, words which I hardly dare to reproduce verbatim, the gist of which was: it was irresponsible enough that soldiers, whose profession and duty it was, after all, to endure such circumstances and risk their lives, had been led into such dangers as had perhaps never been heard of before this; but that I (he was expressing his good opinion of my personality and my works) had had to endure all that alongside them, that was something which he could not accept at all. I presented things from the brighter side, namely from the point of view of having endured these few weeks in order to prove myself in the company of my sovereign, to whom I had not been altogether useless, and so many valiant comrades in arms; but he stuck to his opinion, while a civilian came up to us and expressed his view, in answer to the officer: that people should be thankful to me for having wanted to see all that with my own eyes, because now the public could expect an account and explanation of the whole affair from my talented pen. The old warrior wanted none of that either, and cried out: "Don't believe that, he has too much sense! he won't want to write what he has to write, and he won't write what he would like to write."

Incidentally, one hardly needed to point one's ears in any particular direction, the dissatisfaction was quite general. And if we are irked no end when fortunate people refuse to stop telling us about their good fortune, it is even more intolerable when a great misfortune which we would like to forget completely is dished up again and again. To be pushed out of the country by the French, whom one hated, to be forced to bargain and come to terms with the men of the tenth of August, was just as hard on the mind and soul as our previous physical suffering. Our criticism did not spare the highest generals and the confidence which had been placed for so many years in the famous supreme commander[70] seemed to be lost forever.

Trier, 29 October

Having now reached German soil again and gained hope of disentangling ourselves from this most awful confusion, we received the news of Custine's[71] daring and successful enterprises. A great amount of military supplies had fallen into his hands at Speyer, and following that he had been able to force the surrender of Mainz. These blows seemed to portend endless disasters to come, they evidenced an extraordinary spirit, daring and inexorable, in which case everything was lost. We regarded nothing as more probable or natural than that Coblence was already occupied by the Franks,[72] and how were we then to complete our retreat? In our minds Frankfurt was also lost; we saw Hanau and Aschaffenburg threatened on the one hand, Cassel on the other, and what else did we not fear! The nearest princes were paralyzed by the wretched system of neutrality,[73] while the masses, we feared, seized by revolutionary fervor, would be all the more vigorous and active. Was it not to be supposed that the same kind of agitation going on at Mainz would be extended to that whole area and to the neighboring provinces, taking advantage of preexisting revolutionary sentiments and implanting new ones? All these things were in our thoughts and the subject of our discussions.

I heard the question put repeatedly: would the French have taken such decisive steps without a great deal of forethought and caution, without a strong military force? Custine's actions seemed to be as daring as they were farsighted; we imagined him, his lieutenants, and his superiors to be wise, energetic, and determined. Our danger was great and bewildering, far surpassing the sufferings and cares we had experienced up to now.

In the midst of this tumult and anxiety a delayed letter from my mother found its way to me, a communication that reminded me poignantly of my peaceful youth and its urban domesticity. My uncle, Juror Textor, had died; my close blood relationship to him had excluded me from the possibility of attaining the honorable and influential post of a Frankfurt city councilor as long as he was alive, but upon his death, in accordance with a commendable custom, I had immediately come up for consideration, since I was rather high in seniority on the list of the Frankfurt doctors and licentiates.

My mother had been charged with inquiring whether I would accept the office of city councilor, if I were chosen to be one of those drawing lots and pulled the golden ball. Such an inquiry could hardly have come at a more peculiar moment than now; I was overwhelmed and forced to search my soul, but a thousand images appeared before my eyes and prevented me from collecting my thoughts. I was transported back into other years and spheres, just as a sick man or a prisoner is diverted momentarily by a story that is being told.

I found myself in my grandfather's garden,[74] where the wealth of peaches on the trellises was making my mouth water, and it was only the threat of being expelled from this paradise, the hope of receiving the ripest, reddest fruit from my benevolent grandfather's own hand, that enabled me to control my appetite more or less until the proper time. Then I caught a glimpse of the venerable patriarch busy among his roses, his hands carefully protected against the thorns by the old-fashioned gloves received as tribute from the cities freed from paying the Frankfurt tolls: he resembled Laertes[75] in this scene, except that he was not oppressed by cares and longing. I saw him in full regalia as chief magistrate wearing the golden chain, seated on the throne beneath the emperor's portrait; and sadly enough, I also imagined him in his dotage, the several years he had spent as an invalid, and finally in his coffin.[76]

The last time I had passed through Frankfurt I had found my uncle in possession of house, courtyard and garden.[77] A worthy son of his father, he had also attained to higher positions in the government of our free city. Here, in the intimate family circle, in the unchanged milieu which had been so long familiar to me, those memories of youth had come vividly to mind and now they returned with renewed force. These memories were then joined, I must confess, by other thoughts from childhood days. What citizen of an imperial free city will deny that, sooner or later, he has cast his eye on the city councilors, the jurors and the mayor and striven diligently but cautiously to obtain one of these posts or a lesser one, depending on his talents: for the sweet dream of participating in the government awakens quite early in the breast of every republican, and even more vividly and proudly in the soul of a boy.

But I could not give myself up to such sweet childhood dreams for long. All too rudely awakened by reality I examined the ominous scene around me, the circumstances which so oppressed me and made the prospects for my native city dark and gloomy. Mainz was already in French hands, Frankfurt threatened, if not already captured,[78] the route to Frankfurt blocked and inside those walls, streets, squares, and dwellings the friends of my youth, my relatives perhaps already subjected to the very sort of catastrophe under which I had seen Longwy and Verdun suffering so cruelly; who would have ventured to plunge himself into such a situation!

But even in the heyday of that venerable municipality it would not have been possible for me to consider such a post seriously, and the reasons were not difficult to express. For twelve years I had enjoyed a rare good fortune, the confidence and indulgence of the Duke of Weimar. This sovereign, who was not only richly endowed with natural talents, but also highly cultivated, took some pleasure in my well-meaning, yet often inadequate services to him and gave me opportunity for my own development, something which would not have been possible anywhere else in Germany. My gratitude was boundless, as was my devotion to the Dowager Duchess Amalia and the reigning Duchess, to their growing family, and to a country for which I had, after all, accomplished a number of things. Nor could I forget that circle of newly acquired highly cultivated friends, and so many other domestic joys and comforts which had resulted from my settled estate there. The images and feelings aroused in me by such thoughts suddenly cheered me in this gloomiest moment: for a person is already halfway healed, if, in his oppressive situation in a foreign country, he is stimulated to cast a hopeful gaze on his secure homeland; thus we enjoy, here on earth, what is promised to us beyond the heavenly spheres.

In this spirit I began my letter to my mother, and if my motives seemed to derive from sentiment, personal comfort, and individual advantage, there were yet others I could adduce that took into account the best interests of my hometown and were sufficient to convince my sponsors there. For how could I be expected to be active and effective in that totally specialized circle, something which perhaps required more careful training than any other kind of activity? For so many years I had been accustomed to duties that were suited to my particular aptitudes—aptitudes which were hardly in line with the purposes and demands of municipal government. Indeed, I felt justified in adding that, if only citizens were to be allowed to serve on the council, I had been away from the city so long that I had no choice but to regard myself as a foreigner.

Gratefully I set all this before my mother for her consideration, and she probably had not expected any other kind of reply. I am sure the letter reached her only after much delay.

Trier, 29 October

My young friend, with whom I enjoyed many a pleasant conversation on science and literature, was also well versed in the history of the town and its environs. The walks which we took in fair weather were therefore always instructive, and I was able to absorb a great deal of general information about the place.

The town itself has an unusual character. It claims to have more religious structures than any other of the same size, a claim which probably will not easily be refuted; for the town inside the walls is burdened, not to say overwhelmed, by churches, chapels, cloisters, convents, colleges, and the buildings of chivalric and monastic orders; and outside the walls it is blockaded, even besieged, by abbeys, chapters, and charterhouses.

All this bears witness to the vast sphere of spiritual influence exercised from here by the archbishop, for his diocese extended to Metz, Toul, and Verdun.[79] Nor did the secular realm lack fine things; indeed, the Elector of Trier rules over a wonderful country on both banks of the Moselle, and thus Trier itself has no dearth of palaces testifying that at various times its dominion stretched far and wide.

The origins of the city are shrouded in legend; the pleasant setting probably lured settlers here quite early. The citizens of Trier were incorporated into the Roman Empire, first as heathens, then as Christians, conquered by Normans and Franks, and finally the beautiful land became a part of the Roman-German Empire.

I would like very much to see the city during the good season, during peaceful times, to become better acquainted with its citizens, who have had the reputation since time immemorial of being friendly and cheerful. At the moment there are still traces of the first characteristic, hardly anything of the second; for how is it possible to be cheerful under such adverse circumstances?

To be sure, whoever searches in the annals of the city will find numerous accounts of the misfortunes of war which have visited this area, since the Moselle valley and the river itself favor military undertakings. Even Attila, coming with his vast hordes from the most distant eastern regions, had advanced and retreated through this river valley, like ourselves. The inhabitants suffered greatly during the Thirty Years' War and down to the end of the 17th century, because their ruler had joined with France as the geographically closest ally and was condemned to lengthy imprisonment in Austria as a result. The city also suffered more than once from civil war, as was inevitable in cities ruled by bishops, where the citizen could not always reconcile himself to the temporal rule of ecclesiastics.

My guide, while instructing me about the history of the place, drew my attention to buildings of various periods, which were mostly curious and therefore of some interest, though few appealed to the aesthetic sense or could be praised in the same way as the monument of Igel.

I found the ruins of the Roman amphitheater impressive; but since the structure had collapsed and probably had served as a quarry for several centuries, it was impossible to deduce anything about it. Still, one must admire the wisdom of the ancients in seeking to produce great results with modest means, by taking advantage of the natural layout of a cleft between two hills, where the contour of the terrain saved the architect a good deal of excavation and construction. These ruins lie on the lower slopes of Mars Hill; if one climbs a little higher up, then one can look out over all the shrines of the saints, over cathedrals, roofs and gables to Apollo Hill, and thus the two gods, along with Mercury, perpetuate the memory of their names.[80] Their images could perish, but not the genius of the place.

Trier has monuments of great interest to the student of early medieval architecture. I have little knowledge of such things, nor do they appeal to cultivated taste. Although I paid them some attention, they were ultimately confusing to me; many of them are half buried, in ruins, or have been put to other uses.

I experienced a moment of utter serenity when I was taken across the great bridge, which also dates back to antiquity; here now one can see plainly how the town is built on a space that angles sharply towards the left bank of the river. From the foot of Apollo Hill one can survey the river, bridge, mills, the city, and the environs, where the vineyards, not yet completely bereft of their foliage, made a very pleasing picture at our feet as well as on the lower slopes of Mars Hill and were evidence of the fertility of this region. They awakened a feeling of comfort and well-being which seems to pervade the regions where wine is grown. The best varieties of Moselle wine, which we now had opportunity to enjoy, seemed to have a more pleasant taste after we had obtained this overview.

Trier, 29 October

Our princely commander arrived and took up quarters in the monastery of Saint Maximinus. These monks, rich and otherwise rather fortunate, had had, to be sure, to put up with a great deal of disruption for quite a while; the brothers of Louis XVI had been quartered there, and afterward it had never again been free of guests. Such an institution, founded on peace and calm, meant for peace and calm, took on a very odd aspect under these circumstances, since, no matter how considerately one acted, a sharp contrast was evident between the military and the monks. The Duke, however, here as everywhere, even as an uninvited guest, knew how to make himself and his companions esteemed by virtue of his generosity and his friendliness.

But the evil demon of war was to pursue me even here. Our good Colonel von Gotsch was also quartered in the monastery; one night I found him watching and worrying over his son, who was also seriously afflicted by the grievous sickness. Here again I was subjected to the litany of curses about our campaign from the mouth of an old soldier and a father, who was entitled to criticize with the utmost passion all the errors which he recognized as a soldier and condemned as a father. The pass at Les Islettes was mentioned again, and indeed anyone who grasped the significance of that unfortunate mistake had to despair.

I was glad of the opportunity to see the abbey and found an extensive, truly princely building; the rooms were large with high ceilings, the floors were inlaid, the walls covered with velvet and damask tapestries, there was no lack of stuccowork, gilt, carved wood, and all the other things one is used to seeing in such palaces, everything reflected two- and threefold in large mirrors.

The people billeted here fared quite well, but not all the horses could be accommodated and they had to go without shelter, with neither stalls, mangers, nor troughs. Unfortunately the feedbags had rotted and they had to eat the oats off the ground.

The stables may have been inadequate, but the cellars were all the more capacious. Over and above its own vineyards, the monastery enjoyed the revenue of many tithes. To be sure, many a large cask must have been emptied in recent months, for a pile of them lay in the courtyard.

30 October

Our Duke gave a gala dinner; three of the most eminent clerical dignitaries were invited and had provided priceless table linen and a beautiful porcelain service for the occasion; there was not much silver to be seen, since treasure and valuables had been sent to Ehrenbreitstein[81] for safekeeping. Tasty dishes had been prepared by the Duke's cooks and we enjoyed wine here that had originally been intended to follow us to France and had now been returned from Luxemburg. But it was the delicious white bread that earned the highest praise, and I was reminded of the contrast with the army bread at Hans.

While trying to learn something about the history of Trier in recent days it had been impossible to overlook the Abbey St. Maximinus, and I was therefore in a position to carry on a satisfactory historical conversation with my clerical dinner partner. We agreed on the great age of the institution and reviewed its fluctuating fortunes, its proximity to the city, which had been a source of danger to both, and its burning and complete destruction in the year 1674.[82] I was also told how it had been rebuilt and gradually put in its present state. I was able to respond by saying a number of nice things and praising the institution, which of course the clerical gentleman was glad to hear. He had nothing good to say about the most recent times, however: the French princes had been quartered here for a long while and there were countless tales about their misconduct, insolence, and wastefulness.

To change the subject, therefore, I went back to the field of history; but when I talked about the earliest times, when the abbey had set itself up as the equal of the archbishop and the abbot had had a seat in the Estates of the Holy Roman Empire, he smiled but was evasive, as though he considered such memories somewhat compromising in the present day.

The Duke now demonstrated his great care and concern for the regiment, for when it proved impossible to move the sick men by wagon he rented a ship to transport them to Coblence comfortably.

Now, however, other soldiers arrived who were afflicted in a different way. It had become obvious early in the retreat that moving the cannons would be difficult; the artillery horses died, one after the other, and few teams were to be found. Horses, which had been requisitioned during the march into France and had run away during the retreat, were in short supply everywhere, and it had been necessary to resort to a desperate measure: in every regiment a large contingent of troopers had to dismount and march on foot so that the artillery could be saved. These good men suffered indescribably on the ruined roads in their stiff boots, which were falling apart at the end; but their prospects were to brighten, for arrangements were made to send them too to Coblence by ship.

October

My Duke had delegated me to call on Marquis Lucchesini,[83] in order to take leave of him and to make certain inquiries. Late in the evening, and not without some difficulties, I was allowed to see this important man, who had previously been quite well disposed toward me. The warmth and charm with which he received me were gratifying—not so, however, his responses to my questions and requests. He dismissed me the same way he had received me, without, however, doing the least thing for me, and I can say that is what I had been prepared for.

As I watched the busy preparations for the departure of the sick and exhausted troopers I got the feeling that it would be best if I too were to proceed by water. I left my chaise behind, with great reluctance, having been promised it would be sent after me to Coblence, and hired a one-man boat.[84] When I got into the boat, the sight of all my possessions together in one place, as though for inventory, made quite a pleasurable impression on me, since I had more than once either feared to lose them or actually given them up for lost. A Prussian officer joined us on this trip. I took him on as an old acquaintance whom I remembered well as a page at Weimar; he still had vivid recollections of his days at court and claimed that he had usually brought me my coffee.

The weather was passable, the voyage peaceful, and we appreciated this boon all the more when we watched the columns marching laboriously, and sometimes making no progress at all, on the road, which came close to the water in places. In Trier there had already been complaints that the greatest difficulty on such a hasty retreat was in finding quarters, for it had happened quite often that one regiment had found the villages assigned to it already occupied by another, which caused great hardship and confusion.

The sights along the banks of the Moselle during this journey were quite varied; for though the river stubbornly keeps to its general course from southwest to northeast, it flows through a difficult mountainous terrain and is forced by rock formations jutting into it from the banks to alter its course, now to the right, now to the left, so that its progress is like that of a large snake. This is the reason why a qualified boatman is absolutely indispensable; ours displayed much skill and strength, now by avoiding a rocky shoal, or again by boldly making use of the quick currents along the steep cliffs to speed up the boat. The many villages on either side presented a most charming aspect; the vineyards, everywhere carefully tended, were the sign of a cheerful breed of men who spared no effort to produce the precious juice. Every sunny slope was pressed into service, but we marveled at steep cliffs rising out of the river, where the vines throve the best on narrow ledges that were like natural terraces.

We landed by a nice inn, where we were well received by the innkeeper, an old woman, who complained of many a hardship she had suffered and had particularly harsh words for the émigrés. Often, she said, she had shuddered as she watched these ungodly people at her table, bombarding one another with pellets and morsels of good bread, so that she and her maids had later had to sweep it up with tears in their eyes.

And so we continued down the river smoothly in high spirits until dusk, when we found ourselves caught up in the tortuous meanders winding around the heights of Montroyal.[85] Now night overtook us before we could reach Trarbach, or even catch sight of it. It became pitch dark; when the full and sustained fury of a storm, which had been presaged by gusts of wind, broke upon us, we knew only that we were hemmed in by more or less perpendicular banks. Sometimes the water was whipped up by the wind, at other times vicious squalls whistled fiercely in our ears; one wave after the other broke over the boat and we found ourselves drenched. The boatman couldn't hide his uneasiness, our danger seemed to become ever greater, and our desperation reached its height when the good man announced that he knew neither where we were, nor in what direction to steer the boat.

Our companion became silent, I was composed; we were rocking about in the deepest darkness, except that sometimes it seemed that I could see masses above me that were even darker than the sky—which afforded little comfort or hope. It became ever more frightening to be shut up so between land and cliffs. And so we were thrown back and forth in pitch darkness for a long time, until finally we saw a light and therefore some hope in the distance. Then we steered and rowed toward it as best we could, and Paul worked with all his might.

Finally we landed safely in Trarbach, where we were offered chicken with rice at a passable tavern. A prominent merchant, however, hearing that strangers had landed here at night in such a storm, insisted that we go home with him. There, in tastefully furnished rooms brightly lit by candles, we saw black and white English prints framed under glass, a sight which filled us with joy and deep emotion when we compared this with the dark dangers we had endured only a short time before. The man and his wife, both still young, outdid themselves in caring for us; we savored the finest Moselle wine, especially my companion, who was the one who most needed something to revive him.

Paul confessed that he had already taken off his coat and boots in the boat in order to save us by swimming in the event that we were shipwrecked; in which case, to be sure, he probably would have managed to save only himself.

Once we had dried out and had some refreshment I began to become restless and eager to get under way again. Our friendly host didn't want to let us go, he wanted us to stay the next day as well, said he would take us to a nearby height where we would have the most beautiful panoramic view of a magnificent landscape, and promised any number of other things which would have served to refresh and divert us. But it is a strange thing: just as man accustoms himself to tranquility and wants to cling to it, it is also possible to become accustomed to restlessness; there was within me a compulsion to hurry on without stopping, a compulsion over which I had no control.

Just as we were hurrying off, the good man forced two mattresses upon us, so that we would at least have a bit of comfort in the boat; his wife was not eager to give them to us, for which she could scarcely be blamed, as the ticking was new and of fine quality. It happens frequently in such cases that now the one, and now the other spouse is more or less well disposed to the guest who has been thrust upon them.

We floated gently down to Coblence, and I remember quite clearly that at the end of the trip I saw perhaps the most beautiful nature scene that I have ever experienced. As we were approaching, the Moselle bridge loomed toward us, rugged and black; but through the arches we could see the fine buildings in the valley and above the line of the bridge the castle of Ehrenbreitstein through the blue haze. On the right the town, spreading out from the bridge, formed an impressive foreground. This scene gave us magnificent but only momentary pleasure, for we landed and hastened conscientiously to deliver the mattresses in good condition to the firm named by our worthy Trarbachers.

The Duke of Weimar had been assigned excellent quarters, where I too found good lodging. The army was following in stages; the Duke's servants arrived and could not leave off talking about the hardships they had had to suffer. We considered ourselves fortunate to have come by boat, and the windstorm we had experienced seemed only a minor evil compared to the land route, slowed down by obstacles everywhere.

The sovereign himself had arrived, and many generals gathered around the King; I, for my part, took solitary walks along the Rhine and recapitulated for my own benefit the strange events of the past weeks.

A French general, Lafayette, the leader of a great party, just a short time earlier the idol of his country and enjoying the complete confidence of his soldiers, rebels against that high authority[86] which, after the arrest of the King, alone represents the country; he flees, his army, not stronger than 23,000 men, disorganized, demoralized, remains without a general or other high-ranking officers.

At the same time a powerful king, at the head of an allied army 80,000 strong, invades France and two fortified cities capitulate after only token resistance.

Now a little-known general, Dumouriez, appears on the scene; although he has never commanded an army before, he shrewdly and skillfully takes up a very strong position. That position is broken through, but he manages to retire to another, where he is encircled in such a way that the enemy is positioned between him and Paris.

But because of continual rains the situation is a curiously complicated one; the fearsome allied army, no more than a six hours' march from Châlons and ten hours from Rheims, finds itself prevented from reaching either city, sees fit to retreat, evacuates the two occupied cities, loses more than a third of its men—no more than 2000 of them in action—and now finds itself back at the Rhine. All these events, which verge on the miraculous, transpire in less than six weeks, and France has been saved from the greatest danger ever recorded in the annals of the country.

If one now thinks of the many thousands who participated in such misfortunes, whose grievous bodily and spiritual suffering seemed to give them some right to complain, then one can easily imagine that all this could not be borne in silence, and that no matter how hard one tried to exercise restraint, there were times when feelings welled up and overflowed.

I myself had such an experience. I was sitting at dinner next to an elderly and distinguished general and did not refrain completely from speaking of what had taken place, whereupon he answered me, amiably enough but with a certain decisive tone in his voice: "Do me the honor of calling on me tomorrow morning and we will have a frank and friendly discussion about this." I pretended to accept the invitation, but did not put in an appearance, and I vowed secretly that I would not break my accustomed silence again any time soon.

During my trip on the river and also in Coblence I had made a number of observations that were useful for my study of colors; in particular I had gained new insight into epoptic colors and I could hope more and more to be able to link the physical phenomena among themselves and separate them from other phenomena to which they seemed to have only a more or less distant relationship.

Also, faithful Wagner's diary stood me in good stead in supplementing my own, which I had neglected completely in recent days.

The Duke's regiment had arrived and was encamped in the villages across from Neuwied. Here the Duke showed the most paternal solicitude for his subordinates; every individual was allowed to voice his grievances and aid and redress were granted wherever possible. Lieutenant von Flotow, who was stationed in the city and closest to the benefactor, proved active and helpful. The most crying need, for shoes and boots, was met by purchasing leather and putting all the men in the regiment who were cobblers out to work under the master shoemakers of the city. Care was also taken for cleanliness and appearance, yellow chalk was procured, the men's jackets were washed and dyed, and our troopers were soon trotting around handsomely again.

My studies, however, as well as my casual conversations with my chancellery- and house-mates, were enlivened quite a bit by the excellent Moselle wine which our sovereign was given by the city council and which he gave us permission to enjoy, since most of the time he dined elsewhere. When we got the opportunity to compliment one of the donors, expressing our great gratitude, since they must have given up many a good bottle on our account, we received this reply: we were welcome to this wine and to much more besides, and they only lamented the casks they had had to provide for the émigrés, who, to be sure, had brought much money, but also much unhappiness to the city, and in fact had turned the order of things quite upside down; in particular they were very critical of the émigrés' conduct toward the Elector, for they had more or less usurped his place and undertaken audaciously irresponsible enterprises against his will.[87]

Recently, in the face of impending catastrophe, he too had left for Regensburg, and one fine day at noon I stole up to his wondrously beautiful castle, which lay a little upstream from the city on the left bank of the Rhine and had sprung from the earth since I had last been in this region.[88] It stood all by itself, a brand-new ruin—not architecturally, but politically—and I did not have the courage to ask the castle warden, who was strolling about, to let me in to see it. Its environs, near and far, were delightful, the whole area between the castle and the city under cultivation and dotted with gardens, the view upstream from there calm and soothing, the view toward the city and the fortress, on the other hand, magnificent and impressive.

I went to the flying bridge[89] with the intention of having myself put across, but I was detained, or rather I tarried of my own volition to watch an Austrian wagon convoy which was crossing slowly. I witnessed a dispute there between a Prussian sergeant and an Austrian sergeant which casts a clear light on the character of the two nations.

The Austrian had been posted there to see to it that the wagon train got across as quickly as possible, to prevent any confusion, and therefore to permit no other vehicles to get into the line. The Prussian was demanding loudly that an exception be made for his little cart, on which he had packed his wife and child and a few possessions. The Austrian very calmly refused the request, citing his orders which expressly forbade such a thing; as the Prussian got louder, the Austrian only grew more calm, if that were possible: he wouldn't stand for any gap in the column entrusted to his care, and the Prussian found no space to force his way in. At last the importunate Prussian reached for his saber and challenged the resisting Austrian; with threats and curses he attempted to draw his opponent into the nearest alley to settle the matter then and there. But the totally unruffled Austrian, a man of good sense who knew well the prerogatives of his position, did not stir and continued to maintain order as before.

I would have liked to have the scene done by a portrait painter: for the two differed not only in their behavior, but also in their appearance; the placid Austrian was sturdy and strong, the Prussian—who had flown into a towering rage at the end—was tall and thin, frail and never still for a moment.

Much of the time I had allotted for my walk was already past, and my fear of meeting with similar delays on the way back dispelled all desire to visit the valley I had previously loved so dearly,[90] which would only have aroused in me the feelings of painful loss and stimulated me to reflect fruitlessly on bygone times. Yet I stood a long time gazing across the river, faithfully recalling, in the midst of the confusing press of earthly events, those peaceful days.

It happened by chance that I knew something about the measures being taken to continue the campaign on the right bank. The Duke's regiment was preparing to cross the river and the Duke himself was to follow with all his entourage. I dreaded any continuation of the warfare and was again seized by a desire to flee. I would like to call this reverse homesickness: a yearning for open spaces rather than for circumscribed surroundings. I stood there; the majestic river lay before me and flowed so serenely and invitingly downstream in a broad and expansive landscape. It was flowing towards friends to whom I had always remained loyal in spite of all the twists and turns of life. I had the urge to get out of this strange, violent world, and return to the bosom of friends, and after being granted leave I hastily rented a boat to Düsseldorf. I left my chaise, which still had not arrived from Trier, to be taken care of by friends in Coblence, asking them to have it sent down the river to me.

Once on board with all my possessions and drifting down the river, accompanied by my faithful Paul and a non-paying passenger who had promised to row occasionally, I considered myself a fortunate man, freed of all ills.

Meanwhile some adventures still awaited us. We had not been rowing downstream very long when we noticed that the boat must have a bad leak, because the boatman was quite busily bailing it out from time to time. It was only then we realized that, in our haste to get under way, we had overlooked the fact that on the long trip downstream from Coblence to Düsseldorf the boatmen were in the habit of taking only the very oldest boats, selling them for firewood upon arrival, and returning home very easily on foot, their money in their pocket.

However, we continued on our way without too much concern. A star-filled but very cold night favored our journey, when suddenly the unknown oarsman demanded to be put ashore and began to argue with the boatman about which spot would be the best for a traveler on foot, a point on which they could not agree.

In the course of this dispute, which became quite heated, our boatman fell into the water and was only fished out again with some difficulty. Now he could no longer hold out in the clear, cold night and urgently requested permission to put in at Bonn in order to dry and warm himself. My servant went with him to a boatmen's tavern, but I insisted on staying out under the open sky and had a bed made for me on top of our luggage. The force of habit is so great that after six weeks spent almost entirely in the open I couldn't stand the thought of being in a room with a roof over my head. This time, however, a new misfortune ensued which, to be sure, I should have foreseen: we had pulled the boat up as far as possible on the bank but not far enough to keep water from still coming in through the leak.

After a deep sleep I found myself something more than refreshed, for the water had reached my sleeping place and thoroughly drenched me and my possessions. As a result I was forced to get up, seek out the tavern, and dry myself as well as possible in a room thick with tobacco smoke in the company of men noisily sipping mulled wine; by the time I was done it was practically morning and our delayed trip was speeded along by vigorous rowing.

Excursus

When I see myself now, in memory, floating like this down the Rhine, I hardly know how to say precisely what was going on inside me. The sight of the peaceful water and the feeling of ease connected with this kind of travel made it possible for me to look back on the time just past as on a bad dream from which I had suddenly awakened, and I gave myself over to blissful hopes for the hearty companionship I expected soon to enjoy.

Now, however, if I am to continue with my story, I must choose another method than the one that was appropriate to my narrative so far: for where day after day important events are unfolding before our eyes, when we are suffering and fearing and barely daring to hope, with so many thousand others, the present has definite value, and, related step by step, it renews the past while also pointing toward the future.

But what happens in social interactions can be comprehended only in moral terms, from the outward expressions of inner states of mind; here is the place for reflection. The moment does not speak for itself—

rather, both the memory of the past and later observations must play a role in making it comprehensible.

I lived on the whole without much forethought from day to day, and in recent years had not come off too badly as a result; and so I had a tendency not to think much in advance about a person I was to see or a place where I was to be, instead allowing such encounters and events to affect me without previous preparation. The advantage of this is considerable: a person is never forced to abandon preconceived notions or to erase some pleasing picture he has painted in his mind in order to replace it with an unhappy reality. But there is the disadvantage that in critical moments we may wander around in a daze and not know how to cope spontaneously with unforeseen events.

Likewise, I never paid much attention to the effect my presence and my own state of mind had on other people, with the result that I often discovered with surprise that I had aroused affection or dislike, and often even both at the same time.

Even if one were to refrain from judging this behavior as an individual peculiarity deserving either praise or blame, it remains a fact that in the present case it produced quite unexpected incidents, not always of the pleasantest kind.

I had not been with these friends for many years. They had held faithfully to their own manner of life, whereas it had been my remarkable lot to pass through many stages of trial, activity and endurance, so that, although I remained outwardly the same, I had become a completely different person and appeared almost unrecognizable to my old friends.

It would be a difficult task, even in later years, when we have gained a more impartial overview of our life, to give an exact accounting of those transitions, which appear at one time as progress, and at another as retrogression, and yet are all destined to be of profit and value to a man who is guided by divine Providence. In spite of such difficulties, however, I shall try, for the sake of my friends, to sketch my situation.

A moral man inspires affection and love only insofar as we become aware of a longing in him; this longing is the expression of something he possesses and something which he wishes at the same time: possession of a tender heart, and the wish to discover that same tender heart in others. By virtue of the former we attract other people, by the latter we give of ourselves to others.

The longing that was in my nature, which I had perhaps favored too much in my younger years and sought to combat forcefully as I grew older, was no longer appropriate or sufficient for the grown man, and I therefore sought its final and complete satisfaction. The goal of my most fervent longing, giving rise to a torment which filled my innermost being, was Italy, the image or idea of which had been present in my mind for years, but in vain, until I finally got up the courage to embrace the real thing by means of a daring resolution. My friends gladly followed me in their thoughts to that magnificent country, they accompanied me on the way there and on the way back, and it is to be hoped that they will now also very soon be inclined to share with me my lengthier sojourn in Rome and travel back from there with me again, for then a number of problems will be resolved in a more comprehensible manner.[91]

In Italy I felt myself gradually raised above petty thoughts, lifted beyond the level of false wishes, and in place of longing for the land of the arts I experienced a longing for art itself. I had become aware of art, now I wished to penetrate it, to delve to its very core.

The study of art, like the study of the ancient writers, gives us a certain steadfastness, an inner satisfaction; while it fills us inwardly with great objects and sentiments, it takes control of all those desires that strive for external expression and nurtures every worthy striving of our hearts. It becomes ever less necessary to communicate with others, and in the end the art lover has the same experience as the painter, the sculptor, the architect: he works alone for pleasures which he hardly ever has occasion to share with others.

But at the same time still another idiosyncratic pursuit was to estrange me from my previous world, namely my decided turn toward nature, impelled for urgent inner reasons and in the most personal manner one can imagine. Here I found neither master nor fellows and had to take the responsibility for everything upon myself. I would have remained completely alone in the solitude of forests and gardens and in darkened chambers with my optical experiments, had not a happy domestic relationship been able to revitalize me during this curious period of my life. The *Roman Elegies* and the *Venetian Epigrams* are products of this period.[92]

Now, however, I was also to get a foretaste of military enterprises: ordered to take part in that Silesian campaign which found its negotiated conclusion in the Congress of Reichenbach,[93] I had found myself enlightened and exalted by many an experience in an important part of the world, while at the same time giving myself up to light diversions. But all this time the calamity of the revolution in France, spreading ever farther, forced every single spirit, no matter what its previous bent, to return to the surface of European reality and confronted it with the cruelest possible actualities. Since duty commanded me to take part again with my sovereign master in what were at first only critical, but soon after the sad events of the day and to suffer manfully all those hardships of which I have ventured to give my readers only a moderated account, every delicate and sincere feeling, which had withdrawn into the innermost recesses of my being, might have been expected to be extinguished and to disappear.

If one takes all of this into consideration, then the situation which I have outlined in the following pages will no longer appear so puzzling. This I must desire all the more as it has been difficult for me to resist the urge to rewrite these pages, composed hurriedly many years ago, in the light of my present views and convictions.

Pempelfort, November 1792

It was already dark when I landed in Düsseldorf, and I therefore had to have myself taken by lantern-light to Pempelfort, where, after a momentary surprise, I found the warmest welcome. As is always the case with such reunions, we had a good deal to say to each other, and this took up a good part of the night.

The next day I felt more at home and was answering questions and telling stories; unfortunately the disastrous campaign afforded more than enough stuff for conversation, for no one had expected it to come to such a dismal conclusion. But also no one could begin to express the effect of that awful silence, which had lasted almost four weeks, and the ever growing uncertainty caused by the total lack of information. There was so little news of the allied army that it was as though it had been swallowed up and had disappeared from the face of the earth; everyone, peering into an awful void, was tormented by fear and anxiety, and anticipated with dread the expected continuation of the war in the Netherlands and the threats to both banks of the Rhine.

We were diverted from such reflections by moral and literary discussions, in which my own realism came to the fore and was not particularly appealing to my friends.

Since the revolution, in order to distract myself somewhat from those wild events, I had begun a curious work, the travels of seven brothers who, all quite different, each served the common interest in his own way; it was a thoroughly romantic and fanciful work, masking both outlook and outcome, a parable of our own condition. The group demanded that I read it to them, I needed little urging and dug out my notebooks; but it also did not take very long for me to see that no one was edified by it. I therefore left my wandering family in some convenient port or other and let my manuscript lie.[94]

My friends, however, not ready simply to accept such changed attitudes on my part without further ado, made a number of efforts to use my previous works to rekindle earlier feelings in me, and one night they pressed *Iphigenia* into my hands and wanted me to read from it; but this was not at all to my taste, I felt myself far removed from its delicacy of feeling, and its echo was unpleasant, even when read aloud by other people. And though that play was soon laid aside, it seemed as though they intended to subject me to an even higher degree of torment. They now brought out *Oedipus at Colonos,* the sublimity of which was totally unbearable, hardened as I had been by a horrible campaign and turned against art, nature, and the world; I couldn't take even a hundred lines of it. Then my friends finally resigned themselves to the fact that my opinions had changed—though there were still plenty of topics to talk about.

A number of works from earlier periods of German literature were successfully brought into our conversation, but we never got very far below the surface, because everyone was anxious to avoid a clash of opinions.

The last twenty years, if I may be permitted a general observation, had been a curious period indeed, in which men of significant talent had gotten together and had formed groups on the basis of some shared inclination or other, while in other respects they were totally different: everyone brought along a high opinion of himself and everyone was happy with the mutual praise and forebearance that prevailed.

Talent itself came to be generally and increasingly esteemed, men of talent learned how to maintain themselves and get ahead through social connections, and the advantages gained were no longer due to individuals but to the concerted efforts of groups of like-minded people. It was only natural that there was a certain amount of conscious design involved; they knew as well as anyone else how to manipulate relationships, they forgave each other their idiosyncrasies, the sensitive spots of one were balanced by those of the other, and the mutual misunderstandings remained undiscovered for a long time.

In the midst of all this I was in a rather curious position: thanks to my talents I occupied an honored position in society, but my untamed passion for what I recognized as true and natural led me in a number of instances to behave maliciously towards other people whom I regarded as being caught up in obviously false aspirations; and for this reason I would have a falling-out with other members of the group from time to time, reconcile myself with them wholly or in part, and yet self-righteously keep to my own path. All this time, even in later years, I retained something of the ingenuousness of Voltaire's Huron,[95] and could manage to be insufferable and amiable at the same time.

One field, however, over which we ranged with more freedom and agreement was western and especially French literature. Jacobi,[96] while going his own way, still noticed everything of importance, and because of his proximity to the Netherlands he developed not only literary but also personal and social contacts there. He was a very well-built man with a handsome face, his bearing restrained and yet very agreeable, destined to stand out in any company of cultivated human beings.

It was indeed a strange period, one that is almost impossible to imagine nowadays. Voltaire had really burst the ancient shackles of mankind, and therefore the best minds proceeded to doubt everything that had previously been held in veneration. If the philosopher of Ferney concentrated all his efforts on diminishing and weakening the influence of the clerics, with an eye mainly to Europe, de Pauw[97] projected his spirit of conquest to the far corners of the earth; he wanted to grant neither the Chinese nor the Egyptians the honors that scholarly prejudice had bestowed upon them for many years.[98] He was a canon in Xanten, quite close to Düsseldorf, and he and Jacobi maintained a friendly relationship; but how many others there are who should also be mentioned here!

We should at least include Hemsterhuis[99] who, devoted to Princess Gallitzin,[100] spent considerable time in the nearby city of Münster. Hemsterhuis, along with other kindred spirits, was seeking for his own part a more delicate sort of reassurance, satisfaction in the realm of the ideal, and his Platonic sentiments inclined him toward religion.

While I am engaged in these fragmentary recollections I must also mention Diderot, the vigorous dialectician, who was another of those who enjoyed the hospitality of Pempelfort for a while and asserted his paradoxes with great candor.[101]

Rousseau's views regarding man's natural state were also not unknown to this circle, which excluded nothing, not even me, although as a matter of fact I was only tolerated.

I have already indicated elsewhere how I reacted to the works of others in my younger years. I was able to use other writers to my advantage without actually assimilating them, for which reason I was also unable to reach any agreement about them with my fellows. The case of my own creative productions was just as peculiar. My writings always corresponded closely to the course of my life, and since this was usually a mystery, even to my closest friends, it was very seldom that anyone was able to warm to one of my new works, because they always expected something similar to what they already knew.

If my seven brothers were received badly because they bore no resemblance whatsoever to their sister Iphigenia, I knew full well that my play, *The Great Cophta,*[102] which had already been in print for a while, was actually offensive to my friends. We didn't talk about this drama and I took care to see that the conversation didn't move in that direction. But one will have to grant me that an author who is not in a position to recite his newest works or to be able to talk about them is in the same painful position as a composer who feels he cannot present his newest melodies.

I had little better luck with my nature studies; no one seemed able to understand the passionate earnestness with which I pursued these inquiries, no one could see that they sprang from my innermost being. My friends considered this praiseworthy endeavor a whimsy and a mistake; in their opinion I could do better things than that and should have just let my talent continue on its old course. They believed themselves all the more entitled to this opinion, as my manner of thinking hardly coincided with theirs at all, rather in most points was precisely the opposite of theirs. One cannot imagine a more isolated human being than I was right then and remained for a long time. The doctrine of hylozoism, or whatever one wants to call it, which had a most profound basis that I accepted in all its dignity and sacredness, made me unreceptive and even intolerant toward that other manner of thinking which set up lifeless matter, atoms which were somehow set in motion and forced to react to external causation, as its creed.[103] I had not failed to learn from Kant's natural science that the powers of attraction and repulsion belong to the essence of matter and cannot be separated from each other in our concept of matter; from this I derived my conception of the fundamental polarity of all things, a polarity which permeates and animates the infinite multiplicity of phenomena.

I had already advanced such arguments during the visit Princess Gallitzin, Fürstenberg, and Hemsterhuis had paid earlier in Weimar,[104] only to be brushed aside and condemned to silence as a kind of blasphemer.

No one can blame a circle of people for closing itself off from other influences; and that is something my friends in Pempelfort did quite honestly and openly. They had taken little notice of my *Metamorphosis of Plants*,[105] which had been published a year ago, and when I delivered my thoughts on morphology, no matter how well I knew the subject and no matter how careful I was in its presentation which, it seemed to me, must have been thoroughly convincing, it was unfortunately all too clear that the unyielding proposition, "nothing can come into being which does not already exist" had taken firm hold of their minds. As a result I also had to put up with their telling me that every live thing comes from an egg, in answer to which, in bitter jest, I put the ancient question again as to whether the chicken or the egg had come first. The theory of preformation seemed so plausible to them, and it was so edifying to contemplate nature through the lens of Bonnet![106]

Something had also been said about my *Contributions to Optics*,[107] and I needed little coaxing to entertain the company with some demonstrations and experiments, where it was not at all difficult to present something that was entirely new to them: for everyone there, no matter how educated, had learned only about the refraction of light, and unfortunately they wanted to reduce everything they saw, even those living things that gave them pleasure, to that dead hypothesis.

Yet I put up with all this for a while, because I never presented a lecture without learning something myself as a result; usually I acquired new insights while I was speaking, and in fact the flow of speech itself was the surest medium of invention for me.

To be sure, I could proceed in this manner only didactically and dogmatically—I had no talent for true conversation or for dialectics. I must confess, however, that often a bad habit came to the fore: since I found normal conversation quite boring, because nothing is expressed there except limited, particular modes of representation, I was in the habit of making outrageously paradoxical statements in order to provoke the narrow-minded disagreements that people usually get themselves into, and to force them to extreme conclusions. This was of course usually offensive to the company and annoying on more than one count. For often, to attain my end, I had to play devil's advocate, and since everyone wanted to be on the side of good and wanted me to be good as well, they would not let me do that: what I said could not be taken seriously because it was too superficial, and it could not be a jest either, because it was too bitter. Finally they called me a hypocrite in reverse and soon were reconciled with me. Yet I cannot deny that by this bad habit I alienated a number of people and turned some into outright enemies.

But when I began to talk about Italy I could immediately banish all the evil spirits as though with a magic wand. In going to Italy I had also proceeded without preparation, without any precautions; there was no lack of adventures on my journey and I had firmly imprinted on my memory the land itself along with its charm and its splendor. The very contours, color, and spirit of that landscape, illuminated by the most favorable sky, was still vividly present in my mind. My weak attempts at imitating it through art had sharpened my memory, I could describe it as though I saw it before my very eyes; the landscape I described was teeming with life, and thus they were all content, sometimes even entranced, with the animated pictures I drew for them.

In order to convey the full charm of my stay in Pempelfort it would be desirable if one could also imagine clearly the setting in which all of this took place. It was a large house which stood somewhat apart, in the vicinity of extensive, well-cultivated gardens—a paradise during the summer, and in the winter also quite pleasing. We enjoyed every ray of sunshine outside in a pure and free setting; in the evening, or when the weather was bad, we were glad to retreat to the beautiful large rooms, which, quite comfortable and well furnished without any pretentiousness, afforded a worthy setting for any spirited conversation.

A large dining room, suitable for a large family with its constant guests, cheery and comfortable, contained a long table on which there was never a lack of delicious food. Here everyone assembled, the host always cheerful and stimulating, his sisters kind and caring, the son earnest and promising, the daughter pretty, capable, simple, and lovable, recalling to mind the mother who unfortunately had already passed on, and the earlier days spent with her twenty years ago in Frankfurt. Heinse,[108] practically a member of the family, could parry any joke; there were evenings when we could not stop laughing.

The few hours I had to myself in this most hospitable house I devoted quietly to a curious piece of work. During the campaign, in addition to keeping my diary, I had written down poetic orders of the day, satirical "ordres du jour," and now I wanted to look through them and revise them; but I soon realized that in my shortsighted presumptuousness I had seen a number of things in a false light and judged them incorrectly, and since there is nothing on which a person passes harsher judgment than errors he has just put behind him, and also because it seemed indiscreet to have such papers lying around, I destroyed the whole notebook in a blazing coal fire. Today, of course, I am sorry about this, because the notebook would be worth very much to me in gaining insight into the course of events and into the train of my own thoughts about them.

We paid many visits to friends of the Pempelfort circle who lived in nearby Düsseldorf; we usually met at the gallery.[109] There I could discern a decided predilection for the Italian school and people were quite unjust towards the Flemish. To be sure, the lofty spirit of the Italians exercises an unfailing appeal, arousing enthusiasm in noble minds. Once we had remained a long while in the room where Rubens and the other most important Flemish painters are displayed; as we left this room we saw Guido Reni's *Ascension* hanging just across from us, and someone exclaimed excitedly: "Isn't it just like coming out of the pub and joining polite society!" For my own part I did not mind the fact that the masters who not long ago had held me in thrall on the other side of the Alps were just as magnificent here too and aroused passionate admiration; but still I tried to make myself acquainted with the Flemish also, whose virtues and attainments were represented here to the highest degree; I profited from this for the rest of my life.

What struck me even more was that a certain enthusiasm for liberty, a striving for democracy, had spread among the privileged classes; people did not seem to realize how much would have to be given up for the attainment of some degree of dubious advantage. I saw how people here worshipped Houdon's[110] busts of Lafayette and Mirabeau,[111] which were quite natural and good likenesses of their subjects—the former for his virtues as a gallant cavalier and a citizen, the latter for his immense intelligence and oratorical powers. Sentiment among the Germans was already in a curious state of flux; a number of them had been in Paris themselves, had heard the great men speak and seen them in action, and had been stimulated to imitate them, unfortunately in the German manner, and that precisely at the time when simple concern about the future of the left bank of the Rhine was giving way to panic fear.

The danger seemed to be pressing: Düsseldorf was full of émigrés, even the brothers of the King arrived in town; people hurried to catch a glimpse of them, I ran across them at the gallery and was reminded of how they had been soaked to the skin during the departure from Glorieux. Baron von Grimm[112] and Madame de Bueil also arrived. Since the city was so crowded with people, an apothecary had taken them in; his collection of natural curiosities served as a bedroom, while monkeys, parrots, and other animals watched over the morning slumbers of this most gracious lady; shells and corals encroached upon her dressing-table: the evils of enforced billeting, which we had just recently introduced into France, had now returned to haunt us.

Baroness von Coudenhoven,[113] a beautiful and witty woman who had been the adornment of the Mainz court, had also fled to Düsseldorf. Dohm[114] and his wife arrived from safer German territory in order to gather more exact information about conditions here.

Frankfurt was still occupied by the French and the theater of war operations had been expanded to the area between the River Lahn and the Taunus mountains; in view of the daily fluctuating reports, and news which sometimes was reliable and sometimes not, conversation was lively and witty, but because of conflicting interests and opinions not always pleasant. I couldn't really take anything seriously that was so utterly problematical, uncertain, and exposed to the whims of chance as this situation, and my paradoxical jests sometimes caused merriment and sometimes vexation.

For instance I remember how once at the dinner table the citizens of Frankfurt were praised for their courageous and upright conduct toward Custine; their conduct and their sentiments, it was said, stood in quite favorable contrast to the unpardonable way the citizens of Mainz had behaved and were still behaving.[115] Baroness von Coudenhoven, in a fit of that enthusiasm which was so becoming to her, exclaimed that she would dearly love to be a citizen of Frankfurt! I answered that that could easily be arranged, and I knew how to do it, but would not tell her how. But since they would allow me no peace, I finally declared that the worthy lady need only marry me to be transformed into a Frankfurt citizen on the spot. This produced general laughter!

There was no end to the things we discussed! Once, when we were talking about the ill-fated campaign and especially about the cannonade at Valmy, Baron von Grimm assured me that there had been talk at the King's table about my strange ride into the cannon fire. Probably the officers whom I met on my ride had mentioned it, and the conclusion from all this was that one should never be surprised at my actions, because it was impossible to foresee what an odd fellow like me might do.

There was a very able and clever physician who also took part in our semi-saturnalias, and in my exuberance I never dreamed that I would need his services so soon. He laughed out loud, much to my annoyance, when he found me in bed, almost completely unable to move because of a severe rheumatic condition that I had acquired as the result of a chill. The physician, a student of Privy Councilor Hoffmann,[116] whose eccentricities were known all the way from Mainz and the Mainz court down to the lower Rhine, immediately began a camphor treatment, which was regarded as a cure-all. Blotting paper which had been rubbed with chalk and sprinkled with camphor was applied externally, while small doses of camphor were also administered internally. Whatever may have been the cause of my recovery, I was well within a few days.

The boredom of suffering, however, led me to indulge in many a reflection, while the feeling of weakness that follows all too easily from being confined to bed led me to regard my situation as being somewhat dangerous. The French had made significant progress in the Netherlands,[117] which had been magnified even further by rumors, and there was daily, even hourly talk of newly arriving exiles.

My stay in Pempelfort had been quite long enough, and had it not been for the family's warm hospitality I should long since have felt that I had worn out my welcome. Also I had not intended to stay there so long. But I was eagerly awaiting the arrival of my Bohemian chaise daily, in fact hourly, and I was loath to leave it behind. It had arrived in Coblence from Trier and was supposedly being sent down from there very soon; but because it still had not arrived the impatience that had possessed me during the last few days simply increased. Jacobi offered me the use of a traveling coach, which was a comfortable vehicle, although rather heavy from all the iron in it. We heard that everyone was moving on to the interior of Westphalia, and the King's brothers intended to take up residence there.

And so I departed with strangely mixed feelings: my sympathies made me want to remain with these good friends, who were also beginning to feel quite uneasy now; I had to leave these fine people behind in anxiety and confusion and venture out again, on bad roads and in the most unfriendly weather, into a savage and desolate world, borne along by the stream of restlessly hurrying refugees, feeling like a refugee myself.

And yet I had the prospect of a most agreeable stop along the way: as I was passing so close to Münster, it would have been unthinkable not to visit Princess Gallitzin.

Duisburg, November

And so I found myself, four weeks later, many miles away from the scene of our first disaster, to be sure, but again in the same company, in the same press of émigrés who now, having been definitively routed from the left bank, were flooding across into Germany, helpless and at their wit's end.

Having arrived at the tavern a little late for the noonday meal, I had to sit at the end of the long table. The innkeeper and his wife, who had already confided in me, as a German, their disgust with the French, apologized for the fact that these unwelcome guests had already taken all the good places at table. They also remarked to me that, in spite of all the humiliations, the misery, and the penury that probably awaited them, there was still to be found among them the same obsession with rank and class and the same arrogance as before.

When I looked up the long table I saw sitting at the head, in the seat of honor, a little old man, pleasing in appearance, but placid, not to say vacuous, in his behavior. He had to be someone of consequence, for two people sitting next to him were looking after him with the greatest attentiveness, chose the first and best morsels to put before him, and were practically putting the food into his mouth. It didn't take me long to see that he was far along in senility, a pitiful and mindless robot, dragging the shell of an earlier affluent and honorable existence miserably through the world, while the two devoted companions sought to conjure up for him the dream of his former state.

I looked at the other people at the table; the most serious misfortune could be read in every countenance: they could perhaps be differentiated into soldiers, commissioners, and adventurers. None of them said a word, for each had his own situation to contend with and they all saw endless misery ahead of them.

About the middle of the meal a handsome young man came in, with nothing particularly distinctive about him and no insignia of any kind. It was quite obvious that he was traveling on foot. He sat down quietly across from me, after asking the innkeeper for a cover, and ate without a murmur, everything that was brought out and placed before him. When the meal was over I went to the innkeeper, who whispered in my ear: "Your neighbor won't have to pay much for his meal." I didn't understand what he meant, but when the young man came up and asked what he owed, the innkeeper answered, after glancing fleetingly around the table, that the bill would be twenty kreuzer. The stranger seemed somewhat nonplussed and said that must be a mistake, because he had not only enjoyed a fine meal, but also a glass of wine—surely he must owe more than that! The innkeeper answered in all seriousness that he was in the habit of making out his bills himself, and that his guests were always happy to pay what he demanded. Now the modest young man paid and went away amazed; and the innkeeper immediately solved the mystery for me. "He was the first one of that damnable tribe," he exclaimed, "who ate black bread; that had to be taken into account."

In Duisburg I had only one old acquaintance, whom I did not fail to visit; this was Professor Plessing,[118] with whom, many years ago, I had had a sentimental relationship of the kind that is right out of a novel. I wish to say something about this relationship, for our conversation about it that night took us back from the most turbulent to the most peaceful of times.

When *Werther* came out in Germany it had by no means caused some kind of illness or fever, as was often claimed, but only uncovered the malaise that lay deep down in young souls. During a long and happy period of peace the belles lettres had come into full flower on German soil and in the German tongue. But soon, because this literature was occupied more with the internal than with the external world, it was pervaded by a certain kind of sentimentality in whose origins and progress one cannot fail to discern the influence of Laurence Sterne; even if the Germans were not exactly infused with his spirit, they responded quite eagerly to his feelings. There developed a kind of tender-passionate asceticism, which was usually destined to degenerate into unpleasant self-torment, since it was not given to us to partake of the humoristic irony of the Englishman. I had tried to free myself personally from this evil and intended, according to my convictions, to assist others as well; but that was more difficult than one might have expected, for it was actually a matter of lending support to each individual against himself, where there was no hope of any assistance from the external world, whether in the form of knowledge, instruction, an absorbing occupation, or the favor of others.

Here we must pass over in silence many influential persons and trends, but for our purposes it is necessary to comment at some length on another great aspiration of the time that was more or less independent of the others.

Lavater's *Physiognomy*[119] had turned moral-social interests in another direction. He felt himself in the possession of that most spiritual power, the power of interpreting all the impressions which a person's face and figure make on other people, without the individual himself being able to account for this effect. But since Lavater was not the kind of person to seek any kind of systematic abstraction, he stuck to particular cases and therefore to the individual.

Heinrich Lips,[120] a talented young artist who was especially good at portraits, became Lavater's staunch adherent, and never left his patron's side either at home or on the trip they took down the Rhine. And Lavater, partly in order to still his inordinate hunger for endless experience, and partly in order to initiate as many influential people as possible into his future great work and to link them to it, had likenesses done of everyone he met who was in any way distinguished by rank and talent, by character or actions.

By means of all this, to be sure, many an individual was revealed and increased in value by being included in such a noble collection, the individual's characteristics were pointed out by the interpreting master, people came to believe they had come to know each other better; and thus it resulted in the most curious way that many an individual attained a definite personal value who previously had seen himself as an insignificant cog in the machinery of civil community and state.

This effect was stronger and greater than one can imagine; everyone felt himself entitled to think the best of himself as a separate and complete being, and, thoroughly validated in his separateness, considered himself also to have the right to weave eccentricities, follies, and mistakes into the complex of his beloved existence. It was all the easier to arrive at this result, because throughout the whole undertaking it was only specific, individual nature that was being talked about, without any consideration for that general rationality which is supposed to govern all of nature. The religious element, by comparison, in which Lavater enveloped himself, was not sufficient to attenuate the ever more decisive element of complacency that crept in; instead there developed among the religiously oriented a kind of spiritual pride which was even more presumptuous than the natural sort.

What followed immediately upon that epoch, quite logically and conspicuously, was that individuals began to show each other mutual respect. Older men of note were revered, if not personally, at least in their images; and a young man had only to stand out a bit by virtue of some significant achievement to arouse the desire for personal contact with him—in the absence of which personal contact people were satisfied to have his picture. Silhouettes, carefully and skillfully drawn with highly detailed accuracy, did yeoman service. Everyone knew how to make them, and no stranger passed through without having his shadow outlined on the wall in the evening; the pantographs were never idle.

"Knowledge and love of mankind"[121] had been promised us by this endeavor, there had developed a certain far-flung participation in it, but mutual knowledge and understanding could not be persuaded to emerge so quickly; there was much activity in this respect, however, and it would be pleasant to describe what was undertaken by a certain highly gifted young sovereign[122] and his well-meaning, genial, and lively associates for the purpose of inspiring and furthering the cause far and wide, if it did not seem to be more praiseworthy to leave the beginnings of important developments in honorable obscurity. Perhaps the first leaves produced by that seed may have seemed a little strange; but the harvest, in which the fatherland and the world at large gladly participated, will not fail to be gratefully recognized for years to come.

Whoever bears in mind what I have just said and takes it to heart will find the following adventure, which the two participants happily recalled during their supper, neither improbable nor nonsensical.

Among the many attempts to approach me in person or by mail there was a letter which I received in the middle of 1776. Rather it was practically a whole notebook which had been posted in Wernigerode and was signed "Plessing." This communication was very nearly the strangest example I had ever seen of that self-torment which I mentioned previously. Here was a young man who had been educated in schools and at the university, who had not been able to use anything he had learned to achieve an inner, moral peace of mind. The expert handwriting was easy to read, the style polished and fluent, and though I immediately detected something of the preacher, it was honest and fresh from the heart, and it was impossible not to take some interest in him. But when I sought to gain a better understanding of this interest and took a closer look at the situation of this suffering young man, I thought I detected willfulness instead of forebearance, obstinacy instead of endurance, and a tendency to reject others instead of passionate yearning. In keeping with the temper of those times I developed a strong desire to see this young man in person; but I hardly thought it advisable to invite him to visit me. I had already encumbered myself with a number of young men,[123] under circumstances that are well known, who, instead of accompanying me on my search for a purer and higher culture, all clung to their old ways and were yet no better off than before, while hindering my progress. I let the matter rest for the time being, hoping that time itself would somehow provide a solution. Then I received a second letter which was shorter, but also more insistent and vehement than the first, in which the writer pressed me for an answer and explanation and implored me with all his heart not to refuse him.

But even this renewed onslaught did not ruffle my composure; the second letter moved me no more than the first, but my imperious habit of playing the role of mentor to other young men my age in matters of the heart and spirit would not let me forget him altogether.

The company that had gathered around an excellent young ruler in Weimar was practically inseparable, their occupations and undertakings, jests, joys, and sorrows in common. In November they planned to go hunting for wild boar in the Eisenach territory,[124] which had become necessary because the peasants were complaining so loudly about the depradations of these animals. As a guest[125] I was expected to participate, but I asked leave to make a little detour and join up with them later.

It so happened that I had some curious secret travel plans. I had often heard not only officials, but also other Weimar citizens concerned with the general welfare, wish devoutly for the mines at Ilmenau to be put into operation again.[126] I had only the sketchiest ideas about mining, and of course while my interest in the matter was welcome, no one expected any opinion or report from me about it. But I couldn't get interested in anything unless I had managed first to acquire some direct experience of it. In my opinion it was absolutely mandatory for me above all to see with my own eyes and grasp with my own mind all the facets of mining, even if only briefly, for only then could I hope to understand the arguments for reopening the mine and acquaint myself with its history. Therefore I had long planned a trip to the Harz region, and right now, since this season was to be spent out of doors anyway on the hunt, I felt the urge to take that trip. Besides, at that time winter held a great fascination for me, and as far as the mines were concerned, in their depths there was of course neither summer nor winter. I will also admit frankly that the prospect of seeing my curious correspondent in person and putting him to the test was probably as important in reaching my decision as seeing the mines.

While the hunting enthusiasts were heading off in another direction I rode along toward the Ettersberg and began to compose that ode which, under the title "A Winter Journey in the Harz," has for so long been something of a puzzle to the readers of my shorter poems. There was a buzzard soaring high above me in the gloomy snow clouds that were coming down out of the north. I spent the night in Sondershausen and reached Nordhausen so early the next day that I decided to go on immediately after lunch. I did not reach Ilfeld until very late, however, after passing through some dangerous situations with the aid of guides and lanterns.

An imposing inn was brilliantly illuminated and it seemed there was some special occasion being celebrated. At first the innkeeper did not want to take me in. The representatives of some very high courts, he said, had been working here a long time to reach some important agreements and to coordinate their interests, and, since they had now completed this task successfully, they were giving a general banquet tonight. After some urging on my part, however, and after some hints from the guide that I was not an ungenerous customer, the innkeeper offered to let me have the use of a partitioned area in the taproom, which was actually his own living quarters, equipped with a double bed for which he promised me clean sheets. He led me through the large, brightly lit room where the festivities were going on, and in passing I was able to get a brief look at all the jolly guests.

But a knothole in the wall of my quarters gave me the best opportunity to amuse myself by observing the whole company more closely—a knothole which undoubtedly served the innkeeper himself quite often for the purpose of spying on his guests. I was looking at the long, well-lit table from the lower end, and could survey its entire length; the scene resembled many paintings of the marriage at Cana. At my leisure I mustered the guests from the top to the bottom of the table: presidents, councilors, other participants, and so on down to secretaries, clerks, and assistants. The difficult task that had been successfully completed seemed to have effected an equality of all the active participants. The people were conversing freely among themselves, toasts were flowing, jokes passed back and forth, and several of the guests seemed to be singled out for more than their share of teasing and banter; in short, it was a merry and memorable feast, and in that blazing candlelight I could observe every bit of it calmly, just as though the limping devil[127] were standing beside me and had granted me the privilege of directly seeing and understanding a completely alien world. Those who like such adventures will be able to appreciate how much I enjoyed this after my dark night journey into the Harz. At times the effect was almost spectral, as though merry sprites were disporting themselves in a mountain cave.

After a good night's sleep I hurried early the next day, again accompanied by a guide, towards the Baumann Cave.[128] I crawled through it and observed quite closely the ceaseless working of natural processes. Black masses of marble which dissolved and were transformed into white crystalline columns and surfaces were evidence to me of Nature's tireless weaving at her loom. To be sure, the fanciful images which the gloomy imagination likes to create out of formless shapes vanished before a calmer gaze; but in return, what remained was all the purer and I felt myself greatly enriched by it.

Having returned to the daylight I noted down the most essential things, and at the same time, with a totally reinvigorated spirit, the first stanzas of the poem which under the title "A Winter Journey in the Harz" has won the attention of many friends down to the present day. I would therefore like to make room here for those stanzas which refer to the curious man whom I was soon to see, because they are capable, better than any number of words in prose, of expressing the loving and compassionate state of my soul at that time.

But who is it stands apart?
His path is lost in the brake,

Behind him the shrubs
Close and he's gone,
Grass grows straight again,
The emptiness swallows him.

O who shall heal his agony then
In whom each balm turned to poison,
Who drank hatred of man
From the very fullness of love?
First held, now holding, in contempt,
In secret he consumes
His own particular good
In selfhood unsated.

If in your book of songs
Father of love, there sounds
One note his ear can hear,
Refresh with it then his heart!
Open his clouded gaze
To the thousand fountainheads
About him as he thirsts
In the desert![129]

After arriving at the tavern in Wernigerode I got into a conversation with the waiter and found him to be a sensible man who seemed to know his fellow townsmen rather well. I told him it was my habit, when arriving in a strange place where I had no letters of recommendation, to inquire whether there were any younger people there who were particularly outstanding on account of their intellectual attainments; I asked him if he could name me such a person, so that I might spend a pleasant evening. The waiter replied without hesitation that I would unquestionably enjoy the company of young Mr. Plessing, who was the son of the church superintendent; even as a boy he had distinguished himself in school and he still had the reputation of being an industrious and intelligent young man, although people criticized his gloomy temperament and disapproved the unfriendly manner in which he kept aloof from society. He had been known on occasion, however, to show courtesy toward strangers, and if I wished to announce my presence, that could be done at once.

The waiter soon came back with an affirmative reply and led me there. It was already evening when I entered a large room on the ground floor, such as one meets with in parsonages, and in the dusk I could still make out the young man fairly distinctly. There were some signs that his parents had left hastily in order to make room for the unexpected visitor.

The light that had been brought in enabled me now to see the young man quite clearly, he looked exactly like his letter, and just like his letter he aroused my interest without exerting any power of attraction on me.

To get a conversation going I told him I was a sketch artist from Gotha. Because of family business I was on my way to Brunswick in this unfriendly season to visit my sister and her husband.

In his eagerness he almost interrupted me and exclaimed: "Since you live so close to Weimar, which is becoming so famous, I'm sure you must have visited the place many times." I affirmed this and began to talk about Councilor Kraus,[130] the drawing academy, Legate Bertuch[131] and his tireless work; I also mentioned Musäus[132] and Jagemann,[133] the conductor Wolf[134] and a number of ladies, and I described the circle of which these worthy people were members, in which strangers were always warmly welcomed.

At last he blurted out somewhat impatiently: "And why don't you mention Goethe?" I replied that I had seen him as a welcome guest in the aforementioned circle, and that as an artist from out of town I personally had been received well and helped by him, but I didn't know much else to say about him since he either kept to himself or moved in different circles than I.

The young man, who had been listening with restive attentiveness, now demanded impetuously that I describe for him this strange person about whom there was so much talk. With great ingenuity I delivered myself of the description he demanded, which was not at all difficult for me, because the strange person was standing right there in the strangest possible situation, and had the young man only been endowed by nature with a little more perceptiveness he could scarcely have failed to realize that the visitor standing before him was describing himself.

He had paced up and down in the room several times when the maid came in and placed a bottle of wine and a very nice cold supper on the table; he filled both glasses, we clinked them, and he emptied his at once. I had hardly emptied my own glass at a somewhat more moderate rate when he gripped my arm tightly and exclaimed: "You really must pardon my strange behavior! But you have inspired so much confidence in me that I must tell you everything. This man, as you have described him to me, should have answered me; I wrote him a long and heartfelt letter, described my situation and my sufferings, begged him to take pity on me, to give me counsel, to aid me, and now months have gone by and I have heard nothing from him; I should have deserved at least a negative response to the boundless confidence I placed in him."

I replied to this that I could neither explain nor condone such behavior, but I did know for a fact that this young man, who was otherwise quite well intentioned, benevolent, and ready to lend assistance, suffered so much from the demands made on his emotional as well as his physical constitution that there were times when he was totally unable even to move, much less to have any effect on others.

"Well, since quite by chance we have gotten this far," he answered with some composure, "then I must read you the letter, and you shall decide whether it did not deserve an answer, some sort of response."

I paced back and forth in the room while I waited for him to read the letter, almost completely certain what effect it would have on me and therefore not thinking any more about it, in order not to get ahead of myself in this delicate situation. He was sitting across from me and began to read the pages which I already knew backwards and forwards, and perhaps I have never been more convinced of the claim made by the physiognomists that a living being always acts and behaves in total accord with its own essence, and that every monad which partakes of actuality reveals itself in the perfect unity of all its attributes. The reader was totally identical with what he was reading, and just as this had not appealed to me earlier at a distance, now it was no better face to face. To be sure, I could not deny the young man a certain respect, a certain sympathy, which after all had led me on such a curious journey: there was a seriousness of purpose here, a lofty spirit and intent. But although he was talking about the most delicate sentiments, his reading lacked all charm, and he exhibited strong signs of a totally self-encapsulating egotism. When he had finished, he asked me hastily what I thought of it, and whether such a letter did not deserve, indeed demand an answer?

Meanwhile, the pitiable plight of the young man had become ever clearer to me; it was simply that he had never taken note of the outside world, although educating himself widely in books: but he had turned all his energies and inclination inwards and as good as destroyed himself in this way, since he found no productive talent in the depths of his life. He seemed even to have no sense for diversion and solace such as one can derive so wonderfully from the study of the ancient languages.

Since I had already made the happy discovery in my own case and also in the case of other people that in such a situation the best remedy was to turn swiftly and trustingly to nature and all its infinite variety, I now dared to attempt the same remedy here as well. Therefore, after some reflection, I answered him as follows:

"I believe I understand why the young man in whom you placed so much confidence has remained silent, because his present manner of thinking is too much at odds with yours for him to be able to hope that the two of you could reach any understanding. I myself have been present at a number of conversations in that circle, where I heard it claimed that the only way for a person to save himself and free himself from a painful, self-tormenting, and gloomy state of mind is through the contemplation of nature and genuine participation and interest in the outside world. Even the most elementary acquaintance with nature, from whatever point of view, or an active involvement, whether as a gardner or agriculturist, as a hunter or a miner, draws us out of ourselves; directing our mind to real and true phenomena affords, in time, the greatest pleasure, clarity, and instruction, just as the artist who remains true to nature while seeking to develop his inner resources will certainly achieve the most."

My young friend seemed to become quite restive and impatient during all this, just as we tend to become impatient with a strange or confused language whose sense we do not understand. I continued, without any particular hope of a successful outcome, but rather in order not to lapse into silence: "I, as a landscape painter, had to be the first to understand this, since my art is directly concerned with nature; but since then I have not only been more devoted and eager in contemplating extraordinary and striking scenes and phenomena in nature, I have also tried to show a loving interest in everything and everybody." And so as not to lose myself in generalities, I told him how even this winter trip, which I was taking only out of necessity, was not at all irksome but instead was constantly affording me some pleasure or other. As poetically and picturesquely, and yet as naturally and directly as possible, I described the progress of my journey: the snow-filled clouds above the mountains in the morning, the infinitely various things I had seen during the days; then I offered his imagination the curious towers and walls of Nordhausen seen at dusk,[135] and the waters rushing down the mountain at night, illuminated fleetingly by the guide's lantern, and finally I got to the Baumann Cave. Here, however, he interrupted me eagerly and assured me that he himself regretted the short trip he had taken to see it; it had in no way corresponded to the mental picture he had had of it. After all that had gone before, however, such morbid symptoms did not trouble me especially, for I had often had the experience that a person rejects the worth of clear reality in favor of the dismal phantom of his gloomy imagination. Nor was I surprised when in reply to my question as to just how he had imagined the cave he gave me a description such as the most audacious scenery painter would not have dared to paint of the outer courtyard of Pluto's realm.

After this I tried out a number of other propaedeutic arguments as experimental remedies for effecting a cure; but I was rebuffed so categorically with the claim that there was nothing in this world that could or should ever satisfy him, that my heart closed up. In view of the difficult journey I had undertaken, and conscious that I had come with the best will in the world, I considered my conscience completely clear and myself released from any further obligation toward him.

It was already late when he wanted to read me the second, more vehement communication, which of course was also not unfamiliar to me, but he let me excuse myself because I was so very tired, and extended an urgent invitation on behalf of his family to dine with them the following day. I reserved the right to reply to the invitation early next morning. And so we parted courteously and on good terms. His personality left behind quite a singular impression. He was of medium height, there was nothing attractive about his features, but there was also nothing particularly unattractive about them, his gloomy demeanor did not really seem impolite. He could have been taken for a well-brought-up young man who had quietly prepared himself in school and at the academy for the pulpit and the professorial chair.

Leaving the house, I found the sky quite clear and twinkling with stars, the streets and squares covered with snow; I paused on a narrow bridge and gazed upon the world in this wintry night. At the same time I thought back on my adventure and found myself firmly resolved not to see the young man again. I therefore ordered my horse for daybreak and gave the waiter an anonymous note of apology, written in pencil; and I managed to tell the waiter many good and true things about the young man he had enabled me to meet, which the clever fellow no doubt passed along to good advantage.

Having first visited the Rammelsberg, the brass foundries and other installations of that kind and gotten an impression of them, I rode on along the northeast slope of the Harz mountains to Goslar with a fierce blizzard blowing in my face. I will say nothing more about this part of the trip here, as I hope to give my readers a more detailed account sometime in the future.

I cannot say how much time had passed without my having heard anything more of the young man, when one morning I unexpectedly received a note at my Weimar garden house announcing his arrival; I wrote back a few words to say that he would be welcome. I expected some emotional scene when he recognized me, but when he came in he remained quite calm, and said to me: "I am not surprised to find you here. The handwriting in your note reminded me so much of the lines you left behind for me on departing from Wernigerode that I never doubted for a moment I would find that mysterious traveler again here."

This was already a promising start, and it led to a rather intimate talk during which he sought to explain his situation to me and I did not refrain from giving him my own opinion. I could not say any more to what extent his state of mind had actually improved, but it cannot have been too bad, for after several talks we parted on friendly terms—except that I found myself unable to reciprocate his avid desire for passionate friendship and an intimate relationship.

We kept up a correspondence for some time; I had the opportunity on several occasions to be of real service to him, which he gratefully recalled during our present meeting, and indeed the recollection of those earlier days afforded both of us some pleasant hours. He was as preoccupied with himself as he had always been and had much to tell and communicate about himself. Over the years he had succeeded in establishing a respectable reputation as an author. His special field was the history of ancient philosophy, especially that philosophy which inclined to the mysteries and the occult, from which he sought to derive the origin and primal condition of mankind. To be truthful, I had not read his books, which he sent to me as they came out, for his studies were too remote from the fields which interested me.

Nor did I find his present situation very agreeable; by frenzied effort he had finally stormed the stronghold of languages and history which he had so long neglected and rejected, and he had undermined his health by this intellectual excess. In addition, his economic circumstances did not seem very favorable, or at least his limited income did not permit him to take particularly good care of himself, and the morbid introspectiveness of his youth had never completely subsided. He seemed still to be pursuing the unattainable, and when finally we had exhausted our memories of the old days no other really pleasant exchange was possible. My present mode of being could be considered even more remote from his than before. We nevertheless parted on the best of terms, but him too I left behind in fear and anxiety because of the troubled times.

I also visited the worthy Merrem,[136] whose extensive knowledge of natural history allowed for a much more pleasant conversation. He showed me a number of items of importance and presented me with a copy of his work on snakes, and thus I came to follow his later career, from which I gained some profit for myself. And that is perhaps the most gratifying benefit of travel, that for the rest of our lives we never lose interest in people and places once we have become acquainted with them.

Münster, November 1792

I had announced my impending visit to the Princess and looked forward to comfortable conditions; but first I was destined to undergo another ordeal in keeping with the times: for I was delayed en route for various reasons and reached Münster only late in the night. I did not think it proper to strain her hospitality from the very beginning and appear without warning at such a late hour; so I drove to an inn, where, however, I was flatly refused room and bed; here too the émigrés had arrived en masse and filled up every nook and cranny. Under these circumstances I didn't waste time looking elsewhere and spent the hours on a chair in the taproom, in any case more comfortable than just a short time ago, when in the midst of violent storms it had been impossible to find any shelter at all.

The next morning I was amply compensated for this slight hardship. The Princess came to meet me, and I found everything prepared for my stay in her house. On my side the relationship was quite clear: I already knew the members of her circle quite well, I knew that I was coming into a devout and principled group, and behaved accordingly. They, for their part, proved themselves to be sociable, intelligent, and broad-minded.

The Princess had visited us at Weimar years ago in company with von Fürstenberg and Hemsterhuis; her children too had been along on that trip. At that time we had already ironed out a number of our differences and parted on the best of terms, conceding some things and not hotly contesting others. She was one of those individuals of whom it is impossible to form any picture unless one has actually seen her, whom one cannot judge correctly if one has not observed her individuality, not only when it agreed, but also when it conflicted with the spirit of her times. Von Fürstenberg and Hemsterhuis, two highly estimable men, were her faithful companions, and in such company both the good and the beautiful never ceased to be active and entertaining. Hemsterhuis had died in the meantime, von Fürstenberg was that many years older, but the same noble, understanding, and peaceful man. And what an extraordinary position he occupied in the world! A clergyman and a statesman, he had come within a hair's breadth of ascending the throne.[137]

Our first conversations, once we had finished talking about earlier times, were concerned with Hamann,[138] whose grave I soon saw in the corner of the leafless autumnal garden.

Hamann's great and incomparable qualities were the stuff for profound reflections, but nothing was said about his last days. The man who had been so important and edifying for these friends whom he had finally sought out became something of a burden to them in death—whatever conclusions one reached about his burial, it had been quite irregular.[139]

Seeing the Princess's way of life at close range, one could not but appreciate and respect it. Early in life she had come to believe that the world offers us nothing of great importance, and that it is necessary to withdraw into oneself and to be concerned about time and eternity within the confines of an intimate and limited circle of likeminded friends. She had come to terms with both time and eternity. She found the highest temporal values in what is natural, in which connection one must keep in mind Rousseau's teachings about life in society and child-rearing. She wanted to return to the simple and the true: stays and heels disappeared, powder was banished, hair was allowed to fall into natural curls. Her children learned swimming and running, perhaps also scuffling and wrestling. This time I would hardly have recognized her daughter: she had grown up and become sturdier, I found her sensible and gracious, a good housekeeper, adjusting to and accepting this half-cloistered way of life. That's how it was with the temporal present; they had found their eternal future in a religion[140] which solemnly promises those things which other creeds can only teach their adherents to hope for.

But the most gracious mediator between the worlds of the temporal and the eternal was charity, the gentlest product of earnest self-denial; their life was filled with the practice of religion and with doing good; moderation and frugality were everywhere evident in this domestic environment, daily wants were satisfied amply but simply. The residence itself, the furnishings, and everything else that went with it, appeared neither elegant nor costly; it looked as though it might have been merely a respectable rental place. The same was true of von Fürstenberg's domestic environment: he lived in a palace that was not his own, one that was not destined to be passed on to his children. And thus he demonstrated, just like the Princess, how to live a life that was simple in all respects, moderate, frugal, content to possess inner dignity and rejecting all outward show. The conversations that went on in this atmosphere were rich in warmth and spirit, serious, philosophical, enlivened by art; and if in philosophy people seldom start from the same presuppositions, one is heartened to find agreement most of the time in artistic tastes. Hemsterhuis, a sensitive Dutchman who had been trained in the classics from youth, had devoted his life to the Princess, as well as his writings, which bear throughout imperishable testimony to their trust in each other and to the similarity of their spiritual development.

With a discerning sensitivity all his own, this estimable man was led to strive tirelessly for moral and spiritual as well as for aesthetic values. If it is true that we must be wholly imbued with the moral and spiritual for them to be effective, it is just as true that we should surround ourselves with the beautiful. That is the reason why a collection of carved gems is so valuable for a private person who does not have a great amount of room and who also can't bear to be without the accustomed pleasure of art even when away from home. Something that is highly pleasurable, an instructive treasure that is not bulky or burdensome, can accompany him wherever he goes, and he can enjoy such a noble possession constantly.

But in order to acquire such a collection, more is needed than mere desire for it; in addition to the necessary means, one must above all have the opportunity, and this our friend had to the fullest. Living as he did at the juncture of England and Holland, keeping an eye on the flow of commerce and also on the art treasures that went back and forth, he gradually put together, through purchase and exchange, a beautiful collection of about seventy pieces, whereby he relied heavily on the advice and instruction of the excellent gem cutter Natter.[141]

The Princess had watched the growth of this collection almost from the beginning. She too had acquired a taste and a love for the hobby, as well as a certain amount of knowledge about the subject, and now the collection was in her possession, the bequest of her deceased friend, who seemed still to be always present in these treasures.

The only way I could understand Hemsterhuis's philosophy, his basic principles and his train of thought, was to translate it into my own language. According to his manner of speaking, we experience beauty and pleasure when, without great exertion, we can see and grasp the greatest possible quantity of representations in *one* single moment; I had to say, according to my way of speaking, that we experience the beautiful when we view something living in accordance with the laws of nature in its greatest activity and perfection and, stimulated to reproduce it, feel ourselves to be equally alive and spurred to the highest activity. On closer view the two statements say one and the same thing, only formulated by two different people, and I will refrain from saying more than that; for the beautiful does not give rise to anything as much as it promises something, whereas the ugly, arising from an interruption or a cessation, itself brings about cessation and does not allow us to hope, desire, or expect anything.

I thought that by this means I would be able also to interpret the *Letter on Sculpture* in my own terms; in addition, the little book *On Desire*[142] seemed to be clear when viewed in this light: for when we come to possess the beautiful which we have so ardently desired, it does not always fulfill in every particular what it promised as a whole, and hence that which excited us as a whole will not completely satisfy us in all its particulars.

These reflections were all the more relevant because the Princess herself had seen her friend ardently longing for works of art towards which he cooled once they were in his possession—which is what he had described with so much discerning and grace in the little book *On Desire*. Of course, one must keep in mind the question whether the object is worthy of the enthusiasm it inspires; if so, then our pleasure and admiration while viewing it should never cease growing and should forever be kindled anew. If the object is not completely worthy of our enthusiasm, then the thermometer will decline a few degrees and we gain in insight what we had to take away from our preconceived notion of the object's worth. This is why it is probably true that one must buy works of art in order to get to know them, so that the desire for them will be stilled and their true value can be made out. Here too, however, desire and gratification must alternate in a pulsing rhythm, must reach out, embrace each other and then let go, so that a person who has once been deceived will still not cease to desire.

Anyone who is familiar with Hemsterhuis' works will be in the best position to judge how receptive the group in which I found myself here was to such conversations—for his works had their inception in this circle and owed their life and nurture to it.

It was a great pleasure to return on a number of occasions to the carved gems; and surely it had to appear as the strangest paradox that such a high point of pagan culture should be preserved and esteemed in a devout Christian household. I did not fail to point out the most beloved motifs which sprang to the eye out of these worthy small works. Here too one cannot deny that imitations of great and valuable older works, which would otherwise have been lost to us forever, have been preserved for us like jewels in this small format, and in fact almost every type was represented. The most heroic Hercules, wreathed in ivy, could not deny his colossal origins; a grave head of Medusa, a Bacchus which was once in the Medici collection, charming sacrificial rites and bacchanalia, and in addition to all this the most precious graven heads of personages known and unknown aroused our repeated admiration.

From such conversations, which in spite of all their high points and depth were never in any danger of becoming abstruse, a consensus seemed to emerge, that veneration of a worthy object is always accompanied by religious feeling. Still, we could not deny that Christianity in its purest form is always somewhat at odds with true pictorial art, since the former seeks to distance itself from the world of the senses, whereas the latter acknowledges the sensual element as its most appropriate sphere and is bound to remain in that sphere. In this spirit I wrote down the following poem on the spur of the moment:

Amor, I don't mean the child, but the youth who led Psyche astray,
    Looked 'round on Olympus with pride, bold and always triumphant;
A beauty he spied, without doubt the fairest of all the goddesses,
    Venus Urania it was, and Amor's love was inflamed.
And even this holy person knew not how to withstand him:
    Audacious Amor soon held her fast in the arms of his love.
From the two of them sprang a new and more lovable Amor,
    Passion he got from his sire, morality came from his mother;
Always he is to be found among the fair graces and muses,
    His stinging arrow now serves to implant in us love of true art.

My friends seemed not altogether displeased with this allegorical credo, but the matter really went no farther and both parties made a point of discussing only those sentiments and convictions which everyone shared and which could serve the purpose of mutual instruction and amusement without provoking controversy.

But whenever the conversation threatened to lapse, the carved gems could always be brought up to get it going again. I for my part, to be sure, could appreciate only the poetic element, judging and praising the motif itself, the composition, and the execution, whereas my friends were accustomed to engaging in totally different reflections. For the connoisseur who wants to acquire such jewels and build up a notable collection never satisfies his sense of acquisition merely by appreciating the spirit and meaning of these precious works of art; in addition he is obliged to take into consideration certain external criteria which must be difficult for any but technical experts to apply. Hemsterhuis had corresponded with his friend Natter about this for many years, and many important letters were still preserved. The first topic of discussion was always the kind of stone the artists had used, for they had used different kinds in different periods; another significant point was the amount of detail in the gem. A large amount of detail work showed that it belonged to a major period in the history of art; less detailed work sometimes points to genius, but more often to inferior skill or carelessness and could be a sign of an earlier or a later period. Great value was placed on the amount of polishing in the deepest indentations, which was considered to be irrefutable proof that the gem had been carved in one of the best periods. But no convincing criteria had yet been developed for determining definitively whether a stone was antique or a modern product; even Hemsterhuis had never satisfied himself on this point, except when his able artist friend had concurred with him.

I could not conceal the fact that this field was altogether new to me and that I found it very appealing, regretting only that lack of time kept me from giving my eyes as well as my inner sense sufficient practice in making these distinctions. On one such occasion the Princess remarked quite simply that she was inclined to entrust the collection to me, so that I could study it at home with friends and experts and, with the help of various sulphur and glass impressions of other gems at my disposal, acquaint myself with this significant branch of pictorial art. I turned down this offer, which was no empty compliment and greatly tempted me, with my sincerest thanks; and, to be truthful, I must admit that in my mind my greatest reservation had to do with the manner in which this treasure was stored. The rings were in separate little boxes, one by itself, or two or three thrown together, as chance would have it; when showing the gems it was impossible in the end to determine whether or not any were missing, and the Princess herself confessed that once, in the best of company, a Hercules had got lost and had not been missed until later. And then it seemed quite risky to burden myself with such a valuable collection at the present time and to take on such an important and fearsome responsibility. I sought therefore, while expressing my sincerest thanks, to counter her offer with the most telling reasons for my refusal; she seemed to consider my objections carefully and without taking them amiss, and I moved on to draw her attention more forcefully to the objects themselves insofar as this was at all appropriate.

I was put under the necessity of rendering some account of my scientific studies, which I had rather sought to keep from mentioning in this company, as I thought there was little possibility of finding a favorable audience for them here. Von Fürstenberg mentioned that he had heard in various places, with a surprise that verged on consternation, that I was studying general osteology for the sake of physiognomy, which however, he thought, could hardly hope to offer any assistance in forming judgments of the facial features of humans. Now it may well be that I had told some of my friends about this in order to justify, and more or less introduce them to, the study of osteology, which was thought quite inappropriate for a poet, and said that Lavater's *Physiognomy* had caused me to return to this field of study with which I had first become acquainted during my years at the university. Lavater himself, the most successful observer of facial features, had found it necessary to depict a number of animal skulls in his work and had asked me to produce a brief commentary on them, because he had recognized the fact that the appearance of muscles and skin and their physiognomic effect are dependent upon the all-important internal bone structure. But everything I could recall of this at the moment or adduce in favor of my own method of operation was of very little help to me, because at that time such scientific considerations were too remote, and because, caught up in the social whirl of the moment, everyone accorded a certain importance only to the more mobile facial features, and even that perhaps only in passionate moments, without considering that this might be more than an arbitrary surface phenomenon and that the external, mobile, and changeable appearance should be regarded as the symptom of a meaningful internal structure.

My efforts at entertaining a large company were more successful than these lectures on science; the company included clerics with a good deal of sense and understanding, as well as aspiring young men, attractive and well educated, promising both in intellect and attitudes. Here, without being asked to, I chose to talk about the Roman church festivals, Holy Week and Easter, Corpus Christi, and the Feast of Saints Peter and Paul; on the lighter side there was also the Blessing of the Horses, a boon that was also extended to other domestic animals and pets. At that time these festivals were vividly present in my mind in all their characteristic details, for I was planning a work on "The Roman

Year,"[143] which would have dealt with the whole calendar of religious and secular public events; since I could describe those festivals from my firsthand impressions, I was able to please the devout Catholics as well as the more worldly among the guests with my depiction of the carnival. In fact, one of those present who was not quite clear about all the circumstances had asked confidentially whether I was really Catholic? When the Princess told me about this she also revealed something else: some one had warned her in a letter shortly before my arrival that she should be on her guard with me, because I knew how to make myself appear so devout that people would take me to be a religious person, indeed even a Catholic!

"My dear friend, you must admit," I exclaimed, "that I don't at all pretend to be devout, I really *am* devout where it matters, it is not difficult for me to observe everything with a clear and innocent eye and reproduce it again just as clearly. Every manner of grotesque distortion with which presumptuous people sin against the object while supposedly expressing their own mode of sensual perception was always repugnant to me. I avoid looking at anything I find truly distasteful, but I am happy to recognize the authentic character of many things which I do not exactly approve of; most of the time it turns out that other people are just as right to exist in their own manner as I in mine." And with this, another possible misunderstanding had been cleared up, and this secret attempt to meddle in our relationship, while to be sure it had hardly been justifiable, had produced not suspicion, as intended, but its very opposite, trust between us.

In such an environment it would have been impossible for me to be harsh or unfriendly; on the contrary, I felt in a gentler mood than I had been in for a long time, and I could scarcely have met with better fortune than this opportunity, after the terrible experiences of war and retreat, finally to feel again the effect that pious and moral people had upon me.

In one point, however, I failed to satisfy this good, noble, and morally uplifting company, though I don't understand myself how this could have come about. I had something of a reputation for reading aloud in a felicitous, free, and expressive style; my friends wanted to hear me read something, and since it was known that I was a passionate devotee of Voss's *Luise,*[144] in the version published in the *German Mercury* in November, 1784, and that I loved to recite it, they alluded to it several times without putting any particular pressure on me; they laid out that particular number of the *Mercury* under the mirror and waited for me to take the hint. And I can hardly say what it was that prevented me; it was as though my spirit and my lips were sealed, I simply could not pick up the volume, I could not bring myself to take advantage of any lapse in the conversation to give pleasure to myself and others; the time passed, and I am still at a loss to explain this obstinacy on my part.

The day of my departure drew near; it was time to take my leave. "Now," said the Princess, "I shall not allow any further objections, you simply must take the gems with you, I insist upon it." When I continued to decline in as friendly and polite a manner as I could, she finally said: "Then I must tell you why I asked you to do this. I was advised not to entrust this treasure to your care, and that is precisely the reason why I want to do so, must in fact do it; I was told that I don't know you well enough, after all, to be absolutely sure of you in this matter. But," she went on, "I answered: 'Don't you understand that the opinion I have formed of him is more important to me than these gems? If I had to abandon my high regard for him, then I might as well lose this treasure too.' " There was nothing more for me to say, for by such a statement she managed to honor me and put me under obligation at the same time. She cleared away all remaining obstacles; existing sulphur casts of the gems, which had been catalogued and could be used as a check in case that became necessary, were packed with the originals in a clean little chest, and the easily transportable treasure didn't take up much room.

So we bade one another an affectionate farewell, though we did not part immediately; the Princess said she wanted to accompany me as far as the next post station. She joined me in my carriage while hers followed along behind. We talked again about the most significant aspects of living and believing, I repeated my usual credo calmly and gently, and she remained firm in hers. Then we returned home our separate ways, she expressing the desire to see me again, if not in this life, then in the next.

This form of farewell, used by well-meaning and friendly Catholics, was neither foreign nor distasteful to me; I had heard it used often by casual acquaintances at spas, and otherwise by friendly clerics who wished me well, and I cannot see why I should be upset with anyone who wishes to draw me into his own sysem of belief, which according to his conviction is the only way to attain peace in this life and—since he is sure of eternal salvation—to face death calmly.

I was taken care of quickly by the first postmaster; thanks to my noble friend I was also announced in advance at the other post stations along my way, which was not only very convenient but in fact absolutely necessary. For while I had been enjoying such agreeable, friendly and peaceful diversions, I had forgotten that the refugees were pressing on my heels; and on the way I encountered the swarm of émigrés, who were pushing ever deeper into Germany. They weren't liked by the postillions here any better than they had been in the Rhineland. Often there was no real road at all, we drove now here, now there, encountered or crossed other vehicles. Heather and underbrush, tree stumps and sand, swamps and rushes, the one just as uncomfortable and unpleasant as the other. Tempers flared as well.

We came across a carriage stuck in the mud and Paul sprang down quickly to lend assistance; he believed that it was the beautiful French woman, whom he had met again in Düsseldorf in the most unfortunate circumstances, who again needed his help. The lady had not been able to find her husband, and, terrified and caught up in the general turmoil, she had finally been forced to cross over to this side of the Rhine.

It was not she, however, whom we had found in this wasteland; it was several old and venerable ladies who appealed to our sympathy. But when we tried to get our driver to stop and use his horses to assist them, he said defiantly that we should rather see to our own carriage, loaded down with gold and silver as it was, and take care that we did not get stuck or overturned; for while he intended to do his job properly he could not guarantee anything in this desolate region.

Fortunately for our consciences, a group of Westphalian peasants had gathered around the other carriage and got it back on the road again in return for a nice tip which had been promised in advance.

It was the iron fittings which most weighed down our own vehicle, for the priceless treasure we had aboard was so light that it would not have been noticed at all, even in a light chaise. How I wished for my little Bohemian carriage! The heaviness of our wagon, which seemed to be taken as an indication that we were carrying some important treasure, made me rather uneasy. We had noticed that at the post stations the postillion always told the new driver how heavy the carriage was and that we were probably carrying gold and valuables. But because our horses had been ordered in advance and we were always delayed anyway because of the bad weather, we were rushed through every post station and literally cast out into the night again. As a result we got into the nightmarish situation that in the dead of night the postillion finally swore he could not keep on driving and stopped at an isolated settlement in the forest; the locale and the crudeness of the buildings and the inhabitants would have caused us to shudder even in broad daylight. By comparison, even the gloomiest day was a blessing. I thought back on all the friends with whom I had spent such happy hours just a short time earlier; I regarded them with respect and affection, learned something from their peculiarities, and was impressed by their virtues. But when night fell again I felt myself once more caught up in all my cares and full of anxiety.

However somber my thoughts may have been in the last and darkest of all these nights, they brightened again as I drove into Cassel, which was lit up by hundreds and hundreds of lamps. The sight brought to mind all the amenities of urban living, the comforts each citizen enjoyed in his brightly lit home, and the pleasant accommodations available to travelers. But my spirits were dampened for a while when I drove up to the familiar inn on the magnificent Royal Square, where it was as light as day; my servant, who had gone in to announce my arrival, returned with the news that there was no room to be had. When I refused to budge from the spot, a waiter stepped up to my carriage very politely and apologized, in nice French phrases, for being unable to take me in. To this I replied in good German that it seemed strange to me that a traveler could not get a room for the night in such a place as this, when I knew from experience that it was quite large. "You are a German," he exclaimed, "That's different!" and he immediately allowed the postillion to drive through the gate into the courtyard. When he had shown me into a nice room, he remarked that he was determined to take in no more émigrés. They were both arrogant and niggardly; for in the depths of their misery, when they did not even know where to turn, they had not stopped acting as though they were masters in a conquered land. I left Cassel in peace and found the road to Eisenach less crowded with those guests who had so often and so unexpectedly been forced upon us.

Even my arrival in Weimar was not to remain without some small adventure, for it took place after midnight and was the occasion for a family scene which, had it occurred in a novel, would have lit up and cheered the deepest darkness.

I found the remodeled and well-furnished house my Duke had given me already habitable for the most part, but I was not altogether to be denied the pleasure of helping with and influencing the work. My family was cheerful and healthy, and when we began talking about how things had been there was, in truth, a great contrast between the cheerful and calm tranquility in which they had enjoyed those sweets I had sent them from Verdun and the circumstances in which we, whom they had believed to be in a kind of paradise, had actually had to struggle with every imaginable difficulty. Our quiet domestic circle was now richly and joyously enlarged by the addition of Heinrich Meyer,[145] our housemate, an artist, connoisseur, and collaborator, who took an active part in all my studies as well as my labors.

The Weimar theater had been in existence since May, 1791; the actors had performed in Lauchstädt the past two summers and, by repeating a number of the more important plays current at the time, had pretty well gotten used to working together as a company. Holdovers from the Bellomo troupe,[146] who were already familiar with each other's acting, formed the core of our company; other actors and actresses, some of them already quite accomplished, others still very promising, more than adequately filled in the existing gaps.

At that time acting could still be called a real craft, which made it possible for practitioners from all over to adjust to each other very quickly and work together in harmony, especially if one was fortunate enough to get North Germans for recitations and South Germans for the singing roles; thus one could expect to satisfy the audience, at least for the beginning. I shared the responsibility for directing the theater, and I found it a very pleasant task to look for ways in which to further the enterprise. I soon realized that a certain level of technical proficiency could be achieved by way of imitation, by putting the actors on an equal footing, and by virtue of routine experience, but there was a total lack of what I would call "grammar," which must exist first before one can proceed to rhetoric and poetry. Since I intend to return to this subject[147] and would prefer, for the moment, not to treat it piecemeal, I will only say that I sought to study and analyze thoroughly those techniques which are based wholly on tradition, and in individual cases I instructed the actors according to my insights, without at all going into general principles.

Something that was especially useful for this undertaking was the so-called natural and conversational tone that was becoming prevalent at the time; this manner is of course quite admirable and gratifying if it gets to the point of being a perfected art, a second nature, but not if everyone believes he has only to reproduce his own naked person in order to merit applause. I used this striving for my own purposes, for I was quite satisfied if the actor's natural talent could be brought out gradually, by means of certain rules and precepts, in order to be guided toward a higher degree of cultivation. But I cannot speak any more of this, because what we did and achieved developed little by little from its beginnings and would have to be described from start to finish.

But I must mention some of the circumstances which were favorable to the new theater. Iffland and Kotzebue[148] were in their prime and their dramas were simple and natural, some of them directed at a certain bourgeois smugness, others at loose morality; both these themes were timely and popular; other plays produced while still in manuscript were delightful because they captured so well the flavor of the historical moment. Schröder,[149] Babo,[150] Ziegler,[151] all of them successful and energetic talents, made a significant contribution; Bretzner[152] and Jünger,[153] also in this same period, catered unpretentiously to undemanding cheerfulness. Hagemann[154] and Hagemeister,[155] talents which could not really compete for very long, also strove primarily to please the audience, and while they were not greatly admired they were still perceived as new and welcome. Directors sought to raise the intellectual level of this fermenting mass with Shakespeare, Gozzi, and Schiller. They gave up the practice of learning and playing only new pieces, which then were quickly forgotten; they were careful in their selections and already working to develop a repertory which was influential for many years. But we must also make grateful mention of the man who helped us found this institution, F. J. Fischer,[156] an older actor who understood his craft and was moderate, restrained, happy with his situation, and content to portray only a limited number of roles. He brought along a number of actors from Prague who were content to perform in his manner and he treated the local actors well, so that an inner moderation governed the whole undertaking.

As far as opera is concerned, we were quite well served by Dittersdorf's[157] works. He had put his fortunate talent and good humor to work for a prince's private theater; this imparted to his productions a certain lightness which was of benefit to us as well, because we had had the good sense to conceive our new theater as a place where amateurs too could participate. We put great effort into the verse and prose of the text, in order to make it more accessible to Upper Saxon taste; and thus this light fare garnered approval and ready acceptance.

The friends who had been to Italy sought to adapt the lighter Italian operas of the time, by Païsiello, Cimarosa, Guglielmi, and others for our use, and in the end Mozart's spirit also began to have its effect. If one recalls that very little of this was known at all, and all of it was still fresh and new, then it must be recognized that the beginnings of the Weimar theater very much coincided with the beginnings or the rise of German theater generally and that it enjoyed some advantages which obviously were to facilitate its own natural development.

In order to pave the way for the study and enjoyment of the gem collection which had been entrusted to me, and to keep it more secure, I immediately had two trim little ring cases made, in which the gems stood next to each other and could be surveyed at a glance, so that any empty space would be noticed immediately; and after this was completed multiple sulphur and plaster casts were made and subjected to study under powerful magnifying glasses; in addition, we sought out and consulted all the available copies from older collections. We could see quite well that this was how we had to lay the foundation for our study of the gems, but we only realized gradually what a great favor our friend had done us in letting us have her collection.

Since we are unlikely to turn our attention to this subject again soon, let me summarize here the results of several years of study.

There were inherent artistic reasons why the Weimar friends felt justified in considering, if not quite all, at least by far the largest proportion of these gems to be genuine products of antiquity, and indeed there were a number of specimens in the collection which can be counted among the very finest works of this kind. Several of them actually turned out to be identical with older sulphur casts; we noted others whose subjects coincided with those of other antique gems and could for that reason be considered genuine. In the largest collections there are instances of multiple renderings of the same subject and it would be quite erroneous to insist on regarding one group as originals and the others as modern copies.

We must also always keep in mind the ancients' noble devotion to their art; if a subject had been treated once with great success, they could not repeat it often enough. Those artists considered themselves quite original if they could grasp an original thought and felt in themselves sufficient talent and skill to reproduce it in their own way. A number of gems turned out to have artists' names carved on them, which for years had been considered a mark of great value. Such an addition is certainly remarkable in itself, but most of the time it remains problematic: for it is always possible that the gem is old and the name was engraved later, in order to lend an even higher value to something that was already first-rate.

Although I have refrained here, as is proper, from simply cataloguing the gems, a bare description of such works of art without any illustrations can hardly give a good idea of them and for that reason I offer a few general remarks on some of the finest specimens.

Head of Hercules. Admirable because of the exquisite taste and freedom demonstrated in the work, and even more admirable because of the magnificent idealized features, which are not entirely the same in any of the known heads of Hercules and therefore add significantly to the unique character of this valuable gem.

Bust of Bacchus. The work is as though breathed onto the stone, and with regard to the idealized features one of the noblest works of antiquity. There are a number of pieces similar to this in various collections, and indeed, if we remember correctly, in low as well as high relief; but we know of none superior to this one.

Faun attempting to snatch off the clothing of a bacchante. A fine composition which occurs on a number of old monuments; also very good workmanship.

Overturned lyre, the horns representing two dolphins, the base Amor's head wreathed with roses; Bacchus's panther is an elegant part of the group, holding the staff of Thyrsus in its front paw. The execution of this gem will satisfy the connoisseur, and whoever loves subtlety will also be pleased by it.

Mask with large beard and wide open mouth; ivy entwines the bare brow. This gem is probably one of the finest of its kind.

Another very fine piece is a second mask with a long beard and gracefully gathered-up hair; the carving is unusually deep.

Venus suckling Amor. One of the most attractive groups to be found, handled with much spirit, though without any great expenditure of effort.

Cybele riding on the lion, deeply carved; a work whose excellence is well known to connoisseurs through impressions which are included in almost all collections of reproductions.

Giant dragging a griffin from its cave. A work of great artistic merit, perhaps totally unique in its composition. Our readers will find an enlarged illustration of it as frontispiece to the Voss Program in the *Jena General Literary Journal,* 1804, Vol. IV.

Profile with helmet and large beard. Perhaps it is a mask; but it has nothing at all of the caricature about it, a sturdy heroic face, excellent workmanship.

Homer as herma, represented almost full-face, cut very deeply. The poet is depicted here younger than usual, hardly at the beginning of old age; thus the work is noteworthy not only because of its artistry, but also because of its subject.

In collections of copies one often meets with the head of a venerable elderly man with long hair and beard, who is supposed to represent Aristophanes (without any reasons given for the identification). A similar head, showing only insignificant differences, is to be found in our collection and is in fact one of the best pieces.

The profile of an unknown person was probably found at a later period broken above the eyebrows and recut for a ring. We have never seen a human countenance depicted more nobly or full of life in the small compass of a gem, and seldom have we seen a case in which the artist displayed such consummate skill.

A similar subject is the portrait head of an unknown man in a lion pelt; like the preceding gem this one was broken off above the eye, but the missing part has been restored in gold.

Head of an elderly man of sturdy, strong character with close-cropped hair. Extraordinarily ingenious and masterly workmanship; the daring treatment of the beard is especially to be admired and perhaps totally unique.

Male head or bust, beardless, a band around the hair, a garment with deep folds gathered on the right shoulder. There is a strong and intelligent expression in this work, and features such as one is accustomed to ascribe to Julius Caesar.

Male head, also beardless, the toga drawn over the head as was the custom with sacrificial victims. The face displays extraordinary character and realism, and there can be no doubt that the work is genuine and dates from the period of the first Roman emperors.

Bust of a Roman lady; a double braid of hair around the head, the whole executed with admirable care and as regards character full of realism, contentment, naiveté, and life.

Small head with helmet, heavy beard and powerful character, depicted full-face, admirable workmanship.

In conclusion I should mention an excellent gem from a later period: the head of Medusa, carved in the finest carnelian. It is quite similar to the well-known Medusa of Sosicles and minor differences are hardly noticeable. Certainly one of the very best imitations of ancient works: for it must be considered an imitation in spite of its great merits, since the execution is somewhat less free than in genuine works and besides, an N engraved just below the neck indicates that it may be a work by Natter himself.

The foregoing brief remarks will be sufficient to give true connoisseurs a sense of the great value of this collection. I do not know its present whereabouts; perhaps one could get information about it which would induce some connoisseur of means to acquire this treasure, in case it is for sale.[158]

The Weimar art friends profited from this collection in every imaginable way as long as it was in their hands. Already during the very first winter it afforded pleasant diversion for the cultured group that usually gathered around Duchess Amalia. We all sought to acquire the basics necessary for the study of carved gems, and we were aided considerably by this generosity of the owner, who left it with us for several years. Yet shortly before her death she was able to feast her eyes on the beautiful visual array in which she found the gems laid out in the two little cases. She saw them all together at once for the first time and was thus richly rewarded for the trust she had placed in me.[159]

Our art studies too turned in another direction. I had made many observations on colors under the most varied conditions and had some hope of finally working out a theory of artistic color harmony, which had really been my original aim. My friend Meyer drafted various compositions for our examination and judgment, some of which were arranged in sequence, others in contrast to one another.

This harmony is seen most clearly in the objects in simple landscapes, where the yellow and yellow-red colors always had to be assigned to the light side and the blue and blue-red colors to the shadow side, though because of the variety of natural objects this can also be accomplished by brown-green and blue-green. Great masters had already set an example in the field of landscape painting, more so than in historical painting where the artist is left to his own devices in choosing the colors for garments and tends as a result to fall back upon common practice and tradition. He may even be led astray by some extraneous consideration or other and thus is often prevented from creating a truly harmonious work.

But I feel the need to leave these art studies and return to the subject of the theater in order to make a few observations on my own situation with regard to it, observations which I wish I could avoid having to pass on. One would think that this period would have offered me, as a writer, a great opportunity to make my own contribution to the new Weimar theater and to German theater in general: for it is obvious upon closer inspection that the dramatists mentioned above, and their works, left considerable room that could have been filled out; one only had to lay hold of and claim a wide variety of subjects suitable for simple and natural treatment.

But in order to make clear what I mean, I must recall my earliest dramatic works, which had taken world history for their subject and were consequently too wide-ranging to make really good theater.[160] My more recent works, dedicated to the most profound inner workings of the mind, had not been well received because of the strictness of their form.[161] In the meantime I had been practicing a certain middle style between the two extremes, in which I could have created some passable things for the theater; but I made a poor choice of subject matter, or rather there was one subject which completely laid hold of my inner moral consciousness, and it was a subject which was stubbornly resistant to dramatic treatment.

The diamond necklace affair of the year 1785[162] had already frightened me like the head of Medusa. I saw the dignity of royalty undermined and doomed by this incredibly wicked plot, and unfortunately everything that happened from that time on only confirmed my fearful forebodings. I carried them with me to Italy and returned with them even more intensified. Fortunately, I managed to complete my *Tasso,* but after that my mind was totally absorbed by the historical present.

For many years I had been dismayed at the frauds peddled by bold visionaries and calculating fanatics and had had occasion to curse them roundly; and I had been amazed and repelled by the incomprehensible blindness of otherwise intelligent people in the face of such brazen importunities. Now I saw before me the direct and indirect consequences of such follies, which had led to crimes and offenses against royalty and had an effect powerful enough to shake to its foundations the fairest throne in the world.

To find some solace and diversion I looked for a lighter side to these monstrous events; the *opera bouffe,* which had seemed to me for some time to be one of the best dramatic vehicles, seemed not unsuited for serious subjects as well, as can be seen in the case of *King Theodore.*[163] Consequently I worked up a subject rhythmically and discussed the musical composition with Reichardt.[164] From all this work there still exist rough versions of some fine bass arias which have become known; other pieces of the music which had no real meaning outside of their context were left unused, and the passage which had promised to be the most effective also was never finished. The dazzling finale was to have been the apparitions in the crystal ball in front of Cophta, who was telling prophecies in his sleep.

But the whole venture was ill-starred and threatened to bog down, and in order not to have wasted my time completely I wrote a prose piece for whose leading characters there were really analogous figures in the new theater company, and the company did its best in a very carefully prepared performance.

But precisely because the play was so well performed it made all the worse an impression. A terrifying but at the same time quite tasteless subject, treated boldly and relentlessly, scared everyone and appealed to no one. The fact that the events which I had taken as my model had occurred so recently made it seem all the more harsh; a great and respectable part of the public was alienated, because secret societies believed they had been portrayed unfavorably, just as feminine delicacy was horrified by such an unscrupulous romantic adventure.

I had always been indifferent to the immediate effect produced by my works, and now too I looked on calmly as this latest one, on which I had spent so many years, met with no sympathy at all; in fact I took some malicious delight in the fact that certain people who I knew quite well had often been exposed to deception declared roundly that it was impossible for anyone to be deceived so crudely as in my play.

But I didn't draw any conclusions from this failure. The things that were on my mind continued to appear to me in dramatic form, and just as the necklace affair had seemed to be a sinister omen, so now I was gripped by the revolution itself as its most ghastly fulfillment; I saw the throne overturned and smashed to pieces, a great nation in turmoil, and, in the aftermath of our unfortunate campaign, the whole world out of joint.

While all this was pressing on my mind and causing me anxiety, I was unfortunately forced to observe that in my country, too, there were people who toyed with sentiments which threatened to expose us to a similar fate. I knew plenty of noble souls who had succumbed to certain fanciful hopes and prospects without understanding either themselves or what was at stake; while of course there were also thoroughly unscrupulous elements bent on fomenting and spreading discontent, using it for their own purposes.

As evidence of my irritable good humor I allowed the *Citizen General* to go on the stage. I was seduced into this by an actor named Beck,[165] who had played the role of Schnaps in Anton Wall's[166] adaptation of Florian's *The Two Notes*[167] so well that even his failings redounded to the benefit of his performance. Since this mask was so becoming to him, we produced the first sequel of the very popular little piece, Wall's

Family Tree, and while I was devoting the closest possible attention to the rehearsal, design, and performance of this dramatic trifle it was inevitable that I became so entranced by this ridiculous Schnaps that I got the irresistible urge to reproduce him yet one more time. I did this with great pleasure and detail; and the valise that plays such an important role in the play was a genuine one that Paul had picked up hurriedly during our retreat. In the main scene Malkolmi was not to be outdone in his portrayal of an old, prosperous and generous peasant who can put up with even the most outrageous bit of impudence in fun, and he rivaled Beck in the credibility of his character. But in vain! The play had a thoroughly disagreeable reception, even among my friends and well-wishers, who stubbornly insisted, in order to save both themselves and me, that I was not really the author of the piece, but had only whimsically lent my name and a few revising strokes of the pen to a very inferior product.

But since no external thing could ever turn me from my purpose, but only pointed me back more rigorously into myself, such efforts to encapsulate the spirit of the times remained a kind of agreeably consoling occupation. The *Conversations of the Emigrés*,[168] a fragmentary attempt, and the uncompleted drama *The Enragés* are just a series of confessions of what was going on in my soul at the time. *Hermann and Dorothea* flowed from the same source somewhat later, a source which to be sure then dried up. The poet could not keep up with the headlong pace of history and had to leave the ending open when he saw the puzzle solved in a way that was as decisive as it was unexpected.[169]

Under such conditions there cannot easily have been anyone so far removed from the actual scene of all these catastrophes who was as oppressed by it as I was; the world seemed bloodier and more bloodthirsty than ever, and if the life of a king is to be reckoned equal to the lives of thousands in a battle, that life becomes even more important in a legal battle. A king is prosecuted for capital crimes, and thoughts begin to circulate, relationships begin to be talked about, talk which the monarchy had tried with all its might centuries ago to silence forever.

But I tried to take refuge from this awful catastrophe as well, by declaring the whole world to be worthless, and some special fate delivered *Reynard the Fox* into my hands.[170] Whereas previously I had had to sate myself with street, market, and mob scenes, and had had my fill of them, it was now truly refreshing to cast an eye on affairs at court and on the rulers: because even though the human race is presented here quite naturalistically in all its unmitigated bestiality, the story, if not exemplary, is at least quite merry and good humor prevails.

In order to enjoy this delightful work as thoroughly as possible, I immediately began with my own faithful rendering of it; but the reason for undertaking to write it in hexameters was as follows.

Following Klopstock's example, German poets had been writing quite tolerable hexameters for many years. Voss, while using them himself, hinted here and there that they could be done better, and he even criticized his own poetic works and translations, which had been so well received by the public. I would have been glad to learn this skill myself, but I had no success at it. Herder and Wieland were latitudinarians on this point, and it was not in good taste to mention Voss's efforts in their presence, as those attempts became ever stricter and seemed awkward for the present day. For a long time the public itself admired Voss's early works, which were better known, more than his later efforts; his sincerity could not be called into question, and I myself always retained great confidence in him, so that in my younger days, or in different circumstances, I would probably have made the trip to Eutin to learn his secrets. Out of reverence for Klopstock (a quite honorable motive), as long as the worthy and celebrated poet was still alive, Voss did not want to have to tell him to his face that stricter discipline had to be introduced into German prosody if it was to be worth anything. Meanwhile his utterances seemed to me like the Sibylline books. I still remember gladly the tortures I went through with his preface to the *Georgics*—because of my honest intention of trying to learn something, not because of what I was able to get out of it.

Since I was well aware that I could learn something only by experience, I jumped at the opportunity to write a few thousand hexameters, which could be counted on to meet with a good reception and enduring praise even if the technique were less than perfect, because the subject itself was so interesting. I thought to myself that their deficiencies would ultimately be recognized; and so I spent every free hour on this work which gave me so much pleasure, and in the meantime I kept on building and furnishing my house without thinking much about what was to happen to me, though I might well have been able to foresee it.

Despite the fact that we were far to the east of the momentous world events, a part of the fleeing vanguard of our exiled western neighbors still turned up in Weimar that winter; it was as though they were looking for some civilized place where they could find refuge and protection. Although they were only there briefly they behaved decently in every respect, were patient and contented, prepared to accept their lot and earn a living by their industry, and they were so successful in making a good impression on the citizenry that the failings of the émigrés as a whole were forgotten and antipathy was transformed into good will. And indeed this worked to the benefit of those who came after them and settled in Thuringia, among whom I need mention only Mounier[171] and Camille Jordan[172] in order to explain the good opinion that people had formed of the whole émigré colony there; they were not all equal to these two, but in no case did they prove themselves unworthy of them.

It can be remarked in passing that in political upheavals those spectators who take sides are always best off; they eagerly seize upon everything that is favorable, and whatever is unfavorable to their interests they either ignore or reject, or even manage to turn to their own advantage. But the poet, who by his very nature is and must remain neutral, seeks to comprehend the state of mind of both the opposing sides and must be prepared to end things tragically if reconciliation becomes impossible. And what a cycle of tragedies we saw ourselves threatened with by the turbulent course of events!

Who has not been filled with horror from his earliest youth by the history of the year 1649? Who has not shuddered at the execution of Charles I and consoled himself with the thought that such scenes of partisan fanaticism could never take place again? But now all of that was being repeated, day by day and step by step, even more abominably and furiously, by our most civilized neighbors before our very eyes. One can imagine what the months of December and January meant to those who had taken the field to save the King and now were unable either to intervene in his trial or to prevent his execution.[173]

Frankfurt was again in German hands and all possible preparations were being made to retake Mainz. The army had approached Mainz and taken Hochheim, and Königstein had been forced to capitulate. Now the most important task was to mount a preliminary campaign on the left bank of the Rhine, so as to safeguard the rear. Our forces marched through the Taunus mountains, passed by way of Idstein and the Benedictine cloister at Schönau to Kaub, and then across a well-built pontoon bridge to Bacharach; from there on there was constant skirmishing between the outposts, and the enemy was forced to pull back. Leaving the Hunsrück proper on their right, our forces marched to Stromberg, where General Neuwinger[174] was taken captive. They captured Kreuznach, cleared the area between the Nahe and the Rhine of all French forces, and could now safely march back toward the Rhine. The Austrians had crossed the Rhine at Speyer and it was possible to complete the encirclement of Mainz on 14 April and begin to alarm the inhabitants with the scarcities that ensued as a foretaste of even greater sufferings yet to come.

I received this news at the same time as the command arrived for me to appear in the field. I had participated earlier in a mobile misfortune, and now I was to experience a stationary one. The encirclement was complete, the siege was bound to follow; how unhappy I was about approaching the theater of war again can be seen by anyone who looks at the second etching made from my sketches.[175] The etching copied a very exact pen-and-ink drawing which I had done carefully a few days before my departure. With what feelings I made this drawing is expressed in the few verses I wrote to go along with it:

Here we are for now, peacefully at home,
Enchanting is the view from door to door;
The artist, watching, treasures those quiet glances
Of one beloved harking to the other.
And though we march through distant lands,
Here is where we start from and where we end.
We return, no matter how pleasant the world,
To our cozy home, which alone brings bliss.

Siege of Mainz

Monday, 26 May 1793 from Frankfurt to Höchst and Flörsheim; there was much siege artillery here. The old free road to Mainz was blocked, I had to cross the pontoon bridge at Rüsselsheim; the horses were fed in Ginsheim, which is very shot up; then across the pontoon bridge to the Nuns' Meadow, where many trees lay felled, immediately on across the larger arm of the Rhine on the second part of the pontoon bridge. Went on farther to Bodenheim and Oberolm, where I settled into my billet and immediately rode out with Captain Vent to the right wing by way of Hechtsheim, surveyed the positions of Mainz, Kastel, Kostheim, Hochheim, Weisenau, the Main Point, and the islands in the Rhine. The French had captured one of them and dug in there; that night I slept in Oberolm.

Tuesday, 27 May, I made haste to pay my respects to my Duke at the camp in Marienborn, where I also had the good fortune to wait upon Prince Maximilian of Zweibrücken,[1] my ever gracious lord; then I immediately exchanged my unpleasant billet for a large tent with the regiment. Now I wanted to get acquainted with the middle sector of the blockade semi-circle, rode to the fortifications in front of the Chaussée House, surveyed the situation of the city, the new French redoubt at Zahlbach, and the notably dangerous situation of the village Bretzenheim. Then I retired to the regiment and took care to get some exact outlines down on paper, in order to impress better on my mind the relationship and the distances between the principal localities in the countryside.

I paid a call on General Count Kalckreuth[2] in Marienborn and spent the evening with him; there was much talk about the rumor that there had been a commotion in the other camp the night before, as though a German general had gone over to the enemy, which had even caused a change in the passwords and led to several battalions being put on alert.

We talked further about details of the overall situation, about the blockade and the coming siege.[3] Much was said about the leading personalities and their relationships among themselves, which often have quite an influence without even being mentioned. We took that as evidence of how unreliable history is, because no one really knows why or how this or that thing happens.

Wednesday, 28 May, visited Colonel von Stein[4] at the ranger's house, which is exquisitely located; a truly pleasant place to be. One got an idea how comfortable it would have been to be Master of the Hunt to an Elector of Mainz. From this place one can oversee the entire basin stretching over to Hochheim, where in primeval times the Rhine and the Main turned and eddied and, overflowing, laid down farmland of the best quality before becoming fully free again to flow westward at Biebrich.

I ate at headquarters; we talked about the retreat from the Champagne; Count Kalckreuth let himself go talking about the theoreticians.[5]

After the meal a clergyman was brought in who was suspected of revolutionary sympathies. Actually, he was crazy, or wanted to appear so; he believed he had been Turenne and Condé,[6] and that he had not been born of woman. He claimed that everything was made by the Word! He was in good spirits, and in his madness there was considerable logic and presence of mind.

I asked permission to visit Lieutenant von Itzenplitz, who had suffered both gunshot and sword wounds on 9 May in an encounter outside of the city and had been captured. The enemy had treated him very well and soon set him free again. He wasn't allowed to talk yet, but he was cheered by the presence of an old comrade in arms who had a few things to talk about.

Towards evening the officers of the regiment gathered at the canteen, where everything was much more cheerful than last year in the Champagne: for we drank the local sparkling wine, and in a dry place in the most pleasant weather, at that! They remembered my previous prophecy and repeated my words: "From this time and place a new epoch is beginning, and you will be able to say that you were there." They had seen this prophecy fulfilled, strangely enough, not only in its general sense, but also quite literally and exactly, because the French dated their calendar from those days.[7]

As men always are, but especially in war, so it was here too: people put up with the unavoidable and seek to fill up the intervals between danger, distress, and discontent with pleasure and merrymaking. The musicians of the von Thadden regiment played "Ça ira" and the Marseillaise while we emptied one bottle of champagne after the other.

In the evening at eight o'clock there was a strong barrage from the batteries on the right wing.

Thursday 29 May at nine o'clock in the morning there was a victory celebration for the Austrian triumph at Famars.[8] This general firing of cannon helped me get to know the positions of the batteries and the troops; simultaneously there was a serious encounter at Bretzenheim, for indeed the French had every reason to try to drive us from this village, which was so close to the city.

In the meantime we learned that the rumor about yesterday's desertion had gotten started through a series of strangely illogical conclusions, in impossibly bad taste, but they had still been believed for a while.

I accompanied my sovereign to the left wing and paid a call on the Landgrave of Darmstadt,[9] whose camp was decorated very nicely with pine boughs, and whose tent surpassed anything I have ever seen, well designed, impeccably made, comfortable and imposing.

Toward evening there was a delightful treat in store for us, and especially for me; the princesses of Mecklenburg[10] had dined with His Majesty the King at the headquarters at Bodenheim and visited the camp afterwards. I secreted myself in my tent and was thus able to observe the high personages at close range as they walked back and forth directly in front of me, talking intimately with each other. And in truth, amid the commotion of war these two young ladies could be regarded as heavenly apparitions and the impression they made on me will never fade.

Friday, 30 May, in the morning we heard small arms fire behind the camp, which aroused some apprehension; it turned out the peasants were celebrating Corpus Christi. In addition, salutes were fired from cannon and small arms because of the fortunate turn of events in the Netherlands; this was punctuated by shooting both from and into the city. Thunderstorm in the afternoon.

Dutch artillery flotilla has arrived, waiting at Ebenheim.[11]

In the night of 30 to 31 May I was sleeping peacefully in my tent, fully clothed as usual, when I was awakened by the noise of small arms fire which seemed to be not very far away. I jumped up, went out of my tent, and found everything already astir; it was obvious that Marienborn was being attacked. Soon afterward the cannon of our battery in front of the Chaussée House were fired, which must have been meant for an advancing enemy. The Duke's regiment, a squadron of which was encamped behind the Chaussée House, marched off; it was not at all clear what was going on. The small arms fire at Marienborn, behind our batteries, continued, and the batteries were firing too. I got on my horse and rode farther forward, where I could get an idea of the area in spite of the darkness because I had familiarized myself with it earlier. I expected every minute to see Marienborn in flames and rode back to our tents, where I found the Duke's people busy packing and loading, ready for any eventuality. I entrusted my trunk and portfolio to them and discussed our retreat. They wanted to go toward Oppenheim; I could easily have followed them there, since I knew the footpath through the orchard, but I wanted to wait and see how things would turn out, not leave the place before the village was on fire and the fighting had come closer to us.

In this uncertainty I watched what was going on, but soon the small arms fire died down, the cannon fell silent, day began to break, and the village lay peacefully before me. I rode down towards it. The sun was rising with a melancholy gleam and the night's victims lay stretched out beside each other. Our gigantic well-dressed dragoons made a strange contrast to the dwarflike, fearless, ragged sansculottes; death had mowed them all down without distinction. Our good Major La Viére was among the first to fall, Captain von Voss, Count Kalckreuth's adjutant, was shot through the chest and was not expected to live. I had cause to write a short report about this strange and unpleasant incident, which I will include here, adding a few particulars.

I have the following to report about the French sally against Marienborn during the night.

The Marienborn headquarters are in the middle of the line of camps and batteries which start at the left bank of the Rhine above Mainz and extend back to the river below the city, forming a semi-circle with a radius between one and two miles. The chapel of Heiligkreuz and the villages of Weisenau, Hechtsheim, Marienborn, Drais, Gonsenheim, and Mombach are either on this circle or lie not far outside it. The two wings at Weisenau and Mombach had often been attacked by the French since the beginning of the blockade and the former village burned down, whereas the middle of the circle remained unmolested. No one could expect that the enemy would direct a sally against the middle, because they ran the risk of being attacked from all sides and cut off without achieving anything of significance. Meanwhile our outposts at Bretzenheim and Dalheim, two villages which lie in low country between Marienborn and the city, were skirmishing constantly, and we clung to Bretzenheim all the more tenaciously because the French had set up a battery at Dahlheim, a cloister close to Zahlbach,[12] and were using it to fire on the fields and the road.

We could not have anticipated the enemy's motive for undertaking a sally against the headquarters. We are now convinced from talking to the prisoners that the French wanted either to capture or kill General Kalckreuth, who had his quarters in Marienborn, and Prince Louis Ferdinand, who was quartered in the Chaussée House a few hundred paces from the village. They chose the night of 30 May and marched, perhaps 3000 strong, out of the low ground at Zahlbach, wound their way across the chaussée and through a number of low places in the terrain until they reached the chaussée again, crossed it a second time, and raced for Marienborn. They were well led and made their way between the Austrian and Prussian patrols, which unfortunately were not in direct contact with each other because of the uneven terrain. There was also one other circumstance aiding the French.

The day before, the peasants had been ordered to mow the grain standing between Marienborn and the city that night; when they came back from their work, the French followed them, which confused several of the patrols. They advanced pretty far without being discovered, and when our forces finally noticed them and opened fire, they rushed toward Marienborn and reached the village about one o'clock, when everyone was either asleep or not expecting any trouble. They immediately fired into all the houses where they saw lights, pushed through the street and encircled the village and the cloister where the general was staying. There was great confusion, the batteries began firing, the Wegner infantry regiment advanced immediately, and a squadron of the Duke of Weimar's regiment posted behind the village got there quickly as well as the Saxon hussars. There ensued a very confused engagement.

In the meantime we heard firing from decoy attacks along the whole front of the blockade circle, every unit had to look after itself and none dared to hasten to the aid of the other.

The waning moon gave only a moderate amount of light. The Duke of Weimar rushed up with the rest of his regiment, which was encamped on a hill a quarter-hour's march from Marienborn, Prince Louis Ferdinand led the Wegner and Thadden regiments, and after an hour and a half the French were driven back toward the city. They left thirty dead and wounded behind; it is not known how many they may have carried back with them.

I put the Prussian losses at some ninety dead and wounded. Major La Vière of the Weimar regiment is dead, Captain and Adjutant von Voss mortally wounded. An unfortunate accident led to higher losses on our side: for while our sentries were trying to withdraw from Bretzenheim in the direction of Marienborn they found themselves in the midst of the French forces and were fired upon by our own batteries.

At daybreak we found wreathes of pitch and bundles of twigs coated with pitch all over the village; if they had pulled off their coup they intended to finish their work by setting the village on fire.

We learned that they had simultaneously attempted to get a bridge across from one of the Rhine islands close to the Main Point, where they had been ensconced for some time, to the next island, probably with the intention of moving against the pontoon bridges at Ginsheim. The second ring of the blockade circle was moved closer to the first, and the Duke's regiment is now positioned close by Marienborn.

It is known that national troops led the sally, then came troops of the line, and finally more national troops;[13] this is probably the reason for the rumor that the French were in three columns.

On 1 June the regiment moved closer to Marienborn; the day was spent in changing camp; the infantry too changed its position and we made various dispositions for defense.

I visited Captain von Voss, whose condition I found to be hopeless; he was sitting up in bed and seemed to recognize his friends, but he could not speak. We left after a hint from the surgeon; and a friend informed me on the way back that there had been a heated dispute in that very same room just a few days before, because one man had stubbornly insisted, in opposition to most of the others present, that Marienborn as a headquarters was much too close to the blockaded city, which was soon to be besieged, and that there was even some danger of being attacked there.

But because strong resistance to everything ordered and instituted from above was commonplace, no one thought any more about the matter and this warning, as well as a number of others, was allowed to pass unheeded.

On 2 June a peasant from Oberolm was hanged for having guided the French during the sally: for their circuitous approach would have been unthinkable without an exact knowledge of the terrain; unfortunately for him, he was not as skillful at getting back to the city with the retreating soldiers and was captured by patrols that had been sent out to mount as thorough a search as possible.

Major La Vière was buried before the standards with full military honors. Captain von Voss died. Prince Louis Ferdinand, General Kalckreuth and others dined with the Duke. Firing from the Rhine Point during the evening.

3 June. Large group for lunch with Colonel von Stein at the ranger's house; magnificent weather, indescribably beautiful view, enjoyment of the pastoral setting, saddened by scenes of death and destruction. In the evening Captain von Voss was buried next to La Vière.

5 June. Serious work continues on fortification of the camp.

Large-scale attack and cannonade on the Main Point.

On 6 June the Prussian and Austrian high commands dined with His Most Serene Highness[14] in a large paneled chamber built for just such occasions. A lieutenant colonel from the Wegner regiment sitting diagonally across from me observed me somewhat more attentively than was appropriate.

On 7 June I wrote a lot of letters during the morning. While I was dining at headquarters a major blustered a great deal about the coming siege and spoke indiscretely about what had gone on up to now.

Toward evening a friend took me to visit the aforementioned lieutenant colonel, who had expressed the desire several days earlier to make my acquaintance. We met with no special reception; night had fallen and there wasn't even a candle. Seltzer water and wine, always offered to guests as a matter of course, were wanting, conversation was almost nil. My friend, who ascribed this coolness to the fact that we had arrived too late, stayed behind a moment when we departed to offer his apologies, but the lieutenant colonel confided that it really didn't matter; for yesterday at table he had already seen by my face that I wasn't at all the man he had imagined me to be. We joked about this unsuccessful attempt at making a new acquaintance.

On 8 June I busily continued my work on *Reynard the Fox* and rode with His Most Serene Highness the Duke to the Darmstadt camp. I was glad to pay my respects to the Landgrave, who over the course of many years had never failed to be gracious to me.

In the evening Prince Maximilian of Zweibrücken and Colonel von Stein visited His Most Serene Highness the Duke; a number of things were discussed, finally also the not-so-secret secret of the siege, which was to begin very soon.

On 9 June the French mounted a successful sally against Heiligkreuz; they managed to set the church and the village on fire directly in front of the Austrian batteries, to take some prisoners, and then to retire to the city, although they did have some casualties.

On 10 June the French risked a daylight attack on Gonsenheim which was repulsed, but for a while caused us some anxiety about our left wing and especially the Darmstadt camp.

11 June. The site of His Majesty the King's camp now was selected and laid out, about a thousand paces above Marienborn, just on the slope where the Mainz basin ends in rising clay walls and hills; this provided the opportunity for a number of quite charming improvements. Skillful gardeners took advantage of a soil that was very easy to work, and it did not require much effort for them to create an extremely attractive park: the downhill side was graded and planted with grass, bowers built and climbing and descending paths dug out, surfaces leveled off where the military could show itself in all its splendor and glory, and contiguous groups of trees and bushes were incorporated into the plan, so that, with this splendid view, one could not but wish for the whole vicinity to be treated in like manner. Then we could have enjoyed the most magnificent park in the world. Our Kraus[15] sketched the view very carefully, with all the particulars.

14 June. A small redoubt which the French had built below Weisenau posed an obstacle to the opening of our first parallel;[16] it was to be captured during the night, and a number of people who knew about this went to the fortifications on our side of the right wing, from where one could get a good view of the whole area. Since we knew very well the spot against which our troops were to be directed, we expected that the firing between the attackers and the defenders in the night would afford a worthwhile spectacle. We waited a long time, but in

vain; instead of that spectacle we experienced a much more animated show. All our posts must have been attacked, for we saw heavy firing around the whole circle, without being able to make out any cause for it; but, in the spot where the action was supposed to have been taking place, everything remained dead silent. We returned in consternation, especially Mr. Gore,[17] who had been the most eager to see the troops firing at night. The next day brought an answer to the riddle. The French had planned to attack all our posts during the night and had therefore withdrawn their troops from the fortifications and grouped them for the attack. The troops we had sent out, who approached the redoubt with the greatest caution, had therefore found neither cannon nor resistance; they climbed into it and found it empty except for a single cannoneer, who was quite surprised by the night visit. During the general firing that went on everywhere else except where they were, they had plenty of time to destroy the walls and withdraw. The widespread French attacks had no further effect; the lines that had been alarmed calmed down again at daybreak.

16 June. The siege of Mainz, which had been talked about from the very beginning and kept secret from the enemy, was finally about to begin; it was whispered that the first parallel was to be dug tonight. It was very dark and we were riding along the familiar path to the Weisenau fortifications; we couldn't see or hear anything, but our horses suddenly pricked up their ears, and we became aware of a barely distinguishable procession right in front of us. Austrian soldiers dressed in gray, with gray bundles of sticks on their backs, were marching in silence, the only noise being the sound of shovels and trenching tools banging against each other from time to time. One can hardly imagine anything stranger and more ghostly than this repeated appearance of shapes that could be half seen, but never clearly. We remained where we were until they had passed, for from there we could look toward the place where they were go to work in the dark. Since such undertakings are always in danger of being betrayed to the enemy, we could expect that there would be firing from the city walls toward this area, even if it were only random fire without a definite target. We did not remain long in this expectation, however: instead, small arms fire suddenly broke out, precisely where the trenching was supposed to begin, something no one could understand. Had the French slipped out and dared to advance as far as our outposts, or even beyond them? It was totally incomprehensible. The firing stopped, and everything became utterly silent again. We didn't learn until the next morning that our own outposts had fired on the silently advancing column, thinking they were the enemy; the column faltered, became confused, everyone threw away his bundle of sticks, although they saved their shovels and trenching tools. The French on the walls had taken notice and were

now on their guard, the Austrians returned without accomplishing anything and the whole besieging army was in a state of confusion.

17 June. The French placed a battery on the chaussée. In the night terrible rain and wind.

18 June. When the experts discussed the recent unsuccessful attempt to begin the trenching, it turned out that the position would have been much too far from the fortress; therefore it was immediately decided to dig the first parallel[18] closer than originally planned and thus to gain a decisive advantage from the failure. This was undertaken and carried out successfully.

24 June. When they saw that the siege was on in earnest, the French and the Clubbists,[19] in order to cope with the growing shortage of foodstuffs, ruthlessly tried to rid the city of old people, the sick, women, and children, by sending them across the river to Kastel, where they were just as cruelly turned back by our side. The despair of defenseless and helpless human beings caught between internal and external enemies was beyond belief.

We did not neglect to go and hear the Austrians beat the tattoo, which surpassed that of all the other units in the allied army.

In the afternoon of 25 June no one could understand why there was heavy cannon fire at the end of our left wing; finally it turned out the firing was from the Rhine itself, where the Dutch fleet was carrying out maneuvers for His Majesty the King; His Majesty had gone to Eltville for that purpose.

27 June. Beginning of the bombardment, which immediately set the cathedral chapter house on fire.

In the night our forces made a successful attack on Weisenau and the fortifications above the Carthusian monastery, absolutely indispensable positions for securing the right wing of the second parallel.

28 June, night. Continuing bombardment of the cathedral; tower and roof burn and many houses round about. After midnight the Jesuit church.

We watched this terrible spectacle from the redoubt in front of Marienborn; the night was absolutely clear and full of stars, the bombs seemed to vie with the heavenly lights, and there were moments when it was really impossible to distinguish between the two. The ascending and descending of the incendiary bombs was something new to us; for though they threatened at first to reach the very firmament in a flat circular curve, they always reached a certain height and then fell again on a parabolic path, and soon the rising flames showed that they had reached their target.

Mr. Gore and Councillor Kraus treated this event artistically and made so many sketches of fires that they were later able to produce a translucent model of this night scene; the model still exists, and when well illuminated it is capable of conveying, better than any number of words, the impression made by the misery of a national capital on fire.

And was not such a sight a sign of the sad situation we were in, that in order to save ourselves and more or less to recover our position, we had to resort to such means?

29 June. For a long time there had been talk of a floating battery which had been built at Ginsheim and was to be used against the point of the Main and the islands closest to it and take control of them. In fact it was spoken of so much that we finally forgot about it. I had just arrived on my usual afternoon ride to the fortifications behind Weisenau when I noticed a great deal of movement on the river: French boats were rowing furiously towards the islands, and the Austrian battery, which had been emplaced so as to cover the river down to that point, was continually shooting cannon balls to richochet across the water, something I had never seen before. When the ball hit the water the first time it caused a great splash that went many feet into the air; the first column of water had not yet come down completely when a second spout was thrown up, strong like the first but not quite so high, and then followed a third, a fourth, ever declining in height, until finally the ball reached the vicinity of the boats, skimming the top of the water and posing only a certain incidental danger to them.

I could not get enough of this spectacle, for one shot followed the other, causing new and powerful fountains of water to rise into the air before the first ones had even completely subsided.

Suddenly a strange machine emerged from the bushes and trees over on the right bank; something like a large rectangular room built of beams floated out, to my great surprise, but also to my great delight that I was to be a spectator during this important and much talked-about expedition. But my good wishes seemed to have little effect, my hopes didn't last long: for very soon this thing was turning round and round in the water and it was obvious that it couldn't be steered, the current carried it along, spinning around all the time. Everything was in motion at the Rhine fortifications above and in front of Kastel, hundreds of French were running along the bank and set up a joyous shout as this Trojan water horse, far from its goal, was caught up in the current of the Main where it flows into the Rhine and relentlessly carried along by the merging rivers. Finally the current drove the helpless machine toward Kastel, where it ran aground on a shoal not far from the pontoon bridge. All the French soldiers gathered there, and just as I had so far been able to observe everything very clearly through my excellent spyglass, I now unfortunately saw the trapdoor open and the men inside come out to be taken prisoner. It was an exasperating sight; the plank did not reach to the dry land and the small crew had to wade through the water to reach the circle of their captors. There were forty-six men, two officers, and two cannon; they were treated well, taken to Mainz, and finally brought to the Prussian camp to be exchanged.

Upon my return I did not fail to report on this unexpected happening; no one wanted to believe it, as I myself had hardly believed my own eyes. Quite by chance His Royal Highness the Crown Prince was visiting the Duke of Weimar in his tent, I was called in, and had to tell the story from start to finish; I described exactly what had happened, but very unwillingly, in the knowledge that the messenger who brings bad tidings is always blamed, at least in part, for the misfortunes he has to relay.

Among the misperceptions of various kinds to which we are subject when we meet with unexpected events in an unusual situation there are quite a few that can only be countered at the time they occur. Toward evening I had ridden along the usual path to the fortifications at Weisenau without any problem; the path led through a small depression where there was neither water nor swamp, nor a ditch, nor any other obstacle to be noted. When I was returning, it had become night, and just as I was about to ride into that particular low place I saw a black line drawn across the other side, which could be distinguished quite clearly from the dark brown earth. I had to think it was a trench, but it was incomprehensible to me how a trench could have been dug across my path in such a short time. I had no alternative but to ride up to it.

As I came closer the black line remained, but it seemed to me that in front of it there were things moving, and soon I was hailed and found myself in the midst of familiar cavalry officers. It was the Duke of Weimar's regiment, which had marched out for some reason or other, I do not know why, and taken up a position in this depression, where the long line of black horses had appeared to me to be some kind of a hollow crossing my path. After mutual greetings I hurried back to the tents with no further incident.

And so the endless inner misfortune of a city had gradually become, outside the city and in the vicinity, the motivation for pleasure trips. On Sundays and holidays the fortifications above Weisenau, which afforded a splendid view and were visited every day by individuals who wanted to get a picture of the situation and see what was happening in the large area that could be surveyed from there, became the meeting place of countless persons from all over the countryside. The French could not do much in the way of threatening these fortifications; most of the time when they tried to loft cannon balls into the position they overshot it. When the sentries pacing back and forth on the ramparts noticed that the French were firing their cannon in this direction, they shouted "Duck!" and then it was expected that everyone would go down on hands and knees so as to be protected by the rampart against any cannon ball that happened to come in low enough.

It was great fun on Sundays and holidays to see how the large crowd of dressed-up peasants, often still with prayerbook and rosary in hand, arrived from church and filled up the fortification, looked around, talked, and joked; but when the sentry suddenly called out "Duck" they all quickly fell to their knees before this dangerous and awe-inspiring phenomenon and seemed to be praying to some divine being that was passing overhead. But soon, after the danger had passed, they would pick themselves up and tease each other until they had to kneel again, whenever it so pleased the besieged. It was possible to get a good view of this spectacle if one took up a position on the next hill, somewhat out of the line of fire, looked down upon this unusual crowd, and heard the cannon balls whistling by.

But such cannon balls as flew away over the fortifications did not fail to serve a purpose after all. The road from Frankfurt stretched along the top of these hills, so that from Mainz one could see quite clearly the procession of coaches and chaises, riders and pedestrians, and the balls could strike fear into the people in the fortifications and into the travelers at the same time. Soon after the military had taken note of this they prohibited the presence of so many people in the fortifications, and the people coming from Frankfurt made a detour which allowed them to reach the headquarters without being noticed or shot at.

End of June.—During a restless night I amused myself by listening to the various sounds far and near, and could make out the following quite distinctly:

"Who goes there?" the sentry in front of the tent.
"Who goes there?" the infantry guard.
"Who goes there?" when they made the rounds.
Pacing of the sentry up and down.
Clanging of sabers on spurs.
Barking of dogs in the distance.
Growling of dogs close by.
Crowing of roosters.
Pawing of horses.
Snorting of horses.
Chopping straw.
People singing, talking, and quarreling.
Thunder of cannons.
Cattle lowing.
Mules braying.

Gap

That there is one here shouldn't surprise anyone. Every hour could bring great misfortune; every moment I had cause to worry about my beloved sovereign, my best friends, and I forgot to think of my own safety. Attracted by the wild and boundless danger as though by the stare of a rattlesnake, I plunged without any calling into all the most dangerous areas, rode and walked through the trenches, experienced howitzer shells exploding resoundingly over my head and fragments falling next to me; there was many a badly wounded man for whom one wished speedy release from his awful suffering, and one would not have wanted to bring the dead back to life.

One could say much about the relative positions of the defenders and the attackers. When danger first threatened, the French had taken their precautions in good time and constructed some excellent smaller redoubts out in front of their main fortifications, in order to keep the blockading army at a greater distance from them and to make the siege even more difficult. Now all these obstacles had to be cleared away so that the third parallel could be opened, continued, and secured, as I have recorded, with particulars, in the following narrative.

We however, in the meantime, though we had no orders or calling to do so, were always going with our friends to the most dangerous spots. Weisenau was in German hands and the fortification downstream from there had also been taken; we visited the ruined village and went through whatever diseased bones were left in the charnel house, though the best specimens were probably already in the hands of the surgeons. But because the cannon balls from the French fortifications were continuing to land in the rubble of ruined roofs and walls, we gave one of the soldiers from the outpost there a tip to take us to a well-known and prominent spot from which we could see quite a bit, so long as we exercised a certain amount of caution. We picked our way carefully through ruin after ruin and were finally led up a circular stone staircase to the balcony window of a free-standing gable, which in peacetime must have provided its owner with a truly magnificent view. Here we could see the confluence of the Main and Rhine, along with the Rhine-Main Point, the Lead Meadow, the fortifications at Kastel, the pontoon bridge and then, on the left bank, the magnificent city; the collapsed towers, roofs with holes in them, and smoking ruins were a melancholy sight.

Our guide told us to be careful and to look around the edges of the windows one at a time, because a cannon ball would be shot over immediately if we were seen and he would get into trouble if he were the cause of such firing.

Not satisfied with this we crept down to the nunnery, which indeed was also a desolate enough sight; down in the cellars we were served wine at a good price, while the cannon balls made holes in the rattling roofs from time to time.

But our undisciplined curiosity drove us even farther; we crept into the last redoubt on the right wing, which had been dug deep into the glacis of the fortress above the ruins of the Elector's pleasure palace and the Carthusian monastery, where behind a bulwark of wicker baskets filled with stones cannon fire was exchanged at a range of a few hundred paces—where, to be sure, it was a matter of which side was fortunate enough to be able to silence the other first.

To be quite honest, it was dangerous enough here to satisfy me, and I was not surprised to experience another attack of that cannon fever here; I withdrew now the same way I had come, and yet I returned again and again to the same dangerous place, whenever there was opportunity and occasion to do so.

If one considers the fact that this situation, where I exposed myself to every possible danger in order to drown out the voice of fear, lasted almost three weeks, then I may be forgiven if my account races through these terrible days as though over a bed of hot coals.

---

1 July. The third parallel was in operation and the battery on the Bock immediately came under bombardment.

2 July. Bombardment of the citadel and the Charles fortifications.

3 July. New fires in the Chapel of St. Sebastian; neighboring houses and palaces go up in flames.

6 July. The so-called Clubbist redoubt, which kept us from completing the right wing of the third parallel, had to be captured; but they missed it, attacking some of the fortifications in front of the main wall, and it is not surprising that they were beaten back.

7 July. Finally in control of the terrain; Kostheim is attacked and the French give it up.

---

13 July, night. The city hall and a number of other public buildings burn down.

14 July. Cease-fire on both sides, a holiday and a day for rejoicing; for the French because of the National Confederation[20] established in Paris, for the Germans because of the capture of Condé;[21] the Germans celebrated with cannon and small arms fire, the French with a theatrical celebration of freedom about which there was a lot of talk.

Night of 14–15 July. The French are driven out of a battery in front of the Charles fortifications; terrible bombardment. Firing from the Main Point across the Main sets fire to the Benedictine monastery at the citadel. Firing from the other side of the Rhine sets fire to the munitions factory and it explodes. Windows, shutters, and chimneys on this side of the city break or collapse.

On 15 July we visited Mr. Gore at Kleinwintersheim and found Councilor Kraus in the process of painting a portrait of our dear friend which turned out very well. Mr. Gore was all dressed up, because he was going to put in an appearance at the Duke's table after first looking around the countryside again. Now he was sitting on a chest in a peasant's room in a little German village, surrounded by all kinds of household and agricultural implements, next to him his half-eaten sugarloaf on a piece of paper; he was holding a coffee cup in one hand and a silver drawing pen instead of a spoon in the other; and so the Englishman was quite decently and comfortably established in this simple billet. Because of this painting we can see him and remember him fondly every day.

Since we have mentioned this friend here, we should go on to say more about him. He was very skilled at drawing in the camera obscura and in this manner he had collected the most exquisite souvenirs of his travels on sea and land. Now, living in Weimar, he could not bring himself to give up his accustomed mobility and was always ready to undertake short trips on which Councilor Kraus was in the habit of accompanying him; Kraus had the knack of getting a landscape down on paper easily and successfully, then putting in the shadows and coloring it, so the two of them were always in friendly competition.

The siege of Mainz, a rare and important event in which misfortune itself promised to yield material for the artist, also lured the two friends to the Rhine, where they were never idle for a single moment.

And thus they also accompanied us on one of those dangerous expeditions to Weisenau, where Mr. Gore particularly enjoyed himself. We visited the cemetery again in our search for pathologically interesting bones; a part of the wall facing Mainz had been shot up and one had a view across the open country toward the city. Hardly had the French on the walls taken note of something moving in this sector than they began to send cannon balls richocheting toward this opening; we would see the ball coming, striking the earth repeatedly and kicking up dust; finally we would duck behind what was left of the wall or down into the charnel house and gaily watch the ball rolling on through the cemetery.

Repeating this pleasure seemed somewhat questionable to Gore's old valet. Concerned about his master's life and limbs, he made a strong appeal to our consciences and persuaded the daring group to withdraw.

16 July was a worrisome day for me. I was oppressed by the knowledge of what was to happen in the coming night, which was to be a dangerous one for my friends. The situation was as follows. One of the small enemy redoubts out in front of what we called the "Frog" fortification was quite capably fulfilling its function: it posed the greatest obstacle to our most advanced parallel and simply had to be captured,

no matter what the cost. There was no denying this, but there was one considerable circumstance to be taken into account. In accordance with the intelligence we had, or rather the assumption, that the French had stationed cavalry behind this redoubt, which was protected by the artillery of the fortress, cavalry was to be taken along on this expedition. Anyone can comprehend what this meant: to get out of the trenches and form up a cavalry assault directly in front of the cannon of both the redoubt and the fortress, and for the cavalry to engage in combat in the dead of night on a glacis which was occupied by the enemy; but for me it was cause for great anxiety to know that von Oppen, my very best friend in the regiment, had orders to take part in this assault. Toward nightfall, however, we had to take leave of each other and I hurried to redoubt number four, where I would have a rather good view of the area in question. From a distance we could tell that the action was under way and was quite heated, and it was to be foreseen that many a brave man would not return from it.

But morning told us that the attack had succeeded, our forces had captured the redoubt, razed it, and taken up such a strong position across from it that it would be impossible for the enemy to use it again. My friend Oppen returned unharmed; those who were missing were not such close friends of mine; we were only sorry for Prince Louis Ferdinand, who had daringly led the attack, suffered a wound which, while not dangerous, was quite bothersome, and was very reluctant to leave the scene at such a moment.

17 July. Prince Louis Ferdinand was transported by ship to Mannheim; the Duke of Weimar took over his quarters in the Chaussée House; it is impossible to imagine a more delightful abode.

In accordance with my usual love of order and cleanliness I had the nice plaza in front of the house swept and cleaned. It was littered with straw and shavings and all kinds of refuse because of the speed with which the quarters had had to be vacated.

The afternoon of 18 July, after great and almost unbearable heat, there followed thunder, wind, and rain, all in all a welcome relief, but very much of a tribulation for the men in the trenches.

The commandant makes proposals for a capitulation agreement, but they are rejected.

19 July. The bombardment continues, the mills on the Rhine are damaged and made unusable.

20 July. The French commandant, General d'Oyré, submits a list of conditions and there are negotiations.

Night of 21–22 July. Fierce bombardment, the Dominican church goes up in flames, on our side a Prussian munitions factory also explodes.

22 July. When we heard that there was really a truce we rushed to

headquarters to await the arrival of the French commandant d'Oyré. He arrived, a tall, well-built, slender man in middle age, quite natural in his bearing and behavior. While the negotiating was going on inside, we were all attentive and hopeful; when it was announced, however, that they had reached agreement and the city would be handed over the next day, many of us experienced the strange feeling of suddenly being freed of the previous burdens, pressure, and anxiety, so that a number of my friends and I could not restrain ourselves from mounting our horses and riding toward Mainz. On the way we caught up with Sömmerring,[22] who also was hurrying toward Mainz with a companion; to be sure, his motivation for going was stronger than ours, but he too was oblivious to the danger of such an undertaking. We saw from afar the barrier at the outermost gate and behind it a large mass of people who were chafing at the restraint and pushing against it. Now we saw pitfalls in front of us, but our horses, already accustomed to such things, got us safely through them. We rode directly up to the barrier and the people called out to ask what news we brought. There were very few soldiers in the crowd, it was mostly citizens, men and women alike; our answer, that we could offer them the prospect of a truce, and that tomorrow the city would probably be freed and opened up, was received with loud approval. We traded as much information back and forth as we wanted, and just as we were about to turn around and go back, accompanied by the blessings of the people, Sömmerring arrived and started talking where we had left off, found a number of familiar faces, got into more intimate conversation with them, and finally disappeared without our noticing; but we thought it was time to go back.

The same desire and striving was shared by a number of émigrés from Mainz,[23] who contrived to make their way, carrying victuals, first into the outer works and then into the fortress itself, in order to be reunited with those who had remained behind and to bring them refreshment. We met a number of those passionate wanderers, and this flow reached such intensity that finally, after the number of guards had been doubled, a strict prohibition was issued against approaching the city walls; communications were cut off at once.

23 July. Our army spent this day occupying the outer works of Mainz and Kastel. I took a ride around the city in a light chaise, approaching as close as the sentries would allow. We visited the trenches and inspected the work that had been abandoned as useless, now that we had attained our goal.

While I was driving back, a middle-aged man called to me and asked me to let his son, about eight years old, whom he was leading by the hand, ride with me. He was a citizen of Mainz who had emigrated from the city and now, with great haste and delight, had left the place where he had been staying and hurried, exuberant about the victory, to see the enemy march out of the city, and he swore he would bring death and destruction to any Clubbists who remained behind after the French had departed. I tried to calm him down and explain to him that the return to a state of calm and internal peace should not be marred by new civil war, hatred, and revenge, because then the city's misery would never end. I told him that the punishment of the guilty people would have to be left to the Allies and to the legitimate ruler upon his return, and I said whatever else I could think of to calm him down and make him understand the seriousness of the situation; and I had a perfect right to do this, since I had taken his child into my chaise and had refreshed them both with pretzels and a drink of good wine. I let the boy out at the place we had agreed upon; I could already see the father coming from a distance and he waved his hat to me in a gesture of thanks and blessing for my good deed.

24 July. The morning passed rather calmly, the enemy's departure was delayed, as there were supposedly some financial matters which could not be dealt with so quickly. Finally at noon, when everybody was busy eating and both the camp and the chaussée were quite peaceful, a number of three-horse carriages drove past quickly, a certain distance apart, without anyone noticing or thinking much about them; but soon the rumor spread that it had been some of the Clubbists who had made their escape in this bold and clever fashion. Their most passionate enemies claimed that we had to chase after them, others were inclined to accept the chagrin of having let them escape, while yet others were intrigued by the idea that along the whole stretch there had been no sign of a guard, or pickets, or any observers whatsoever; from which they claimed that it was quite clear that our people, from the top on down, had been inclined to look the other way and leave things to chance.

These reflections, however, were interrupted and given new direction by the actual departure of the enemy. Here again the windows of the Chaussée House stood us in good stead. We watched the procession approaching in all its solemnity. The French garrison, conducted by Prussian cavalry, was the first to pass by. There was nothing more curious than the way this part of the march began; a column of troops from Marseilles, small, dark, many-colored and ragged in dress, tripped by, as though King Edwin[24] had opened up the mountain and sent forth a high-spirited army of dwarves. They were followed by somewhat more regular army troops, somber and out of sorts, but not depressed or shamed by their defeat. Everyone agreed, however, that the mounted fusiliers presented the most memorable sight; they had marched quietly until they got very near to us, and then their musicians began playing the Marseillaise. This revolutionary Te deum has something sad and eerie about it, no matter how briskly it is played; but this time they took the tempo very slowly, corresponding to the creeping pace at which they were riding. It was gripping and terrible, and a very solemn sight, when these riders, tall thin men, all of them middle-aged, approached, the expression on their faces in keeping with those sounds; any single one of them could have been compared to Don Quixote, but en masse they were very impressive.

The French commissars made up a noteworthy group. Merlin de Thionville,[25] dressed in a hussar costume, was distinguished by his wild beard and eyes. On his left was a figure in identical costume; the crowd of Mainz refugees, outraged, shouted the name of one of the Clubbists and surged forward to attack him. Merlin stopped, reminded them of the respect due a representative of the French people and the vengeance that would be meted out to anyone who insulted him: he advised them to restrain themselves, for this was not the last time they would see him here. The crowd stood as though transfixed, not a single person daring to approach. Merlin had spoken to several of our officers who were standing there, reminding them of the King's word of honor, and as a result no one dared make a move either to attack him or to come to his defense. The procession passed without any interference.

25 July. In the morning I noted that again, unfortunately, there had been no measures taken to prevent disorders on or near the chaussée. Such measures seemed all the more necessary today, as the poor, endlessly miserable Mainz émigrés, now arriving from all around the area, thronged the chaussée, relieving their torment and anxiety with curses and threats of vengeance. The ruse that had facilitated the escape of some of the Clubbists yesterday could therefore not succeed again. Individual vehicles sped down the road again, but these Mainz refugees had taken up positions everywhere in the ditches alongside the road, and whenever the fugitives managed to escape one such ambush they were caught up in another.

A conveyance would be stopped, and if they found French men or women in it they would allow them to go their way, but no known Clubbists. A very handsome three-horse traveling coach rolls up, a friendly young lady hastens to show herself in the window and waves to left and right; but the postillion is halted, the door opened, and an arch-Clubbist next to her is immediately recognized. To be sure, it was impossible not to recognize him, short and plump, with his broad, pockmarked face. He is quickly dragged from the coach by the heels, they close the door and wish the beauty a safe journey. They drag him out into the field and pound him mercilessly, all his bones are broken, his face is unrecognizable. Finally some guards have pity on him, he is taken to a peasant's house, where he lies on straw and is safe from the physical abuse of his enemies, but not from their curses, threats, and malevolence. Finally that too reached the point where the officer refused to let anyone else enter the house. He would not have turned me away, for he was an acquaintance of mine; but he implored me too to forego this saddest and most disgusting of all spectacles.

Also 25 July. At the Chaussée House we were now occupied with the continued orderly departure of the French. I stood at the window with Mr. Gore, below us a large crowd had gathered; but nothing on the spacious plaza outside could escape the observer.

Infantry, high-spirited and handsome troops of the line, approached; a number of young women from Mainz departed with them, some of them alongside, some marching in their ranks. Their acquaintances greeted them now with headshaking and taunts: "Well, Miss Lieschen, do you intend to see the wide world?" and then "Your soles are still new, they won't last long!" Or "Did you also learn French while you were at it?—Have a good trip!" And thus it went as they passed through this gauntlet of tongues; the young women, however, seemed cheerful and confident, some of them bade their female neighbors farewell, most of them were quiet and fixed their eyes on their lovers.

In the meantime the crowd had become quite agitated; they shouted curses and threats. The women criticized their men for letting these worthless creatures pass without incident, for they were certainly carrying in their bundles many a piece of property that rightfully belonged to true citizens of Mainz, and only the steady pace of the soldiers, kept in order by the officers marching alongside them, prevented an outburst; the anger and unrest were terrible.

Precisely in this most dangerous moment there appeared a procession which certainly would have wished to be far away from this scene. A handsome man rode up on horseback without any special protective detachment, his uniform not precisely a military one, at his side a well-formed and very beautiful woman in men's clothing, behind them followed a number of four-in-hands packed with boxes and crates; the quiet was ominous. Suddenly there was a murmur in the crowd and a cry: "Stop him! kill him! that's the scoundrel of an architect who plundered the cathedral chapter and then set fire to it!" It would have taken only one determined person to set off the crowd.

Without thinking of anything else than preserving the peace in front of the Duke's quarters, and imagining in a flash what the sovereign and general would say if he returned and had trouble reaching his front door because of the debris left by such unlawful vengeance, I sprang downstairs, raced outside, and cried out with an authoritative voice: "Halt!"

The crowd had already moved closer; to be sure no one dared to lower the barrier, but the path itself was blocked by the crowd. I repeated my "Halt!" and absolute quiet ensued. I went on speaking loudly and vehemently: these were the quarters of the Duke of Weimar and the plaza was sacred; if they wanted to make a disturbance and wreak vengeance, then they should go somewhere else. The King had promised safe conduct to all the French, and if he had wanted to set conditions and except certain people from the safe conduct, he would have stationed observers and either turned back or taken prisoner those who were guilty; but there was no indication that this was the case and there was not a patrol in sight. And they, the people in the crowd, no matter who they were and how they got there, had no other role to play here in the midst of the German army than to remain peaceful spectators; their misfortune and their hatred, I said, gave them no rights here, and once and for all I would not allow any violence in this place.

Now the crowd was astounded, was silent, then there was another surge of grumbling and curses; a few individuals became furious, some men pushed forward to grab the reins of the horses. Strangely enough, one of them was that wigmaker whom I had already warned yesterday when I did him a good turn.—"What!" I called out to him, "have you already forgotten what we talked about yesterday, have you not considered the fact that whoever takes revenge into his own hands becomes guilty himself, that we are to leave the punishment of criminals to God and the constituted authorities, just as we had to rely on them to bring about the end of this misery?" and I said whatever else I could think of that was brief and to the point, loudly and with conviction. The man, who recognized me immediately, stepped back, the child clung to his father and looked over toward me in a friendly way; now the crowd had already retreated and left the plaza somewhat freer and the way through to the barrier was clear again. The two figures on horseback hardly knew how to react. I had made my way rather far into the plaza; the man rode up to me and said he would like to know my name, to know to whom it was he owed such a great service, he would never forget it all his life and gladly be of service in return. The beautiful woman also rode up to me and expressed her heartfelt thanks. I told them that I had only done my duty and maintained the security and sanctity of this place; I motioned to them, and they passed on. The crowd, now confused in its eagerness for vengeance, remained where it was; thirty paces farther on no one could have controlled it. But that's the way it is in the world: whoever has managed to get past one obstacle can get past a thousand. Chi scampa d'un punto, scampa di mille.

When I went back upstairs to join friend Gore after my sally he said to me in his English-French: "What kind of bug has bitten you, you got yourself into something that could have turned out badly."

"I wasn't afraid of that," I answered, "and don't you find it nicer that I kept the plaza clean in front of the house? What would it look like if it were all full of little bits and pieces of things which made everyone angry and excited, got them all worked up, and were not of any use to anybody—regardless of whether or not the man deserves to have the things that he has now so comfortably carted off?"

In the meantime the procession of departing French continued past our window; the crowd, which had no further interest in what was going on, dispersed; whoever could do so was looking for a way to slip into the city, to find his loved ones again with whatever might have been saved of their property, and rejoice. But they were driven even more by the highly pardonable urge to punish their hated enemies, the Clubbists and the Committee members,[26] and to destroy them totally, as they more than once loudly threatened to do.

But my good Gore still could not get over his unhappiness at having seen me, at some danger to myself, venture so much for the sake of a stranger who was perhaps also a criminal. I kept pointing out to him in jest the clean plaza in front of the house, and finally I said impatiently: "It is simply in my nature, I prefer to commit an injustice rather than endure disorder."

26 and 27 July. Already on the twenty-sixth we succeeded in entering the city on horseback with some friends; there we found a most lamentable situation. Things that had been built over the course of centuries were now in ruins, in a place, the most beautiful location in the world, where the riches of whole provinces had been brought together and where religion had endeavored to preserve and increase the possessions of its servants. This was painfully disorienting for the spirit, much sadder than if one had simply wandered into a city that had been burned down by chance.

Because the functioning of the municipality had broken down completely there was, in addition to the sad rubble, all sorts of refuse piled up in the streets; there were also obvious signs of plundering that had taken place as a result of civil strife and discord. High walls threatened to cave in, towers were on the point of collapsing, but why does one need individual descriptions when I have already mentioned the main buildings one by one as they went up in flames. I hurried to the chapter house,[27] my old favorite, which I remembered as an architectural paradise; the portico with its pediment was still standing, but all too quickly I found myself walking in the rubble of the beautifully vaulted ceilings; the wire screens, which formerly had been like nets protecting the windows that let in the light from above, now lay in my way; here and there some relic of the old splendor and elegance was still to be seen, but this magnificent building was really destroyed for ever. All the buildings on the square around it had shared the same fate; on the night of 27 June their destruction had lit up the whole countryside.

After this I found myself in the vicinity of the palace, which no one dared to approach. Lean-to shacks built against the outer walls were an indication of the desecration suffered by this princely dwelling; on the square in front stood a jumble of useless cannon, some of them knocked out by the enemy, others destroyed by their own too rapid firing.

Many a magnificent building with all its contents had been destroyed by the enemy from outside the walls, but there had also been much destruction from within the city due to vandalism, desecration, and wantonness. The Ostheim palace was still intact, but it had been transformed into tailors' quarters, billets, and guard rooms: a subversion execrable to behold. The halls were full of rags and scraps, plaster and marble walls were defaced by hooks and large nails, weapons were hung up and strewn all around.

The Academy still looked quite attractive from the outside, but a cannon ball had smashed a window jamb in Sömmerring's quarters on the third floor. There I found my friend again; one could not exactly say he had moved in, because the beautiful rooms had been vandalized by uncouth guests. Not only had they ruined the bright blue wallpaper as high as they could reach; they must have used ladders or stacked-up tables and chairs in order to smear the rooms with bacon or some other fat all the way to the ceiling. These were the same rooms where we had sat together in such friendly company the year before, jesting and conversing so cheerfully and intimately. Meanwhile, in spite of this misfortune, there was one comforting thing to report: Sömmerring had found his cellar untouched and all the anatomical specimens he had stored there were unharmed. We went to inspect them, and they were the occasion for a profitable conversation.

The new governor had issued a proclamation. I found it to be wholly consonant, in fact the words were almost identical, with my own exhortations to that émigré wigmaker; every act of taking the law into one's own hands was forbidden; the right to draw the distinction between obedient and disobedient citizens was reserved to the ruler alone upon his return to the city.[28] Such a pronouncement was absolutely necessary, for, in the present state of disorder occasioned by the truce of several days ago, the most daring of the émigrés were forcing their way into the city and even inciting and egging on the siege soldiers to plunder the houses of the Clubbists as they marched in. The proclamation had used the mildest possible language, as was only fitting, in order not to condemn out of hand the righteous anger of these people who had been so unbelievably insulted and humiliated.

How difficult it is to calm an excited crowd! Irregularities occurred even in our presence. A soldier went into a shop, asked for tobacco, and took all of it while it was being weighed out. Our officers intervened in response to the citizens' cries for help, and that was how we got through an hour or a day of disorder and confusion.

On our wanderings we found an old woman in the doorway of a low hut that was little more than a hole in the ground. We expressed our surprise that she had already returned to the city, whereupon she replied that she had never gone away, although she had certainly received hints that she should. "Those clowns came to me too," she said, "with their pretty sashes,[29] threatened me and ordered me about; but I always just told them the plain truth: 'God will keep me, a poor woman, alive in my simple hut and people will still respect me when I have long since seen the likes of you in shame and disgrace.' I told them to go somewhere else with their foolishness. They were afraid my cries might upset the neighbors, and they left me alone. And so I spent the whole time partly in my cellar, partly out in the open, I got by with just a little bit to eat, and I am still alive to praise God. But those people will have a rough time of it."

Then she pointed to the house on the corner across the way, to show how close the danger had been. We were able to see into the lower corner window of that impressive building, and what a curious sight it was! An old collection of curiosities had been kept there for many years, figures of porcelain and stone, Chinese cups, saucers, bowls, and pitchers; there must have been objects made of ivory and amber, as well as other things that had been either carved or turned on a lathe, pictures made of moss, straw, and other things, and whatever else one can imagine having been in such a collection. All this had to be surmised from the bits and pieces that remained: for a bomb had passed through all the upper stories and exploded in this room; the force of the air pressure had thrown everything in the room from its place, also blowing out the windows and wire screens, which now seemed to be bent out, like so many stomachs, between the iron bars. The good woman told us she had truly believed that she too would perish in this explosion.

We had our noon meal at an inn; with all the talk that was going back and forth, it seemed to us that it was best to remain silent. It seemed rather strange to us, however, that the patrons asked the musicians there to play the Marseillaise and the "Ça ira"; they all seemed to hum or sing along with the tunes and to be cheered by them.

In our wanderings we could hardly make out the spot where the pleasure palace had stood. In August of the previous year this promenade situated directly on the Rhine had been a most delightful place with its majestic garden room, terrasses, orangery, and fountains. Here had been the tree-lined walks where, as the gardener told me, his most gracious Elector had hosted the most distinguished rulers, with their entire retinues, at tables so long one could hardly see from one end to the other; and the good man had much more to say about damast tablecloths, silverware, and place settings.[30] Contrasted with that memory what we now saw made only a still more unbearable impression.

The neighboring Carthusian monastery had likewise all but disappeared, for the stones from the buildings had immediately been taken away and used in the important Weisenau fortifications. The little nunnery had only recently been reduced to rubble, hardly capable of being rebuilt.

I accompanied my friends Gore and Kraus to the citadel. There the Drusus monument was still standing, just about the same as when I had drawn it as a child; this time too it had remained unshaken, no matter how many incendiary shells had flown past or even struck it.

Mr. Gore immediately set up his portable camera obscura on the wall, with the intention of drawing the whole city as it appeared after the siege. He worked very conscientiously and meticulously on the drawing, starting in the middle at the cathedral; toward the sides it is less perfectly done, as we can still see from the neatly ordered papers left behind at his death.

Finally our paths turned toward Kastel; on the Rhine bridge we could still get a breath of fresh air just as we had long ago, and it was possible for a moment to imagine that those times could return. The defenders had worked on the fortifications of Kastel throughout the siege; we found a trough full of fresh lime, next to it bricks, and a piece of unfinished wall; after the truce and capitulation everything had simply been left standing and lying as it was.

The obstacles that had been erected around the Kastel fortifications were strange-looking as well as saddening; to this end they had cut down all the fruit trees in the area. These had been cut off at the roots and trimmed of their smallest and most delicate branches, and then the stronger, regularly shaped tops had been shoved into each other to form a last impenetrable barrier in front of the fortifications. They seemed to be trees that had all been planted at the same time and had grown under the same favorable conditions, but now, abandoned to their fate, they had been used for hostile purposes.

However, it was not possible to spend a long time over such regrets, for the innkeeper and his wife and every inhabitant we spoke to seemed to forget their own sorrows in talking at length of the boundless misery endured by those citizens of Mainz who had been forced to leave the city and found themselves caught between the internal and the external enemy. For it was not the war alone, but rather the dissolution of the bonds of civil society through acts of lunacy, that had paved the way for and brought about such misfortune.

Our spirits recovered somewhat from all this woe and sorrow when we were told of some of the heroic deeds performed by sturdy citizens of the city. At first they had regarded the bombardment as an unavoidable evil; the destructive power of the incendiary shells was so great, and the approaching misfortune so inescapable, that no one had believed anything could be done to counter it. But finally, when they had become more familiar with the danger, they had decided to do what they could. They jested daringly about putting out bombs that had fallen into houses with water stored for that purpose; people told wonders of heroines of this sort who had been so fortunate as to save themselves and others. But there were also the deaths of some brave and sturdy people to be deplored: an apothecary and his son had been killed while trying to put out one such bomb.

Although we were now expressing our sadness and congratulating ourselves and others for having endured these sufferings, we were nevertheless amazed that the fortress had not been held longer. In the nave of the cathedral, the roof of which was still intact, lay a huge store of untouched sacks of flour; people also told of other supplies of foodstuffs and practically inexhaustible quantities of wine. We therefore conjectured that the early capitulation of the fortress had something to do with the most recent revolution in Paris, which had brought to power the party to which the Mainz commissioners belonged.[31] Merlin de Thionville, Reubel,[32] and others wanted to be present in Paris, where, once their enemies had been overcome, there was nothing more to fear and everything to gain. For the present it was necessary for them to take part in this change of power and secure their places in the new order of things, rise to important posts, lay their hands on large fortunes, and only then take part once more in the continuing feud with the foreign enemy. When the fortunes of war changed again, as was to be hoped, they would march out to spread the restless sentiments of their countrymen over other countries, with an eye to regaining possession of Mainz, and indeed, of much more than that.

There was no more reason to remain in this wasted and desolate land. The king left first with his guards; the regiments followed. It was not demanded of me that I take any further part in the hardships of war; I was given leave to return home, but first I wanted to visit Mannheim again.

The first thing I did there was to visit His Royal Highness, Prince Louis Ferdinand, whom I found in good spirits stretched out on his sofa, not completely comfortable, because his wound made it difficult for him to lie down; at the same time he also could not conceal his eagerness to appear again in person in the theater of war as soon as possible.

Afterward I had quite an amusing adventure in the inn. I sat at one end of the long and very full table. The king's chamberlain, von Rietz,[33] sat at the other end, a tall, well-built, strong, broad-shouldered man, with a figure that was very appropriate for the man who was Frederick William's personal servant. He and his fellows had been quite loud and were in high spirits as they got up from the table. I saw Rietz coming towards me; he greeted me in a friendly way, expressed his pleasure at finally making my acquaintance, which he had wanted to do for a long time, added a few flattering remarks, and then finally said: I should pardon him, but he had a certain personal interest in running across me here and seeing me. He had always been told that intellectuals and persons of genius had to be small and gaunt, and look sickly and as though they were unhappy with the world, and he had heard of plenty of such people. That had always upset him, for he figured he was well enough endowed with brains himself, and yet he was healthy and strong and well built; but now he was very happy to find that I was a man who also looked like something, and whom no one considered any less a genius on that account. He was glad of that and hoped we would both enjoy such well-being for a long time to come.

I answered with some courteous words of my own; he shook my hand, and I could console myself with the thought that even though that well-meaning lieutenant colonel at Mainz had rejected me (for he too had probably expected to find in me a person who was out of sorts with the world), I had now received some honor, albeit in a completely opposite category.

In Heidelberg, at the home of my devoted old lady-friend Delph,[34] I encountered my youthful companion and brother-in-law, Schlosser. We talked about a number of things and he too had to put up with a presentation of my theory of colors. He listened earnestly and sympathetically, although he could not bring himself to leave off his accustomed way of thinking on this subject, and he insisted above all on knowing to what extent my thinking could be reconciled with Euler's theory, which impressed him very much. Unfortunately, I had to confess that on the path I was taking there was no reason to ask such questions, that for me it was a matter of collecting and distilling countless experiences, putting them in order, so as to ascertain their relationships and their positions relative to each other, and making this comprehensible to myself and to other people. But it was difficult to make him understand this manner of investigation, since I could not point to very many real experiments as yet.

The difficulty of the enterprise becoming apparent in the course of our discussion, I showed him an essay I had written during the siege, where I had outlined how a group of men with quite different fields of interest might cooperate, each attacking the problem from his own point of view, in order to further such a difficult and wide-ranging undertaking. For help I had called upon the philosopher, the physicist, mathematician, painter, instrument maker, the cloth dyer, and God knows whom else; when I talked about all this in general terms, Schlosser listened patiently; but when I wanted to read him the essay for the details, he declined to listen to it and laughed at me instead: he claimed that even at my age I was still just a child and a novice, that I was just dreaming if I thought anyone would take a part in anything I was interested in, or that anyone would embrace a new manner of proceeding and make it his own, or that it was at all possible for there to be any common effort or cooperation in Germany!

He expressed similar opinions with regard to other subjects; to be sure, he had experienced and suffered much personally, as a man of affairs and as an author, which was the reason why his earnest character had shut itself up and ill-humoredly renounced every cheerful, happy, and often helpful illusion. But it made a most unpleasant impression on me to think that, returning now from the most horrible scenes of war to my peaceful private life, I should not even dare to hope for peaceful cooperation and collaboration in an undertaking that was so important to me and that I considered so useful and interesting for the whole world.

At that the old Adam asserted himself again; my ironic way of speaking, my frivolous statements, paradoxical theses, and all the rest quickly gave rise to apprehensiveness and unease between the two of us: Schlosser vehemently refused to listen to more of it, our hostess didn't know what to make of us, and her attempts to mediate at least had the effect that I indeed departed sooner than planned, but without appearing to be too much in haste.

There is not much to say about my stay in Frankfurt, or about the rest of my journey home; the end of that year and the beginning of the next brought us only news of the atrocities committed by a nation that had lapsed into barbarism and was drunk with victory at the same time. But soon I too was to experience a quite unexpected change in my accustomed way of life. The Duke of Weimar left the Prussian service upon completion of the campaign; there was great lamenting everywhere in the regiment, for they were losing their leader, sovereign, adviser, benefactor, and father all at the same time. I too was suddenly to take my leave of excellent men with whom I had formed strong bonds, and this leavetaking took place not without tears on the part of the best of them. Our love and respect for this extraordinary man and leader had brought us together and sustained us, and we seemed to be losing our own selves when forced to do without his leadership and our lively and mutually rewarding intercourse with each other. The area around Aschersleben along with the nearby Harz, so easy to reach from there, seemed to be lost for me, and in fact I never afterward ventured far into those areas.[35]

And so let us close, in order not to slip into reflections about the fateful world events that threatened us for another twelve years until we finally saw ourselves flooded, if not in fact totally engulfed, by the same tides.[36]

NOTES

Poetry and Truth

Part Four

[1] See Vol. 4, p. 183 and note. During the 18th century Bayle's article on Spinoza was probably the most influential critique of the philosopher's work.

[2] Petrarch.

[3] Christian Friedrich Himburg, 1733–1801, a Berlin publisher, was one of the most notorious pirate printers of the 18th century. In 1775–1776 he brought out an unauthorized three-volume edition of Goethe's collected works, with second and third printings in 1777 and 1779. This at least attests to the popularity of Goethe's works. Himburg introduced numerous errors into the texts and standardized Goethe's German to approximate North German norms.

[4] Karl Friedrich, 1728–1811. Karl Friedrich's encouragement of pirate printing must be seen in the context of the mercantilist economic theory of the time and the ruler's efforts to establish domestic industries in Baden. Such an undertaking necessarily stressed economic development over nebulous rights to intellectual property, which, under the legal conditions obtaining in Germany at the time, could not be enforced in any event. Karl Friedrich Macklot was the most important Baden pirate and is mentioned a number of times by Goethe as the very epitome of the pirate publisher, but he never printed any work by Goethe. Goethe has possibly confused Macklot with a Karlsruhe pirate printer, Christian Gottlieb Schmieder.

[5] The Holy Roman Emperor Joseph II supported the development of a publishing industry in Austria for the same mercantilistic reasons as Karl Friedrich in Baden. The recipient of Joseph's support and encouragement was Johann Thomas von Trattner, 1717–1798, the Viennese court printer who also published school books and prayer books.

[6] In Richard Cumberland's drama, *The West Indian,* a German translation of which appeared in 1772, the hero is a youth who has grown up in Central America and cannot appreciate European culture.

[7] It is typical of Goethe that throughout the Lili episodes there is no mention of the family name. Lili was Anne Elisabeth Schönemann, 1758–1817. Her father, the merchant and banker Johann Wolfgang Schönemann, born in 1717, had died in 1763. His widow continued the business with the aid of a partner. Lili married a Strassburg banker, Bernhard Friedrich von Türckheim, in 1778.

[8] Friedrich Maximilian von Lersner, 1736–1804, a Danish legation secretary and later an official and burgomaster of Frankfurt.

[9] "God finishes the job in just a few hours."

[10] Nicolas Bernard, 1709–1780, a merchant and tobacco manufacturer and a member of the Calvinist congregation in Offenbach.

[11] Jean George d'Orville, a cousin of Lili, a merchant and also a member of the Calvinist congregation.

[12] Johann André, 1741–1799, originally a silk manufacturer, switched to music.

He founded a music publishing house in Offenbach in 1774 and went to Berlin as an opera director in 1777, where he stayed until 1784. André composed music to two of Goethe's early plays.

[13] Theobald Marchand, 1741–1800, was a theater director in Frankfurt from 1771 to 1777 and staged one of the early Goethe-André musicals.

[14] André Ernest Modeste Grétry, 1741–1813, a French composer whose opera *Beauty and the Beast,* 1771, was also translated into German.

[15] André's *Potter* was first performed in 1773.

[16] Johann Ludwig Ewald, 1747–1822, Calvinist pastor in Offenbach. He later became a church official in Karlsruhe and was a popular devotional writer.

[17] Gottfried August Bürger's ballad, "Lenore," was published in 1773, about the same time as Goethe's *Götz von Berlichingen.* André's musical setting is generally considered to have been of some significance for the development of the German "Lied," or art song.

[18] Johann Wilhelm Liebholdt, who continued to work for Goethe's father and later for his mother. It was Liebholdt who put together the auction catalogue of the father's library after his death.

[19] On the date in question, 23 June 1775, Goethe was in Switzerland. He has probably confused the birthday with some other festive occasion.

[20] Song of Solomon, 5:2.

[21] Helena Dorothea Delph, who died in 1808 at the approximate age of eighty. She was a businesswoman, visited the Frankfurt fairs regularly, and may have quietly carried out diplomatic and political assignments for several German princes.

[22] Although Goethe declined to join this particular Masonic lodge, he did become a Mason in Weimar in 1780.

[23] The war between Turkey and Russia, Catherine's first attempt to break the power of the Turks, lasted from 1768 to 1774. The naval battle of Cheshme took place in 1770.

[24] After the close of the Russo-Turkish war, Jacob Philipp Hackert, 1737–1807, was commissioned by the Russians to paint a six-part series depicting the battle of Cheshme. The Russians were pleased with the first five parts, but Admiral Orloff complained that exploding ships looked quite different from what Hackert had painted in the sixth. When Hackert replied that he had never seen an exploding ship and therefore had no idea what one really looked like, Orloff arranged to blow up a Russian ship anchored at Leghorn for Hackert's benefit. Afterward the Russians were satisfied with Hackert's new version of an exploding ship. Goethe became acquainted with Hackert during his Italian journey 1786–1788, became his close friend, and later wrote his biography.

[25] Gustav III of Sweden, 1746–1792, who came to the throne in 1771. With the help of the military he put an end to the corrupt power of the Estates. He sponsored reforms which amounted to the creation of a constitutional monarchy in Sweden.

[26] Pasquale Paoli, 1725–1807, a Corsican patriot who led the struggle against Genoese rule. Tired of the struggle, Genoa sold Corsica to France in 1768 and, since France was much better equipped to put down the rebellion, Paoli was forced to flee to England, where he was treated as something of a popular hero.

[27] Johann Philipp Bethmann, 1715–1793, founded a leading Frankfurt banking house.

[28] Louis XVI.

[29] Ulrich von Hutten, 1488–1523, an imperial knight, a humanist scholar, and an early German patriot and adherent of Martin Luther. Willibald Pirckheimer, 1470–1530, was a Nuremberg patrician and fellow humanist.

[30] The House of Limpurg was a Frankfurt aristocratic society which had the right to elect 14 of the 42 Frankfurt senators. The House of Frauenstein, another aristocratic corporation, elected six senators.

[31] Until 1788 the Calvinists were not allowed to hold services in the city of Frankfurt. They had a church in the village of Bockenheim, northwest of the city, where they held their services.

[32] Hans Sachs, 1494–1576, the best known of the Nuremberg Meistersingers. Sachs's particular verse form, the "knittel" verse, was in disrepute until past the middle of the 18th century, primarily because of its lack of elegance. Goethe and his Storm and Stress comrades valued Sachs and the knittel verse precisely because of its archaic qualities and its old-fashioned "Germanness." In addition to a number of the playlets and sketches mentioned in Book Eighteen, long stretches of *Faust,* which had its origins in these years, were composed in this meter.

[33] Christian zu Stolberg, 1748–1821, and his younger brother Friedrich Leopold, 1750–1819, had grown up in Denmark and studied in Göttingen in 1772–1773, where they were members of the group of young poets associated with the *Poetic Almanac.* Friedrich Leopold (Fritz) was the more significant as a poet. They arrived in Frankfurt on their way to Switzerland in the middle of May, 1775. In the course of the 1780s they became more and more conservative and associated themselves with pious groups for whom Klopstock, as the epitome of a religious poet, was the ideal.

[34] Christian August Heinrich Kurt von Haugwitz, 1752–1831, was, at the time Goethe was writing, a well-known public figure, as he had been a Prussian minister from 1792 to 1807.

[35] Spanish for "governess," also the name of the mother in the chapbook, *Children of Aymon.*

[36] This is faulty recollection on Goethe's part. Klopstock had been in Karlsruhe from October, 1774 to March, 1775, whereas Goethe and his traveling companions stayed there from 17 to 21 May. Goethe *had* met with Klopstock both when Klopstock passed through Frankfurt on his way to Karlsruhe and on his return trip to Hamburg.

[37] Princess Louise was the niece of the ruling margravine of Baden, Caroline Louise of Hesse-Darmstadt, 1723–1783. She had been betrothed to Carl August of Saxe-Weimar since 1774. The marriage took place on 3 October 1775.

[38] Johann Georg Gehrock (usually spelled Gerock), a merchant, died in 1796. His wife was acquainted with Goethe's mother. They had three daughters.

[39] Lavater's *Physiognomic Fragments for the Purpose of Furthering Knowledge and Love of Mankind* were published in four volumes between 1775 and 1778.

[40] Jacob Ludwig Passavant, 1751–1827, was from Frankfurt. At the time of

Goethe's visit Passavant was a student of Calvinist theology and worked as Lavater's personal assistant.

[41] Johannes Hotz (or Hotze), 1734–1801, was a physician in Richterswil and a friend of Lavater.

[42] Maria Einsiedeln, in the canton of Schwyz, was a Benedictine abbey to which many pilgrims journeyed. The first building activity dated from 934 A.D.

[43] St. Meinrad, a hermit who had been murdered by robbers in this vicinity in 861 A.D.

[44] Martin Schongauer, born around 1420, died 1480.

[45] Also called Gross and Klein Mythen.

[46] Lake Lucerne.

[47] According to legend, at least, Walther Fürst, Werner Stauffacher, and Arnold an der Halden, the three leaders who had met at the Rütli to renew the ancient pact of friendship and cooperation between the cantons.

[48] Built in 1708, it was 64 meters long.

[49] Andermatt.

[50] In actuality, the valley of the Reuss.

[51] The St. Gotthard hospice.

[52] Heinrich Julius Freiherr von Lindau, a young man who had left Hamburg because of an unfortunate affair of the heart and taken up a hermit's existence in Switzerland. In 1776 he entered the Hessian military, was sent to America and was killed in the Battle of Manhattan.

[53] Here, again, Goethe's recollection is faulty. Goethe returned to Zurich on 26 June; the Stolbergs were still there, not leaving until 5 July.

[54] The exact title is *Letters From Switzerland,* which resulted from Goethe's second trip to Switzerland with Carl August in 1779. They were first published in 1796 in Schiller's journal, *Die Horen.* In preparing the letters for publication in his collected works Goethe invented the fiction that they were "Werther's" letters written on a trip which he had taken prior to his involvement with Lotte.

[55] The work was published in Zurich in four volumes between 1768–1778. The subject is Lavater's expectations with regard to the afterlife, and Goethe's characterization is not unjust. There were chapters in the work such as "On the Perfection of Heavenly Bodies" and "On Language in Heaven."

[56] A work by Lavater in four volumes, 1782–1785.

[57] Abraham a Santa Clara, 1644–1709, a Catholic Baroque preacher famed for his pithy wit and unexpected turns of phrase.

[58] The Stolbergs. This passage was presumably of interest to the contemporary audience because of controversies between Friedrich Leopold Stolberg, who had become Catholic in 1800, and Johann Heinrich Voss, one of his old Göttingen comrades.

[59] These phrases are reminiscences, although not exact quotations, of Stolberg's poetry.

[60] There is no contemporary evidence to indicate that Goethe or Lili thought of starting together anew in America. In several of Goethe's late works, however, America represents a land of new beginnings and escape from encroaching dehumanizing industrialization.

[61] *Erwin and Elmira, a Play with Songs,* was published in Georg Jacobi's journal *Iris* in March, 1775.

[62] Georg Melchior Kraus, born either 1733 or 1737 in Frankfurt, died 1806 in Weimar. He is known for many colored etchings of Weimar landscapes and views, and for his portraits of a number of leading Weimar personalities. He had been a guest at the courts in Gotha and Weimar during the winter of 1774–1775, and was appointed ducal drawing-master in Weimar effective 1 October 1775.

[63] On Hackert see note 24 above. Johann Georg Wille, 1715–1808, had lived in Paris since 1736 and was in the business of making engravings from paintings. Carl August had visited him on his trip to Paris.

[64] François Boucher, 1703–1770; Jean Antoine Watteau, born in 1684, could hardly have been very helpful to Kraus in Paris, as he died in 1721! Boucher and Watteau were both esteemed highly in the second half of the 18th century.

[65] Jean Baptiste Greuze, 1725–1805. Goethe's artist friend Heinrich Meyer esteemed Greuze for his touch of sentimentality and for his depiction of scenes from bourgeois life.

[66] Johanna Louise vom Stein, 1752–1816, married Jacob Friedemann von Werthern, a Thuringian count. They played an important role in Weimar social circles.

[67] Ernst Wilhelm Wolf, 1735–1792, was in charge of music at the court of Weimar. His wife, Caroline, 1742–1820, was a singer.

[68] Friedrich Justin Bertuch, 1747–1822, an author and theater writer, became Privy Secretary to Carl August in 1775. He was later an enterprising and successful businessman, publisher of a long-running journal.

[69] Johann Karl August Musäus, 1735–1787, professor at the Weimar Gymnasium, was also an author. His best-known work was a collection of fairy tales. Franz Kirms, 1750–1826, was a privy secretary. Hieronymus Dietrich Berendis, 1719–1782, was a Weimar administrator and had been a friend of Winckelmann. Twenty-seven letters of Winckelmann to Berendis came into the possession of Anna Amalia after Berendis' death and they were published by Goethe in 1805 along with his important essay on Winckelmann. Johann August Ludecus, 1742–1801, was a privy secretary and later a court councilor.

[70] The son mentioned by Goethe was the writer August von Kotzebue, 1761–1819, one of the two most popular German dramatists of the late 18th and early 19th century.

[71] Duchess Anna Amalia.

[72] "No one opposes God except God himself."

[73] Carl August and Louise of Hesse-Darmstadt had been married on 3 October and were on their way to Weimar. They arrived in Frankfurt on 12 October.

[74] Ferdinand Joseph von Wrede, 1722–1792, was a Palatine official in Heidelberg.

[75] Elector Charles Theodore of the Palatinate, 1724–1799.

Campaign in France 1792

[1] Johann Friedrich Reichsfreiherr vom Stein, 1749–1799, was an older brother of the celebrated Prussian reformer of the era of the Wars of Liberation. He was the Prussian diplomatic representative at the court of Mainz and a ferocious opponent of the French Revolution.

[2] Louis Philippe Joseph d'Orléans, 1747–1793. The proprietor of the Palais Royal in Paris and fabulously wealthy, he was suspected of using his wealth to influence the course of events during the French Revolution, and of harboring ambitions to usurp the throne. He became a member of the National Convention in 1792 and adopted the name Egalité, voting for the execution of Louis XVI, but was nevertheless executed himself in 1793 after the fall of the Gironde.

[3] Louis Joseph de Bourbon, Prince of Condé, 1736–1818, leader of one of the two principal groups of armed French émigrés.

[4] The vivaciously intriguing female character in *Wilhelm Meister's Apprenticeship*. The Princess of Monaco, however, had been divorced since 1770 and would have been close to fifty years old by the time Goethe encountered her in Mainz. Perhaps Philine is a state of mind.

[5] The French National Assembly expropriated much of the property of the Roman Church with the intention of selling it in order to shore up the national finances. The assignats were a kind of security issued in anticipation of the income from these properties; they were to be redeemed and retired upon completion of the sales. The assignats, however, quickly came to be treated as legal tender and were printed in ever smaller denominations instead of being retired as originally planned. As more and more were printed, they of course became worth ever less. Counterfeit assignats also were put into circulation, for example by the émigrés. On at least one occasion the émigrés even sought the assistance of the Austrian government in producing an issue of 50 million livres in counterfeit assignats, but the Austrians disdainfully refused to participate in the scheme. It is unclear whether the émigrés thought of this as a form of economic warfare or simply wanted to profit by the fraud, but the counterfeiting wreaked havoc in border areas. Assignats and the desirability of possessing cash (coin) are a recurring theme in this work.

[6] Samuel Thomas Sömmerring, 1755–1830, a professor at the university in Mainz, was perhaps the leading anatomist of the period. At the time of this meeting in Mainz he and Goethe had already carried on a scientific correspondence for several years.

[7] Ludwig Ferdinand Huber, 1764–1804, was secretary at the Saxonian legation in Mainz. After Mainz was occupied by the French in October, 1792, he moved to Switzerland and made his living during the 1790s by publishing a number of journals devoted to France and French affairs.

[8] Georg Forster, 1754–1794, a natural scientist who had sailed with Captain James Cook on his second voyage around the world, was librarian of the university. When the French occupied Mainz Forster became one of the leaders

of the attempt to convert Mainz into a republic, was one of the delegates sent to Paris in March of 1793 to petition the National Convention for annexation to the French Republic, and died in Paris in January, 1794. His wife, Theresa, was already living with Huber in Switzerland and married him after Forster's death.

[9] Ludwig Heinrich Gottlieb von Fritsch, 1772–1808, was the son of one of Goethe's colleagues in the Weimar government.

[10] Illustrations of the monument at Igel are contained in Alfred G. Steer, Jr., *Goethe's Social philosophy as Revealed in Campagne in Frankreich and Belagerung von Mainz* (Chapel Hill: University of North Carolina Press, 1955).

[11] A military order established in 1693 by Louis XIV. Since the order was conferred only after a great number of years of service, Goethe is referring to a rather elderly contingent.

[12] The two brothers of Louis XVI, the Counts Provence (later King Louis XVIII from 1814–1824) and Artois (later King Charles X from 1824–1830), had established themselves at Coblence after emigrating from France. The Elector of Trier, whose residence was in Coblence, was their uncle.

[13] Johann Conrad Wagner, 1737–1802, accompanied Carl August on a number of his trips and expeditions. Goethe relied heavily on Wagner's diary while writing *Campaign in France 1792.*

[14] Carl August's Prussian regiment was normally stationed at Aschersleben, in the Harz vicinity.

[15] The reigning Duke of Brunswick, Karl Wilhelm Ferdinand, 1735–1806, was a Prussian field marshal and the nominal commander of all Allied forces involved in the campaign in France. He had a high reputation because of his military record in the Seven Years' War and his enlightened government of his territory, Brunswick-Wolfenbüttel. After the death of Frederick II he had been regarded by many who were apprehensive about the capacity of Frederick William II to govern intelligently as the best hope for stability and for the continuation of Frederick's policies, if he would only interest himself in participating in Prussian government, but he preferred to remain at home in Brunswick. He came out of retirement to command Prussian forces again in 1806 and was mortally wounded at the battle of Jena and Auerstedt.

[16] François Claude Amour de Bouillé, a French general who had emigrated after the beginning of the revolution. After the meeting between King Frederick William, Emperor Leopold II, and the French princes at Pillnitz in August, 1791, Bouillé was given the task of drawing up plans for a campaign against France. It is impossible to determine how much of Bouillé's plan was incorporated into the strategy eventually worked out by the Duke of Brunswick. Bouillé's memoirs, published in London in 1797, were one of Goethe's sources for *Campaign in France 1792.*

[17] Carl August's second son and eventual successor, 1792–1862, had been born on 30 May.

[18] The main manifesto of 25 July (supplemented by a second manifesto on 27 July) had been drafted by the émigrés but was issued under the name of the Duke of Brunswick. The manifestos threatened severe reprisals against any and all French citizens who resisted the invading armies or threatened the safety of Louis XVI or members of his family. The manifestos were often credited

with having precipitated the so-called Second Revolution of 10 August and the massacre of the Swiss Guards in the Tuileries, which led to the imprisonment of the king and the abolition of the monarchy.

[19] One Austrian army marched from the Netherlands and joined the Prussian army in the vicinity of Longwy. A second Austrian army marched from Mannheim by way of Thionville, a French border fortress which it was supposed to capture. This Austrian force did not, however, succeed in taking Thionville and was finally ordered deep into French territory to support the Allied advance towards Paris, thus weakening German defenses in the border areas and making possible the later counterthrust by the French into the Rhineland.

[20] Nikolaus Heinrich Julius von Grothaus, 1747–1801, a Prussian jurist and officer with whom Goethe was fairly well acquainted. In actual fact, it was not Grothaus who was entrusted with opening negotiations for the capitulation of Verdun.

[21] Georg Agricola, 1490–1555, a humanist and mineralogist.

[22] In actuality Heinrich XVI of Reuss-Greiz. The Austrian ambassador at Berlin since 1785, he participated in the campaign, accompanying the Prussian headquarters group for the purpose of coordinating affairs between the Allies and keeping Vienna informed of the progress of the campaign.

[23] Nicolas Joseph de Beaurepaire, 1740–1792. The commandants of French fortresses were under strict orders to hold out at all costs, and in the campaign of 1792 the French held all their fortresses except Longwy (which was in a state of disrepair) and Verdun. Beaurepaire is mentioned widely in the contemporary literature for his act, which even Goethe calls a "patriotic sacrifice," and was made a French national hero. Modern French historians, however, lean to the view that he did not commit suicide, but was murdered by the Royalists.

[24] Presumably Goethe is referring to objections and prohibitions against the burial of suicides in hallowed ground.

[25] It was the postmaster of Ste.-Menehould who had recognized Louis XVI on 20 June 1791 on his flight from Paris and alerted other authorities, which led to his arrest and return to Paris. Goethe is mistaken here, however: it was not the postmaster of Ste.-Menehould who was arrested by the Prussians at the instigation of the émigrés, but the mayor of Varennes, who was a former member of the National Assembly and had given the order for the arrest of Louis XVI. Much outrage is expressed in accounts of the campaign about his treatment at the hands of the émigrés and the Prussians.

[26] Jean Paul Gilbert Motier, Marquis de Lafayette, 1757–1834, the friend of George Washington and hero of the American Revolution, was one of the leading figures of the early stages of the French Revolution. Assigned to the command of one of the armies on the eastern front, he attempted to lead his troops over to the enemy on 19 August 1792 after receiving news of the fall of the monarchy on 10 August. Only a small number of his soldiers followed him, however, and instead of being received with open arms by Austrian officials in the Netherlands he was imprisoned until 1797 because they viewed him as an enemy of monarchy and one of the instigators of the revolution.

[27] Charles François Dumouriez, 1739–1823, had been foreign minister during the spring of 1792 and minister of war in the summer. After Lafayette's defection

he was appointed to overall command of the eastern armies facing Germany and the Netherlands. His autobiography, a self-justifying document published in 1793 after his own defection in the Netherlands, was one of Goethe's sources for *Campaign in France 1792*.

[28] The most direct and the best road from Verdun to Paris was that through the pass at Les Islettes. While it could be argued that it would have been impossible for the Allies to capture the pass in any case, their failure to move on Les Islettes immediately after the capitulation of Verdun was possibly the single most damaging error of the campaign, and Goethe highlights this moment in his account. While the Allied army was marching north around the Argonne Forest in search of another usable pass, Dumouriez succeeded in gathering his forces at Ste.-Menehould and Valmy.

[29] Philipp Karl von Alvensleben, 1745–1802, a Prussian diplomat and cabinet minister in the king's retinue during the campaign.

[30] Christian Georg Karl Vogel, 1760–1819, one of the Weimar chancellery officials accompanying Carl August.

[31] François-Sébastien-Charles-Joseph de Croix, Comte de Clerfait, 1733–1798, Austrian field marshal and commander of the troops that had marched from the Netherlands to join the Prussians. Goethe gives the wrong impression in making it appear as though the Austrians had just now appeared on the scene: Clerfait's forces had joined up with the Prussians near Longwy.

[32] Friedrich Ludwig Christian, Prince of Prussia, 1772–1806, a nephew of Frederick William. A dashing and popular figure, he was killed in 1806 in the campaign preceding the battle of Jena and Auerstedt.

[33] Karl Joseph Emmanuel von Ligne, 1759–1792, an Austrian colonel and son of the Austrian field marshal Karl Joseph von Ligne, 1735–1814, with whom Goethe was acquainted after 1803. On Ligne's body was found an unfinished letter expressing drastic disillusionment with the campaign and with Allied prospects for victory, a letter which was later of some propaganda value to the French.

[34] The *Gazette nationale ou Moniteur universel,* which began to appear in Paris in 1789 and printed debates of the National Assembly and other documents. It was a prime source of information about developments in France and was widely read in Germany.

[35] "The Prussians will be able to reach Paris, but they will not leave it again."

[36] Anton Frans van der Meulen, 1632–1690, a Dutch painter of landscapes and battle scenes, depicted events of Louis XIV's campaigns.

[37] Marc Marie, Marquis de Bombelles, 1744–1822, was a French diplomat before the revolution.

[38] Anna Amalia, mother of Carl August. On this second journey to Italy in the company of Anna Amalia Goethe had not gotten farther south than Venice.

[39] Franz Christoph Kellermann, 1735–1820, later a French field marshal and created Duc de Valmy by Napoleon, commanded the army that had been stationed at Metz at the beginning of the campaign and had just effected a link-up with Dumouriez's army west of the Argonne Forest.

[40] The young man in question was the son of Julie Auguste Christianne von Bechtolsheim, 1751–1847, one of the ornaments of Weimar society.

[41] In Book XIV of the *Odyssey* Odysseus, concealing his true identity, invents a tale of woe to see whether or not he can get the faithful swineherd Eumaios to lend him his cloak for the night, and succeeds.

[42] In actuality it was not the secretary of the Duke of Brunswick, but Johann Wilhelm Lombard, 1767–1812, at the time cabinet secretary to Frederick William. Lombard was later exchanged for the mayor of Varennes. The letters Lombard wrote to his wife during the campaign are of considerable interest, although Lombard unfortunately says relatively little about political matters and offers no insights as to the intentions of Frederick William and the Duke of Brunswick.

[43] Friedrich Adolf von Kalckreuth, 1737–1818, one of the most respected Prussian generals.

[44] Johann Wilhelm von Manstein, 1729–1800, was not a general, but a colonel and Frederick William's adjutant. He gained ever greater influence over the king from the period of the campaign on.

[45] An Alsatian who entered Prussian service after emigrating from France, he died in 1801.

[46] The French made great efforts to encourage desertions and win over the German common soldiers, promulgating a decree, before the outbreak of hostilities, which offered deserters the choice of serving in the French armies or of receiving a generous stipend to live in France. In their propaganda they painted a favorable picture of conditions in France and of service in the French army since the beginning of the revolution.

[47] "Good bread, good soup, good meat, good beer."

[48] A French coin, so-called "écu de six livres," worth somewhat less than the customary German taler, which was struck between 1726 and 1790. It was in general circulation in the southern and western parts of Germany. "Laub" refers to the laurel wreath which surrounded the shield of lilies on the reverse side of the coin.

[49] Nikolaus, Graf Luckner, 1722–1794, a Bavarian, had been in overall command of the eastern front before Dumouriez took over. Because of his advanced age and some doubts as to his political loyalty he was assigned to depot service training the volunteers streaming out from Paris to join the army, although he was by far the most prestigious general available to the French. He was accused of treason and executed in 1794.

[50] St. Louis, the French King Louis IX, 1226–1270. Jean Sire de Joinville, 1224–1309, participated in Louis' Sixth Crusade and completed his *Life of St. Louis,* Goethe's source for the story he tells at Valmy, in 1309.

[51] In actuality, 451 A.D.

[52] Here Goethe indulges in devastating irony at the expense of the Duke of Brunswick. In reality, the document in question was a proclamation drafted by Marquis Lucchesini (see note 83 below), with the assistance and approval of Prince Reuss. Dumouriez broke off these particular negotiations after receiving news from Paris that the newly convened National Convention had proclaimed the Republic on 20 September. There were, however, continuing and somewhat murky negotiations between the French and the Prussians throughout the period of the retreat to which the Austrians were not a party; the French were making efforts to drive a wedge between the Prussians and

the Austrians, which resulted in a good deal of suspicion on the part of the Austrians. Dumouriez even addressed a memoire to Frederick William urging him to leave his Allies in the lurch and renew the traditional Franco-Prussian friendship at Austria's expense.

[53] The later King Frederick William III.

[54] Louis Ferdinand.

[55] The work mentioned by Goethe, the author of which was Johann Carl Fischer, did not begin to appear until 1798. Scholars speculate that the volume in question was one of the volumes of Johann Samuel Traugott Gehler's physical lexicon, which appeared between 1787 and 1796.

[56] Friedrich Wilhelm of Brunswick, 1771–1815, the youngest son and later successor of Karl Wilhelm Ferdinand who fell in the Battle of Waterloo, was a Prussian major at the time.

[57] Clearly an oversight: Goethe certainly means "yesterday morning."

[58] After the departure of the Prussians the inhabitants of Verdun were dealt with sternly for having so quickly surrendered the city, and there were treason trials. The young women who had so charmed Frederick William were condemned by the Revolutionary Tribunal in Paris and guillotined.

[59] Wilhelm René Baron de l'Homme de Courbière, 1733–1811, later a Prussian field marshal.

[60] It is clear from Wagner's diary that Goethe shapes the narrative here to his own ends. Goethe himself had delivered the letter and knew perfectly well what was in it: it was a request by Carl August that the commandant warn Goethe and the members of his party in good time of any plan to evacuate the city.

[61] Louis August Le Tonnelier de Breteuil, 1733–1807, had been a minister before the revolution.

[62] Louis-René, Prince de Rohan, 1734–1803, a cardinal since 1778, became Bishop of Strassburg in 1779 and thus the ruler of a territory which extended onto the German side of the Rhine. After the abolition of feudalism by the National Assembly Rohan withdrew to the German part of his principality, where he was an active supporter of the French émigrés and allowed them to recruit and train troops.

[63] An intriguer, the Countess de la Motte, had given Cardinal Rohan to believe that the queen, Marie Antoinette, desired to purchase a certain very expensive diamond necklace, but was in no position to deal directly with the jewelers herself. Rohan, in an attempt to gain the favor of the queen, agreed to act as the go-between, negotiated the purchase and took delivery of the necklace, which, however, never reached the queen, who knew nothing of the whole business. The countess and her accomplices managed to get their hands on the necklace and spirit it away. The affair came to light in August, 1785, when the first payment came due, which was supposed to be made by the queen. Breteuil had Rohan arrested and imprisoned in the Bastille; Rohan was acquitted in the ensuing trial, but the queen and the court had been cast in a devastating light. Goethe claimed to the end of his life that the necklace affair had given him a premonition of all that was to happen in the course of the revolution. He was, however, far from alone among his contemporaries in seeing a direct relationship between the necklace affair and the beginning of the revolution.

[64] Louis XVI and his minister, Turgot, convened the Assembly of Notables in 1787 in an attempt to resolve the financial crisis by gaining voluntary tax concessions from the nobility. When the Assembly disbanded without agreeing to anything that would have improved the situation Louis was forced to summon the Estates General for May, 1789.

[65] Christian August Heinrich Kurt von Haugwitz, 1752–1831, had accompanied Goethe on his trip to Switzerland in 1775. The "malicious pleasure" recounted by Goethe at having seen Haugwitz lumbering down the street in his large coach is unmotivated unless perhaps Goethe knew why Haugwitz had been at Verdun in the first place. Haugwitz, who shortly after the campaign became Prussian foreign minister, was Prussian ambassador to Vienna at the time. Incredibly enough, Prussia and Austria were negotiating about compensation for their war expenses in the middle of a losing campaign which promised no trophies or compensation at all! Haugwitz had traveled especially from Vienna to meet with Frederick William at his campaign headquarters in order to work out the definitive Prussian position on the question of reparations, and an Austrian representative was waiting in Luxemburg to be summoned to meet Haugwitz at Verdun in order to try to conclude these negotiations between the two courts: Prussia wanted a piece of Poland (which it eventually received in the Second Polish Partition in 1793) in exchange for supporting the Austrian project to trade the Netherlands for Bavaria. Before Haugwitz and the Austrian representative could negotiate seriously at Verdun the city was surrendered to the French and the two negotiators were forced to flee to safety.

[66] A comedy by Louis Benoît Picard, 1769–1828, which was published in 1801. *Die deutschen Kleinstädter* was a comedy about German small-town life by August von Kotzebue, 1761–1819, based on Picard's play.

[67] Nicolas Poussin, 1593–1665, a French painter.

[68] "Valley of the Priests."

[69] The Archbishop-Electors of Trier, Cologne, and Mainz, as well as a number of less important rulers, fled to safety before the French advance.

[70] That is, the Duke of Brunswick.

[71] Adam Philippe de Custine, 1740–1793, went on from Mainz to capture Frankfurt and threatened in a blustering manifesto to invade Hesse-Kassel in retribution for the atrocities perpetrated by the Hessians and their ruler, the landgrave, on French soil during the invasion. Custine's army was too small, however, to threaten such a large territory and he was soon forced to concentrate on holding Frankfurt and Mainz. After the recapture of Frankfurt on 2 December his army withdrew to Mainz and the left bank territories. Custine, whose military talents were perhaps somewhat questionable, managed not to be in Mainz when it was besieged, was soon accused of treason and executed in 1793 after the recapture of Mainz by the Allies.

[72] From 1789 on German writers often refer to the French as "Franks." In most cases this usage is a sign of admiration and recalls the Germanic origins of the French state under the Merovingians and Carolingians.

[73] The campaign of 1792 was undertaken by Prussia and Austria on the basis of their defensive alliance. They were joined or supported only by a small number of other German princes (for example the Landgrave of Hesse-Kassel contributed troops to the campaign and led them in person in return for a Prus-

sian promise to support him in his ambition to be raised to the rank of elector). The war was not declared to be a war of the Holy Roman Empire, requiring the allegiance and support of all German Estates, until after this campaign. Understandably, many of the Rhenish princes, none of whom had any significant military forces, made every effort to remain neutral, or at least to appear to remain neutral, towards the French. Carl Theodore, the Elector of Palatine-Bavaria, in particular, was so careful not to offend the French that he drew down upon himself sharp criticism from other German rulers.

[74] See *Poetry and Truth,* Volume 4, p. 41.

[75] Laertes, the father of Odysseus, is working in the garden and wears gloves to protect his hands against the thorns (*Odyssey,* Book XXIV, 11. 230 ff).

[76] Goethe's grandfather Textor had died in 1771 and his uncle, Johann Jost Textor, 1739–1792, had that year become a city councilor.

[77] It is unclear just which visit to Frankfurt Goethe has in mind. He had in fact spent several days in Frankfurt in August, 1792, before proceeding to catch up with the army.

[78] Mainz capitulated to Custine on 21 October and Frankfurt was occupied the next day. See note 71 above.

[79] The archbishop and the elector were of course one and the same person. However, his spiritual authority as archbishop extended well past the limits of his territorial power. The French seizure of Lorraine in Louis XIV's time had led to the anomalous situation that there were French bishops under the ecclesiastical supervision of a German archbishop of Trier. During the struggle over the institution of a constitutional oath for the French clergy the archbishop had forbidden his French bishops and priests to swear the oath.

[80] In this passage Goethe seems to be relying on a topographical work by Matthias Merian published in 1646, in which Merian wrote of Mars Hill and Apollo Hill, and of a palace built by Archbishop Albero in the twelfth century which was supposedly named "Mount of Mercury." With regard at least to Mars Hill and Apollo Hill Merian had mistakenly tried to find learned equivalents for popular names ("Martinsberg" and "Polsberg").

[81] The principal fortress of the Electorate of Trier.

[82] Trier was occupied by the French in 1673. In order to facilitate its defense, the French leveled much of the surrounding countryside, including the cloister of St. Maximin, in 1674.

[83] Girolamo Marquis Lucchesini, 1751–1825. Originally librarian and reader to Frederick II, he became a diplomat and minister under Frederick William II and was one of the King's most influential advisers. He was Haugwitz's successor as ambassador in Vienna.

[84] That is, a craft operated by one boatsman.

[85] A fortress built by order of Louis XIV in 1687 and razed in 1698.

[86] The Legislative Assembly (the second French national assembly) and the interim executive committee which exercised authority from the time the Legislative Assembly was dissolved after 10 August until the convening of the National Convention in September, 1792. This, and the following three paragraphs, are based on Dumouriez' autobiography.

[87] The Elector of Trier was in the extremely unfortunate position of being the uncle of Louis XVI and his two brothers, the Counts Provence and Artois.

His hospitality, understandable in the light of his family ties, had quickly been abused by the two princes and their followers; and in spite of all the elector's efforts, Coblence came to contain the largest number of émigrés anywhere within the borders of the Empire. It was the efforts of the émigrés to establish a military force to intervene in France that had most embittered Franco-German relations and was the principal cause for the French declaration of war on 20 April 1792. Goethe by no means says everything in this passage that he could justifiably have said about the machinations of the émigrés.

[88] See *Poetry and Truth,* Volume 4, p. 414. The elector had resided in Trier until completion of the new castle at Coblence, which was built between 1778 and 1786.

[89] According to the Voyle *Military Dictionary* a flying bridge "consists of one or more barges moored by a long cable to a point in the centre of the stream. When the barge is properly steered in a current sufficiently strong, it is swept by it from one bank to the other."

[90] The much-admired author Sophie la Roche had lived here until 1780 and Goethe had visited her in 1772 and 1774. See the beginning of Book Thirteen of *Poetry and Truth.*

[91] The first two parts of Goethe's *Italian Journey* had appeared in 1816–1817. The end of this passage announces the third part, which contains the account of Goethe's second sojourn in Rome. The third part of the *Italian Journey* did not appear "soon," as hoped here, and was only published in the last authorized edition of his collected works, in 1829.

[92] The *Roman Elegies* were an erotic breakthrough in Goethe's poetry and caused a certain amount of scandal. See the *Elegies* and the *Epigrams* in *Goethe. Selected Poems,* ed. by Christopher Middleton, Boston (Suhrkamp/Insel), 1983, pp. 102–119 and pp. 125–7.

[93] A flare-up of tensions between Prussia and Austria in the spring of 1790 led to mobilization of forces and a confrontation in Silesia. Carl August's regiment had been among those mobilized and Goethe had spent part of the summer with the Duke in Silesia. The dispute was resolved in an agreement signed on 27 July 1790 in Reichenbach.

[94] The work in question was entitled *The Journey of the Sons of Megaprazon* and was never finished. Only a short fragment survives.

[95] Goethe is referring to Voltaire's novel, *L'Ingénu,* of 1767. The hero is a young man who has grown up among the Huron Indians and is unable, because of his openness and naiveté, to deal with the conventions and prejudices of civilized society.

[96] Friedrich Heinrich Jacobi, 1743–1819. Goethe and Jacobi had been acquainted since Storm and Stress days (see *Poetry and Truth,* Volume 4, p. 456 and note). They had had various misunderstandings and controversies over the years and by 1792 their relationship, while friendly, was not what it had been previously—which is the point of this section of Goethe's memoir. Goethe refrained from writing anything seriously critical of Jacobi until after Jacobi's death.

[97] Cornelis de Pauw, 1739–1799, was known for his works on the philosophy of culture: *Recherches philosophiques sur les Egyptiens et les Chinois,* 1773–74, and *Recherches philosophiques sur les Anciens Grecs,* 1787–88.

[98] It is not entirely clear what Goethe means here. "Scholarly prejudice"

for many years (at least since the days of Christian Wolff) had credited the ancient Chinese with having been a thoroughly moral people, though they had adhered to an atheistic philosophical system (Confucianism). De Pauw had questioned such notions and in turn was attacked energetically by Voltaire in his *Lettres chinoises, indiennes et tartares à M. Paux, par un bénédictin,* 1776.

[99] Francis Hemsterhuis, 1721–1790, a Dutch official, philosopher, and art lover who had been close to Princess Gallitzin since 1775.

[100] Adelheid Amalia Princess Gallitzin (1748–1806) was born Countess of Schmettau. She was married in 1768 to Dimitri Prince Gallitzin, Russian ambassador in The Hague, but from 1774 on she lived a secluded life dedicated to the education of her children and to her own philosophical and scientific studies. She moved to Münster in 1779, attracted by the policies and educational innovations of Fürstenberg (see note 137 below).

[101] Diderot had visited in Pempelfort in 1773 on his way to St. Petersburg.

[102] Written and performed in Weimar in 1791, the play intertwines the machinations and exposure of the "Great Cophta," a mystical swindler modeled on the adventurer Cagliostro, with the diamond necklace affair of 1785.

[103] For Goethe's reaction to materialism, as propounded for example in Holbach's *Système de la nature,* see *Poetry and Truth,* pp. 363 f.

[104] Princess Gallitzin had visited Weimar with Fürstenberg and Hemsterhuis in the autumn of 1785.

[105] The *Metamorphosis of Plants* had been published in 1790 and Goethe had sent Jacobi a copy.

[106] Charles Bonnet, 1720–1793, a philosopher and natural scientist in Geneva. His writings, which combined observation of nature with mystical speculations and religious edification, were much read in the 18th century. His most popular work was the *Contemplation de la nature,* which appeared in two volumes in Amsterdam in 1764 and was also translated into other languages.

[107] Goethe had published the first part of his *Contributions to Optics* in 1791, the second part in the spring of 1792. He had sent Jacobi copies of both parts. This was Goethe's first publication on colors.

[108] Wilhelm Heinse, 1749–1803, had translated Petronius' *Satyricon* and was the author of other works leaning toward erotic explicitness. The best-known of these, his novel *Ardinghello,* had appeared in 1787. Heinse also wrote extensively on art. He was a close friend of Jacobi and had lived with him before becoming reader and librarian to the Elector of Mainz in 1786. When the elector fled and Custine occupied Mainz Heinse had returned to Pempelfort and the Jacobis.

[109] Düsseldorf had a well-known gallery with collections both of Italian and Flemish art. When Düsseldorf became Prussian after the Congress of Vienna the paintings were removed to Munich, where they are now part of the Alte Pinakothek.

[110] Jean Antoine Houdon, 1741–1828.

[111] Honoré-Gabriel-Victor Riqueti, Comte de Mirabeau, 1749–1791, the vastly influential and inspiring orator of the early days of the French Revolution, had a large following among German liberals of the time. Mirabeau had spent considerable time in Germany. In addition to his famous dispatches on the situation at the Prussian court following the death of Frederick II (the *Secret History of the Berlin Court*), he had written a multi-volume treatise on the Prussian state.

[112] Friedrich Melchior Baron von Grimm, 1723–1807, lived for many years in Paris and was a collaborator of Diderot and his circle, while also serving to publicize French developments in Germany through his correspondence. After leaving France during the revolution he settled in Gotha in 1792.

[113] Sophie Freifrau von Coudenhoven, born Countess of Hatzfeldt, 1743–1825, the widow of a Mainz general, exerted considerable influence on the Elector of Mainz and was rumored to be his mistress.

[114] Christian Wilhelm von Dohm, 1751–1820, had been a professor at the academy in Kassel before entering Prussian civil service in the late 1770s. At this time he was the Prussian diplomatic representative at the court of the Elector of Cologne (who was also Bishop of Münster) and had accompanied the elector when he fled to Münster to escape the invading French.

[115] French efforts to win over the citizens of Frankfurt to their cause were fruitless, in contrast to what happened in Mainz. Immediately after occupying Mainz Custine had encouraged the formation of a Jacobin club which began to agitate in favor of republicanizing the city. The elector, after having done everything possible to encourage the outbreak of war, harboring and entertaining numerous French émigrés, and making available most of his armed forces to support the Allied invasion, had collected his valuables and stolen away in the middle of the night, leaving his subjects in the lurch. Government officials in the Electorate had not even been given any guidelines as to how to conduct themselves vis à vis the French (in contrast to the situation in Electoral Cologne, where the elector had explicitly instructed his officials to do everything demanded of them by the French as long as they remained loyal to him). There was understandably considerable resentment against the elector, which the French and their Jacobin allies set about to exploit.

[116] Christoph Ludwig Hoffmann, 1721–1807, sought to bring about medical reforms.

[117] During and after the Prussian retreat from French territory Dumouriez had led most of his forces against the Austrian Netherlands, which had been his major goal from the very beginning of the war. The French occupied most of modern-day Belgium by the end of the year, forcing the Austrian army to retreat.

[118] Friedrich Victor Lebrecht Plessing, 1749–1806. After the personal crisis and the studies described by Goethe in the account of his journey to the Harz, Plessing had received a doctorate in 1783 and became professor of philosophy in Duisburg in 1788.

[119] See *Poetry and Truth,* Volume 4, pp. 445 ff., and Volume 5, pp. 565 f.

[120] Heinrich Lips, 1758–1817, a painter and etcher from Zurich and a former professor at the Weimar drawing academy. See *Poetry and Truth,* p. 566.

[121] Lavater's title was *Physiognomic Fragments for the Purpose of Furthering Knowledge and Love of Mankind.*

[122] Carl August is meant.

[123] Goethe is referring particularly to Jakob Michael Reinhold Lenz, 1751–1792 (see *Poetry and Truth,* Volume 4, pp. 440 ff.), and Friedrich Maximilian Klinger, 1752–1831 (see *Poetry and Truth,* Volume 4, pp. 443–45 and note 130). Both had visited him in Weimar in 1776, and Lenz especially had made himself so unwelcome there that Goethe had had to take steps to make him leave.

[124] Saxe-Eisenach, a separate territory from Saxe-Weimar, was also ruled by Carl August.

[125] Goethe is mistaken in his recollection. The hunting trip in question and Goethe's first trip to the Harz took place in November, 1777, a year after his arrival in Weimar, by which time he had already been appointed to the privy council and was serving in the government.

[126] The state mines at Ilmenau had not been in operation since 1739, and it was one of the major projects of the Weimar government to open them again. Goethe was made a member of the mining commission in 1777 and spent considerable time on the project in the following years. The ore from the mines was not rich enough, however, to justify continued operation, and after years of effort and much expense they were finally closed down in 1800.

[127] Title character of the novel *Le Diable boiteux* by Alain René Lesage, 1707.

[128] A cave near Rübeland in the Harz. Goethe visited it again on 12 September 1783 and on 7 September 1784.

[129] These three stanzas are taken from Middleton's translation in *Goethe. Selected Poems,* pp. 67–9.

[130] Georg Melchior Kraus, 1733–1806, an artist, director of the Drawing Academy in Weimar. See also *Poetry and Truth,* pp. 594 f., and *Siege of Mainz,* passim.

[131] Friedrich Justin Bertuch, 1747–1822. See *Poetry and Truth,* p. 596 and note.

[132] Johann Karl August Musäus, 1735–1787, professor at the gymnasium in Weimar. See also *Poetry and Truth,* p. 596 and note 69.

[133] Christoph Joseph Jagemann, 1735–1804, librarian in Weimar.

[134] Ernst Wilhelm Wolf, 1735–1792, court music director in Weimar. See also *Poetry and Truth,* p. 595.

[135] According to the itinerary recounted above, Goethe arrived in Nordhausen at midday!

[136] Blasius Merrem, 1761–1824, professor of mathematics and physics in Duisburg, later in Marburg.

[137] Franz Freiherr von Fürstenberg, 1729–1810, was a canon of the Münster cathedral. He had functioned as minister for secular affairs and as general vicar for ecclesiastical affairs and was at one time widely regarded as the most likely successor as Bishop of Münster. In 1780, however, the Habsburg house succeeded in having Archduke Max Franz, the youngest son of Maria Theresa, who was already coadjutor with right of succession to the Elector of Cologne, elected coadjutor and successor for Münster as well. After 1780 Fürstenberg was no longer minister, but retained the general vicariat and was in charge of educational affairs in the territory.

[138] Johann Georg Hamann, 1730–1788, the so-called "magus of the north," was a Prussian official in Königsberg and the author of philological, speculative, and quasi-philosophical treatises. He was much revered by the young writers and intellectuals of Goethe's generation, and spiritually akin to Hemsterhuis, Princess Gallitzin, and their circle. See also *Poetry and Truth,* Volume 4, pp. 379–82.

[139] Hamann retired in 1787 and was finally able to travel to Münster and

Düsseldorf to visit his friends. He arrived in Münster on 16 July 1787, visited Jacobi in Pempelfort for a while during the autumn, then returned to Münster. He had been in poor health for a long while and died in Münster on 21 June 1788. The cemeteries of Münster were officially reserved for Roman Catholics, although exceptions were not unheard of. Princess Gallitzin, however, was determined to have Hamann buried in her garden, using the official exclusion of Protestants from the cemeteries as a pretext. After much difficulty she finally got the permission of the authorities to bury Hamann, but only on condition that she have it announced in the papers that Hamann was being interred on private property not because of any intolerance on the part of the authorities, but because it was her express desire.

[140] Catholicism, in contrast to other creeds and confessions which apparently seem to offer less certainty of heaven.

[141] Johann Lorenz Natter, 1705–1763.

[142] *Lettre sur la sculpture,* 1769, and *Lettre sur les désirs,* 1770, were in Goethe's library, along with a number of other works by Hemsterhuis which he had obtained with the assistance of Jacobi and Princess Gallitzin.

[143] Goethe never wrote such a work, but a number of church festivals are described in the *Italian Journey.*

[144] Johann Heinrich Voss, 1751–1826, a member of the group of Göttingen poets in the early 1770s, became rector of the gymnasium in Eutin in 1782 and professor of classics in Jena in 1802. Voss was the son of a serf and one of the more democratically minded of his generation; one of the respected classical scholars of the age, he was an expert on metrics and had translated Homer.

[145] Johann Heinrich Meyer, 1759–1832, an artist and art historian, professor at the drawing academy in Weimar from 1792 on and its director after 1807, lived in Goethe's house from 1791 to 1803 and collaborated with him on a number of art-historical projects.

[146] A troupe of actors under the directorship of Giuseppe Bellomo had been in Weimar and performed regularly from 1784–1791.

[147] Goethe wrote a set of *Rules for Actors* which were not published until after his death.

[148] August Wilhelm Iffland, 1759–1814, an actor and dramatist, director of the Mannheim theater in 1779, director of the Berlin theater from 1796 on. He wrote numerous "bourgeois" dramas and was, along with August von Kotzebue (see note 66 above), one of the most popular dramatists of the period.

[149] Friedrich Ludwig Schröder, 1744–1816, an actor and theater director in Hamburg, also wrote plays.

[150] Joseph Marius Babo, 1756–1822, director of the court theater in Munich from 1797 on.

[151] Friedrich Wilhelm Ziegler, 1756–1827, writer and actor at the Burgtheater in Vienna.

[152] Christoph Friedrich Bretzner, 1748–1807, a Leipzig merchant and author of comedies. Mozart used a drama by Bretzner as the basis of his *Abduction from the Seraglio.*

[153] Johann Friedrich Jünger, 1759–1797, a Viennese novelist and dramatist.

[154] Friedrich Gustav Hagemann, 1760–1835, an actor and dramatist in Breslau.

[155] Johann Gottfried Lukas Hagemeister, 1762–1806. With the exception of

Kotzebue and Iffland, none of the authors mentioned by Goethe in this passage were important for the further development of German literature. Schröder was extremely influential as a director and important for his role in the development of acting style during this period.

[156] Franz Joseph Fischer, born around 1740, acted and directed in Weimar from 1791 to 1793, later in Innsbruck and other Austrian cities.

[157] Karl Ditters von Dittersdorf, 1739–1799, a conductor and extremely popular composer of the time.

[158] After the death of Princess Gallitzin Goethe had had no further information about the fate or whereabouts of the gem collection. As a result of this passage in *Campaign in France 1792* he subsequently learned that the collection had been acquired by the King of the Netherlands.

[159] Goethe has not, for whatever reason, been entirely candid in his account. Princess Gallitzin was not being at all so altruistic in entrusting the collection to Goethe. She hoped to sell it and use the proceeds for philanthropical purposes, and she entrusted it to Goethe for the express purpose of making its existence and value more widely known and assisting her in finding a buyer.

[160] Here Goethe is thinking primarily of his first play, *Götz von Berlichingen*.

[161] Goethe is referring here to *Torquato Tasso* and *Iphigenia at Tauris*, both of which are in blank verse.

[162] See above, p. 678 and note.

[163] *Il re Teodore*, an opera by Paisiello which Goethe very much admired.

[164] Johann Friedrich Reichardt, 1752–1814, a Berlin composer and conductor who wrote music for a number of Goethe's poems and musical comedies.

[165] Johann Christoph Beck, born 1754, acted in Weimar from 1793 to 1800.

[166] Pseudonym of Christian Leberecht Heyne, 1751–1821.

[167] The French writer Claris de Florian's *Les deux billets* came out in 1779. The German adaptation by Anton Wall dates from 1782.

[168] Goethe has misquoted his own title. The exact title is *Conversations of German Refugees*.

[169] A reference to the rise of Bonaparte.

[170] Goethe's inspiration and source was Johann Christoph Gottsched's prose translation of the Low German animal fable.

[171] Jean Joseph Mounier, 1758–1806, had been president of the National Assembly for a short while in 1789. He came to Thuringia in 1795 and established a school for young Englishmen in Weimar.

[172] Camille Jordan, 1771–1821, an author and member of the Council of Five Hundred under the Directory, lived abroad from 1797 to 1800.

[173] Louis XVI was executed on 21 January 1793.

[174] The French general Joseph Victorin Neuwinger, 1736–1808, was captured by the Austrians on 27 March 1793.

[175] In 1821 Goethe had published a set of etchings based on his sketches, each etching accompanied by verses. The second etching, which is accompanied by the poem with which he concludes the text of *Campaign in France 1792*, shows a young woman looking from the front door down the steps at her young son, who is sitting in a downstairs or cellar doorway, looking up toward the mother. No effort has been made to reproduce the metrics or the rhymes of Goethe's poem.

Siege of Mainz

[1] Maximilian of Pfalz-Zweibrücken-Birkenfeld, 1756–1825. The head of the Zweibrücken line of the house of Palatine-Bavaria, he became Elector in 1799 when the ruling line died out, and King of Bavaria in 1806 upon the dissolution of the Empire.

[2] See *Campaign in France 1792,* note 43. Kalckreuth was overall commander of the blockading and siege force.

[3] Goethe distinguishes carefully between the blockade of Mainz (that is, the attempt to cut off the city from reinforcement and resupply), and the actual siege itself. There was in fact considerable controversy in the high command about whether or not to conduct a siege, with all the attendant destruction by bombardment that would entail. The siege did not begin, in a technical sense, until construction of the siege trenches and fortifications had begun.

[4] The same Johann Friedrich Reichsfreiherr vom Stein with whom Goethe had visited on his way through Mainz to join the army in August of 1792. Stein was present throughout the blockade and siege.

[5] Kalckreuth was disdainful of the theoretically oriented, hesitant strategy of his superiors in the high command, especially the Duke of Brunswick. (Brunswick was still in overall command of the Prussian forces in the summer of 1793, but is nowhere mentioned in Goethe's account of the siege of Mainz!)

[6] Henri de Latour d'Auvergne, Vicomte de Turenne, 1611–1675, and Louis II de Bourbon, Prince de Condé, 1621–1686, were French commanders who had ravaged the Rhineland during the wars of Louis XIV.

[7] Strictly speaking, this is an anachronism, as the French revolutionary calendar was not officially adopted until October, 1793, some months after the date of the conversation Goethe describes. However, when the National Convention had proclaimed the Republic in September, 1792, it decreed also that from then on official documents should be dated from Year 1 of the Republic.

[8] The Austrians had won a victory in the Netherlands at Famars on 23 May.

[9] Ludwig X of Hesse-Darmstadt, 1753–1830, was the brother-in-law of Carl August.

[10] Luise and Friederike von Mecklenburg-Strelitz. Luise, 1776–1810, the later greatly beloved Queen Luise, was at this time engaged to be married to the Crown Prince. Friederike, 1778–1841, was engaged to be married to the younger Prussian Prince Friedrich Ludwig Karl.

[11] Goethe's information is inaccurate, but there is no agreement on the correct site, possibly Eltville or Erbach.

[12] Goethe's text actually reads "Zahlbach, a cloister close to Dahlheim," but that is incorrect—he has confused the cloister and the village.

[13] Troops of the line were troops of the old regular army; "national" troops were national guard or volunteer troops who had entered the army since the summer of 1792 and had had little military training. At this period the two types of units were kept more or less separate, but later they were merged into a single force.

[14] Namely Carl August.

[15] Namely Georg Melchior Kraus.

[16] A "parallel" was a network of siege trenches running parallel to the defensive fortifications—in this case, a rough half-circle extending from the Rhine above Mainz back around to the Rhine below Mainz. Contemporary military strategy called for a total of three parallels, concentric siege rings excavated at ever closer range, connected with each other by trenches. In this usage, the first parallel is that farthest away from the defensive fortifications, the third parallel the one closest to them.

[17] Charles Gore, 1729–1807, a wealthy Englishman who had retired to Weimar with his daughters. He and Kraus shared artistic interests and were close friends.

[18] Goethe actually writes "the third parallel," but it is obvious that he means the outermost siege ring, i.e., the first.

[19] The members of the Jacobin Club, who zealously supported the French and took part in the administration of the city and the left bank occupied territories.

[20] 14 July was the anniversary of the storming of the Bastille. From 1791 on there was a festival celebrating national unity and brotherhood on that date every year.

[21] Condé, a fortress in the Netherlands, had been captured by the Austrians on 10 July.

[22] See *Campaign in France 1792,* note 6. Sömmerring had left Mainz before the French occupation and was apprehensive about the condition of his valuable anatomical specimens, which, as we learn later, had survived the occupation and the revolutionary fervor intact—probably due in large part to intervention by Georg Forster to protect them.

[23] The French and the Mainz revolutionary authorities had followed a ruthless policy of demanding an oath of allegiance of all citizens who desired to remain in the city. As a result, a very large number of citizens were expelled or left the city voluntarily. Now they were streaming back, hoping to recover their possessions and take revenge on their persecutors.

[24] Goethe is probably referring to the dwarf King Eckwald in the Siegfried chapbook.

[25] Antoine Christophe Merlin de Thionville, 1762–1833, a Jacobin and one of the members of the National Convention sent as a commissioner to Mainz. He had arrived in Mainz on 17 December 1792 and represented, along with his Convention colleagues, the highest authority in the occupied city.

[26] The Rhenish-German National Convention which had proclaimed Mainz and much of the left bank territory to be a republic at the end of March had instituted a "Security and Surveillance Committee" on the French model. This committee had been most active in denouncing and expelling those who refused to take the loyalty oath and had thus gained the bitter enmity of the citizens now seeking to return to the city.

[27] The cathedral chapter was a neoclassical structure built by the French architect Charles Mangin between 1782 and 1786. The furnishings had not been completed until 1791.

[28] In contrast to the hope expressed here that justice would be fair and even-handed in dealing with those Clubbists who did not manage to escape from the

city with the departing French, the reality was quite unpleasant and reflected badly on the Elector of Mainz and his government. A number of the Clubbists were kept in prison, in Erfurt and in the fortress at Königstein, without ever being tried on any charges, and the French commandant, d'Oyré, was imprisoned until 1794 instead of being allowed to depart with his troops. Many of the Clubbists were finally set free, on condition that they emigrated from Mainz territory, in exchange for the freedom of hostages from Mainz who had been taken to France during the occupation. Because the elector had fled without giving any instructions to his officials there were discrimination and even legal proceedings against some quite conscientious officials who had considered it their duty to cooperate with the occupiers in order to protect the interests of the elector and their fellow citizens. There was considerable controversy in the contemporary press about the treatment of the Clubbists and proceedings against Mainz officials.

[29] Sashes were the symbol of office of the municipal authorities who had gone from house to house demanding that the citizens take the oath.

[30] Following the coronation of Francis II as Holy Roman Emperor in Frankfurt in mid-July, 1792, Francis and Frederick William had met in Mainz at the invitation of the elector, and many other rulers had assembled there as well. At the height of the festivities the elector seems to have had the table set for at least 200 people.

[31] The fall of the Gironde and the rise to power of the Mountain faction in May and June, 1793.

[32] Jean François Rewbel, or Reubel, 1747–1807, an Alsatian and one of the National Convention commissioners in Mainz. Reubel later became a member of the Directory and was its strongest advocate of the policy of Rhineland annexation. The rest of this paragraph is of course not a "conjecture," but rather a capsule history of the years 1793–1797.

[33] Johann Friedrich von Rietz, whose marriage to Frederick William's mistress Wilhelmine Enke had been arranged solely for the king's convenience.

[34] See *Poetry and Truth,* p. 546 and note, and pp. 602–05.

[35] Goethe paints a somewhat rosier picture of Carl August's military career than was actually the case. Carl August suffered a number of slights and disappointments at the hands of Frederick William and the high command, and he was also rather quickly disillusioned with the war and with the Prussian war aims. In addition, his younger brother, Prince Konstantine, who had also participated in the campaigning, had taken ill and died in late 1793. Carl August returned to Weimar on leave shortly before Christmas, 1793, then asked to resign his commission and was given permission to leave the service by Frederick William on 5 February 1794, shortly after he had been promoted to lieutenant general.

[36] A reference to Napoleon, the campaigns of 1806, and the Prussian collapse. This ended the neutrality of northern Germany, which had so benefited Weimar in the period following the Treaty of Basel signed in 1795.

GPSR Authorized Representative: Easy Access System Europe - Mustamäe tee 50, 10621 Tallinn, Estonia, gpsr.requests@easproject.com

www.ingramcontent.com/pod-product-compliance
Lightning Source LLC
LaVergne TN
LVHW102157101026
849957LV00026B/217
9780691292229